Cases in Business Policy

BRIAN KENNY, EDWARD LEA,
STUART SANDERSON AND
GEORGE LUFFMAN

Basil Blackwell

First published 1987

Basil Blackwell Ltd
108 Cowley Road, Oxford, OX4 1JF, UK

Basil Blackwell Inc.
432 Park Avenue South, Suite 1503
New York, NY 10016, USA

BRITISH LIBRARY CATALOGUING IN PUBLICATION DATA
Cases in business policy.
1. Management – Case studies 2. Business enterprises – Case studies
I. Kenny, B.
685.4'012'0722 HD31
ISBN 0-631-15544-9

LIBRARY OF CONGRESS CATALOGING IN PUBLICATON DATA
Cases in business policy.
1. Strategic planning – Case studies.
2. Management – Case studies. I. *Kenny*, B.
HD30.28.C379 1987 658.4'012 87-6607
ISBN 0-631-15544-9 (pbk.)

Typeset in 10 on 11.5pt Times
by Columns
Printed in Great Britain by Page Bros (Norwich) Ltd

Contents

Preface

This case book draws on the authors' experience of teaching business policy to students and managers over a number of years. Thus all the cases have been tested in the market place.

The use of case material as a learning medium is, we believe, endemic to the study of business policy, and thus this book should be seen as a valuable companion volume to *Business Policy – An Analytical Introduction* by the same authors, which has been purposely designed to help the student understand and evaluate the case material.

For the student of business policy, we hope the cases will be interesting, rewarding and challenging, but we would point out that they do not preclude reading round the topics or widening the student's reading of the financial press. The study of business policy will hopefully engender an increased interest in business.

For the teacher, we hope that the cases will provide a valuable resource for courses. To help in course design we have produced an accompanying set of teachers' notes which attempt to show those issues which the authors feel are important in the cases and some of the important teaching ideas we have discerned from their use. The teachers' notes are available to *bona fide* teachers from the publisher. The potential of business policy for differing types of teaching approach appears to us to be substantial. We have successfully used both teacher- and student-led discussion, role playing, case writing and simulation as learning vehicles.

To both student and teacher we would stress that there is no substitute for careful and comprehensive preparation of case material and that the sharing and challenging of ideas is fundamental to the learning experience.

We believe that with such a holistic subject as business policy it is essential to gain a broad understanding of strategic analysis before proceeding to some of the more specialized areas of the subject. It is often difficult for students coping with business policy studies for the first time to come to terms with its integrative nature and with its concentration on top management decision-making. The former problem is often resolved by repeated exposure to case material with the constant application of models of strategic analysis, whilst the latter problem requires more sensitive treatment in order to demonstrate how the handling of strategic problems improves the students' ability to make decisions and to appreciate the significance of such decisions, as well as improving their ability to handle seemingly difficult data and opinions. Perhaps the greatest benefit of the case method is that students can potentially develop themselves as managers in a risk-free environment without the imposition of the school of 'hard knocks'.

For many students, particularly those who are to be examined in the subject, the learning style of the case method comes as something of a challenge. Often they cannot get specific answers from textbooks, they may feel they cannot revise for an examination in the usual sense, and they face the constant pressure of case analysis and report writing on a regular basis. Thus the role of the teacher in extracting the lessons and principles from case material becomes crucial. Further, the choice and sequence of case material becomes an important aspect of course design in business policy.

The cases in this book have been grouped into topic areas where we feel there is an important theme contained within individual cases. However, cases invariably contain more than one theme or topic and thus may be utilized to demonstrate differing aspects of strategic management. We nevertheless feel strongly that a great deal of emphasis should be placed on analysis in the early part of a course.

The cases are grouped under the following seven broad headings:

1 Strategic Analysis
2 Growth
3 Management Styles
4 Strategies for Declining Environments
5 New Business Development
6 Turnaround
7 Industry Notes.

The first section comprises the scope and variety of case histories through which students can thoroughly develop both an understanding of the concept of strategy and the associated skills of strategic analysis, for example: setting business objectives, analysing the business environment, internal company analysis and strategy evaluation and formulation.

In the remaining sections, cases have been assembled under more specific headings in order to indicate a main theme upon which the respective cases may be focused. These groupings, however, have to some extent been designed for the convenience of presentation as many of the cases are structured to provide additional focal points for analysis.

Thus the headings, although assisting in course design, should not be interpreted as a rigid classification of content or of application.

On a final note the authors stress that all of the cases making up this text have been written for the purpose of student instruction rather than to convey the notion of effective or ineffective management of a business.

Brian Kenny
Edward Lea
Stuart Sanderson
George Luffman

Acknowledgements

We are grateful to the following for permission to include case material, without which the scope and quality of the cases would have been that much less: John Edwards and Graham Inman, the School of Management University of Bath (Westbury Homes Group); Colin Clarke-Hill, Huddersfield Polytechnic (Habitat-Mothercare); Caroline Thompson, formerly research assistant, Huddersfield Polytechnic (House of Fraser); John L Heath, Leicester Polytechnic, (Ariel Industries).

We also gratefully acknowledge the co-operation of the many companies whose case histories form the body of the text.

We would further like to thank the following for permission to reproduce copyright material: *Caterer and Hotel Keeper*; Euromonitor Publications; *Investors' Chronicle*; Extel Statistical Services Ltd, *Financial Times*; Times Newspapers Ltd; Mintel Publications Ltd; ICC Information Group; *Wool Record*; Wood Mackenzie; British Carpet Manufacturers' Association; Pickfords Travel; Economist Intelligence Unit; Central Statistical Office; *International Management*; Thomas Cook; Birds Eye; *Sunday Times*; Data Stream; Monopolies and Mergers Commission; *MEAL; Journal of Long Range Planning*; Textile Statistics Bureau; Wool Industry Bureau of Statistics; *Silberston Report*; British Textile Confederation; CAITS Unit, NELP; Sir George Young.

PART I

STRATEGIC ANALYSIS

1 GKN

By 1984 Guest Keen and Nettlefold (GKN) had grown to be the biggest engineering group in the UK. Originally the group was a manufacturer of steel and steel products such as industrial fasteners (nuts, bolts, screws), but with the emergence of the automobile industry the company moved into component manufacture through a series of takeovers. The company currently employs some 34,000 people, which is less than half the number employed ten years ago. Current turnover is some £1974.5m, with profits of £119.4m (see Appendix 1).

The company comprises some 216 subsidiaries which are organized into four operating divisions, namely Automotive components and products representing in 1983 43% of turnover, Industrial supplies and services representing 24% of turnover, Wholesale and industrial distribution representing 25% of turnover, and Special steels and forgings with 8% of turnover (see Appendix 2).

Automotive Components and Products This sector of GKN produces transmission equipment for the car, truck, tractor and other vehicle manufacturers, together with axles, bearings, pistons, military vehicles and a whole range of automotive components from cabs and chassis to couplings and disc brakes. The principal area of production is the UK, but the company also owns plant in W. Germany, Italy, USA, France and Denmark.

Industrial Supplies and Services This business is varied, having interests in pallet hire, scaffolding, vending machines, threaded metal fasteners, tools, piling, soil improvement and specialist foundation services. Its principal areas of operation are the UK, South Africa, USA, W. Germany, Holland, France and Belgium. The group further includes home improvement systems, aluminium and plastic extrusion, safety footwear and clothing, water treatment, locks, hinges, steel reinforcement, brewery kegs and racking and storage systems.

Wholesale and Industrial Division This division is concerned with replacement parts for vehicles, steel stockholding and processing, together with distribution of hardware, gardening equipment and tools, DIY and leisure goods to supermarkets. Its activities are based in the UK, France, USA and Ireland.

Special Steels and Forgings Based in the UK, this division is responsible for electrically melted alloy and special carbon steels as well as forged steel products for the automotive, agricultural, aerospace, mining and railway industries. Its products include camshafts, crankshafts, gas turbine discs, steering and suspension joint assemblies.

STRATEGY

In the annual report in 1980 Sir Trevor Holdsworth referred to 'the general thrust of our programme for strategic change and development' which was to

1 concentrate upon the manufacture of technologically orientated products of high added value;
2 direct the company's thrust to world rather than national markets;
3 increase substantially the group's involvement in the services sector both wholesale and industrial distribution and in a variety of problem-solving services to industry.

The decline of the motor industry and problems with steel have created difficulties for GKN. The response was to close capacity as part of a general process of rationalization. The company's growth in automotive components had been via a series of takeovers of such firms as Birfield, Vandervell and Sheepbridge. Such growth by acquisition has continued, and it was only the intervention of the Monopolies Commission in 1983 which thwarted GKN's bid for AE, which would have increased their stake in autoparts by a third. Such a process of rationalization has not been without cost. It is estimated that since 1980 rationalization costs amount to some £200m. This partly explains the poor financial picture of the 1980s. Sir Trevor Holdsworth, commenting on other potential problems for the company, is on record as saying 'If we look back at the record in 20 years' time the UK recession will be no more than a blip'. The company, despite these problems, has continued to invest, for example £100m in 1980 and £92m in 1983 and, despite the rationalization programme the company has strengthened its stake in its traditional businesses. Roy Roberts, the group managing director, has commented that what the recession did was to accelerate action which would have taken place in any case over a longer period.

GKN's view is perhaps best summed up by a quote from Roy Roberts who said, 'the motor industry is basically a mature industry but the technology is by no means mature'. Sir Trevor Holdsworth added, 'once you're in, the market's there . . . and there are not a lot of people wanting to get in . . . the technological change that's taking place is so rapid that the big assemblers can't keep up'. One of the reasons for GKN's bid for AE being turned down by the Monopolies Commission was its failure to convince the Commission of its technological competence.

The company had grown into the auto business by taking over existing companies, and further changes in the design of cars had greatly assisted the company. In the 1960s GKN had bought Birfield and Hardy Spicer, which brought the company the Laycock clutch business and a 37% stake in a German prop shaft specialist Uni-Cardan. All three companies supplied the car, truck and tractor industry. One of the important products made by the group was constant velocity joints which are indispensable for front-wheel configurations on vehicles. Since the early beginnings with the Austin Mini, CV joints have been increasingly used for both front-wheel drive and independent rear suspension. GKN's products are heavily used in this market, either wholly, as in the case of BMW or as part of an assembly – indeed only Citroen of the European car manufacturers don't use GKN products. US manufacturers were slow to move to front-wheel drive but, after the oil crises, began to adopt this configuration. GKN opened a factory in North Carolina tied to Ford, with a second plant opening just in time for the all-time low in US car production, but components from this plant were exported to Germany. Uni-Cardan as a group of companies have been financially successful throughout the recession. It is now variously estimated that the world-wide earnings in transmission products are some £560m, half of which is accounted for by CV joints.

In addition to the important transmission business, the fastest growing sector of GKN's business has been in distributing motor components and accessories. As a business it has one inherent risk, namely that any incursion into the aftermarket can be seriously resisted by GKN's own customers who want to keep such sales under their own control. In 1979 GKN purchased Parts Industries Corporation in Tennessee, the fourth largest parts distributor in the US; later the same year Sheepbridge and the distribution activities of Armstrong Equipment were purchased in the UK. Later a similar company was purchased in France, giving GKN a £100m business in parts distribution across three countries. Throughout the recession GKN has continued to expand its activities in distribution, particularly in the US where PIC is now third largest, specializing in truck parts and spares for Japanese cars. The French market continues to be dominated by car producers, and in the UK the fragmented nature of the market led the Monopolies Commission to suggest that it be tidied up, which is happening with AE selling its distribution business to Unipart and GKN's recent addition of Smiths Industries parts subsidiaries making them a leader in that part of the industry not dominated by car manufacturers. The UK parts operation now accounts for one-fifth of GKN's total sales to the vehicle aftermarket worldwide, which is estimated to be worth £400m.

GKN's traditional business in bolts and nuts has been severely pruned, leaving it much smaller than before. Further the company has divested itself of interests in welding, central heating, air conditioning, car parking, filtration, together with a plastics machinery company in Germany. Now developments include research and development into composite materials for the manufacture of springs, which are being developed in the Group Technology Centre in Wolverhampton. So far £7m has been spent on the project and plans are advanced for the production of a composite leaf spring for commercial vehicles, which is half the weight of a traditional steel spring. GKN also have a proposal for producing systems rather than discrete components such that when an engine is redesigned all the components could be redesigned as a system. This relied upon car companies giving up their control over design, but some companies have shown some interest. The major area where GKN can demonstrate this ability is in the design and manufacture of their own vehicles, the Saxon armoured personnel carrier and the MCV 80 tracked personnel carrier. These two vehicles are a new departure for GKN for they not only supply the transmission but the chassis and bodywork. So far the company has sold the Saxon to developing nations as well as the Dutch army and 500 to the British army. The MCV 80 is currently on trial with 50 units being in use with the British army.

ORGANIZATION AND CONTROL

Up until the 1970s GKN's 200 subsidiaries were organized into sub-groups whose chief executives had seats on the main board. This system has been abolished, leaving a board composed of chairman and managing director plus two deputy managing directors and the finance director. Five executive directors make up a group policy committee which meets weekly. 'We don't do an annual exercise on policy', Roberts is on record as saying. The major aim of the policy committee is to ensure flexibility. The deputy managing directors have no operational responsibility but have general oversight of the divisions. Roberts has said that despite any leanings they might have 'they met as a trio'.

The next tier of management is made up of six 'corporate management directors' who are managing directors of the principal divisions. The responsibilities of corporate management directors (average age 44) differ widely in size, scope and importance. As one corporate manager put it, 'it has no synergy except that you need certain skills and perceptions to run certain businesses.'

Despite the differences in size and scope GKN lays down targets for the groups: 20% return on net assets and 10% on sales. These are stressed as targets not financial budgeted forecasts.

Although GKN has substantial overseas holdings, senior staff are based in the UK; some UK executives sit on boards overseas but the company's policy is not to post senior people overseas.

PLANNING

In its early history GKN planned, basing its ideas for the future on one-year financial forecasts and budgets. In 1965 a planner was hired who investigated a full corporate planning procedure of rolling five-year plans, a strategic policy committee and a planning procedure manual. Subsidiaries had to submit plans to head office for approval and consolidation into a master plan for the whole company. The system did force subsidiaries to take a strategic view of the business, but the system collapsed due to an overload of paper and the fact that head office tended to ignore subsidiaries' plans because they often appeared unconvincing or were difficult to reconcile. Further plans for large investments tended to be taken outside of the planning procedures.

In 1977 the planning function was disbanded, to be replaced by a business development function which was smaller in size and more limited in scope. The five-year plan was to be replaced by three-year plans and annual budgets based on forecasts of the motor industry. This system was then subject to changes in the top management structure and changes in the structure and size of the company. The board became much smaller and the company began divesting itself of certain businesses in forging and casting and 35,000 of a workforce of some 80,000 were dispensed with. Similarly business became more difficult so that personal decision making by senior staff could no longer be tolerated.

Currently there is a three-tier planning system. At the top there is the group policy committee (GPC) which replaced the old system in 1982 and comprises the five executive directors who meet weekly. The committee has no direct profit responsibility nor does it focus on operating efficiency; instead it concerns itself with shaping the future of GKN. Once a year this group goes away for a 'brainstorming' session of two days to review group stategies.

The next tier is composed of six corporate management directors. Their function is to vet the three-year plans and budgets which all of the profit centres under their control produce. At their meetings they are joined by people from the finance and business development departments.

Business development grew from the old planning department, has a staff of ten, and is responsible for economic forecasting, and capital expenditure monitoring (any project over £2m). Further, business development acts as a secretariat which links the GPC and corporate management directors. For example, business development lays down the guidelines for the three-year profit centre plans, the guidelines coming from the GPC. Further, business development is responsible for special investigations.

The planning cycle begins in May when the GPC meets for its 'brainstorming' session and produces a report on future developments in strategy, together with resource implications for investments or cutbacks. In July this report is discussed by the whole board. As one director puts it, 'We don't aim to have a grandiose ten-year plan for GKN, festooned with what turned out in the past to be spurious figures. We simply spell out how we see the company, and how we see ourselves going forward'.

The conclusions of this board meeting are then given to the six corporate management directors (CMD) who are told what their capital expenditure should be and what projects will be supported. This information is then passed to the profit centres providing parameters for subsidiaries' future strategy.

By October each subsidiary produces an annual budget which is vetted by the appropriate CMD together with executives from the finance and business development departments. After a careful check on the budgets they are approved by the December meeting of the board.

Three-year plans are submitted separately from annual budgets and are spaced out through the year. Not more than four per month are dealt with by the GPC. According to the GPC, 'the ideal plan is short and not too heavy on figures . . . we want some numbers on the implications of the plan for resources and profits . . . but not too many, because the figures are likely to be wrong anyway. What we want much more are ideas for acquisitions, divestments or new projects – and the clear identification of problem areas, together with the action to remedy them.' Where the environment is stable, three-year plans are called for annually. Where this is not the case there may be a six-month update. Three-year plans are vetted by CMDs with the finance and business development departments. The role of business development is the same as with budgets, namely, to act for the GPC, looking for weaknesses and difficulties. The GPC then puts the profit centre boss and his CMD through a two- to three-hour interrogation, at the end of which the plan is not ousted but indications are given whether or not the plan fits general corporate strategy. The net result, as one GKN executive director put it, is that 'by the time the plans get to us the CMDs have crawled all over them, so have finance and business development and, perhaps because we've gone through such rough times, there's a hell of a lot more realism in them anyway.' Further, it is claimed 'GKN is not a planned company is the sense that we try to spell out everything in detail for five years ahead – and it is all the better for that, because we don't bemuse ourselves with a mish-mash of useless figures which bear no relation to reality. We believe it is much better to know exactly what is happening, to have clear in our minds the area which we are going to make a major effort – but always be willing to look at areas which we haven't thought about'.

Appendix 1 Financial information: GKN

PROFIT AND LOSS ACCOUNT (£m)

	1983	*1982*	*1981*	*1980*	*1979*
Turnover	1975	1892	1855	1923	1961
Trading profit	119	90	83	37	138
Profit after interest	88	41	35	(1)	126
Taxation & minorities	53	40	34	39	51
Net earnings	35	1	1	(40)	75

BALANCE SHEET

	1983	*1982*	*1981*	*1980*	*1979*
Fixed assets	571	604	597	594	579
Stocks	403	430	450	466	518
Debtors less creditors	(52)	(43)	(68)	(19)	28
Net operating assets	922	991	979	1041	1125
Investments	133	101	103	33	44
Taxation & dividends	(47)	(28)	(20)	(21)	(62)
Net borrowings	(240)	(366)	(329)	(329)	(261)
Provisions	(42)	(41)	(35)	(30)	(27)
Net assets	726	657	698	694	819
Equity	650	591	650	653	778
Minority interests	76	66	48	41	41
	726	657	698	694	819
E.P.S. (pence)	17.4	0.5	0.4	–	46.2
Dividend per share (pence)	9.0	8.0	8.0	8.0	19.4
Trading profit to net assets (%)	13.0	9.1	8.5	3.6	12.3
Earnings to equity interest (%)	5.4	0.1	0.1	–	9.6

Appendix 2

BUSINESS SECTOR (£m)

	1983	*1982*
Turnover		
Automotive products	846	755
Industrial supplies	483	503
Wholesale	487	467
Special steels	159	167
	1975	1892
Profit		
Automotive products	81	59
Industrial supplies	23	20
Wholesale	10	11
Special steels	5	0
	119	90

BY AREA

	1983	*1982*	*1981*	*1980*	*1979*
Turnover					
UK	1007	990	1066	1259	1339
Europe	480	488	422	411	430
America	303	239	161	95	58
Rest of world	185	175	206	158	134
	1975	1892	1855	1923	1961
Profit					
UK	27	11	13	(18)	83
Europe	55	50	36	39	45
America	31	21	12	2	–
Rest of world	6	8	22	14	10
	119	90	83	37	138

BUSINESS SECTORS

	1981	1980	1979
Turnover			
Automotive Components	682	677	696
Wholesale & Industrial distribution	446	452	388
Special steels	217	225	270
Fasteners	120	128	141
Industrial services	137	129	135
General steels	46	134	174
Other	261	333	344
	1909	2078	2148
Profit			
Automotive components	44	25	59
Wholesale & Industrial distribution	6	11	18
Special steels	10	(9)	19
Fasteners	5	5	9
Industrial services	12	12	11
General steels	(6)	(12)	4
Other	12	5	18
	83	37	138

SALES TO THE UK MARKET (£m)

	1983	1982	1981	1980	1979
Industrial supplies and services	205	N/A	N/A	N/A	N/A
Automotive components	255	N/A	N/A	N/A	N/A
Wholesale & Industrial distribution	245	N/A	N/A	N/A	N/A
Special steels & forgings	103	N/A	N/A	N/A	N/A
	808	803	885	1064	1140

Appendix 3 Directors

EXECUTIVE DIRECTORS

Chairman: Sir Trevor Holdsworth (aged 56), a chartered accountant, joined the group in 1963 and was successively group chief accountant, general managing director of the UK screws and fasteners operations and group controller. He was appointed to the board in 1970, a deputy chairman in 1974 and (additionally) managing director in 1977. On 1 January 1980 Sir Trevor was appointed chairman of the company. He is also non-executive chairman of Allied Colloids group P.L.C., a non-executive director of Midland Bank plc and Thorn EMI plc, a former chairman of the British Institute of Management and a holder of honorary doctorates conferred by the Universities of Aston, Bradford and Loughborough.

Managing director: Roy E.J. Roberts (aged 55), a chartered engineer, joined the group as a management trainee in 1951. He served in a number of senior executive appointments, including the chairmanship of the engineering and construction services operations, before being appointed to the board in 1975. Roy Roberts became managing director of the company on 1 January 1980. He is also a part-time member of the United Kingdom Atomic Energy Authority and a vice-president of the Institution of Production Engineers.

Deputy managing director: Ian F. Donald (aged 55) joined the group in 1972 on the acquisition of Firth Cleveland Ltd (of which he was a managing director), was appointed to the board of the company in 1974 and became a deputy managing director on 1 January 1982. His main areas of responsibility are the operations in the automotive components sector, and the American and Pacific regions. Ian Donald is chairman of the Hong Kong Trade Advisory Group.

Deputy managing director: Basil J.P. Woods (aged 61), an economist, joined the group in 1962 and held a number of senior corporate executive posts before being appointed to the board in 1974 as director of corporate planning and economic affairs. He became a deputy managing director of the company on 1 January 1982. Basil Woods's main areas of responsibility are the distribution and industrial services sectors and the group's wholly owned and related steel interests and affairs, as well as South Africa.

Finance director: David B. Lees (aged 47), a chartered accountant, joined the group in 1970. After successive appointments as chief accountant and controller of one of the major manufacturing divisions, he was appointed general manager – finance at group headquarters. On 1 January 1982 he was appointed to the board as finance director. David Lees is also responsible for the Scandinavian security systems business. He is a member of the Government-appointed Audit Commission.

The executive directors form the group policy committee which is responsible for the development and monitoring of basic strategies for the group and for taking major policy decisions. Reporting to them are six corporate management directors, who hold full executive and profit responsibility for most of the group's operating activities worldwide.

NONEXECUTIVE DIRECTORS

E. Philip Chappell, CBE (aged 54), appointed to the board as a non-executive director in January 1974, is vice-chairman of Morgan Grenfell Holdings Ltd.

Antony R. Pilkington (aged 48), appointed to the board as a non-executive director in May 1982, is chairman of Pilkington Brothers plc.

David A.S. Plastow (aged 51), appointed to the board as a non-executive director in September 1978, is managing director and chief executive of Vickers P.L.C.

The non-executive directors comprise the audit committee of the company.

Life president: Lord Brookes, chairman of the company from 1965 until 1974.

CORPORATE MANAGEMENT DIRECTORS

The corporate management directors, the operations for which they are responsible and the parts of the world in which those operations have their principal places of business are as follows:

Trevor C. Bonner (aged 40), joined GKN in 1968. GKN Automotive Components Inc. (USA); Transmissions UK Division (UK); Uni-Cardan AG (81.9% owned) (West Germany, France, Italy).

Michael J.C. Borlenghi (aged 40), joined GKN in 1966. Fasteners Division (UK, Belgium, Holland, France); General Industries Division (UK, Holland); Hardware Distribution Division (UK).

Jeremiah J. Clancy (aged 48), joined GKN in 1978. Autoparts European Division (France); Autoparts UK Division (UK); Autoparts US Division (USA).

Alexander Daly (aged 48), joined GKN in 1978. Axles Division (UK); Engine Parts Division (UK, Italy); Forgings Divsion (UK); GKN Technology Ltd (UK); Laycock Engineering Ltd (UK); Sankey Division (UK).

Brian D. Insch (aged 42) joined GKN in 1963. Powder Metallurgy Division (UK, Italy); Special Steels Division (UK); Steelstock Division (UK); Firth Cleveland Steel Strip Ltd (UK).

R. John B. Jessop (aged 45), joined GKN in 1971. Foundations Division (UK, West Germany, North America, Australia); GKN Birwelco Ltd (UK, USA); Industrial Services Division (UK, Europe, Australia).

Appendix 4 Principal divisions and subsidiaries

The issued share capitals of the companies which comprise the GKN group are held indirectly by Guest, Keen and Nettlefolds, plc through intermediate holding companies which are registered or incorporated in England, Holland, USA, West Germany, Australia and South Africa.

There are 216 subsidiaries, which for management purposes are organized in operating divisions. The principal divisions and subsidiaries within business sectors are as follows:

AUTOMOTIVE COMPONENTS AND PRODUCTS

GKN Automotive Components Inc. USA
GKN Axles Ltd.
Engine Parts Division
  GKN Vandervell Ltd.
  GKN Sheepbridge Stokes Ltd.
Laycock Engineering Ltd.
Powder Metallurgy Division
  GKN Bound Brook Ltd.
GKN Sankey Ltd.
Transmissions UK Division
  BRD Company Ltd.
  Hardy Spicer Ltd.
Uni-Cardan AG (81.9% owned) West Germany
  Gelenkwellenbau GmbH (81.9% owned) West Germany
  Glaenzer Spicer SA (81.1% owned) France
  Jean Walterscheid GmbH (81.9% owned) West Germany
  Lohr & Bromkamp GmbH (77.5% owned) West Germany

INDUSTRIAL SUPPLIES AND SERVICES

GKN Birwelco Ltd.
Fasteners Division
  GKN Screws & Fasteners Ltd.
Foundations Division
  GKN Keller GmbH West Germany
  GKN Keller Ltd.

General Industries Division
  BKL Extrusions Ltd.
  Sankey Laminations Ltd.
Industrial Services Division
  GKN Chep Ltd. (70% owned)
  GKN Kwikform Ltd. (60% owned)
  Sankey Vending Ltd.
GKN Australia Ltd Australia
GKN South Africa (Pty) Ltd (75% owned) South Africa
GKN-Stenman AB (91.3% owned) Sweden

WHOLESALE AND INDUSTRIAL DISTRIBUTION

Autoparts International Division
  Parts Industries Corporation USA
  GKN Replacement Services Ltd.
  Unigep SA (73.9% owned) France
Hardware Distribution Division
  Stern Osmat Ltd.
GKN Steelstock Ltd.

SPECIAL STEELS AND FORGINGS

Brymbo Steel Works Ltd
GKN Forgings Ltd.

Except where otherwise indicated, the subsidiaries are wholly owned and incorporated in England. The country of incorporation or registration is also the principal country in which the subsidiaries operate.

Appendix 5 Motor component and accessory manufacturers: key ratios

	1983	*1982*	*1981*
Return on capital	(1.0)	1.9	12.7
Profitability	(0.6)	1.2	7.5
Profit margin	(0.5)	0.9	5.7
Return on equity	(1.4)	2.5	15.1
Sales to total assets	128.4	132.2	132.8
Sales to fixed assets	3.9	4.2	4.4
Stock turnover	3.9	3.8	3.7
Credit period	74.0	71.0	74.0
Liquidity ratio	1.5	1.6	1.6
Quick ratio	0.7	0.7	0.7
Gearing			
Debt to net worth	0.5	0.4	0.4
Equity to total liabilities	0.4	0.5	0.5
Gross interest as a percentage of EBIT	127.0	68.1	18.4

Source: ICC Information Group Limited, 28–42 Banner Street, London EC1Y 8QE

Appendix 6 Smiths Industries plc

Smiths Industries is a larger company than GKN and has a wide diversity of products. In 1983 their product base was as follows:

MARKET ANALYSIS (£000)

	Sales	*Profit*
Aerospace	97,200	12,642
Automotive	47,250	(1,112)
Marine	30,200	2,260
Industrial	57,300	4,821
Medical	42,750	10,731
Distribution	55,800	1,337
Australia/South Africa	50,200	731
Total sales	380,700	31,410

Their interests in the automotive components industry comprise machinery parts, bearings, seals and part transmission products. In addition they own a car radio manufacturer as well as a paint and refinish company. In the chief executive's review of 1983 it was stated that 'The results of our UK motor vehicle original equipment businesses have been a cause for concern for some years'. The results for this division for 1982 and 1983 show a trading loss in both years.

Appendix 7 The motor vehicle market

UK ANNUAL REGISTRATIONS (JANUARY – DECEMBER)

	1978	*1979*	*1980*	*1981*	*1982*	*1983*
Cars	1,618,193	1,731,882	1,536,882	1,513,875	1,785,990	1,038,907
Motor cycles	229,412	289,323	316,207	275,411	234,663	177,271
Goods vehicles	270,889	314,190	271,132	218,705	61,046	67,310
Public transport	9,282	9,258	8,935	7,650	7,203	7,544
Agricultural	52,608	49,896	38,146	33,798	40,215	44,007
Other	42,245	45,483	44,782	35,795	40,764	49,123

Source: *Business Monitor*

TOTAL MOTOR VEHICLES LICENSED (in 000s)

1971	*1972*	*1973*	*1974*	*1975*	*1976*	*1977*	*1978*	*1979*	*1980*	*1981*
15,478	16,117	17,014	17,252	17,501	17,832	17,772	18,625	19,210	19,355	19,770

Source: CSO Transport Statistics

CONSOLIDATED BALANCE SHEETS (£m) AE plc

	30 Sept 1982	*30 Sept 1983*
Fixed Assets		
a Tangibles	94.3	95.3
b Investments	5.5	6.3
	99.8	101.6
Current Assets		
c Stocks	104.7	102.4
Trade debtors	74.0	75.3
Other debtors	4.1	6.9
Prepayments, etc.	6.1	6.2
Deposits	2.6	4.4
Cash	1.7	1.4
	193.2	196.6
Creditors (due within one year)		
Bank loans & overdrafts	30.7	32.7
Trade creditors	35.1	41.6
Bills of exchange	1.6	2.6
Tax	1.7	1.6
Payroll tax & social security	5.3	6.7
Other creditors	15.9	17.1
Accrued charges	14.9	15.6
Dividend	0.6	1.4
	105.8	119.3
Net current assets	87.4	77.3
Total assets less current liabilities	187.2	178.9
Creditors (due after one year)		
Deb. Stocks	6.6	6.6
Other Loans	30.2	20.8
Govt Grants Reserve	3.1	2.8
Other Creditors	5.1	5.1
	45.0	35.3
	142.2	143.6

CONSOLIDATED BALANCE SHEETS (£m) continued

	30 Sept 1982	*30 Sept 1983*
Capital	24.5	24.5
Share premium a/c	25.0	25.0
Revaluation reserve	20.1	21.7
Capital redemption reserve	3.7	3.7
Other reserves	3.0	3.0
Profit & Loss a/c	62.1	60.7
Minority interests	3.8	5.0
	142.2	143.6

Source: Reproduced by arrangement with Extel Statistical Services Limited, 37–45 Paul Street, London EC2A 4PB

Appendix 8 A.E. plc

A.E. is principally concerned with the manufacture and distribution of components. The company's principal divisions are:

After market group: sells bought-in parts such as filters, spark plugs, transmission equipment, electrical parts, bearings, gaskets, valves, etc, as well as products manufactured by A.E. such as bearings and cylinder components.

This group has overseas interests in Austria, Canada, USA, Germany, Singapore, France, Portugal, Sweden, Italy, Ireland and Costa Rica.

Bearings division: manufactures all types of bearing and ancillary products as well as machinery for manufacturing bearings. Chief amongst the subsidiaries is Glacier Metal with subsidiaries in France, Holland, Germany and the USA.

Cylinder components: manufactures pistons, cylinder liners, valve guides, machine tools and castings. The company has overseas holdings in France, Germany and USA.

Industrial products division: this group manufactures springs, valve seats, camshafts and cruise controls.

Turbine components division: Turbine blades and precision castings.

In addition the company owns plant in South Africa making a range of vehicle components, as well as other engineering companies in Europe. The group employs some 17,500 people worldwide which is a considerable change from 1974 when the company employed some 30,000. The major change in employment appears to have been in the UK.

OUTPUT: PASSENGER CAR PRODUCTION – BY COUNTRY (in millions)

	1973	*1974*	*1975*	*1976*	*1977*	*1978*	*1979*	*1980*	*1981*	*1982*	*1983*[a]
World	29.76	25.50	25.00	28.90	30.60	31.72	31.56	29.24	27.99	27.20	–
USA	9.67	7.32	6.72	8.50	9.21	9.18	8.43	6.38	6.25	5.07	6.35
Canada	1.23	1.18	1.05	1.15	1.16	1.14	0.99	0.85	0.80	0.87	0.90
Japan	4.47	3.93	4.57	5.03	5.43	5.75	6.18	7.04	6.97	6.88	7.00
W. Germany	3.65	2.84	2.91	3.55	3.79	3.89	3.93	3.52	3.58	3.76	3.93
France	2.87	2.70	2.55	2.98	3.09	3.11	3.22	2.94	2.61	2.78	2.60
Italy	1.82	1.63	1.35	1.47	1.44	1.51	1.48	1.45	1.26	1.30	1.35
UK	1.78	1.53	1.27	1.33	1.33	1.22	1.07	0.92	0.95	0.89	0.97
Spain	0.71	0.71	0.70	0.75	0.99	0.99	0.97	1.03	0.86	0.93	1.00
Sweden	0.34	0.33	0.32	0.32	0.24	0.25	0.30	0.24	0.26	0.29	–
Brazil	0.73[b]	0.86[b]	0.93[b]	0.99[b]	0.92[b]	0.54	0.55	0.60	0.41	–	–

[a] forecast [b] cars & CVs

Source: SMMT, Economist Intelligence Unit

AE plc RESULTS

		1980	*1981*	*1982*	*1983*
Gross profit (£m)		20.8	15.0	16.6	14.2
Net profit before tax (£m)		15.7	10.7	6.7	5.0
Sales (£m)		442	441	382	370
of which	UK	311	280	257	244
	Overseas companies	131	161	125	126
	Exports	75.7	76.6	75.2	79.3
Analysis of sales (%)					
Market:	Cars	8	6	6	7
	Trucks & buses	6	4	5	4
	Industrial & marine engines	7	6	7	6
	Agricultural	4	3	3	3
	Aircraft	7	9	7	5
	General engineering	6	5	5	5
	Replacement parts	17	16	17	18
		55	49	50	48
Direct exports					
	Replacement parts	7	7	9	9
	Engine & vehicle mfg	10	10	11	12
		17	17	20	21
Overseas subsidiaries					
	Replacement parts	17	20	20	21
	Engine & vehicle mfg	11	14	10	10
		28	34	30	31

GEOGRAPHICAL SALES (£m)

	UK	*EEC*	*Rest of Europe*	*N. America*	*S. America*	*Africa*	*Rest*
1979	219.5	50.6	25.3	12.3	3.5	43.3	13.3
1980	243.8	74.9	28.6	14.8	4.2	58.6	16.8
1981	214.9	77.1	28.5	20.5	5.1	79.9	15.1
1982	191.8	70.5	29.4	18.3	7.0	51.1	13.6
1983	176.2	77.6	29.2	20.0	6.6	44.5	15.5

2 Sirdar

The company was founded in 1880 in the West Riding of Yorkshire as a worsted spinning company under the family name of Fred Harrap. One hundred years later the company had changed its name to Sirdar Plc, and was the brand leader in the UK hand-knitting yarn market, a product area to which it had swapped in the early part of the twentieth century. This was followed by a marketing decision to sell their product direct to the many retail shops around the country which stocked the various colours and qualities, even holding them for their own customers who sometimes preferred to buy them ball by ball on a weekly basis as their knitting progressed rather than lay out all the cash in advance.

Fred Harrap died in 1960 and his daughter, Jean Tyrrell, took over, and in 1971 brought in a new managing director (K. Palmer), followed by the appointment of new board members, G. Lumb as secretary, and G. Hampton as marketing director. The 1970s proved to be a difficult decade for most of British industry, marked as it was by the major recession of 1973/4, following the quadrupling of the price of oil by the Organization of Petroleum Exporting Countries (OPEC), and the later recession beginning in 1979.

Wool, as the basic raw material used by Sirdar, had always been a volatile commodity in price terms, and when the year to year changes in the price of specific wools are examined with respect to the average price for a given period, they are seen to be second only to rubber for fluctuations. Not only was the wool price a volatile variable, but the industry faced difficulties over the qualitative variability of wool and other fibres used which made successful buying and blending critical. Indeed the wool industry was famous for people and firms where fortunes were based on wool-buying expertise rather than woollen manufacturing.

In 1973 the company made two further significant moves. It decided to reduce its dependence upon wool by increasing the proportion of synthetic fibres used, and it acquired the business of 'Hayfield Yarns', retaining it as a different brand of knitting yarns to Sirdar, which tended to be of higher quality and higher price. Hayfield was also interested in hosiery manufacture, but this was discontinued within two years, allowing further expansion of the hand-knitting yarn capacity.

The UK hand-knitting yarn market had experienced a large decline in volume terms in the first half of the 1970s, when it fell by over 30% between 1970 and 1976, and only really recovered in 1978 with the advent of a fashion trend towards more chunky garments. These garments use more wool, and hence lead to higher sales by manufacturers, so the market demand is led by fashion design as much as by interest in hand knitting as a pastime. Market size was estimated to be approximately £200 million at retail prices in the early 1980s.

Of this market about one-third was sold as unbranded products and the balance shared by a number of manufacturers, of which the most important were Sirdar, which (including its Hayfield brand) had a 35% market share, Patons with 25% and Robin (including Emu) with about 20%. (These market shares refer to the branded sector.) The most significant importers were Phildar from France, and Three Swifts from Belgium. Phildar sold through its own chain of 82 specialist wool shops.

About half the market sales were retailed through small specialist wool shops which concentrated mainly on the branded, higher priced yarns, and the balances through other retail outlets like department stores and variety chains. Within the latter group, Littlewoods played a significant role as retailers of about 10% of the market, concentrating on own-brand labels.

By 1985 Sirdar had sales revenue of over £36 million and profits before tax of nearly £10 million (see Appendix 1), and attributed their success to three major factors:

1 The small and hence flexible organization of the company, based as it was on a board of directors with only five members.
2 Brand leadership of the market which they achieved in 1981 and had maintained since.
3 Continuing expenditure on the latest available equipment.

This was inspired, in part at least, by the Wool Textile Industry Scheme begun by the UK government in 1973 (with a second stage in 1976) with the aim of improving the industry's competitive position by providing assistance to: (i) modernize production facilities; (ii) improve industrial structure; (iii) eliminate uneconomic excess capacity. Thus by the mid 1980s Sirdar was established as a leading company in the UK hand-knitting yarn market. Its major competitors were Patons (which was a part of Coats Paton) and Robert Glew & Co Ltd (whose major brands were Robin and Emu). Appendix 2 shows financial data for Robert Glew.

Appendix 1 Sirdar plc

PROFIT AND LOSS ACCOUNT, YEAR ENDED 30 JUNE (£000)

	1985	*1984*	*1983*
Turnover	36,495	33,122	30,021
Costs and overheads	27,437	24,762	22,854
Operating profit	9,058	8,360	7,167
Interest and other income received	475	648	479
Profit on ordinary activities before taxation	9,533	9,008	7,646
Taxation	3,504	3,004	2,813
Profit on ordinary activities after taxation	6,029	6,004	4,833
Extraordinary item	–	247[a]	–
Profit for year	6,029	5,757	4,833
Dividends	1,983	1,566	1,196
Profit retained	4,046	4,191	3,637

[a] Extraordinary item arose from closure of subsidiary company in Switzerland which had been making losses. (Sirdar had closed other subsidiary companies in South Africa and Australia in 1974.)

GEOGRAPHICAL ANALYSIS OF TURNOVER (£000)

	Total	*UK*	*Eire*	*Europe*	*Asia*
1982	27,282	24,167	996	865	493
1983	30,021	25,956	1,016	947	920
1984	33,122	28,049	1,092	1,235	1,147

	Africa	*N. America*	*Australasia*	*Rest of world*
1982	106	304	337	14
1983	32	455	631	64
1984	30	826	728	16

BALANCE SHEET AS AT 30 JUNE (£000)

	1985		1984		1983	
Fixed assets						
Tangible		16,091		14,540		11,997
Investment		730		336		
		16,821		14,876		11,997
Current assets						
Stocks	8,638		7,611		5,907	
Debtors	6,216		5,446		5,185	
Investments	8,678		8,752		6,668	
Cash at bank and in hand	377		129		60	
	23,909		21,938		17,820	
Creditors (due within one year)	9,806		10,594		7,194	
Net current assets	14,103		11,344		10,626	
Creditors (due after one year)	2,671		2,002		2,599	
Net working capital		11,432		9,342		8,027
		28,253		24,218		20,024
Capital and reserves						
Called-up share capital		12,167		12,167		6,184
Profit and loss account		16,086		12,051		13,840
		28,253		24,218		20,024

13-YEAR RECORD (£MILLIONS – EXCEPT EMPLOYEES)

Year	*Sales*	*PBT*	*Fixed assets*	*Net current*	*No. of employees*	*Capital expenditure*	*Stocks*
1972	6.6	0.635	1.316	1.276	1051	N/A	2.147
1973	9.5	0.842	2.640	1.432	1601	N/A	3.168
1974	10.5	0.609	2.739	1.482	1535	N/A	2.789
1975	11.57	0.812	2.977	1.815	1565	0.443	3.338
1976	13.51	0.942	3.640	2.146	1512	0.952	4.674
1977	16.43	1.136	4.472	3.505	1484	1.250	4.880
1978	19.28	2.110	5.851	3.080	1457	1.896	4.860
1979	21.35	3.197	7.640	3.445	1414	2.640	5.290
1980	22.99	3.726	8.825	3.997	1278	2.209	5.370
1981	27.65	5.314	9.879	5.199	1243	2.349	5.650
1982	29.63	6.175	11.401	6.540	1212	2.911	5.650
1983	30.02	7.646	11.997	10.626	1152	2.861	5.907
1984	33.12	9.008	14.540	11.344	1137	4.168	7.611
1985	36.49	9.533	16.091	14.103	1157	3.346	8.638

Appendix 2 Robert Glew & Co. Ltd

CONSOLIDATED PROFIT AND LOSS ACCOUNT, YEAR ENDING DECEMBER (£000)

	1980	*1981*	*1982*	*1983*	*1984*
Turnover	12,246	13,537	15,200	17,934	21,695
Changes in stocks	N/A	N/A	(352)	(484)	(2,448)
Raw materials	N/A	N/A	6,413	7,858	10,820
Other external charges	N/A	N/A	3,814	4,500	6,232
Staff costs	N/A	N/A	3,486	3,807	4,464
Depreciation	140	207	254	358	454
Interest payable	269	113	121	150	266
Profit (loss) before tax	1,092	1,446	1,464	1,745	1,907
Corporation tax	347	351	522	567	761
Deferred tax	–	–	–	–	130
ACT recoverable	(26)	–	–	–	–
Overseas tax	–	–	4	13	36
Prior year adjustment	(7)	(41)	(16)	(17)	(26)
Total taxation	314	310	510	563	901
Profit (loss) after tax	778	1,136	954	1,182	1,006
Preference dividends	1	1	1	1	1
Profit after preference dividends	777	1,135	953	1,181	1,005
Ordinary dividends	36	53	60	69	90
Extraordinary items	–	–	–	–	118
Retained profit (loss)	741	1,082	893	1,112	797

Notes

Staff costs					
Wages and Salaries	N/A	N/A	3,022	3,335	3,907
Social security	N/A	N/A	320	297	358
Pensions	N/A	N/A	144	175	199
			3,486	3,807	4,464

CONSOLIDATED PROFIT AND LOSS ACCOUNT, YEAR ENDING DECEMBER (£000) continued

	1980	*1981*	*1982*	*1983*	*1984*
Average no of employees	621	588	563	554	612
Interest payable					
Bank	236	112	104	128	199
Loan	31	1	–	–	–
Other	2	–	17	22	67
	269	113	121	150	266
Profit before tax is after charging/(crediting)					
Auditors' remuneration	22	25	21	19	26
Plant hire	143	160	180	190	194
Sale of assets	(2)	(10)	(4)	–	–
Dividends	(1)	(1)	–	–	–
Regional development grant	(19)	(10)	–	–	–
Sale of investments	–	(1)	–	–	–
Directors					
Emoluments	87	119	146	160	173
Loss of office	–	–	–	–	50
Corporation Tax rate %	52	52	52	52	46.4
Extraordinary items					
Compensation costs	–	–	–	–	65
Tax credit	–	–	–	–	(30)
	–	–	–	–	35
Deferred tax	–	–	–	–	83
	–	–	–	–	118

GEOGRAPHICAL ANALYSIS OF TURNOVER (£000)

	Total	*EEC*	*Others*
1982	15,200	13,702	1,498
1983	17,934	16,070	1,864
1984	21,695	19,389	2,306

STATEMENT OF SOURCE AND APPLICATION OF FUNDS (£000)

	1980	*1981*	*1982*	*1983*	*1984*
Source of funds					
Operations	1,215	1,632	1,718	2,105	2,288
Asset disposal	17	18	N/A	N/A	N/A
Regional development grants	59	6	(10)	(10)	138
Loan	–	–	–	–	591
Investments	–	47	–	–	–
Net liquid funds					
Cash	43	(12)	8	(1)	(307)
Overdraft & advances	(575)	(313)	84	(143)	2,465
Decrease (increase)	(532)	(325)	92	(144)	2,158
Total	759	1,378	1,800	1,951	5,175
Application of funds					
Dividends	27	35	51[b]	60[b]	81[b]
Fixed assets	311	740	596	828	1,052
Taxation	23	149	259	487	676
Loans	353	21	–	–	–
Investments	46	–	–	–	–
Stocks	197	158	352	484	2,448
Debtors	(158)	208	1,052	(365)	1,347
Creditors	(40)	67	(510)	273	(429)
Working capital[a]	(1)	433	894	576	3,366
Total	759	1,378	1,800	1,951	5,175

[a] Excluding net liquid funds.
[b] Net of disposals.

CONSOLIDATED BALANCE SHEET, YEAR ENDED DECEMBER (£000)

	1982	*1983*	*1984*
Fixed assets			
Tangible	2,109	2,578	3,178
Current assets			
Stocks	3,436	3,920	6,368
Debtors	4,454	4,795	6,217
Prepayments	201	226	151
Investments	1	1	1
Cash	17	18	324
	8,109	8,960	13,061
Creditors			
(Due within one year)			
Bank overdraft	401	242	1,787
Advances	158	175	1,095
Creditors	2,232	2,469	2,858
Tax provision	937	1,023	1,136
Accruals	198	225	301
Dividends	70	80	90
	3,996	4,214	7,267
Net current assets	4,113	4,746	5,794
Net assets			
(Total assets less current liabilities)	6,222	7,324	8,972
Creditors			
(Due after one year)			
Government grants	152	142	266
Loans	–	–	507
Employees benefit fund	34	34	34
Deferred tax	–	–	213
	186	176	1,020
	6,036	7,148	7,952
Capital	1,580	1,580	1,580
Profit and loss account	4,456	5,568	6,732
	6,036	7,148	7,952

Source: Reproduced by arrangement with Extel Statistical Services Ltd, 37–45 Paul St, London EC2A 4PB

TABLE 2.1

Using the information in Appendices 1 and 2, complete the following:

	Sirdar plc			*Robert Glew*	
	1985	*1984*	*1983*	*1984*	*1983*
Gearing					
Return on capital employed[a]					
Stockturn					
Net asset per share					
Gross profit margin[b]					
Earnings per share[c]					
Dividend cover					
Price/Earnings ratio				–	–
Share price	123p[d]	135p[e]	101p[e]	N/A	N/A

[a] Using EBIT.
[b] Using 'Operating Profit'.
[c] Number of ordinary shares = 47.868 million (Sirdar) and 6.32 million (R. Glew).
[d] On 16 October 1985.
[c] Average for each year.
(1985 figures are not available for R. Glew.)

TABLE 2.2 Sirdar plc

Using the information in Appendix 1 complete the following:

Year	*Actual sales £m*	*Inflation adjusted sales*[a] *£m*	*Actual PBT £m*	*Inflation adjusted PBT £m*	$\frac{PBT}{sales}$ *as %*	*Stock turnover rate*	*Fixed asset turnover*	*Net asset turnover*[b]	*ROCE as % (PBT*[c] *net assets)*
1972	6.6		0.635						
1973	9.5		0.842						
1974	10.5		0.609						
1975	11.137		0.812						
1976	12.961		0.942						
1977	15.636		1.136						
1978	18.174		2.110						
1979	20.028		3.197						
1980	21.37		3.726						
1981	25.384		5.314						
1982	27.282		6.175						
1983	30.021		7.646						
1984	33.122		9.008						
1985	36.495		9.533						

[a] Corrected to 1972 base e.g. 1985 = 1985 sales × $\frac{0.213}{0.860}$ – use inflation index (see annexe).

[b] Fixed assets plus net current assets.

[c] Using PBT as 'EBIT' is not always available.

Annexe

Inflation

Year	*Index*
1970	1.000
1971	0.940
1972	0.860
1973	0.803
1974	0.735
1975	0.633
1976	0.510
1977	0.437
1978	0.377
1979	0.349
1980	0.307
1981	0.274
1982	0.253
1983	0.238
1984	0.226
1985	0.213

Example 1

Year	*1970*	*1971*	*1972*	*1973*	*1974*	*1975*
Figures	120	170	204	310	502	590
Corrected figures (to 1970 base)	120	160	175	249	369	373
	(× 1.000	0.940	0.860	0.803	0.735	0.633)

Example 2

Year	*1974*	*1975*	*1976*	*1977*	*1978*	*1979*
Figures	502	590	620	690	710	720
Corrected figures (to 1974 base)	502	508	430	410	364	342
	(× $\frac{0.735}{0.735}$	$\frac{0.633}{0.735}$	$\frac{0.510}{0.735}$	$\frac{0.437}{0.735}$	$\frac{0.377}{0.735}$	$\frac{0.349}{0.735}$)

3 Marks and Spencer

For the financial year end in March 1985 Marks and Spencer (M & S) reported sales of over £3 billion and pre-tax profits of over £300 million, and whilst they remained Britain's largest retailer the growth in profits over the previous year was disappointing. (See Appendix 1 for financial information on Marks and Spencer Plc.)

The centenary of M & S was in 1984, as it was known that Micheal Marks set up his first 'Penny Bazaar' on Leeds market in 1884. A Leeds wholesaler called Isaac Dewhirst gave Michael Marks trade credit and the business relationship formed then still existed over 100 years later, with I.J. Dewhirst Plc being one of the major suppliers to M & S. Tom Spencer, although he knew Michael Marks in 1884, did not become a business partner until 1894, and the work of those two founders was carried on by Simon Marks and brother-in-law Israel Sieff, with a member of the family as chairman of the company until 1984 when Lord Raynor took over, following the retirement of Lord Sieff (grandson of Michael Marks).

The trading principles of M & S were established in 1884 and restated in 1984 in the chairman's annual report. These are directly quoted, as follows:

1 To offer our customer a selected range of goods of high quality and good value.
2 To work in close co-operation with our suppliers to develop this catalogue.
3 Always to buy British providing the goods the British suppliers produce represent high quality and good value.
4 To develop and maintain good human relations with our staff, our suppliers, and our customers.

He went on to say 'Our principles are sacrosant, our policies flexible – which departments to expand, which to contract, what new departments to introduce, where to build stores and what their size should be.'

The basis of M & S success over the years had been founded on textiles and clothing products, although the more recent years had seen most growth in foods and housewares. By building close relationships with clothing manufacturers M & S had been able to enjoy most of the benefits of having its own manufacturing base whilst having few of the responsibilities, and in turn many of the clothing manufacturers had prospered. In this way the company had demonstrated the ability of the UK clothing industry to provide well-designed clothes giving good value for money.

M & S issued 'demand specifications' to their suppliers, many of whom supplied a high proportion of their output to the retailer, e.g. S.R. Gent (ladies outerwear) 95%, I.J. Dewhirst (mens' suits) 90%, N. Corah (underwear) 75%. In return for their loyalty, M & S took an interest in their profitability and assisted in ensuring healthy progression. There was a never-ending search for efficiency allied with strict quality control in order that M & S could claim their 'St Michael' brand provided the best value for money rather than the highest quality. That being a supplier to M & S was considered of value was shown in the fact that 45 suppliers had done so for over 40 years, and 134 for over 25 years. By 1984 M & S had 264 stores in the UK with a total sales area of 6.97 million square feet, a further 262,000 square feet of sales area in mainland Europe (nine stores), and 2.22 million square feet in Canada (in 213 stores).

Each week over 14 million customers shopped at M & S UK stores, and this very success pointed to the company's problems in maintaining the growth rate expected of it. Providing for such a large market meant that it couldn't afford to make many mistakes and this encouraged them to be rather conservative when it came to fashion clothing. M & S had introduced 'Miss Michelle' clothes in 1979 aimed at the more fashion-conscious teenage market, but the customers had decided the clothes offered were not fashionable enough and far too expensive. At the same time they had offered more expensive clothing to other age groups, e.g. silk blouses, but the timing proved wrong as the onset of the recession made it more difficult to sell at higher prices.

Textiles was one of the three trading groups in the company, the others being foods and housewares, but textiles was much the biggest. The organizational structure for these trading groups involved a senior executive in charge supported by two merchandise managers and several selectors (the M & S name for buyers). New product ideas were generated in two ways: first by developing ideas out of existing areas, and second by moving into totally new product areas. The latter route was obviously more risky and was an area where Marks and Spencer expertise at laying down specifications could not be so predominant. Having found new product areas, through various methods, the company needed to divide good ideas from bad. The company did not undertake quantitative or qualitative marketing research, but preferred to put new products straight into the High Street by trying them in about 20 stores, always including the two major London stores.

M & S had begun to respond to the new challenges in the clothing sector by:

1 cutting lead times for orders;
2 ordering in smaller quantities;
3 moving towards more co-ordinated fashion ranges, especially for the 25 to 35 year old market;
4 including new, more fashionable clothing products;
5 taking advantage of the new technology to increase control over stock-holding and provide better sales information.

These challenges in the clothing sector were exemplified firstly by the growth and development of the so-called 'lifestyle' retailers such as 'Next' which had segmented the clothing market and aimed specifically at certain age-groups; secondly, by the relatively slow growth of consumer expenditure on clothing generally in the UK; and thirdly, by the increased penetration of the clothing market by overseas manufacturers in the face of the M & S policy to buy British.

Consumer expenditure on clothing in the United Kingdom represented a significant proportion of total expenditure. However, a number of environmental changes throughout the 1970s and 1980s had posed both opportunities and threats to retailers. Although total consumer expenditure continued to grow, expenditure on clothing exhibited a different pattern and volume (see table 3.1).

TABLE 3.1 Consumer expenditure on clothing £m (current prices)

Year	*Clothing expenditure*	*Total consumer expenditure*
1980	8,103	136,789
1981	8,406	152,125
1982	8,854	166,477
1983	9,804	182,420
1984	10,637	194,954

Source: CSO.

Appendix 2 gives further information on clothing expenditure.

Changes in clothing retailing had been profound, with the entry into the market of food retailers and fundamental changes in strategy by existing clothing retailers. Superstores, those with over 25,000 sq ft of selling space, had grown rapidly from 24 in 1971 to 369 by 1984. These stores needed a large minimum population to sustain their profitability and cost, some £7m to £8m. The saturation level of such stores was expected to be some 600 in the UK by the end of the decade. Over 90% of these stores sold clothing which was a relatively new product line for them. Clothing was the sixth most common item in these stores, after food, meat, vegetables, liquor and confectionery. A major reason for this entry into clothing by superstores was the slowdown in the growth of food sales in the 1970s.

A further major change was the trend to more casual clothing. Large chains of menswear retailers, which had grown to prominence with the made-to-measure suit, suffered because of this trend.

During the 1970s and early 1980s the UK economy suffered two major recessions due to the oil crises of 1974 and 1979, with consequent effects upon the retail sector including clothing.

The major factors influencing clothing sales remained population size and composition and income. (See Appendix 3). Changes in these variables coupled with changes in habits (e.g. towards more casual clothing) had contributed to changes in the pattern of demand for clothing.

There were approximately 10,000 shops specializing in menswear and 22,000 specializing in womenswear. The numbers in both markets had been slowly decreasing over the decade (see Appendix 4 for principal companies and their market shares). Major changes have taken place in both markets, where there has been a general trend away from formal wear in the menswear market and the emergence of new classes of customer in the womenswear market. Generally the womenswear market has been more resilient to environmental pressures. The 1980 government 'Retailing Inquiry' found that gross margins in menswear were 40% with a stockturn of 4.2, whilst for womenswear the comparable figures were 37% and 4.8.

A number of important developments took place during the 1970s, beginning with the development of boutiques and the significant growth of the variety chains, e.g. M & S which built up large market shares by negotiating output and price levels with clothing manufacturers although they tended not to be leaders in fashion. Also during this period some specialist clothing multiples, e.g. Burtons and J. Hepworth, took a greater interest in the womenswear market and began developing specialist chains to cater for specific age-groups.

Many of the major retail chains turned to design specialists such as 'Conran Associates' (e.g. Hepworths and Miss Selfridge) or 'Fitch' (e.g. Burton) to help them not only in attracting the right kind of consumer, but also to get them to spend more money. This showed an appreciation that it was not sufficient to maintain volume increases by relying on inflation. Thus the Habitat Stores of Terence Conran beginning in the 1960s had set standards for design and image creation, whilst lessons were also learned from the food retailers with respect to productivity (higher rates of sales per square foot of sales space). As a consequence, the clothing retailers had to achieve a balance between attracting the appropriate target audience and then giving them sufficient space to enable clothes shopping to be a pleasurable experience.

Information on major retailers follows.

BURTONS

Burtons menswear retailing was divided into 'Top Man' with 166 outlets catering for the 15 to 25 age group and 'Burtons' with 309 outlets catering for 20 to 44 year olds. Womenswear retailing was more segmented into four distinct chains.

'Top Shop' had 104 outlets for the 15–30 age group, 'Peter Robinson' with three stores was for the 25–44 age group, 'Dorothy Perkins' with 271 outlets catered for 20–35 year olds, and 'Evans' had 104 outlets for the larger sized.

During 1984 Burtons opened 166 new clothing retailing outlets which increased the sales area of the group by 400,000 square feet. By the end of 1984 the group had 957 outlets with sales turnover of £416 million and more than a 5% share of the UK retail clothing market, and during 1984 the group had launched 'Principles' with 19 outlets, with plans to expand, as a competitive response to 'Next' (see below).

'Principles' opened its first outlets in September 1984 aimed at the 25–40 year old women, with plans to open 50 stores within a year and 200 in total. The intention was to provide a wide range of co-ordinated clothing in spacious surroundings.

HEPWORTH'S/NEXT

J. Hepworth was, like Burton's, one of the original menswear tailors producing made-to-measure suits, and with its own manufacturing capacity, but unlike Burton's did not change its competitive stance until the early 1980s. In 1981 it bought the Kendall's chain of 79 womenswear outlets and converted them into 'Next' for women between 25 and 40 years selling a co-ordinated range of clothing. The 'Next' stores which first opened in 1982 were designed to have a continental look, with cool colours and a racking system and no models which gave customers easy access to the merchandise. The staff chosen were deliberately of the same age group as the target of customers. 'Next' also learned from Marks & Spencer's success, whereby the latter demanded high-quality finished products at competitive prices from its suppliers. The outlets were a great success and by the end of 1984 there were 176 'Next' outlets achieving annual sales per square foot of £400. The original Hepworth outlets for menswear had fallen to 375 by the end of 1984 and had produced annual sales per square foot of £160.

In August 1984 Hepworth's expanded the 'Next' idea to menswear retailing and opened the first 'Next for Men' outlet, and by the end of the year had opened 50 with plans to reach 100 within a year. As with womenswear, the target age group was 25 to 40 and design of the store was important.

Following the relatively poor financial results in 1984, M & S decided to re-establish itself in the retailing area as the major force, and in particular against the inroads made by chains such as Burton's and 'Next'. A number of changes were announced, including the appointment of a new chairman in 1984, and the announcement that the company had decided to seek out and develop out-of-town sites in co-operation with the Tesco Supermarket chain in order to provide more selling space and parking convenience for customers. This would also mean the need for more products, for M & S was unusual in having a fairly narrow product range for such a large retailing presence. These changes were part of a two-year plan to set the company back on a high-growth course. Other parts were:

1 Capital expenditure on a large scale to refurbish existing stores, and extend selling areas where possble. A 700,000 square foot increase was planned for.

2 Introduction of the M & S charge-card with expectations of having three million cardholders by 1990 (Visa had four million), and proifits from it by 1988. M & S had piloted the charge-card in Scotland and registered 6% of sales recorded to it in the larger Scottish city stores. The initial start-up costs were estimated to be £2 million.

3 Change in the role of some stores. For example, the Camden Town store would sell only food and homewares, and the Chiswick store only women's fashion wear and foods.

4 Introduction of shops-within-shops (e.g. houseplants).

5 Opening of 'satellite stores', i.e. smaller stores close to original M & S stores which would concentrate on specific product areas. The first two of these were the 'man's shop' in Huddersfield, and 'childrens-wear' shop in York. The latter would compete directly with Mothercare, had 5,000 square feet of selling area and was 200 yards from its parent store.

Appendix 1 Financial information: Marks and Spencer Plc

PROFIT AND LOSS ACCOUNT (£ THOUSANDS)

Year ended March

	1982	*1983*	*1984*	*1985*
Turnover				
Clothing	1,226,000	1,353,00	1,493,600	1,611,800
Homeware, footwear and accessories	172,400	216,300	261,800	385,300
Foods	774,700	902,900	1,060,600	1,215,900
General merchandise	25,600	33,300	38,500	–
Total	2,198,700	2,505,500	2,854,500	3,213,000
Profit before tax	222,100	239,300	279,300	303,400
Attributable profit	120,700	135,200	166,400	181,100

BALANCE SHEET (£ THOUSANDS)

	1983	*1984*	*1985*
Fixed assets	1,075,700	1,293,700	1,373,500
Current assets			
Stocks	163,300	194,100	229,700
Debtors	57,600	61,900	67,400
Investments	108,900	58,400	108,300
Cash	63,200	73,400	83,800
Current assets	393,000	387,800	489,200
Current liabilities	432,500	396,400	477,300
Total assets less current liabilities	1,212,600	1,285,100	1,385,400
Financed by			
Shareholders funds	1,140,000	1,226,800	1,325,300
Minority interests	7,300	8,800	10,800
Deferred taxation	12,900	–	–
Long-term debt	52,400	49,500	49,300
	1,212,600	1,285,100	1,385,400

Number of ordinary shares: 2,639.7 million

SEVEN-YEAR RECORD (£m)

	1979	*1980*	*1981*	*1982*	*1983*	*1984*	*1985*
Turnover	1,473.0	1,667.9	1,872.9	2,198.7	2,505.5	2,854.5	3,213.0
Profit before tax	161.6	173.7	181.2	222.1	239.3	279.3	303.4
Attributable profit	85.5	93.9	99.5	120.7	135.2	166.4	181.1
Number of stores							
UK	253	251	252	256	260	262	265
Europe	4	5	6	7	8	9	9
Canada[a]	178	190	198	203	209	213	227
Total sales area ('000 square feet)							
UK	6,267	6,374	6,443	6,624	6,825	6,971	7,216
Europe	119	154	163	200	236	262	266
Canada	1,719	1,881	1,910	2,116	2,195	2,220	2,304

GEOGRAPHICAL ANALYSIS OF TURNOVER AND PROFIT (£m)

	1982	*1983*	*1984*	*1985*
Turnover				
UK: stores	2,024.3	2,276.2	2,596.7	2,900.2
Europe: stores	43.6	64.4	74.4	80.9
Canada: stores	103.3	137.3	150.2	175.0
Exports	26.5	27.6	33.2	38.2
Profits before tax				
UK	216.4	231.0	265.3	288.7
Europe	3.1	3.7	6.7	7.1
Canada	2.6	4.6	7.3	7.6

[a] Marks and Spencer plc own 57% of the equity of the Canadian company which operated three divisions.

Source: Derived from Company Annual Reports

Appendix 2

THE CLOTHING MARKET

Year	Current prices (£ billion)	1980 prices (£ billion)
1973	3,232	6,860
1974	3,773	6,750
1975	4,365	6,828
1976	4,834	6,838
1977	5,520	6,961
1978	6,488	7,596
1979	7,555	8,149
1980	8,103	8,103
1981	8,406	8,334
1982	8,854	8,676
1983	9,804	9,405

Year	*Men's & boys' wear*	*1980 = 100 Index*	*Women's*	*1980 = 100 Index*	*All items*	*1980 = 100 Index*
1973	2,903	107	4,023	74	127,436	93
1974	2,838	105	3,975	74	125,630	92
1975	2,794	103	4,083	76	124,748	91
1976	2,721	101	4,152	77	125,175	92
1977	2,682	99	4,300	80	124,564	91
1978	2,803	104	4,793	89	131,373	96
1979	2,880	107	5,269	98	137,256	100
1980	2,702	100	5,401	100	136,789	100
1981	2,680	99	5,654	105	136,714	100
1982	2,798	104	5,878	109	138,135	101
1983	3,049	112	6,356	118	144,008	105

Source: Central Statistical Office (1984)

Appendix 3 Population and income

SELECTED DEMOGRAPHIC INFORMATION ON POPULATION SIZE AND STRUCTURE

(1) AGE DISTRIBUTION IN THE UK (THOUSANDS)

	Enumerated[1] population		*Home population*			
	1961	*1971[a]*	*1971[b]*	*1975*	*1978*	*1980*
Persons	52,709	55,515	55,610	55,901	55,836	55,945
Under 5	4,213	4,505	4,503	3,950	3,408	3,411
5–14	8,123	8,882	8,909	9,118	8,879	8,417
15–29	10,258	11,678	11,714	12,124	12,281	12,567
30–44	10,526	9,759	9,751	9,860	10,424	10,744
45–64	13,400	13,389	13,389	13,021	12,716	12,477
65+	6,189	7,307	7,345	7,827	8,128	8,329

[1] Figures for 1961 and 1971 [a] are for the 'Enumerated' population, i.e. counted at the census, whereas figures for 1971 [b] to 1980 are for the 'Home' population. The two are not strictly comparable.
Source: CSO Annual Abstract 1983

(2) PROJECTED TOTAL POPULATION STRUCTURE (THOUSANDS)

	1979 (base)	*1986*	*1991*	*1996*
Persons	55,946	56,416	57,192	57,939
Males				
Under 14	6,191	5,728	6,082	6,572
15–29	6,368	6,846	6,576	5,954
30–44	5,367	5,711	5,985	6,225
45–64	6,126	5,953	5,954	6,298
65+	3,213	3,294	3,363	3,328
Females				
Under 14	5,859	5,417	5,755	6,215
15–29	6,090	6,526	6,270	5,673
30–44	5,254	5,638	5,902	6,094
45–64	6,466	6,190	6,147	6,508
65+	5,012	5,113	5,158	5,072

Source: CSO Annual Abstract 1983

(3) THE LABOUR FORCE IN BRITAIN

	1977	*1981*
Labour force estimates (m)		
All men	15.9	15.9
All women	10.3	10.4
Married women	6.9	6.7
Non-married women	3.3	3.7
All persons	26.1	26.3
Labour force composition (%)		
All men	60.7	60.4
All women	39.3	39.6
Married women	26.5	25.5
Non-married women	12.8	14.0
All persons	100.0	100.0

Source: Equal Opportunities Commission

(4) ECONOMIC ACTIVITY RATES OF MARRIED WOMEN (%)

	1911	*1921*	*1931*	*1951*	*1961*	*1971*	*1977*	*1981*
All ages above school leaving age	9.6	8.7	10.0	21.7	29.7	42.3	50.4	49.5

This was a trend, which, in view of the number of women entering into higher education, looked likely to continue.

(5) UK PERSONAL DISPOSABLE INCOME

Year	*Current prices (£m)*	*1984 prices (using DOI price index) (£m)*
1974	59,907	59,907
1975	74,005	61,722
1976	84,949	57,436
1977	96,300	55,858
1978	113,404	59,843
1979	136,802	66,024
1980	160,820	65,560
1981	174,491	59,149
1982	190,766	59,539
1983	205,442	61,308
1984	220,524	61,651

Source: D.O.I.

(6) INDEX OF PRICES (1974 = 100)

	All items	*Clothing retailers*
1980	263.7	205.4
1981	295.0	208.3
1982	320.4	210.5
1983	335.1	214.8
1984	357.7	216.2
	Average increase = 18.8% p.a.	Average increase = 2.16% p.a.

Appendix 4

(1) MENSWEAR RETAILERS: 1984 MARKET SHARES (%)

Marks & Spencer	14.0
Burton Group	5.8
C & A Modes	3.8
British Home Stores	2.9
Littlewoods	2.6
Hepworths	2.3
Foster Brothers	2.0
G.A. Dunn	1.4
Greenwoods	1.0
Cecil Gee	0.6
Mail order	7.0
Department stores	5.5
Independent specialists	28.7
Others	22.4
	100.0

Source: Euromonitor (1984)

(2) WOMENSWEAR RETAILERS: 1982 MARKET SHARES (%)

Marks & Spencer	20
C & A Modes	6
Burton Group	5
British Home Stores	4
Littlewoods	3
Other multiple specialists	12
Independent specialists	24
Department stores	11
Mail order	11
Other retailers	4
	100

Source: Mintel and press reports

Burton Group PLC: financial information

PROFIT AND LOSS ACCOUNT, YEAR ENDED AUGUST
(£ THOUSANDS)

	1980	*1981*	*1982*	*1983*	*1984*	*1985*
Turnover	196,451	189,623	231,944	299,174	415,989	551,001
Cost of sales	–	–	188,601	238,918	332,277	432,364
Gross profit	–	–	43,343	60,256	83,621	118,637
Distribution costs	–	–	(5,476)	(6,892)	(9,129)	(12,769)
Admin expenses	–	–	(13,596)	(15,624)	(19,062)	(24,314)
TRADING PROFIT	14,729	18,656	24,271	37,740	55,430	81,554
Interest	(5,224)	(4,128)	(128)	1,168	976	(2,407)
Other income	3,125	1,846	164	215	2	1,055
PROFIT BEFORE TAX	12,630	16,374	24,307	39,123	56,408	80,202
Taxation	(1,949)	(2,336)	(4,900)	(11,100)	(19,700)	(28,650)
PROFIT AFTER TAX	10,681	14,038	19,407	28,023	36,708	51,552
Dividends	(4,262)	(5,193)	(6,460)	(8,628)	(11,440)	(21,505)
Extraordinary items	(10,328)	2,027	–	–	–	–
RETAINED PROFIT (LOSS)	(3,909)	10,872	12,947	19,395	25,268	30,047

ANALYSIS OF TURNOVER/PROFIT (£ THOUSANDS)

	Turnover				*Profit*			
	1982	*1983*	*1984*	*1985*	*1982*	*1983*	*1984*	*1985*
Menswear	121,573	155,202	222,116	283,323	15,600	23,272	34,563	47,963
Womenswear	106,384	139,198	188,012	259,177	8,656	14,166	20,482	32,972
Manufacturing	353	591	–	–	(87)	91	–	–
Other activities	3,634	4,183	5,770	8,501	102	211	385	619
Totals	231,944	299,174	415,898	551,001	24,271	37,740	55,430	81,554
Interest					(128)	1,168	976	(2,407)
Plus other income					164	215	2	1,055
Profit before tax					24,307	39,123	56,408	80,202

BALANCE SHEETS

	1982	*1983*	*1984*
Fixed assets	227,533	248,871	302,591
Current assets			
Stock	27,630	38,373	64,006
Debtors	5,276	5,496	7,414
Others	16,775	26,381	12,781
Total current assets	49,681	70,250	84,201
Total assets	277,214	319,121	386,792
Less current liabilities	47,120	66,479	103,281
Net assets	230,094	252,642	283,511
Shareholders' funds	216,192	239,056	260,758
Loans	5,612	4,736	4,606
Others	8,290	8,850	18,147
	230,894	252,642	283,511

Source: Reproduced by arrangement with Extel Statistical Services Ltd, 37–45 Paul Street, London EC2A 4PB

J. Hepworth PLC – financial information

(i) PROFIT AND LOSS ACCOUNT (£ THOUSANDS)

	1975	*1976*	*1977*	*1978*	*1979*	*1980*	*1981*	*1982*	*1983*	*1984*	*1985*
Turnover	29,890	27,880	33,735	41,786	50,457	61,923	75,692	83,370	98,603	108,331	146,045
Interest	(1,031)	(1,101)	(1,289)	(838)	(1,272)	(1,587)	(1,631)	(2,681)	(967)	(280)	(690)
Profit before tax	3,410	2,804	3,559	5,225	6,603	5,705	4,083	3,860	8,561	13,616	20,063
Taxation	(1,874)	(1,623)	(971)	(2,568)	(1,770)	(2,856)	(748)	(92)	(2,423)	(6,518)	(8,271)
Profit after tax	1,536	1,181	2,588	2,651	4,815	2,849	3,335	3,768	6,138	7,098	11,792
Dividends	(902)	(902)	(992)	(1,102)	(1,619)	(1,687)	(1,716)	(1,815)	(2,502)	(3,513)	N/A
Extraordinary items	917	469	1,246	430	518	48	120	1,529	808	451	2,147
Retained profit	634	279	1,596	1,549	3,196	1,162	1,619	1,953	3,636	3,585	N/A

(ii) TURNOVER AND PROFIT (£ THOUSANDS)

Year ended August	*Retailing*[a]		*Manufacturing*[a]		*Property*[a]		*Total*	
	Turnover	*Profit*	*Turnover*	*Profit*	*Turnover*	*Profit*	*Turnover*	*Profit*
1980	60,235	2,120	11,692	(466)	5,117	2,550	61,923	5,705
1981	73,503	(62)	6,608	320	8,012	2,017	75,692	4,083
1982	81,920	(309)	5,238	296	9,762	2,617	83,370	3,860
1983	97,122	2,727	5,073	204	10,212	2,537	98,603	8,561
1984	106,018	6,580	4,041	(434)	11,621	3,043	108,331	13,616

[a] Does not sum to total due to intergroup sales.

(iii) BALANCE SHEET (£ THOUSANDS)

	1983	*1984*
Fixed assets	108,965	120,774
Current assets	24,958	38,766
Current liabilities	17,427	30,604
Total assets less current liabilities	116,496	128,935
Financed by		
Shareholders' funds	111,848	122,020
Debentures	990	990
Deferred tax	3,658	5,925
	116,496	128,935

Source: Reproduced by arrangement with Extel Statistical Services Limited, 37–45 Paul Street, London EC2A 4PB

4 Imperial Group

In 1902 Imperial Tobacco was formed when a group of British tobacco companies including John Player's of Nottingham and W.D. and H.O. Wills of Bristol combined when faced with the entry to the UK market by an American tobacco-cigarette manufacturer. This resulted in an agreement whereby the UK firms and the American firm formed a new company (British American Tobacco Ltd) with the rights to use the Imperial brand names in overseas countries. Following the entry of the UK into the European Economic Community in 1973, this holding by Imperial in BAT was sold in two stages in 1975 and 1979. This had a twofold effect in that, on the one hand, Imperial (having sold its BAT shares) thus became more dependent on the UK market and, on the other hand, the resulting tax changes made the UK market easier to enter for overseas companies because EEC tax harmonization made price competition more effective.

By the mid 1970s the UK method of taxing cigarettes by the weight of the tobacco in them had led to the UK market being dominated by small-size but high-quality cigarettes, and Imperial brands 'Players' No 6' and 'Player's No 10' were the brand leaders. However, the European Economic Community, in order to rationalize the method on which tobacco duty was based throughout the Community, determined that the duty should be paid on the number of cigarettes (regardless of size) plus a percentage of the retail price. This created a revolution in the British market as smokers switched to King Size cigarettes very rapidly as they became relatively less expensive, and the tobacco companies began a price war as they fought for market share in the new market. Gallahers had previously sold their King Size 'Benson and Hedges' brand in an attempt to find a market niche not dominated by an Imperial brand and they found themselves with an overnight brand leader with 15% of the whole cigarette market, as King Size cigarettes grew from 10% of the market to 80% in a period of three years. Imperial introduced King Size brands and by 1981 had spent £13 million promoting 'John Player Special' in order to get a 12% share of the market. By 1982 Imperial recorded a market share down to just under 50% of the total market (from 68% in 1972) and 45% of the King Size market.

A problem for both Imperial and Gallaher (a part of American Brands), as original British-based manufacturers largely dependent on the UK economy for sales, was intensified competition from BAT industries and Rothmans International which were both heavily export-oriented. Rothmans took a 14% share of the UK market and BAT 6%. Table 4.1 shows the trends in market shares.

TABLE 4.1 UK cigarette market share by company (%)

	1973	*1975*	*1977*	*1979*	*1980*	*1981*	*1982*
Imperial	65	66	61	54	51.5	49.1	26.2
Gallaher	27	26	29	28	28.3	28.8	29.9
Rothmans	7	7	9	13	13.7	12.1	14.0
BAT	–	–	0.2	2.9	4.0	5.9	5.9
Morris	–	0.4	0.5	1.6	2.1	2.6	2.6
Other[a]					0.4	1.5	1.5

[a] Own labels/generics and minor brands

Source: Review by brokers Wood, Mackenzie & Co

By 1982 the proportion of men smoking cigarettes in the UK had fallen to 38% compared with 52% for 1972. Comparative figures for women were 33% and 41%. The Office of Population Census reported that consumption of cigarettes in the same period had risen from 120 cigarettes per week to 121 for men and up to 98 for women from 87. Although individual consumption by smokers had risen, the fall in the proportion of the population smoking meant that between 1972 and 1982 there was an overall fall in the sales of cigarettes from 128 thousand million cigarettes in 1972 to 100 thousand million in 1982 (following a rise to 139 thousand million in 1974). Appendix 1 gives further detail on cigarette smoking over the period 1972 to 1982.

Over the same period the price of cigarettes rose from 30 pence for a packet of 20 Benson and Hedges King Size to 104 pence, often due to large increases in duty added by the Chancellor of the Exchequer in the annual budget. In 1981, for example, the price of a packet of 20 rose by 23 pence, of which 17 pence was additional tobacco duty, and in 1982 a 7 pence increase included 5 pence in duty. Appendix 2 gives information on inflation rates 1972–1982 and the Retail Price Index for those years.

It was difficult to know whether the falling trend in cigarette sales was the result of the steep tax/duty increases, or because of health fears growing since the report of the Royal College of Surgeons twenty years previously associating cigarette smoking with various illnesses, or more recent increasing consciousness about healthy living (as shown by jogging, gyms and high-fibre diets), or effective lobbying by anti-smoking pressure groups such as Action on Smoking and Health (ASH) or by government decisions to restrict cigarette advertising especially on television. Probably all of these factors had some impact and the net result was that for companies such as the Imperial Group, BAT Industries, Rothmans and Gallahers the cigarette industry, though still large, was an industry in long-term decline. Imperial alone had the capacity in 1982 to manufacture over 100 thousand million cigarettes a year. During 1982 the tobacco industry had been negotiating with the UK government over advertising agreements for their products and had lobbied fiercely against legal constraints; and finally at the end of 1982 the government announced the new voluntary advertising agreement. The main points were:

1 a 50% cut in the amount spent on poster advertising by 1984 as compared with expenditures in the year to March 1980;
2 a 60% cut in the amount spent on cinema advertising by 1986 as compared with expenditure in the year ending January 1981;
3 an increase from 9% to 15% in the space devoted to the health warnings on poster and press advertisements;
4 a health warning on point-of-sale display material;
5 a reduction in the tar ceiling above which brands could not be advertised at all;
6 an undertaking not to advertise in videos or by planes towing banners.

The general view in the industry was that the new voluntary agreement could just about be workable, but any further restrictions would have broken down the voluntary nature of the agreement which was negotiated between the government and industry and intended to last for three and a half years. The opponents of the industry (ASH and the British Medical Association) were united in condemning the agreement as being far too lenient.

The Imperial Group (in common with other companies dependent upon an industry in long-term decline) had in the 1960s diversified into first 'Foods' (e.g. Golden Wonder Crisps, HP Sauce, Ross Frozen Foods, Buxted Chickens) and subsequently in 1972 into 'Brewing' (Courage and John Smiths) but was still dependent for its sales and profits on the UK economy. The next major diversification was the purchase in 1980 of Howard Johnson in the USA for £280 million, which comprised over 1,000 restaurants and 500 hotels and motor lodges. Organizationally by this time Imperial had formed four divisions: Tobacco, Brewing and Leisure, Food, and Howard Johnson (USA), reporting to a group policy committee which had a membership of the chairman of the board, the group finance director, and the chairman of each of the four operating subsidiaries. (There was a further operation in packaging and paper.) This group policy committee was a sub-committee of the board of Imperial Group which at that time had 19 members but which by the end of 1983 had been reduced to 14 members. (See Appendix 3.)

The performance of the company was important not only to shareholders and employees, but also to UK consumers who spent 4½% of their consumer expenditure on Imperial products.

Details of the financial performance of the Imperial Group are given in Appendix 4, and figure 4.1 shows the relative contribution to the group's various trading activities over the period 1971 to 1982.

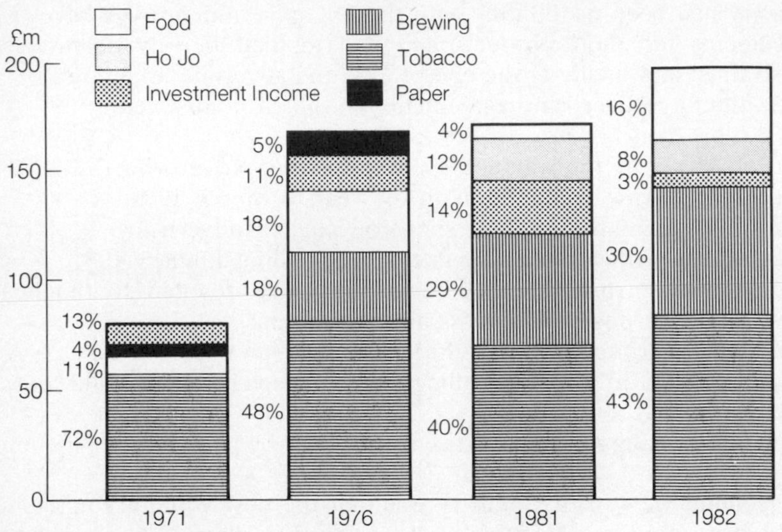

FIGURE 4.1 **Distribution of pre-interest profits**
Source: Wood, MacKenzie & Co.

Appendix 5 gives information on BAT Industries (formerly British American Tobacco) for comparative purposes.

As figure 4.1 shows, the group was still very dependent in the early 1970s upon the tobacco industry, and in the late 1970s and early 1980s the group set out to clarify its corporate strategy. In the 1979 Company Annual Report, the chairman of Imperial Group wrote,

> . . . we have been making a very careful reassessment of ourselves and of systems for evaluating risks and opportunities in every field, for formulating business plans and for resource allocations. This process of critical self analysis has been beneficial on a number of counts, not the least of which is our deepening perception of our own strengths and weaknesses and what must be done to build upon the former and cure the latter . . . . for the past fifteen years we have been diversifying in order to lessen our dependence on a single market, tobacco, which we dominated, and (that) our bid to acquire a platform for the growth of such earnings. Dependence on a single

> economy has become unusual for a company of our size.. . . We will need to concentrate more of our assets in businesses with higher growth potential. . . .

In 1980 the new chairman (he was previously deputy chairman) wrote in the Company Annual Report for that year:

> Our objective is by careful and constructive allocation of our resources and by energetic and enterprising management to sustain a steady growth in earnings per share. . . . For Imperial Group, as for the rest of British Industry, the present recession has sharpened the need to look critically at all its operations, to redeploy its assets and to redirect its efforts, so as to build its earnings power for the future. We are doing this with thoroughness and resolution, while remaining well aware that we must not base long-term strategic decisions on short-term economic factors. . . .

The financial editor of the *Times* commented:

> Imperial Group is perhaps the best example of a company, which in the 1980s, should be operating in the Third World, rather than in the United Kingdom. The demand and the growth prospects for its products are in the developing countries. The United States route to expansion has failed to date. Imperial Group needs to be a smaller, leaner company and shareholders deserve to be consulted on the painful strategic decisions being considered by the board. (3 Nov. 1981)

In 1981 Mr Geoffrey Kent (previously chairman of the Brewing Division) took over as chairman of Imperial Group and proposed a new approach. First stage was that of short-term recovery to overcome the main reasons for the decline of the past few years, second was to be a period when the business areas would be given the target of matching the 'best practice' return on capital in the sectors and countries in which they operated and finally to attain a growth rate equal to or better than other leading UK companies. Mr Kent wrote in the 1982 Company Annual Report:

> One of my priorities was to improve our central planning capability and during 1982, to institute the concept of management by strategy throughout the Group. The aim of that process is to have a Group-wide strategic plan, designed to achieve our objectives, with each Division having a commitment to them. An early task was to declare certain key principles to govern the shape and content of the strategic plan. The central goal is to re-establish Imperial Group as a leading and successful British Company. Its achievement depends upon

- obtaining a high and sustained return on capital employed;
- producing a reliable and growing stream of profits with consequent benefits for shareholders;
- ensuring demanding and consistent standards of performance and integrity;
- developing professional management of the highest calibre;
- motivating a workforce with a firm belief in innovation and achievement.

Deliberately, I did not at the outset establish financial targets. I asked, first, that each Division should examine, critically and in a disciplined way, the businesses in which it was engaged, assessing their strengths and weaknesses and identifying growth points for future development. This is a painstaking and exacting process but the groundwork is essential to the formulation of the strategic plan. . . . Although the details of that plan are not yet ready, I see it based on the following criteria

- to make our businesses stronger;
- to recycle the cash generated by those which are mature into those which are growing;
- to realise assets such as land and buildings which have ceased to have commercial use;
- to continue to divest companies which are neither cash generating nor operating in growth sectors;
- to concentrate on a profits turnaround in Howard Johnson's.

Consequently a reorganization of central planning was implemented during 1982 to prepare the group for sustained growth through 'management by strategy'. This concept aimed to develop a group-wide strategic plan from each division's internal and external assessment.

Tobacco Division Traditionally Imperial's tobacco companies had maintained independent operations selling in competition with each other as well as with the external tobacco companies. In August 1981 an administrative reorganization of the companies was announced, leading to a loss of 1,000 white-collar jobs.

In March 1982 plans to close three tobacco factories were announced, which would end with the loss of 1,700 jobs in addition to the general fall in the workforce from over 18,000 in 1978 to 12,400 in 1983.

In August 1982 it was announced that the Player's Wills and Ogdens companies would be brought together for marketing purposes. Previously these Imperial Group tobacco companies had been distinct companies and sold in competition with each other.

Brewing and Leisure Division Early in 1983 reorganization created a new structure dividing the business into Courage Ltd (production and wholesaleing of beer, wines and spirits to the tied estate and free trade), and Imperial Leisure and Retailing (for all the managed houses, shops, restaurants and hotels) both reporting to the division.

Howard Johnson Division The American Howard Johnson (Hojo) chain comprised over 500 hotels and over 1,000 restaurants, and the new management began to work on improving the efficiency of the various units.

Foods Division This comprised crisps and snacks (Golden Wonder), frozen vegetables (Ross Foods), frozen fish (Young's Speciality Frozen Seafoods), sauces and baked beans (HP Foods), eggs and poultry (Daylay). The Daylay business had a 23% share of the UK poultry business and 14% of the UK egg market but had suffered losses in 1981 of £8m on sales of £382m. Daylay assets were valued at £98m (which represented about one-third of all Imperial's Food Division assets) but were sold for £48m in 1982.

The new chairman of the Imperial Group was attempting to bring about the recovery of the company. Imperial had found itself dependent on a product in long-term decline, had diversified widely, but by the 1980s still found itself heavily dependent on one product. Its new objectives of recycling cash generated by the mature businesses into its growth businesses was dependent upon having growth businesses. If the rest of Imperial's business areas were already mature and facing low growth prospects, then the strategy might have to be modified to acquire some growth areas.

Appendix 1 Cigarette smoking in Britain, 1972–1982

Average weekly cigarette consumption per smoker by sex and age

	Men					
Age	*1972*	*1974*	*1976*	*1978*	*1980*	*1982*
16–19	109	110	106	98	99	87
20–24	123	132	135	122	113	114
25–34	129	136	138	134	135	121
35–49	132	138	141	138	140	137
50–59	124	127	130	137	130	129
60 and over	96	100	108	104	102	109
All aged 16 and over	120	125	129	127	124	212

	Women					
Age	*1972*	*1974*	*1976*	*1978*	*1980*	*1982*
16–19	76	86	89	90	84	76
20–24	91	89	110	101	102	100
25–34	97	108	109	113	111	109
35–49	94	104	112	109	115	108
50–59	87	91	108	101	105	101
60 and over	60	68	75	79	73	77
All aged 16 and over	87	94	101	101	102	98

Source: The *Times*, 7 July 1983

Appendix 2 Index of retail prices (1972 = 100)

		Inflation index
1972	100	1.000
1973	120.4	0.830
1974	130.7	0.765
1975	162.4	0.615
1976	189.2	0.528
1977	219.2	0.456
1978	237.4	0.421
1979	269.2	0.371
1980	317.2	0.315
1981	355.4	0.281
1982	386.0	0.259

Source: Derived from Table 18.6 Index of Retail Prices Annual Abstract 1985, H.M.S.O.

Appendix 3 Imperial Group

BOARD OF DIRECTORS, END 1983

Mr Geoffrey C. Kent	Group chairman and chief executive
Sir Campbell Adamson	Non-executive
Dr Herbert R. Bentley	Deputy chairman and managing director; director, Imperial Tobacco Ltd
Mr Martin B. Bunting	Deputy chairman, Imperial Brewing and Leisure Ltd
Mr Peter M. Davies	Director of administration and group secretary
Sir Robin Haydon KCMG	Director of group public affairs
Mr James H. Higgins	Non-executive
Mr G. Michael Hostage	Chairman and chief executive officer, Howard Johnson Company
Mr James McKinnon	Finance director
The Hon Sara A.S.F. Morrison	Non-executive
Mr J. Michael Pickard	Chairman, Brewing and Leisure Division and chief executive, Imperial Brewing and Leisure Ltd
Mr Andrew M. Reid	Director of group planning and chairman, Tobacco Division and Imperial Tobacco Ltd
Mr T. Gerry Sharman	Chairman, Food Division and Chairman and chief executive, Imperial Foods Ltd

Appendix 4 Imperial Group PLC

CONSOLIDATED PROFIT AND LOSS ACCOUNT, YEAR ENDED 31 OCTOBER 1982

	£m
Turnover	4,097.7
Cost of sales	3,683.1
Gross profit	414.6
Distribution costs	126.6
Administration expenses	111.4
Other operating income	(5.3)
Companies sold	(9.3)
Assoc. cos profits	(1.7)
Investment income	(6.8)
Interest	45.4
Profit (loss) before tax	154.3
Corporation Tax	57.1
DTR	(2.1)
ACT	
Current year	–
Prior year	(7.9)
Deferred tax	
Current year	(5.8)
Prior year	0.1
Overseas tax	(4.4)
Assoc. cos tax	0.4
Prior year's tax	(1.6)
Total taxation	35.8
Profit (loss) after tax	118.2
Minority interest	0.3
Attrib. to members	118.2
Ordinary dividends	52.2
Extraordinary items	66.8
Retained profit (loss)	(0.8)

Extraordinary items	
Reorganization costs	36.7
Sub. disposal	74.1
Invest etc disposal	(13.5)
Debs etc purchased	(1.6)
Property sale	–
Assoc. co. disposal	–
Goodwill	–
Other	–
	95.7
Taxation	(28.9)
	66.8

CONSOLIDATED BALANCE SHEETS (£m) YEAR ENDED 31 OCTOBER 1982

Fixed assets	
Tangibles	865.1
Investments	83.8
	948.9
Current assets	
Stock	420.8
Debtors (due within one year)	
Trade	301.6
Due by assoc. cos	0.1
Other	34.8
Prepayments etc	18.5
Debtors (due after one year)	
Other	6.4
Prepayments etc	5.8
Deferred tax	38.3
Investments	38.7
Cash	22.5
	887.5

Creditors (due within one year)	
Debentures	1.5
Overdrafts	29.2
Bank loans	20.7
Trade creditors	165.8
Bills of exchange	6.0
Due to assoc. cos	0.6
Other creditors	332.7
Tax & social security	39.9
Accruals	51.1
Dividends	52.2
	699.7
Net current assets	187.8
Total assets less curt liabs	1,136.7
Creditors (due after one year)	
Loan stocks (unsecured)	163.2
Debentures	62.8
Bank loans	3.7
Trade creditors	6.3
Taxation	16.7
Reorganization	
Costs provn	58.0
Minority interest	1.9
	312.6
	824.1
Capital	179.9
Share premium a/c	143.6
Other reserves	68.5
P & L a/c	432.1
	824.1

SALES, PROFIT BEFORE TAX AND SUMMARY OF BALANCE SHEETS – TEN YEAR RECORD (£ MILLION)

	1973		*1974*	
Sales (external)	1,522.2		1,793.7	
Sources of funds – ordinary operations				
Depreciation	20.9		25.6	
Group profit before taxation	100.6		77.5	
Net current assets (excl borrowing)		209.7		290.7
Fixed assets		304.2		338.8
Interest in associated companies		41.8		45.4
Operating capital employed at book value	555.7		674.9	
Investments	247.6		147.2	
	803.3		822.1	
Financed as follows:				
Issued capital	176.5		176.5	
Reserves including shares premium account	232.2		155.1	
Shareholders funds		408.7		331.6
Minority interests in subsidiaries		0.8		0.9
Loan capital		305.2		284.9
Short-term borrowings		50.6		170.4
Future taxation-deferred taxation		14.2		34.6
tax payable		23.8		(0.3)
	803.3		822.1	
Earnings per 25p ordinary share equivalent to:				
pence per share before taxation	14.2		10.9	
pence per share after taxation[a]	74.		5.5	
Dividend per 25p ordinary share equivalent to:				
pence per share	4.3		4.3	

[a] Because of changes in the group's accounting policy on deferred taxation in 1977 and 1978 figures for reserves, deferred taxation, interest in associated companies and earnings per share after taxation for the last five years, though comparable with each other, are not comparable with those for earlier years. Similarly, the 1976 figures are not comparable with earlier years, nor do they strictly correspond with those for 1977 due to the subsequent change of deferred taxation policy in relation to associated companies.

1975		1976		1977	
2,249.0		2,734.2		3,052.9	
29.4		30.9		31.5	
112.6		137.2		132.7	
	321.7		330.3		386.7
	343.6		364.2		402.8
	49.1		56.8		68.2
714.4		751.3		857.7	
240.0		242.3		285.8	
954.4		993.6		1,143.5	
176.5		176.5		176.6	
259.4		389.2		497.8	
	435.9		565.7		674.4
	0.9		1.4		1.5
	282.3		281.0		275.5
	160.2		132.7		190.1
	66.4		(1.1)		(0.8)
	8.7		13.9		2.8
954.4		993.6		1,143.5	
15.9		19.3		18.7	
8.2		13.1		15.1	
4.6		5.1		5.7	

	1978		1979	
Sales (external)	3,267.3		3,621.0	
Sources of funds – ordinary operations				
Depreciation	33.8		40.6	
Group profit before taxation	139.1		142.3	
Net current assets (excl borrowing)		301.0		312.6
Fixed assets		506.6		571.1
Interest in associated companies		69.8		66.6
Operating capital employed at book value	877.4		950.3	
Investments	261.0		254.2	
	1,138.4		1,204.5	
Financed as follows:				
Issued capital	176.6		177.4	
Reserves including shares premium account	558.9		609.0	
Shareholders funds		735.5		786.4
Minority interests in subsidiaries		1.8		2.0
Loan capital		276.2		269.7
Short-term borrowings		122.5		150.2
Future taxation-deferred taxation		(18.2)		(18.9)
tax payable		20.6		15.1
	1,138.4		1,204.5	
Earnings per 25p ordinary share equivalent to:				
pence per share before taxation	19.5		20.0	
pence per share after taxation[a]	15.5		18.1	
Dividend per 26p ordinary share equivalent to:				
pence per share	6.3		7.3	

[a] Because of changes in the group's accounting policy on deferred taxation in 1977 and 1978 figures for reserves, deferred taxation, interest in associated companies and earnings per share after taxation for the last five years, though comparable with each other, are not comparable with those for earlier years. Similarly, the 1976 figures are not comparable with earlier years, nor do they strictly correspond with those for 1977 due to the subsequent change of deferred taxation policy in relation to associated companies.

1980		*1981*		*1982*	
3,929.1		4,525.6		4,614.3	
54.6		77. 3		76.7	
126.9		106.0		154.3	
	246.3		119.8		97.9
	805.5		902.6		865.1
	18.8		5.5		6.2
1070.6		1027.9		969.2	
265.0		57.1		96.3	
1,335.6		1,335.6		1,065.5	
178.7		178.8		179.9	
558.4		617.2		644.2	
	737.1		796.0		824.1
	2.8		2.1		1.9
	263.0		249.6		231.2
	309.5		37.2		29.9
	0.7		(2.5)		(38.3)
	22.5		2.6		16.7
1,335.6		1,085.0		1,065.5	
17.7		14.8		21.4	
11.3		12.8		16.4	
7.3		7.3		7.3	

Sales analysis by activity (£m)

	1978	*1979*	*1980*	*1981*	*1982*
Tobacco	1951.3	1998.2	2051.1	2204.2	2304.2
Food	856.1	1081.7	1172.0	1247.8	1090.5
Brewing	449.9	481.7	539.9	733.9	815.2
Paper, board, etc.	230.0	84.4	87.0	61.9	53.6
Howard Johnson	–	–	107.5	329.8	403.4
less: internal sales	(36.9)	(25.0)	(28.4)	(52.0)	(52.6)
effect of foreign currency changes	(17.6)	–	–	–	–
Total	3432.8	3621.0	3929.1	4525.6	4614.3

Profit analysis by activity (£m)

	1978	*1979*	*1980*	*1981*	*1982*
Tobacco	66.3	78.5	80.4	68.7	84.0
Food	27.1	24.5	10.3	7.5	32.2
Brewing	37.1	38.6	42.4	50.4	58.5
Paper, board, etc.	15.9	1.5	(3.3)	0.1	0.9
Howard Johnson	–	–	11.5	20.5	15.6
Effect of foreign currency changes	(2.4)	–	–	–	–
Total	144.0	143.1	141.3	147.2	191.2

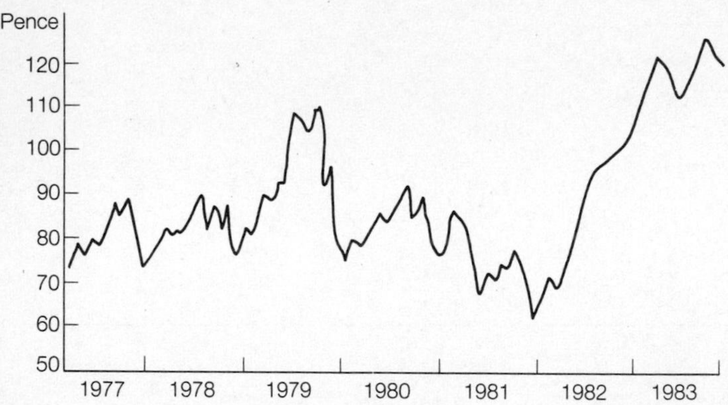

IMPERIAL GROUP SHARE PRICE

Appendix 5 BAT Industries

BAT was a multinational corporation with 118 tobacco factories in 54 countries, cosmetic products (Yardley) sold in 143 countries, retailing outlets in the USA, the UK and West Germany, and a variety of other businesses run from the company headquarters in Millbank, London. The company was the world's largest manufacturer of cigarettes, although as a result of history it held only 6% of the UK market in 1981 with its State Express, du Maurier, Kent and Kim brands.

Retailing in the UK included International Stores, a 750-strong chain of supermarkets and 25 Mainstop Superstores, and also the Argos catalogue showroom chain with 116 showrooms and 9 million catalogues issued annually.

Financial statistics for BAT Industries, 1982

CONSOLIDATED PROFIT AND LOSS ACCOUNT (£m) YEAR ENDED 31 DECEMBER 1982

Turnover	11,507
Duty & excise taxes	3,890
UK VAT	189
	7,428
Change in stocks	(32)
Other operating income	(68)
Raw materials etc	3,867
Staff costs	1,411
Depreciation	179
Other operating charges	1,288
Assoc. cos profits	(102)
Investment income	(18)
Interest receivable	(115)
Interest payable	162
Profit (loss) before tax	856
Corporation Tax	156
DTR	(138)
ACT written off	28
Deferred tax	26
Overseas tax	235

Assoc. cos tax	39
Total taxation	346
Profit (loss) after tax	510
Minority interests	56
Attrib. to members	454
Ordinary dividends	100
Extraordinary items	4

CONSOLIDATED BALANCE SHEETS (£m) YEAR ENDED 31 DECEMBER 1982

Fixed assets	
Tangibles	1,871
Invests in assoc. cos	434
Other invests & loans	36
	2,341
Current assets	
Stocks	2,147
Trade debtors	1,005
Other debtors	157
Prepayments etc	70
Listed investments	157
Unlisted investments	59
Deposits	270
Cash	161
	4,026
Creditors (due within one year)	
Trade creditors	555
Sales taxes, duty & excise	357
Bills of exchange	39
Accrued charges etc	299
Dividend	55
Taxn on profits	228
Other taxn & social security	57
Sundry creditors	130
Borrowings	462
	2,182

Net current assets	1,844
Total assets less curt liabs	4,185
Creditors (due after one year)	
Sales taxes, duty & excise	2
Bills of exchange	2
Accrued charges etc.	1
Taxn on profits	6
Sundry creditors	2
Borrowings	867
Provns for liabilities & charges	314
	1,194
	2,991
Capital	91
Share premium a/c	10
Other reserves	409
P & L a/c	2,001
Assoc. cos	210
Minority interests	270
	2,991

SIX-YEAR SUMMARY

Turnover and profits (£m)

			12 months to 31 December			12 months to 30 September	
	1982	*1981*	*1980*	*1979*	*1978*	*1978*	*1977*
Turnover	11,507	9,265	7,645	7,288	6,844	6,719	6,212
Trading profit	783	634	467	466	441	438	412
Share of profit of associated companies	102	87	60	53			
Profit before taxation	856	684	479	481	435	433	416
Profit after taxation	510	403	262	286	250	244	258
Attributable to BAT Industries							
Net profit before extraordinary items	454	363	234	259	226	219	235
Dividends – ordinary (pence)	100	84	69	60	50	49	44
Earnings per ordinary share (pence)	–	99.9	64.4	71.3	62.2	60.4	64.8
Dividend per ordinary share (pence)							
Net of ACT credit (pence)	–	23.0	19.0	17.5	15.0	14.5	13.0
Adjusted by the retail price index (pence)	–	23.0	21.3	22.6	22.7	22.4	21.6

Balance sheet (£m)							
Interest of ordinary shareholders	2,484	2,218	1,746	1,689	1,637	1,635	1,604
Interest of minority shareholders	480	210	177	171	134	114	110
Shareholders funds	2,964	2,428	1,923	1,860	1,771	1,749	1,714
Deferred taxation	41	39	28	28	16	12	13
Provisionos for unfunded pensions	286	207	171	174	159	148	138
Borrowings – due beyond one year	867	589	431	504	504	506	528
Borrowings – due within one year	462	346	451	462	372	211	184
Other current liabilities	1,720	1,379	1,054	1,022	1,022	957	765
Funds employed	6,367	4,988	4,058	4,050	3,824	3,601	3,342
Fixed assets	1,871	1,388	1,169	1,092	920	859	770
Investments	470	424	334	324	368	368	356
Future tax relief	52	43	38	45	53	28	
Stocks	2,147	1,731	1,407	1,438	1,383	1,354	1,285
Other current assets	1,827	1,402	1,110	1,151	1,100	992	931
Total assets	6,367	4,988	4,058	4,050	3,824	3,601	3,342

INDUSTRIAL AND GEOGRAPHICAL ANALYSIS[a]

Industrial analysis (£m)

	1981	*1980*	*1979*	*1978*	*1977*
Tobacco					
Turnover	5,322	4,331	4,240	4,477	4,104
Trading profit	469	336	320	327	339
Assets emp.	2,114	1,707	1,732	1,792	1,576
Retailing					
Turnover	2,180	1,772	1,732	1,455	1,391
Trading profit	72	42	40	24	22
Assets emp.	864	689	652	592	601
Paper					
Turnover	798	709	672	549	401
Trading profit	47	52	79	60	41
Assets emp.	544	476	470	426	273
Packaging/printing					
Turnover	525	465	262	182	151
Trading profit	20	21	18	13	11
Asets emp.	301	270	262	180	146
Other activities					
Turnover	440	368			
Trading profit	26	16			
Assets emp.	310	257			

Geographical Analysis (£m)

	Turnover		*Trading profit*		*Assets emp.*	
	1981	*1980*	*1981*	*1980*	*1981*	*1980*
UK	2,034	1,757	46	18	862	833
Europe	1,979	1,755	77	78	706	612
North America	2,542	1,871	283	212	1,626	1,161
Latin America	1,731	1,495	131	78	486	429
Asia	566	425	59	44	228	177
Africa	355	300	35	35	198	165
Australia	58	42	3	2	27	22

[a] Excludes data regarding associated companies and concentrates on main BAT Industries companies.

Source: Company Reports

5 Thomas Tilling

INTRODUCTION

Thomas Tilling started business with a horse and cart in Walworth, London in 1845. On his death in 1893 he owned 2,500 horses and many carts. Tilling was incorporated as a limited company in 1897 and the shares first listed on the London Stock Exchange in 1904. After the turn of the century, motor buses and lorries replaced the horses and carts, and Tilling became Britain's leading passenger and freight transport company. In 1948, under the threat of possible nationalization, the transport assets were sold to the government. In 1949, the first year that Tilling operated as an industrial holding company with diverse interests, sales were less than £10 million and profit before tax was only £¾ million. The ensuing years have seen steady expansion of the group, largely in the UK, but increasingly overseas.

THOMAS TILLING – 1982

Thomas Tilling is a holding company owning a wide variety of companies throughout the world. The current shape and structure of the company is as a result of a number of acquisitions the company has made since the Second World War. The company has a stated policy of becoming a conglomerate for, as Sir Patrick Meaney, managing director has said, 'We believe that the raison d'etre for a conglomerate is to grow, even in recessionary conditions . . . unless we can make our units, and the totality, grow faster than those units would grow if they were independent we have not got a reason for holding them.'[1]

The company was one of the first conglomerates in the world and comprises 22 companies and 42,600 employees worldwide. The activities of the companies in the group are described elsewhere in the case. The Tilling management philosophy has been to encourage the companies 'to

[1] *International Management*, May 1983.

manage their own affairs subject only to central guidance on corporate policy, planning, investment and finance'.[2] This style of management allows the operating companies considerable freedom, and 'interference' from the centre would only occur in exceptional circumstances. This philosophy of independence was also seen in the organization of the company in that one of four main board directors based in London would act as chairman of each major subsidiary. The chairmanships held by any one of these directors would not necessarily be in companies with related interests, as expertise in any one field, say construction, was considered to be unnecessary. Also Tilling has been unwilling, until recently (1981), to divest itself of any major businesses. However, in 1981 it did reluctantly dispose of some businesses in the automotive sector and an insulation bususiness.

In 1973 when Meaney became managing director, only 5% of group sales were outside the UK and he decided that expansion overseas, and in particular in the USA, would be a key strategy. Another feature of group policy was that Tilling would not become involved in buying low performers and turning them round, nor would it get involved in high technology markets, preferring to supply the companies in such markets with component products and/or services.

ACTIVITIES OF SECTOR BUSINESSES

Builders' Merchants This division comprises Graham Building Services, a nationwide builders' merchants business in the UK which is significantly influenced by the mortgage rate and local authority expenditure on housing repairs, maintenance and improvements. There is a US supply group within this division which is similarly significantly affected by changes in the housing market. Higher interest rates and a severe recession in the US have caused a decline in the construction industry, but there was a significant improvement in 1982.

Construction Materials and Services This division is composed of two major activities. firstly, the hire and distribution of contractors' plant and access equipment and scaffolding. The second arm of the business is the production and supply of construction materials and services and agricultural and industrial minerals. This division is affected by the same economic factors as the builders' merchants in both the UK and the US.

Engineering The companies in the engineering group are divided into three subgroups, Electronic Equipment and Supplies, Energy Equipment and the long-established Manufacturing Engineering.

The Electronic Equipment and Supplies group manufactures electronic

[2] Ibid.

accounting and data systems and is a leader in special solders and related chemicals for the electronics and communications industry. Also it produces special laminates for these and other hi-tech industries.

The Energy group is heavily dependent on the US energy market, which dropped steeply in 1982 as drilling exploration programmes were cut back. the group supplies a variety of components to the oil, gas and mining industries for use in exploration, extraction and distribution.

The Manufacturing Engineering division produces a range of equipment for industrial and commercial hygiene, environmental control, agricultural and industrial equipment and power transmissions. This broadly based group is in many markets but is affected overall by the general level of investment which was low in both the UK and US in 1982. A new Japanese trading company has been purchased to extend the sales of group products in that country.

Furniture This is a small division in which the major products are bedroom furniture and beds. It also manufactures a range of other furniture and has recently expanded into the hotel refurbishment business. Sales are significantly affected by changes to factors affecting credit such as hire purchase controls and the interest rate, and stocking and de-stocking by retailers.

Industrial Equipment Division The major part of the UK business of this division is supplying electrical contractors, industrial users, local authorities and nationalized industries through its nationwide network of 100 branches. A similar but smaller operation is operating through 60 branches in the US.

Insurance Cornhill Insurance PLC is a leading insurance company with branches throughout the UK and in many parts of the world. There is also a small American company. Profitability is affected by the weather, and the industry is fiercely competitive.

Medical The companies in the medical group are specialist manufacturers and suppliers of medical, dental, veterinary, rehabilitation and other health care products. Apart from general recessionary factors, the division is affected by government cost restraint measures.

Publishing The publishing interests are focussed on Heinemann. A wide range of segments are covered and Pan Books provide a significant contribution from the sale of paperbacks. Business is affected by local authority spending on education and libraries.

Textiles This division is concentrated on the ladies' hosiery market under the brand name Pretty Polly, which is top of the branded market.

Tiles and Pottery The products manufactured by this division are decorative ceramic tiles and pottery.

Appendix 1

STATEMENT BY THE CHAIRMAN, 1982 COMPANY REPORT

Worldwide recessionary conditions in 1982 created a most difficult trading environment for the Group, particularly in the Energy Equipment sector in the USA. Nationally, there was modest economic improvement in the UK but the US economy suffered its worst setback for more than thirty years. Overall output in the industrialised countries fell by ½% and the volume of world trade by 2%.

One of the few good features of the economic situation was the decline in the annual rate of inflation. By the end of the year, the UK rate had fallen to 5½%, the lowest level since 1969, and the US rate was down to 4%. This was accompanied by a welcome fall in interest rates in the second half of the year, although real rates remain historically high.

Most of the Group's trade sectors contributed higher profits in 1982. Trade sectors which performed particularly well in the circumstances of the year were Builders' Merchanting, Construction Materials and Services. Industrial Equipment Distribution, Insurance, Manufacturing Engineering, Publishing and Textiles.

The notable, indeed dramatic, exception to this overall performance was the Energy Equipment sector which experienced a severe downturn in common with the oil market. In the USA a combination of recession, unstable prices of oil and gas, the uncertainty of future prospects, and changes in tax structure greatly reduced exploration and production activity. As a result, the Energy Equipment sector swung from a profit, before interest and tax, of £30.4 million in 1981 to a loss of £4.1 million in 1982. At the pre tax level, a profit of £24.8 million in 1981 was replaced by a loss of £16.4 million in 1982. The setback in this sector thus accounted for more than the whole of the drop in Group profits.

Action costing £20 million in extraordinary items was taken to restructure unprofitable parts of the Group and to dispose of loss making companies. Their pre tax losses on trading, which will not recur in future, amounted to £4.2 million.

The Group profit before interest and tax fell from the record level of £107.7 million in 1981 to £93.6 million and, after higher net interest, the Group profit before tax fell from £73.6 million in 1981 to £43.7 million. Group sales rose to a new high of £2.2 billion.

On a geographical analysis, the UK contribution to Group profit before interest and tax rose to £65.8 million. The USA performance, with its heavy Energy Equipment loss, resulted in a profit before interest of £15.1 million which was insufficient to cover interest costs. Operations in the rest of the world made a higher contribution, partly through acquisitions, of £12.7 million.

The earnings per ordinary share were 8.8p, compared with 18.6p in 1981. A final dividend of 4.5p per ordinary share is now proposed by the Board and this, together with thc interim dividend of 3.5p paid in January, will maintain the total dividend for 1982 at 8.0p per ordinary share.

During 1982 we invested £57 million in fixed assets for future expansion, modernisation and replacement of obsolete assets with the objectives of greater operational efficiency, productivity and profitability. We also spent £53 million on new acquisitions to strengthen our profitable operations and to establish our new trade sector, Electronic Equipment and Supplies. Excluding acquisitions, the Group had an operational cash outflow of £4 million.

Despite new acquisitions and sales expansion, the number of people employed by the Group fell for the third year running. Employees now number 42,600 worldwide and, on behalf of the Board, I wish to express appreciation to our managements and workforces for their application during a most difficult and challenging period when change has been managed and executed with skill.

We have carried out a significant amount of restructuring in 1982 by reorganisation and divestment, and we plan further actions to ensure that each principal operating company is able to meet the long term growth objectives of the Group. We are continuing to review the organisation and further development of the Group. We believe that our corporate philosophy of decentralising the operating responsibility of our companies to their Managing Directors and managements, whilst retaining the Tilling Board's overall responsibility for corporate policy, planning, investment and finance, is still the best formula for higher profitability in the 1980s.

At the forthcoming Annual General Meeting I shall be retiring from the Board, having reached the age of seventy. I have been on the Board for thirteen years, the last seven as your Chairman and during that period I have seen the Group expand from a mainly UK business with sales of some £200 million to an international business with sales in excess of £2.2 billion. Whilst I am departing in a year when the disappointing results of the Energy Equipment sector have overshadowed an encouraging performance by the remainder of the Group I am confident that Tilling has a sound foundation for profitable progress from 1983 onwards. I shall be succeeded as Chairman by Sir Arthur Norman, who was appointed Deputy Chairman last December, having served as a non executive Director since 1979. We also welcomed Mr David Rae Smith to the Board in 1982 as a non executive Director.

After an extremely testing period in 1982, particularly in the USA, current indicators point to economic improvement in the UK and the

USA during 1983. Although the energy market is unlikely to revive as quickly or as strongly as we should wish there is growing confidence that a more stable trading pattern will be resumed through the year in most of the trade sectors and countries in which we operate.

I expect that our plans to resume profit growth will result in a significant recovery in 1983.

R.M. Taylor
16 March 1983

Appendix 2

BRIEF DETAILS OF THE EXECUTIVE DIRECTORS

Sir Patrick Meaney (aged 57) is the group managing director and chief executive. He joined Tilling in 1961 and was appointed to the Tilling Board in 1964. He was appointed group managing director in 1973 and was knighted in 1981.

Colin Draper (aged 58) is deputy managing director and president of Thomas Tilling Inc. He joined Tilling in 1963 and has been resident in the USA since Tilling established a New York office in 1977. He was appointed to the Tilling Board in 1968 and made deputy managing director in 1973.

Francis Black (aged 49) is finance director. A chartered accountant, he joined Tilling in 1960 and was appointed to the Tilling Board as finance director in 1976.

David Sawyer (aged 56) is an executive director and head of the company's legal department. A solicitor, he joined Tilling in 1956 and was appointed to the Tilling Board in 1970.

Peter Ryan (aged 51) is an executive director and chairman of a number of principal operating companies in the group. He is a chartered engineer and before joining Tilling in 1973, he was managing director of Ideal Toy Company. Prior to that he was for nine years managing director of Stephenson Mills, a subsidiary of the then British Match Corporation. He was appointed to the Tilling Board in 1979.

Hugh Laughland (aged 50) is an executive director and chairman of a number of principal operating companies in the group. He is a chartered accountant, and prior to joining Tilling in 1980 he was for four years with Scottish & Universal Investments, the last two as chief executive, having previously spent eighteen years with Scottish Aviation, the last six as managing director. He was appointed to the Tilling Board in June 1981.

Appendix 3 Five-year record 1978 to 1982

SALES, PROFIT EARNINGS AND DIVIDENDS (£m)

	1978	*1979*	*1980*	*1981*	*1982*
Group sales	1,026.4	1,416.2	1,696.6	2,050.1	2,237.6
Group profit before interest and tax	74.7	103.6	98.7	107.7	93.6
Group profit before tax	64.9	81.1	70.7	73.6	43.7
Net profit available for distribution	52.5	67.1	52.0	42.0	5.7
Transfer top/(from) reserves	41.7	48.5	31.7	19.8	(18.1)
Earnings per ordinary share	24.6p	29.4p	21.5p	18.6p	8.8p
Dividend per ordinary share	4.818p	7.0p	7.5p	8.0p	8.0p
Dividend cover – times	5.1	3.9	2.8	2.3	1.1

GROUP FUNDS EMPLOYED

	1978	*1979*	*1980*	*1981*	*1982*
Fixed assets	158.8	251.4	277.6	310.0	336.7
Net assets of Cornhill Insurance	24.4	30.1	35.7	39.4	43.0
Associated companies	4.2	4.0	5.9	5.5	12.8
Net trading assets	176.3	257.4	265.0	322.8	368.8
Goodwill	45.4	58.5	62.3	63.6	77.9
Total funds employed at the year end	409.1	601.4	646.5	741.3	839.2
Represented by:					
Ordinary capital and reserves	303.3	434.9	475.2	506.5	516.3
Preference capital and minority interests	14.9	14.6	13.7	13.2	15.5
	318.2	449.5	488.9	519.7	531.8

Debenture and other loan capital	83.9	202.5	203.9	199.4	243.9
Bank overdrafts and short term loans	67.2	78.8	91.1	198.7	274.0
Investments, bank balances, etc.	(60.2)	(129.4)	(137.4)	(176.5)	(210.5)
Net borrowings	90.9	151.9	157.6	221.6	307.4
Analysis of increase in net borrowings:					
Per generation and application of funds (below)	32.1	37.9	16.3	18.1	28.4
Net borrowings assumed on acquisitions less disposals	4.3	34.7	3.6	3.7	5.9
Exchange rate variation[a]	(1.2)	(11.6)	(14.2)	42.2	51.5
	35.2	61.0	5.7	64.0	85.8
Return on average funds employed[b]	20.3%	20.5%	15.8%	15.5%	11.8%
Gearing[c]	25.0%	28.0%	27.0%	32.7%	40.4%
Net tangible assets per ordinary share	120.2p	145.8p	156.6p	163.7p	150.6p

[a] The exchange rate variations were broadly counterbalanced by similar changes in total funds employed.

[b] The return on average funds employed is the Group profit before interest and tax as a percentage of average funds employed, being the mean of the funds at the beginning and end of each year.

[c] Gearing is the net borrowings as a percentage of total funds employed, less goodwill.

GENERATION AND APPLICATION OF FUNDS

Operational cash flow – inflow/(outflow)	(8.8)	(22.0)	24.1	2.3	(3.8)
Acquisitions less disposals of subsidiaries	(28.7)	(74.1)	(49.4)	(32.3)	(52.3)
Total – (outflow)	(37.5)	(96.1)	(25.3)	(30.0)	(56.1)
Finance:					
Increase in net borrowings	32.1	37.9	16.3	18.1	28.4
Rights issue	–	57.4	–	–	–
Securities issued for acquisitions	5.4	0.8	9.0	11.9	27.7

Appendix 4

GROUP SALES (£m)

	1977	*1978*	*1979*	*1980*	*1981*	*1982*
Builders' merchanting	201.5	240.5	303.8	316.1	341.1	418.8
Construction, etc.	138.1	169.5	264.0	277.5	250.7	280.4
Engineering	111.1	143.7	238.2	346.8	544.8	529.4
Furniture	15.7	20.8	22.4	21.1	19.6	27.5
Industrial equip. dist.	123.1	176.8	241.0	349.0	411.7	464.5
Insurance	84.2	97.6	123.7	143.5	156.5	177.5
Medical	61.3	82.6	120.9	131.8	171.6	200.2
Publishing & printing	22.1	27.4	21.9	23.8	28.4	30.8
Textiles	22.3	27.7	33.0	38.0	38.1	40.0
Tiles & pottery	19.2	20.9	25.0	30.2	33.7	33.2
Vehicle distribution	12.6	18.9	16.5	12.5	–	–
Group total	811.2	1026.4	1410.4	1690.3	1996.2	2202.3

GROUP PROFIT BEFORE INTEREST & TAX (£m)

	1977	*1978*	*1979*	*1980*	*1981*	*1982*
Builders' merchanting	11.2	14.8	21.1	15.6	10.8	12.7
Construction, etc.	14.2	15.1	23.6	13.8	12.1	14.1
Engineering	10.3	12.5	16.4	20.3	40.8	15.0
Furniture	2.1	2.5	2.3	1.2	1.2	1.2
Industrial equip. dist.	6.7	9.6	14.8	17.7	13.4	15.3
Insurance	7.7	8.2	6.5	9.3	12.6	12.3
Medical	5.2	6.0	9.0	9.9	13.1	11.1
Publishing & printing	3.6	4.2	3.4	2.2	3.8	4.3
Textiles	0.9	1.7	3.7	4.8	2.3	2.8
Tiles & pottery	1.6	0.6	1.2	3.1	3.7	2.4
Vehicles distribution	0.5	0.6	0.5	0.1	–	–
Group total	64.2	75.8	102.5	98.0	113.8	91.2

GROUP FUNDS[a] (£m)

	1977	1978	1979	1980	1981	1982
Builders' merchanting	63.6	73.5	91.8	79.9	97.8	102.2
Construction, etc.	63.1	79.5	137.0	153.7	143.6	140.4
Engineering	53.8	72.2	114.5	140.7	182.5	267.4
Furniture	3.7	4.6	6.0	5.4	5.7	7.2
Industrial equip. dist.	26.0	44.4	60.2	76.8	82.8	90.4
Insurance	29.6	33.1	38.8	44.5	47.9	51.6
Medical	27.9	31.5	50.4	52.8	63.4	79.1
Publishing & printing	14.9	16.2	16.4	19.6	19.2	20.9
Textiles	8.0	6.7	10.6	10.2	10.1	12.4
Tiles & pottery	13.8	13.3	14.2	17.1	22.4	23.2
Vehicle distribution	1.5	2.9	4.4	3.2	–	–
Total	305.9	377.9	544.3	603.9	657.4	794.8
Unallocated to trade sectors[b]	20.4	31.2	57.1	42.6	65.9	44.4
Group total	326.3	409.1	601.4	646.5	741.3	839.2

[a] Group funds comprise total share capital and reserves, minority shareholders interests, debenture and other loan capital, bank overdrafts and short-term loans, less investments, certificates of tax deposit, bank balances, short-term deposits and cash.

[b] There are some activities which are not allocated to the divisions shown; therefore, figures are different to Balance Sheet and Profit and Loss Account.

Appendix 5 Breakdown of engineering sector

SALES (£m)

	1977	1978	1979	1980	1981	1982
Electronic eqpt and supplies	–	–	–	–	5.8	62.8
Energy equipment	–	–	91.2	195.7	383.4	283.8
Manufacturing engineering	111.1	143.7	147.0	151.1	155.6	182.8

Appendix 6 Acquisitions

	Price paid (£m)	*Net assets acquired (£m)*	*Pre-tax profit*[a] *(£m)*	*Notes*
1978	32.2	25.0	N/A	
1979	75.9	62.9	17.4	Mainly in the USA
1980	51.4	46.7	7.0	Mainly in the USA
1981	34.7	21.5	4.8	Mainly in the USA
1982	53.3	35.2	10.0	W. Germany, USA, Japan

[a] Pre-tax profit is the combined value of profit before tax in the last published accounts prior to acquisition.

Appendix 7

GROUP SALES (£m)

<table>
<tr><th></th><th>1978</th><th>1979</th><th>1980</th><th>1981</th><th>1982</th></tr>
<tr><td>UK</td><td>821.2</td><td>982.7</td><td>1065.3</td><td>1058.8</td><td>1193.7</td></tr>
<tr><td>USA</td><td>89.9</td><td>315.5</td><td>505.7</td><td>850.8</td><td>852.1</td></tr>
<tr><td>Rest of Europe</td><td>86.6</td><td>93.3</td><td>89.6</td><td>86.0</td><td rowspan="2">191.8</td></tr>
<tr><td>Other areas</td><td>28.7</td><td>24.9</td><td>36.0</td><td>54.5</td></tr>
<tr><td>Group total</td><td>1026.4</td><td>1416.2</td><td>1696.6</td><td>2050.1</td><td>2237.6</td></tr>
</table>

GROUP PROFIT BEFORE INTEREST AND TAX (£m)

<table>
<tr><th></th><th>1978</th><th>1979</th><th>1980</th><th>1981</th><th>1982</th></tr>
<tr><td>UK</td><td>63.0</td><td>72.4</td><td>62.6</td><td>47.3</td><td>65.8</td></tr>
<tr><td>USA</td><td>4.1</td><td>23.3</td><td>28.9</td><td>52.3</td><td>15.1</td></tr>
<tr><td>Rest of Europe</td><td>6.6</td><td>7.2</td><td>4.9</td><td>3.9</td><td rowspan="2">12.7</td></tr>
<tr><td>Other areas</td><td>1.0</td><td>0.7</td><td>2.3</td><td>4.2</td></tr>
<tr><td>Group total</td><td>74.7</td><td>103.7</td><td>98.7</td><td>107.7</td><td>93.6</td></tr>
</table>

GROUP FUNDS (£m)

<table>
<tr><th></th><th>1978</th><th>1979</th><th>1980</th><th>1981</th><th>1982</th></tr>
<tr><td>UK</td><td>324.7</td><td>414.6</td><td>419.6</td><td>402.1</td><td>418.6</td></tr>
<tr><td>USA</td><td>28.4</td><td>132.2</td><td>174.4</td><td>268.5</td><td>319.0</td></tr>
<tr><td>Rest of Europe</td><td>43.5</td><td>45.1</td><td>39.4</td><td>44.1</td><td rowspan="2">101.6</td></tr>
<tr><td>Other areas</td><td>12.5</td><td>9.5</td><td>13.1</td><td>26.6</td></tr>
<tr><td>Group total</td><td>409.1</td><td>601.4</td><td>646.5</td><td>741.3</td><td>839.2</td></tr>
</table>

Appendix 8 Consolidated statement of income and reserves Thomas Tilling plc and subsidiaries

CONSOLIDATED PROFIT AND LOSS ACCOUNT FOR THE YEAR TO 31 DECEMBER 1982 (£m)

		1982		*1981*
Group sales		2,237.6		2,050.1
Group profit before interest and tax		93.6		107.7
Interest		49.9		34.1
Group profit before tax		43.7		73.6
Tax		17.4		23.5
Group profit after tax		26.3		50.1
Deduct:				
Amount attributable to minority shareholders	0.5		–	
Extraordinary items	20.1		8.1	
		20.6		8.1
Net profit available for distribution		5.7		42.0
Dividends				
Preference dividends	0.5		0.5	
Ordinary dividends:				
Interim of 3.5p per share (3.5p per share)	10.2		9.5	
Final of 4.5p per share (4.5p per share	13.1		12.2	
	23.3	23.8	21.7	22.2
Transfer (from)/to Reserves		(18.1)		19.8
Earnings per ordinary share		8.8p		18.6p

MOVEMENTS IN CONSOLIDATED RESERVES DURING THE YEAR (£m)

	1982	*1981*
Balance at the beginning of the year	323.2	303.8
Transfer (to)/from Profit and Loss Account	(18.1)	19.8
Exchange surplus on fixed assets overseas	0.3	0.1
Sundry items	(0.1)	(0.5)
Balance at the end of the year	305.3	323.2

Appendix 9 Balance sheets at 31 December 1982

	Consolidated Balance Sheet		*Parent Company Balance Sheet*	
	1982	*1981*	*1982*	*1981*
Capital Employed				
Tilling ordinary shareholders' interests				
Ordinary shares issued	58.2	54.1	58.2	54.1
Premiums on issues of shares	152.8	129.2	152.8	129.2
Reserves	305.3	323.2	45.0	58.1
	516.3	506.5	256.0	241.4
Preference shares issued	10.5	10.5	10.5	10.5
Total share capital and reserves	526.8	517.0	266.5	251.9
Deduct: Goodwill – premiums less discounts on acquisitions	77.9	63.6	–	–
	448.9	453.4	266.5	251.9
Minority shareholders' interests	5.0	2.7	–	–
Debenture and other loan capital	243.9	199.4	226.8	185.2
	697.8	655.5	493.3	437.1
Use of Capital				
Fixed assets	336.7	310.0	–	–
Cornhill Insurance PLC – Net assets	43.0	39.4	–	–
Associated companies	12.8	5.5	–	–
Investments	71.3	112.5	64.2	107.5
Investment in subsidiaries	–	–	392.2	329.0
	463.8	467.4	456.4	436.5

Current assets				
Stocks and work in progress	388.5	337.9	–	–
Debtors	385.2	353.3	3.8	7.3
Tax recoverable	15.0	9.9	0.2	0.9
Owing by subsidiaries, including proposed dividends	–	–	229.4	166.7
Certificates of tax deposit	7.5	1.2	7.5	1.2
Bank balances, short term deposits and cash	131.7	62.8	94.2	28.6
	927.9	765.1	335.1	204.7
Deduct: Current liabilities				
Creditors	385.3	352.6	15.1	9.3
Due to subsidiaries	–	–	39.2	34.3
Bank overdrafts and short term loans	274.0	198.7	218.3	134.6
Tax	11.1	3.8	2.1	4.0
Dividends – Thomas Tilling plc	23.5	21.9	23.5	21.9
	693.9	577.0	298.2	204.1
Net current assets	234.0	188.1	36.9	0.6
	697.8	655.5	493.3	437.1

Signed on behalf of the Board, who approved the Financial Statements on 16th March 1983

R.M. Taylor
Patrick Meaney } Directors

Appendix 10

INDEX OF OUTPUT OF THE PRODUCTION INDUSTRIES – SELECTED COMPONENT INDICATORS[a] (AVERAGE 1980 = 100)

	Group heading[b]	*1980 Weights*[c]	*1973*[d]	*1974*[d]	*1975*[d]	*1976*[d]	*1977*[d]	*1978*	*1979*	*1980*	*1981*	*1982*
Coal extraction and solid fuels manufacture	111	*40*	112.3	92.9	108.8	100.9	98.0	97.0	97.0	100.0	97.5	93.4
Oil and gas extraction	130	*123*	1.5	−0.8	−1.1	15.4	47.8	68.7	98.4	100.0	110.0	125.7
Mineral oil processing	140	*15*	126.8	124.2	104.4	111.1	109.4	110.2	113.3	100.0	93.3	93.7
Iron and steel manufacture	221	*7*	186.6	165.7	140.2	151.0	153.6	155.0	165.4	100.0	120.5	114.9
Steel tubes	222	*3*	220.0	195.4	165.4	155.1	145.5	148.8	146.7	100.0	124.0	134.8
Drawing, cold rolling/forming of steel	223	*4*	139.8	135.8	118.3	130.3	126.9	125.2	124.7	100.0	97.7	95.5
Non-ferrous metals	224	*11*	113.4	109.5	103.6	105.1	105.1	103.2	105.6	100.0	96.9	89.8
Building products	241–246	*23*	141.0	127.3	119.1	114.5	109.1	109.7	108.7	100.0	88.3	90.5
Glass	247	*7*	110.1	107.6	98.5	102.7	104.6	108.3	110.6	100.0	91.8	89.6
Basic industrial chemicals	251	*24*	106.4	109.3	92.8	106.5	108.4	107.7	111.3	100.0	98.4	96.4
Paints, varnishes and printing ink	255	*5*	99.2	93.2	90.2	98.9	104.6	106.8	109.2	100.0	98.4	98.4

Chemical products mainly for industry	256	*11*	86.1	89.1	85.3	93.4	101.1	104.4	109.2	100.0	99.1	97.6
Pharmaceutical products	257	*16*	77.3	86.8	88.4	97.2	101.7	104.7	103.9	100.0	102.7	107.1
Soap and toilet preparations	258	*7*	83.3	91.5	88.9	94.2	97.4	104.6	103.6	100.0	98.7	101.7
Other household and office chemicals	259	*3*	88.4	95.6	79.6	84.8	94.4	101.9	109.1	100.0	90.6	90.6
Metal foundries	311	*10*	168.7	158.0	142.8	143.4	139.8	134.3	131.2	100.0	86.3	79.5
Forgings, pressings and stampings	312	*6*	167.6	164.7	154.3	145.2	144.3	129.1	116.9	100.0	104.1	114.1
Hand tools and finished metal goods	316	*21*	113.2	116.8	108.6	115.2	123.9	119.2	115.1	100.0	95.9	99.0
Industrial plant and steel work	320	*15*	98.0	104.7	103.9	105.1	103.0	99.4	110.7	100.0	91.9	106.9
Machine tools and engineers' tools	322	*10*	129.5	132.6	131.7	112.8	112.0	112.6	106.3	100.0	73.2	68.0
Machinery for classes 25, 41 and 42[e]	324	*13*	106.9	112.8	113.7	116.8	118.7	112.7	109.2	100.0	94.6	95.3
Mining, construction and handling machinery	325	*14*	99.8	107.5	118.9	111.5	109.6	108.1	108.9	100.0	82.9	82.5
Mechanical power tranmission equipment	326	*6*	137.4	141.0	128.8	120.9	118.7	116.0	112.6	100.0	81.2	76.7
Other machinery and mechanical equipment	328	*33*	115.3	115.9	111.4	107.8	110.2	108.8	105.2	100.0	87.5	87.0
Ordnance, small arms and ammunition	329	*4*	64.4	65.1	71.4	84.1	89.3	103.5	92.7	100.0	114.2	131.4
Computers and office machinery	330	*10*	50.0	53.4	57.7	58.5	66.3	77.7	93.0	100.0	85.5	96.5
Basic electrical equipment	342	*14*	112.5	115.2	120.0	115.8	120.5	121.4	100.5	100.0	83.3	86.5
Electrical equipment for industrial use	343	*9*	105.1	107.5	104.6	106.0	110.5	115.2	112.3	100.0	81.3	85.2
Telecommunication equipment etc	344	*31*	77.8	82.2	78.6	78.3	81.4	84.8	93.2	100.0	99.5	103.0

continued

continued

	Group heading[b]	1980 Weights[c]	1973[d]	1974[d]	1975[d]	1976[d]	1977[d]	1978	1979	1980	1981	1982
Motor vehicles and their engines	351	*18*	162.6	150.1	126.9	126.1	127.8	124.1	114.6	100.0	80.2	77.2
Motor vehicle parts	353	*20*	113.6	107.5	105.3	106.6	121.0	116.6	117.7	100.0	88.3	86.3
Shipbuilding and repairing	361	*10*	122.3	127.3	128.5	124.2	123.1	113.8	106.5	100.0	104.2	110.4
Instrument engineering	370	*10*	90.2	96.4	97.6	95.4	97.7	103.6	102.3	100.0	100.1	97.7
Preparation of milk and milk products	413	*8*	85.9	83.2	84.1	88.2	96.5	101.4	100.7	100.0	100.6	104.7
Bread, biscuits and flour confectionery	419	*13*	108.5	105.3	103.2	101.4	102.0	99.2	101.5	100.0	101.1	99.9
Ice cream and chocolate/sugar confectionery	421	*8*	107.4	106.5	95.7	104.3	104.5	109.3	106.4	100.0	97.8	105.1
Animal feeding stuffs	422	*5*	91.9	86.9	87.1	94.2	93.4	95.4	99.1	100.0	98.6	106.2
Miscellaneous foods	423	*11*	92.4	96.2	94.1	97.0	92.7	96.4	96.5	100.0	98.7	103.3
Spirits	424	*5*	91.9	96.4	90.4	86.7	90.3	100.1	100.8	100.0	91.5	88.3
Brewing and malting	427	*12*	93.6	97.4	99.8	100.9	100.8	102.9	104.1	100.0	95.6	92.5
Soft drinks	428	*5*	70.9	71.5	80.5	88.1	85.8	92.8	101.7	100.0	93.9	96.2
Tobacco	429	*8*	95.0	94.2	91.8	92.2	90.9	98.1	97.3	100.0	97.2	90.3
Woollen and worsted	431	*5*	171.3	139.6	123.2	123.9	128.4	124.3	115.6	100.0	90.4	86.0
Hosiery and other knitted goods	436	*7*	111.8	109.6	106.5	112.5	112.9	110.6	108.3	100.0	96.0	93.5
Leather and leather goods	440	*3*	158.1	145.5	148.6	153.8	148.1	144.8	125.3	100.0	87.2	78.8
Footwear	451	*5*	119.2	117.1	111.8	110.5	116.4	115.3	114.3	100.0	88.4	82.1
Clothing, hats and gloves	453	*17*	102.7	100.7	101.7	98.0	104.6	108.3	110.7	100.0	91.3	90.2
Timber and related industries (excluding furniture)	461–466	*11*	151.2	126.5	121.0	129.4	117.9	116.2	117.3	100.0	91.7	94.4

Pulp, paper and board	471–472	*22*	122.9	123.4	99.5	104.1	107.7	109.6	111.5	100.0	92.8	88.4
Printing and publishing	475	*45*	101.6	101.3	92.0	92.9	97.3	99.8	104.9	100.0	95.1	91.5
Rubber products	481	*11*	105.0	100.7	98.5	107.7	111.3	113.7	113.0	100.0	86.6	79.1
Processing of plastics	483	*17*	99.4	96.1	85.4	95.3	102.5	106.7	110.6	100.0	94.7	94.5

[a] These indices are components of the index of output of the production industries (revised definition) (see Table 14.6) *however*, they do not include an adjustment to correct mixed sales and production data to true production index numbers: consequently, they are not strictly comparable with index of output of the production industries series. See paragraphs 11 to 16 of the notes on pages 247 and 248.

[b] The Group numbers are those of the Standard Industrial Classification 1980.

[c] Parts per 1,000 of index of output of the production industries (revised definition) shown in Table 14.6.

[d] Figures for years prior to 1978 have been linked to data based on minimum list headings of the Standard Industrial Classification 1968 and are therefore only approximations.

[e] Machinery for food, chemical and related industries; process engineering contractors.

BUILDING MATERIALS AND COMPONENTS: PRODUCTION[a], GREAT BRITAIN

	Unit	*1972*	*1973*	*1974*	*1975*	*1976*	*1977*	*1978*	*1979*	*1980*	*1981*	*1982*
Building bricks (excluding refractory and glazed)[b]	Millions	6,938	7,183	5,575	5,046	5,046	5,067	4,842	4,887	4,562	3,725	3,517
Cement[c]	Thousand tonnes	18,048	19,986	17,781	16,891	15,780	15,457	15,916	16,140	14,805	12,729	12,962
Building sand[d,e]	Thousand tonnes	21,314	23,619	20,295	21,444	20,431	18,608	18,510	18,983	18,005	15,675	16,592
Concreting sand[e]	Thousand tonnes	33,147	37,587	32,468	32,667	31,118	27,483	29,1664	29,455	26,699	25,427	23,809
Gravel[e,f]	Thousand tonnes	62,873	67,943	59,876	63,069	58,405	53,1238	54,426	54,056	51,454	48,351	47,092
Manufactured lightweight aggregates[b,g]	Thousand m³	1,050	1,091	1,012	1,274	1,546	1,399	1,402	[n]			
Crushed rock aggregates:[h]												
used as roadstone (coated)	Thousand tonnes	18,187	20,308	18,435	17,146	14,577	13,374	13,,910	13,413	14,366	13,179	
roadstone (uncoated)	Thousand tonnes	27,945	54,246	49,122	41,216	37,548	37,756	37,807	41,785	42,896	35,949	
fill and ballast	Thousand tonnes	34,836	30,481	33,737	34,301	29,973	29,227	31,131	31,722	31,619	31,049	
concrete aggregate	Thousand tonnes	18,705	21,403	16,958	16,930	16,227	15,259	15,872	15,588	13,663	11,205	
Ready mixed concrete[c]	Million m³	27.1	31.7	27.8	26.7	24.5	23.5	23.8	24.4	22.4	19.9	20.7
Asbestos cement products:												
Corrugated sheets	Thousand tonnes	395.7	433.9	406.0	291.1	301.7	313.4	309.0	330.0	284.5	219.4	217.7
Flat sheets	Thousand tonnes	48.5	46.8	48.4	41.7	49.2	45.6	45.4	27.6	17.0	11.4	13.2
All other products	Thousand tonnes	117.3	118.8	93.5	89.1	93.0	90.9	74.4	47.9	50.7	34.7	30.8
Clay roofing tiles[c,i]	Thousand m²	1,151	1,238	1,195	1,108	1,170	1,192	1,207	2,265	1,698	1,635	1,632[n]
Concrete roofing tiles[b]	Thousand m²	30,144	30,669	27,359	25,942	29,839	24,151	27,899	28,263	28,813	23,345	25,561

Concrete building blocks:[b]												
dense aggregate	Thousand m^2	18,823	20,849	17,533	18,407	18,092	19,206	20,780	22,298	21,014	18,911	23,918
lightweight aggregate	Thousand m^2	34,329	35,034	23,196	26,015	31,210	27,118	29,937	28,407	23,779	20,896	23,395
aerated concrete	Thousand m^2	15,252	16,,885	15,813	17,715	20,461	20,542	20,343	22,385	22,027	15,758	16,372
Concrete pipes[c,i,j]	Thousand tonnes	1,271	1,470	1,330	1,424	1,374	1,111	1,158	1,063	692	663	690[o]
Pitch fibre pipes and conduits	Thousand tonnes	31.7	30.1	24.5	16.8	17.4	13.1	11.0	[n]			
Roofing slates	Thousand tonnes	16.4	17.0	18.0	17.4	15.8	14.3	15.0	14.5	17.7	16.3	22.7
Slates (damp-proof course)	Thousand tonnes	0.9	0.9	0.6	0.5							
Gypsum (excluding anhydrite)	Thousand tonnes	3,396	3,689	3,115	3,206	3,148	3,136	3,144	3,396	3,264	2,667	2,566
Plaster	Thousand tonnes	1,019	1,125	1,038	1,047	1,053	988	975	949	960	775	764
Plasterboard	Thousand m^2	103,241	112,801	110,861	104,396	116,999	101,827	114,120	113,961	111,132	101,987	106,147
Hardboard and insulation board[c,i]	Thousand tonnes	36.4	35.3	29.3	24.6	30.2	31.3	31.4	30.8	29.5	[o]	
Unglazed floorquarries[c,i]	Thousand m^2	1,259	1,325	1,241	1,146	1,019	1,155	1,273	1,220	1,123	1,007	949[o]
Unglazed tiles[c,i]	Thousand m^2	1,528	1,840	1,906	1,704	1,769	1,900	2,025	2,099	2,332	2,084	1,366[o]

continued

continued

	Unit	1972	1973	1974	1975	1976	1977	1978	1979	1980	1981	1982
Cast iron pipes and fittings[c,k,l]	Thousand tonnes	46	43	40	40	50	38	43	34	[n]		
Pressure pipes and fittings[c,l]	Thousand tonnes	389	350	340	291	267	222	278	278	[n]		
Copper tubing[c,m]	Thousand	74	79	66	64	74	73	80	79	69	68	72

[a] The figures are summaries of returns made by manufacturers and producers. They represent total production and not merely the quantities available for building purposes.
[b] From 1975 figures include additional sites. The change has had the following effects: Building bricks production increased by 1 per cent; concrete building blocks production increased by an average of 11.0 per cent; manufactured lightweight aggregate 24 per cent and concrete roofing tiles production increased by less than 1 per cent.
[c] United Kingdom
[d] Including sand used in the production of sand lime bricks.
[e] From 1975 the figures relate to production derived from the Annual Minerals Raised Inquiries. These include additional sites not covered by the quarterly inquiries on which data prior to 1975 is based. From 1979 figures represent volumes sold, not production.
[f] Figures include hoggin, concrete aggregate, other purposes (excluding fill) and fill.
[g] Including aglite, foamed slag, leca, lytag and solite.
[h] From 1979 figures represent volume sold, not production.
[i] Figures represent volumes sold, not production.
[j] From 1974 figures relate to manufacturers' sales by firms employing 11 or more persons. From 1975 figures relate to manufacturers' sales by firms employing 25 or more persons.
[k] Including rainwater, hot water and soil pipes and gutters.
[l] 1975 was a 53-week year.
[m] Figures relate to the production of copper tubes for all purposes including those used in the construction industry.
[n] Series discontinued.
[o] Provisional.

CONSTRUCTION: VALUE OF OUTPUT IN GREAT BRITAIN (£m)

	1972	*1973*	*1974*	*1975*	*1976*	*1977*	*1978*	*1979*	*1980*	*1981*	*1982*
All work: total	6,752	8,613	9,733	11,077	12,176	13,309	15,702	18,871	22,052	21,547	22,540
New work: total	4,794	6,128	6,804	7,724	8,477	8,972	10,313	11,722	13,055	12,354	12,629
New housing: total	1,874	2,485	2,536	2,963	3,521	3,545	4,124	4,384	4,296	3,738	3,920
For public sector	683	849	1,100	1,453	1,760	1,717	1,749	1,711	1,711	1,222	1,021
For private sector	1,191	1,636	1,436	1,510	1,761	1,828	2,375	2,673	2,585	2,516	2,899
Other new work: total	2,920	3,643	4,268	4,761	4,956	5,427	6,189	7,338	8,760	8.616	8,709
For public sector	1,494	1,814	2,001	2,347	2,568	2,603	2,764	3,068	3,524	3.572	3,671
For private sector: total	1,426	1,829	2,267	2,414	2,388	2,824	3,425	4,270	5,236	5,044	5,038
Industrial	675	825	1,050	1,150	1,187	1,512	1,802	2,351	2,806	2,382	2,087
Commercial	751	1,004	1,217	1,264	1,201	1,312	1,623	1,919	2,430	2,662	2,951
Repair and maintenance: total	1,958	2,485	2,929	3,353	3,699	4,337	5,389	7,148	8,997	9,193	9,911
Housing	927	1,255	1,474	1,625	1,755	2,069	2,571	3,601	4,480	4,568	4,970
Public other work	737	860	974	1,208	1,338	1,528	1,854	2,269	2,920	3,026	3,286
Private other work	294	370	481	520	606	740	964	1,278	1,597	1,599	1,666

Output by contractors including unrecorded estimates by small firms and self-employed workers and by the public sectors' direct labour departments classified to construction in the *Standard Industrial Classification*, Revised 1980

Source: *Annual Abstract of Statistics*, 1984

Appendix 11 Ten-year record (£m) – BTR

	1973	*1974*	*1975*	*1976*	*1977*	*1978*	*1979*	*1980*	*1981*	*1982*
Sales										
Europe	44.6	74.5	99.0	130.1	161.5	243.7	284.1	310.0	325.0	399.4
Western region	2.0	2.6	7.2	30.0	35.4	42.3	59.5	77.1	134.8	146.8
Eastern region	23.8	33.4	44.7	52.3	51.0	65.1	89.0	122.7	177.7	178.7
	70.4	110.5	151.8	212.4	247.9	351.1	432.6	509.8	637.5	724.9
Profit before taxation										
Europe	4.4	7.9	11.8	16.5	21.2	31.1	39.1	41.0	42.0	61.8
Western region	0.3	0.6	0.6	4.9	6.3	7.8	11.7	17.8	33.5	39.9
Eastern region	2.6	3.8	6.1	6.6	5.3	6.2	11.2	18.4	28.2	24.3
Finance costs	(1.3)	(2.4)	(2.5)	(3.8)	(3.1)	(5.0)	(4.8)	(6.9)	(13.6)	(19.3)
	6.0	9.9	16.0	24.2	29.7	40.1	57.2	70.3	90.1	106.7
Earnings for BTR shareholders	2.8	4.6	6.7	13.0	18.1	23.4	32.1	43.2	57.1	68.6
Capital employed										
Fixed assets and investments	24.0	28.6	39.8	65.4	74.2	114.0	123.6	220.2	285.4	321.2
Net current assets	17.4	24.8	27.3	35.7	32.1	67.7	67.5	82.5	117.6	120.8
	41.4	53.4	67.1	101.1	106.3	181.7	191.1	302.7	403.0	442.0

Financed by										
Issued capital	8.1	8.1	9.9	11.0	13.6	17.4	26.2	40.0	60.0	60.0
Reserves	13.2	16.2	28.0	44.6	67.5	117.5	123.1	181.5	200.6	257.0
BTR shareholders' interests	21.3	24.3	37.9	55.6	81.1	134.9	149.3	221.5	260.6	317.0
Minority interests	5.3	7.0	8.5	10.4	7.6	10.1	10.2	15.7	19.4	21.1
Deferred taxation and other provisions	1.9	3.9	6.7	1.8	1.1	2.4	1.9	1.4	1.6	–
Long-term borrowings	7.2	9.0	13.7	25.1	21.2	20.9	24.3	68.4	107.0	79.5
Short-term borrowings net	5.7	9.2	0.3	8.2	(4.7)	13.4	5.4	(4.3)	14.4	24.4
	41.4	53.4	67.1	101.1	106.3	181.7	191.1	302.7	403.0	442.0
Shareholders' interests (pence per share)										
Earnings	2.1	3.4	4.7	8.2	9.9	12.1	15.1	19.7	23.9	28.6
Dividends net	0.7	0.9	1.6	1.8	2.7	3.6	5.7	7.1	8.8	10.0
Net assets	15.7	17.8	23.7	34.6	43.3	63.0	69.7	92.3	108.5	132.0

The above figures reflect adjustments both for bonus and rights issues and to conform to Statements of Standard Accounting Practice – deferred taxation (1976 onwards) and accounting for acquisitions (1978 onwards).

CONSOLIDATED PROFIT AND LOSS ACCOUNT (£000) – BTR

	1982	*1981*
Sales	724,942	637,512
Operating profit	118,805	97,425
Other income	7,230	6,319
	126,035	103,744
Finance costs	19,374	13,590
Profit before taxation	106,661	90,154
Taxation	34,114	27,057
Profit after taxation	72,547	63,097
Minority interests	3,964	5,972
Earnings for the year	68,583	57,125
Extraordinary items	9,975	4,071
Attributable to BTR plc	58,608	53,054
Dividends	24,031	20,976
Retained	34,577	32,078
Earnings per ordinary share	28.6p	23.9p

Earnings per ordinary share are calculated on earnings of £68,583,000 (£57,125,000) and 239,965,000 (239,404,000) ordinary shares in issue, which is the average for the year.

CONSOLIDATED BALANCE SHEET AT 1 JANUARY 1983 (£000) – BTR

	1982	*1981*
Capital employed:		
Fixed assets	271,577	236,406
Investments	49,651	49,013
	321,228	285,419
Inventories	149,994	157,225
Accounts receivable	162,150	156,686
Cash	20,240	17,384
Total current assets	332,384	331,295
Accounts payable	154,861	158,281
Bank loans and overdrafts	44,681	31,800
Taxation	23,839	27,270
Dividends	12,607	10,787
Total current liabilities	235,988	228,138
Net current assets	96,396	103,157
	417,624	388,576
Financed by:		
Issued capital of BTR plc	60,034	60,000
Reserves	256,987	200,587
BTR shareholders interests	317,021	260,587
Minority interests	21,061	19,398
Deferred taxation		1,630
Loan capital	79,542	106,961
	417,624	388,576

Approved by the Board on 16 March 1983

David Nicolson Director

Owen Green Director

6 Horizon Travel

The package tour holiday companies begin their advertising for the following season before the customers have finished their Christmas dinner, and the colder the weather in Britain, then the more attractive a two-week stay in the summer sun of Spain and the Mediterranean seems. Generally, most of the booking is done by the end of February, but early 1983 turned out to be a bit more difficult. The well-known tour companies, Thomson, Horizon, Intasun and Cosmos and others were a little more cautious after a 1982 season in which holiday package bookings were down by about 3% according to the British Market Research Bureau, and most of the travel companies had given discounts off their normal prices.

In 1965 Bruce Tanner, chairman of Horizon, who was operating a small Birmingham tour operator (as Horizon Midlands) joined with the London-based Horizon Holidays. The result was Horizon London operating from the south and Horizon Midlands operating from Birmingham and this geographical expansion partly explained the early growth of Horizon. At the time when Clarksons, the market leader, went into liquidation in 1974 as a result of offering holidays at too low a price, the Horizon London end of the Horizon operation ran into difficulties as all the tour operators struggled with the problems arising from the quadrupling of oil prices and the devaluation of sterling. Bruce Tanner set about carefully rebuilding the business, conscious that quality control and product consistency were becoming more important in the holiday business, and by 1978 Horizon was able to consider setting up its own airline.

Thus by the holiday season of 1979 Horizon had joined the other three big tour operators running their own airline. Thomson Holidays owned Britannia Airlines, Intasun Leisure owned Air Europe, and Cosmos was the owner of Monarch Airways. Horizon's airline was called Orion Airlines and it immediately contributed to company profitability with £1m of the company's £7.38m pre-tax profit for 1980; in 1981 Orion contributed £4m to pre-tax profits of £13.3m on sales of £97m (a market share of the package tour business of 9%).

Prior to the establishment of Orion Airlines the company had been paying approximately one-third of its sales revenue to Britannia Airlines (owned by Thomson), and the economics of the industry did not pose serious difficulties to paying out for aeroplanes. Package holiday customers paid, on average, about £35 when booking their holiday (often six months in advance) and the balance eight weeks before departure. Since the foreign hotel bills are settled when the holidaymakers have returned, at certain times of the year the tour operators have a very large/positive cash flow.

In the early days the original Horizon Midlands had bought ten retail travel agents in main cities which sold competitors' holiday tours as well as Horizon tours.

In 1980 Horizon Travel, as by that time the company had been renamed, bought two hotels at Mojacar in Spain which was not at that time on the tourist map; the hotels were thus virtually worthless unless a big tour operator took an interest in them. Horizon bought them for less than £1m and subsequently bought and developed a surrounding 20-acre site for self-catering units at a projected completion price of £4.5m, with the forecast contribution of the Pueblo Indalo holiday village, as it would be known, of £1m per year. It was planned to offer holidays at Pueblo Indalo by 1983 for Spanish holidaymakers as the village reached completion, and subsequently to offer holidays there for UK holidaymakers in 1984.

Following its 1981 financial performance Horizon expected to continue growing, and in 1982 produced record profit figures of £14.3m even though the 1982 season had not been good for the industry generally. Unlike the other tour operators, however, Horizon had not had to indulge in discount sales of its holidays although its load factor[1] had fallen to 87% from 94% in 1981. Each percentage point fall meant roughly an overall fall in profits for the industry as a whole of £500,000 as the gross profit margin of 'top-slice' customers[2] was over 40%. In 1983 Horizon Travel planned to offer 525,000 holidays, which was a 16% increase over 1982.

Thus by 1983 Horizon Travel was involved in all the stages of the package tour holiday from retail travel agent (although selling only a minute proportion of their own holidays) to hotel/village ownership and airline transport. (See Appendix 1 for financial information on Horizon Travel PLC)

[1] The 'load-factor' referred to the planning by the companies regarding the proportion of holidays sold. The typical load-factor plan in the industry was 90% whereas Horizon planned on 85%.

[2] Once the load factor had passed 90% the industry called the percentages above that the 'top-slice customers'.

BACKGROUND TO THE INDUSTRY

The air-inclusive tour holiday developed after the Second World War such that whereas 600,000 UK residents went abroad by air on a package holiday in 1962, the number had risen to 1.7 million by 1969 and over 4 million by 1982. (Table 6.1 shows the developments in the 1970s). The rapid growth of the industry in the 1960s attracted many entrants and by 1965 there were over 300 companies offering air-inclusive package holidays. However, by the late 1960s the industry had evolved into a small group of companies who had survived the development and 'shake-out' periods of the industry growth. In addition large companies had bought their way into what they saw as a profitable growth market. For example, the Thomson Organization (well-known for its newspapers and television) bought three tour operators in 1965, and by 1982 was the largest UK operator.

TABLE 6.1 Holidays abroad

	Summer inclusive tours (thousands)	*Winter inclusive tours (thousands)*	*All holidays (thousands)*	*Inclusive tours as % of all holidays*
1974	2,400	737	6.75	46
1975	2,680	782	8.00	43
1976	2,710	761	7.25	48
1977	2,525	851	7.25	47
1978	2,992	1,105	9.00	46
1979	3,638	1,231	10.25	48
1980	4,164	1,107	12.00	44
1981	4,372	1,052	13.25	41
1982	4,153	N/A	N/A	N/A

Source: Pickford's Travel, November 1982

Although the industry continued to grow through the 1970s, there were often problems to be overcome. The industry was particularly susceptible to fluctuations in sterling, and when sterling was floated by the UK Government in 1972, the operators had continually to consider its value from one year to the next. Also by this time the economy and industry growth rates had begun to slow down and profits were not always as easy to make. Clarksons, the industry leader, reported losses of £2.7 million in 1971 and went into liquidation in 1974.

As the *Financial Times* reported on 5 July 1972:

> (the companies) are well aware that the last year or so has seen the basis on which package tourism has grown in Britain changed somewhat. Assorted factors have contributed to this, and the

problem of the pound is simply the last in a long line. Broadly speaking, the companies have found that:

(a) Size gave them greater management problems than they had anticipated,
(b) Continued growth could not be taken for granted,
and
(c) Inflation (and now effective devaluation) plays havoc with long-term pricing policies.

The companies which coped best in those difficult times were the Horizons and Wings of the business. It was arguable that this was not necessarily due to the management quality, but rather that they had concentrated on up-market growth by aiming at white-collar, middle-class executives who had suffered less in the recessions. In addition, at that time Horizon was more of a regional operator based in the Midlands, and a part of its success may be attributed to the general prosperity of the area at that time. The bigger companies seemed unable to deal with the problems posed. With hindsight it was easy to criticize the tour operators for not buying their currencies or their beds forward, but the situation was more complex than it appeared. Some had completed favourable deals; for example Thomson fixed its beds in Jamaica and Jugoslavia in dollar currency and when the dollar fell they emerged with a profit. But the currency crisis of 1972 arrived at the very worst part of their year, with the summer rush about to start, leaving little time to reorganize. The result was the operators had to involve themselves in the messy business of collecting surcharges at the airports to cover both currency losses and fuel price changes levied by the airlines.

These problems of the early to mid-seventies emphasized the advantages of longer-term planning to the tour operators and resulted in changes relating to both flights and beds.

Some of the larger companies had recognized that they could cut costs by entering into longer-term (i.e. five to ten years rather than just a holiday season) contracts with the airlines, and eventually they began to integrate vertically with an airline company. Thomson Holidays bought Britannia Airways, Cosmos bought Monarch Airways, Intasun owned Air Europe, while Laker Holidays and Arrowsmith Holidays were subsidiaries of Laker Airlines before Laker went into involuntary liquidation in February 1982. All the holiday tour operators maintained a policy of runnng their airlines as separate companies from the mainstream holiday business and even chartering flights seats to other holiday tour operators; for example Intasun used only 50% of their seats for their own package holidays, and the balance was used by 25 different tour operators.

Changes in the methods of acquisition of hotel beds also occurred, particularly in the second half of the 1960s as there was a shortage of beds in the most popular resorts. Not only were British companies in competition with each other, but they also competed directly with the Scandinavians and the Germans. The tour companies also discovered that British holidaymakers did not take kindly to being accommodated in a hotel dominated by fellow-guests of a different nationality – different social habits led to friction and ill-feeling.

The original method of obtaining beds was to have an annual contract with the hotelier and to renew that contract each year. The growing competition for beds led to rapid increases in prices and consequent uncertainty for the companies. Furthermore, no company could be confident that the beds it had used one year would be available the following year: the hoteliers were in a strong position to negotiate last-minute contracts with competing companies.

As a result, the practice of contracting with a hotelier for a block of beds in his hotel for seven to ten years became increasingly common. The normal contract had three particular features: first, an initial deposit was required, usually amounting to between 10 and 20% of the total value of the contract (sometimes it was as high as 50%), to be repaid over the length of the contract; secondly, the negotiated rate per bed per night increased by an agreed fixed percentage every year to allow for inflation; thirdly, the company had to give a guarantee that there would be an agreed level of occupancy of the beds, averaged over the whole summer season, below which a financial penalty was incurred.

A third method of obtaining beds also developed. This was the long-term (15–25 years) turnkey lease, in which the company took over a complete hotel, fully equipped and furnished, and was entirely responsible for providing the management. Usually, a deposit was required, amounting to perhaps three years' rent in advance. This scheme guaranteed beds for years ahead, and allowed total control over the quality of service provided. There were, however, some problems. Local hoteliers resented a hotel leased and managed by a tour company, because the company tended to favour its own hotel, especially in lean years.

A distinctive feature of the air-package holiday industry in the UK was the high proportion of holidays sold through general retail travel agents. A survey by the Economist Intelligence Unit (EIU) in 1968 had estimated this proportion as 83%, as against 77% for airline seats and 68% for sea passages. The sale of air package holidays by travel agents represented the most profitable part of their business, since they normally received a commission of 10% on each sale and occasionally an overriding commission of a variable 2½%. As a result, any attempt by the companies to bypass the travel agent, by selling direct to the public or using some other outlet, met with strong resistance.

The travel agents were in a powerful position. Since many companies marketed almost identical holidays, and 'brand loyalty' was low, the agents had great influence on whose holidays were sold. They could effectively 'black' any company they chose without seriously affecting their volume of business. Furthermore, all the largest travel agents (25% were responsible for 78% of business in 1968) were closely linked through the Association of British Travel Agents (ABTA) and could, in theory, if they so wished, act together against any individual company. This was unlikely, but the threat remained.

For the tour companies, which operated on load factors of 85–90%, and for which each additional sale after breakeven represented almost pure profit, the maximization of outlets was increasingly important. The EIU survey had suggested that the number of outlets could be increased by the use of supermarkets, banks, mail order houses, etc.

One strategy open to the tour companies was the acquisition of a chain of independent travel agents. Vertical integration had not proceeded far in this direction, possibly because of the threat of boycott from other travel agents should a tour company make a serious move towards such a policy. The EIU survey found that little capital was normally required to set up an agency and that staff costs accounted for between 60 and 65 per cent of the total running costs. Significantly, the EIU study revealed that provincial and country town agents were generally very profitable: 75% showed profits in excess of 20% of total revenue (total value of ticket sales less remissions to carriers and tour operators); 40% of suburban agents showed profits in excess of 20% of total revenue, but city shopping centre agents showed small profits.

By the end of the 1970s there had been a distinct move in favour of the largest tour operators, as holidaymakers had seen companies associated with the industry collapse in the 1970s, for example, Clarksons, Courtline, Horizon London, and in 1982 Laker Airlines (including Arrowsmith Holidays and Laker Holidays). Fear of such events had encouraged the shift to the industry's more established names. As a consequence 1981 results gave Thomson Travel, the biggest tour operator a pre-tax profit increase of 24% on a turnover of £334m, and sales for the first time of over one million holidays. (See Appendix 1). 1982 saw the economic recession biting deeper, and overall sales of holidays were down 3%, but by then the planning for 1983 had been put under way.

A gradual move by the tour operators was for some of them to sell their holidays direct to the holidaymakers, thus bypassing the travel agent. For many years they had held off making such a move, fearing retaliation from the travel agents, but the situation was upset when a new tour company entered the market from abroad with experience of direct selling and no connections with the travel agents. This was the Scandinavian company Tjareborg. Of the major UK tour operators only Thomson, the largest with over 20% share of the market, launched its own direct selling operation called 'Portland' in 1980. This showed a £500,000 profit in 1981, but it did not endear Thomson to the travel agents.

In the early 1980s there was a brisk demand for retail travel agencies. Consequently, the membership of ABTA (necessary if air-inclusive tours were to be sold) had grown. The Thomas Cook group, having hived off to its parent company the traveller's cheque business, was concentrating on becoming an effective retail chain. There were few economies of scale in retail travel agency, and increased turnover could only be sought by increasing the number of outlets. It may be that too much 'capacity' in retailing was being put on the market and some degree of concentration of ownership might be expected. In the early 1980s the travel agents were also faced with a variety of problems apart from the looming threat of the relaxation of ABTA regulations. The managing director of Pickford's Travel, which operated the country's second largest chain of 200 retail travel outlets, proposed one way of cutting the number of travel agents down by suggesting that the travel agents, instead of operating on their 10% commission, should be allowed to set their own prices for holiday packages (and hence their own profit margins). This would enable a multiple travel agent to negotiate the numbers and prices of holidays bought from the tour operator and resell them at its own price.

By 1982 there were approximately 4,500 retail travel agents in the UK, and typically, at least 60% of a travel agent's turnover was air-related business, either through the sale of airline tickets or through the sale of air inclusive tours. The role of retailing was supplemented by the sales offices of the major airlines and tour operators, and by agents not appointed by the International Air Travel Association (IATA) airlines (such entrepreneurs are often referred to as bucket shops).

The conventional travel agent was appointed by the IATA airlines to handle the tickets of the IATA airlines operating in the country concerned. Agents' commission on ticket sales was only allowed to the IATA-appointed travel agents. The IATA appointment was thus highly prized. Deregulation in the airline field extended into this area too: for example, the withdrawal of the large US airlines from the IATA fares-setting traffic conferences meant that they would not see themselves bound by the IATA resolutions on travel agency relations, including the setting of agents' commission.

OPERATION 'STABILIZER'

A quite different situation existed in the case of the retailing of air inclusive tours. In the UK, the Association of British Travel Agents (ABTA), the trade association, partly with quite laudable consumer protection considerations in mind, had operated an exclusive dealing scheme whereby ABTA retailers may only sell the air inclusive tours of ABTA tour operators who in turn may only retail their tours through ABTA retailers (apart from direct sales they may make through their own offices). In view of the importance of tour operation to outward tourism, membership of ABTA was virtually a necessary condition of being a travel agent.

In late 1982 this exclusive dealing arrangement (known as Operation Stabilizer) was scheduled to be examined under the restrictive trades practices legislation. It was hard to see how Stabilizer could be defended, and if it could not, then retail price maintenance for inclusive tours and the restriction on retail outlets would disappear, and the retail travel trade would become something of a free-for-all. It could be argued that Stabilizer had brought order and discipline to the tourism market at a time of rapid expansion, that it had protected the public to some extent from the less stable tour operator and travel agent, and that it had not worked in restraint of trade, at least not on any large scale.

If Stabilizer was abolished by the Court, a wholly new situation could appear in tourism and travel retailing. If one considered what had happened in other retail trades, an argument by analogy suggested that the balance of power would shift from the manufacturer (the tour operator) to the retailer (the travel agent). One would expect that the multiple travel agency chains such as Thomas Cook would assume much greater importance, particularly in the inclusive-tour field, where the market demand is highly price inelastic. (See Appendix 5 on ABTA and 'Stabilizer').

THE PROBLEMS OF PLANNING

The planning for the 1983 season brochures issued by Thomson, Horizon, Intasun, Cosmos and the other package tour operators had begun in November 1981. By that time the major operators had already issued their 1982 brochures and had begun to get some idea of what their sales would be like for 1982, as bookings came in from the 4,500 travel agents around the country who sold the holiday packages for a 10% commission. By early 1982 the tour operators had decided what strategic moves they should make. Intasun, for example, left its main programme of holidays unchanged for 1983, but had branched out into camping, coach holidays and the teenage market. The four major ingredients of the packaged holiday were the hotels, the resorts, the UK airports and the length of stay, and these were determined a year in advance. The brochures, usually led by Horizon or Thompson, went to press in July with prices worked out on the basis of the cost of the four basic ingredients, plus a contribution to overheads and profit. None of the variables was straightforward. The cost of the hotel bed was affected by the exchange rate between sterling and the local currency. Air flight contracts were subject to the price of fuel (always calculated in dollars). Overheads were controllable, but the company had to estimate how many holidays it would sell in order to work out how thinly to spread out the fixed costs. Fuel and foreign exchange could be covered by 'buying forward', but there remained the imponderable factor of how many holidays the public would buy. Horizon had always planned on the basis of a load factor of

85%, that is they priced on the basis of selling at least 85% of the holidays they offered. Other companies planned for a load factor of 90%.

The economics of the industry and the slim margins were such that even a slight fall below anticipated demand could cause severe problems for some of the package tour operators. In Autumn 1982 Horizon launched its 1983 brochures, followed a week later by Thomson, with the latter offering one million holidays. By November 1982 the whole trade was reported to be 30% down on bookings compared with the previous year, and Thomson had sold only 200,000 compared with 240,000 at the same time a year earlier. Horizon, Intasun and Cosmos were each offering about 500,000 holidays, and frequently the latter two had awaited Thomson's announcements before making final commitments on prices, thus expecting in autumn 1982 to offer comparable holidays at slightly lower prices than the market leader.

When Intasun and Cosmos produced their 1983 brochures the price differential was more marked than usual, for they priced comparable holidays, often in the same hotels, up to £15 cheaper (a summer package cost between £175 and £300) with prices guaranteed. Thomson responded by withdrawing its original brochure and issuing a new one with price reductions ranging from £5 to £74 on more than half the holidays on offer, with no surcharges guaranteed at a 'paper' cost to the company of £6 million. Thomson had prepared for the possibility of a price war as forecasts for the 1983 holiday season were of falls of 5% to 20%, by splitting its brochure print run into two parts. The company usually produced 2.75 million copies of its 300-page brochure, but for 1983 it had produced only 1.15 million and had been able to respond to its competitors by producing the second run with the new prices in December 1982. As well as a general fall in demand for holidays in 1982 they had had to contend with an increasing tendency by the buyer to book later and later, such that at one point in summer 1982 it was estimated that the average period between booking and departure had fallen to 20 days. (See figure 6.1.)

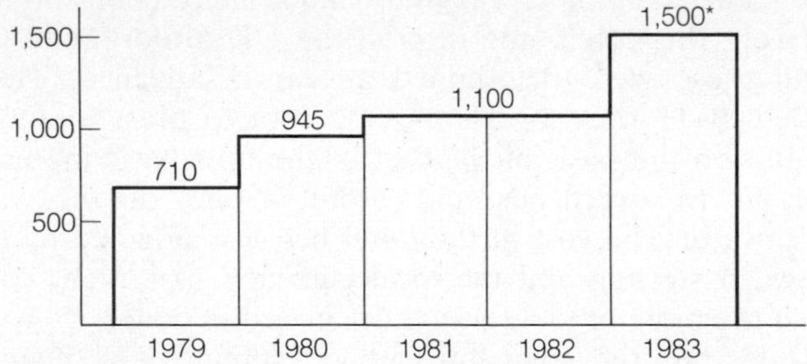

FIGURE 6.1 Number of bookings (in thousands) after 30 April for the summer of each year
* estimated
Source: Thomas Cook

The problem facing Horizon, Intasun and Cosmos, not to mention the many smaller tour operators, was how to respond to the reissue of Thomson's 1983 brochure. The problem was one of timing as well as cost. Thomson had been able to plan its whole Christmas press and television advertising around the new prices, and it was impossible for the others to produce a new brochure in time to get it out to the 4,500 travel agents.

Traditionally the first two months of a year produced most of the summer's bookings[3] so the tour operators had always begun their major advertising efforts at Christmas, aware that by March they would have to start releasing hotel beds and flights or pay for them with the hope of selling them, but perhaps only at a discount.

As each year progressed, those tour operators who got their initial capacity plans wrong had to write to customers explaining changes in departure or return dates, airports and even hotels and resorts (with opportunity for the customer to back out), and this would involve giving the customer an *ex gratia* payment for the inconvenience. Those holidays bought by the tour operator but not sold would have to be heavily discounted because by the summer any contribution would be better than nothing. Horizon, however, had a policy of not discounting its holidays.

THOMSON TRAVEL LTD

Thomson Travel Ltd was a fully owned subsidiary of the International Thomson Organization PLC, and it operated package tours, aircraft charter and travel retailing in the UK through the following travel companies: Thomson Holidays, Portland Holidays, Lunn Poly and Britannia Airways. Thomson Holidays was one of the world's largest package tour operators, and by far the largest in the UK, organizing and selling approximately one million holidays a year covering Europe, Asia, Africa and America. It offered every conceivable kind of resort and hotel from the large luxury to the tiny intimate. Thomson was also the leader in skiing holidays, the number two in villa holidays and in 1980 entered the short weekend breaks market (e.g. to Paris). Portland Holidays was launched in 1980 as a tour operator selling direct to the public and in 1981 sold over 100,000 holidays. Lunn Poly was an expanding retail travel agency with over 60 outlets.

International Thomson PLC was involved in the publishing of newspapers, periodicals and books, and natural mineral exploitation and interests in Canada, Australia and the USA as well as the UK. It had disposed of its interest in Scottish Television in 1977 and the *Sunday*

[3] By end of January 1979, 63% of those who eventually took a foreign holiday had booked, and by the end of January 1982 this had fallen to 42%. Eventually in 1982, 15% of all holidays were discounted, although Horizon had not discounted any.

Times in 1981. It had taken up its interest in the travel industry when it bought Thomson Travel in 1965. For the year ended December 1981, the turnover of International Thomson PLC was £609 million and profit before tax £32.5 million. (See Appendix 2 for financial information on Thomson Travel Ltd.)

INTASUN LEISURE GROUP

The company began operations in 1971 when Harry Goodman, Stephen Matthews and Michael Prior started Vacation Apartments Ltd. In 1972 they acquired the Intasun name and by 1977 were operating package holidays from airports all over the UK. In 1978 they decided to acquire their own airline and formed Air Europe which by 1981 was a wholly owned subsidiary of Intasun and contributed 28% of the group's profit before tax. Table 6.2 shows the growth of the Intasun business since it began operating nationally in 1977.

TABLE 6.2 Growth of the Intasun business

Year ended 31 March	1977	1978	1979	1980	1981	1982
Holidays sold (000's)	124	238	339	296	417	468
Load factor (%)	88	92	89	90	91	95

Air Europe planes were chartered to a further 25 other tour operators, although 50% of the capacity was used by Intasun in the peak holiday seasons, but none of them accounted for more than 8% of the airfleet's capacity. Like other tour operators, Intasun sold its holidays through ABTA travel agents around the country who accounted for 95% of the Intasun holidays sold. As a matter of policy the company had made no investments in hotels, and negotiated fixed tariffs with hoteliers on a seasonal basis and kept advance contractual commitments to a minimum. Intasun did sometimes place deposits with hotels, but only when it had already taken sufficient bookings to cover the deposit. It avoided undue dependence on any one hotel group and believed that its buying power as the second biggest UK tour operator and its record of taking up its allocations enabled it to reserve accommodation in advance and to pay only for those rooms occupied.

In common with other overseas inclusive air tour operators the company was required to hold a licence issued by the Civil Aviation Authority, and to hold a bond guaranteeing payment of up to 7% of its estimated gross turnover in the event of failure to meet liabilities to passengers.

Like its competitors Intasun had planned for growth in the 1983 season, and had increased its number of holidays available by 19% to 634,000 and offered a no-surcharge guarantee for all bookings made before the end of February. Thomson and Horizon had countered this offer by giving a no-surcharge guarantee regardless of booking date. Such a move was considered by Intasun as contrary to commonsense as they felt that no-surchage guarantees should be offered to encourage early booking.

The history of no-surcharge guarantees is complicated, but in several seasons Horizon had managed to avoid surcharges by getting its 'buying forward' right at times when other operators had been obliged to levy surcharges. The complications arose when an operator found itself in a position of surcharging with the left hand whilst discounting with the right within the same season. This had befallen Intasun in the past. (Appendix 3 gives financial information on Intasun).

Appendix 1 Horizon Travel PLC

PROFIT AND LOSS, YEAR ENDING NOVEMBER

	1982	*1981*
Turnover	118,486,963	96,833,711
Group profit before taxation	14,367,373	13,401,523
Share of result of associated company	(66,556)	(68,182)
	14,300,817	13,333,341
Provision for taxation	4,543,021	7,062,265
Profit after taxation	9,757,796	6,271,076
Attributable to minority interests	39,702	7,830
Attributable to members	9,718,094	6,263,246

Number of ordinary shares 42.25 million

BALANCE SHEETS

	1982 £	*1981* £
Fixed assets	50,113,615	32,739,391
Investments	37,558	45,122
Current assets		
Debtors and prepayments	3,806,543	2,888,629
Corporation Tax recoverable	518,740	–
Short-term deposits	15,291,005	16,095,000
Bank balances and cash	1,378,008	2,076,530
	20,994,296	21,060,159
	71,145,469	53,844,672
Deduct – Current liabilities		
Cash received in advance	8,399,316	7,730,719
Creditors and accrued expenses	10,533,723	7,775,762
Corporation Tax	1,100,482	1,526,585
Dividend	1,183,284	1,024,321
	21,216,805	18,057,387
	49,928,664	35,787,285
Representing		
Share capital	10,565,036	5,280,006
Capital reserve	2,122,547	7,426,510
Retained profits	15,285,820	7,089,091
Shareholders' funds	27,973,403	19,795,607
Minority interests	502,812	287,263
Provision for aircraft maintenance	3,723,602	1,937,724
Deferred taxation reserve	17,728,847	13,766,691
	49,928,664	35,787,285

FIVE-YEAR FINANCIAL STATEMENT

	1982 £	*1981* £	*1980* £	*1979* £	*1978* £
Group turnover	118,486,963	96,833,711	72,577,000	50,178,618	31,269,252
Profit before taxation	14,367,373	13,401,523	7,381,491	3,815,069	2,951,342
Associated company	(66.556)	(68,182)	–	–	–
	14,300,817	13,333,341	7,381,491	3,815,069	2,951,342
Taxation	4,543,021	7,062,265	4,076,396	2,004,047	1,557,409
Profit after taxation	9,757,796	6,271,076	3,305,095	1,811,022	1,393,933
Minority interests	39,702	7,830	–	–	–
	9,718,094	6,263,246	3,305,095	1,811,022	1,393,933
Dividends	1,521,365	1,267,201	646,860	431,200	331,056
Profit retained	8,196,729	4,996,045	2,658,235	1,379,822	1,062,877

Fixed assets	50,113,615	32,739,391	18,921,317	11,359,655	6,029,396
Investments	37,558	45,122	–	–	–
Current assets	20,994,296	21,060,159	8,844,328	6,979,177	6,548,694
	71,145,469	53,844,672	27,765,645	18,338,832	12,578,090
Less Current liabilities	21,216,805	18,057,387	11,463,224	8,549,882	6,001,134
	49,928,664	35,787,285	16,302,421	9,788,950	6,576,956
Representing					
Share capital	10,565,036	5,280,006	1,466,668	293,333	293,333
Reserves	17,408,367	14,515,601	6,394,820	5,013,406	3,633,584
Shareholders funds	27,973,403	19,795,607	7,861,488	5,306,739	3,926,917
Minority interests	502,812	287,263	–	371	388
Provision for aircraft maintenance	3,723,602	1,937,724	307,616	–	–
Deferred taxation reserve	17,728,847	13,766,691	8,133,317	4,431,840	2,599,651
Staff pension reserve	–	–	–	50,000	50,000
	49,928,664	35,787,285	16,302,421	9,788,950	6,576,956

Appendix 2 Thomson Travel Ltd (£ million)

Year ending 31 December	*Turnover*	*Profit before tax*	*Dividend*
1977	124	4	N/A
1978	152	17	N/A
1979	208	22.5	N/A
1980	270	27.3	15.0
1981	334	35.3	63.0

BALANCE SHEETS (£ MILLION)

	1981	*1980*
Assets employed		
Fixed assets	63.4	61.6
Goodwill	4.5	4.4
Investments	2.5	4.8
Net current liabilities	(4.3)	(18.7)
	66.1	52.1
Financed by		
Share capital	3.0	3.0
Reserves	9.9	30.4
	12.9	33.4
Shareholders' loan	49.0[a]	14.0
	61.9	47.4
Deferred liabilities	4.2	4.7
	66.1	52.1

[a] On 16 October 1981 £35m of loan stock was issued to the holding company at 8% p.a.

Appendix 3 Intasun Leisure Group PLC

PROFIT AND LOSS STATEMENT, YEARS ENDED 31 MARCH (£000)

	1982	*1981*	*1980*	*1979*	*1978*
Turnover	114,118	101,653	48,755	40,238	25,452
Profit before tax and extraordinary items	14,075	10,258	3,024	2,590	1,963
Earnings per share (pence)	19.6	14.6	8.0	4.8	2.3
Dividends per share (pence)	3.5[a]	–	–	–	–

1982 (year ending 31 March)

	Turnover %	*Turnover £000*	*Profit before tax (£000)*
Holidays	80.8	92,168	8,685
Airline	19.2	21,950	5,390
	100.00	114,118	14,075

[a] The shares were first issued to the public in April 1981.

BALANCE SHEETS AT 31 MARCH (£000)

	1982		*1981*	
Assets employed:				
Fixed assets		39,764		32,058
Investments		91		43
Deferred expenditure		4,769		3,380
Current assets:				
Debtors and prepayments	10,481		8,610	
Bank deposits and cash	31,902		20,958	
Taxation recoverable	–		315	
	42,383		29,883	
Current liabilities:				
Cash received in advance	16,046		13,977	
Creditors and accruals	11,524		7,433	
Short-term loans	624		1,024	
Taxation	782		92	
Dividend	1,084		–	
	30,060		22,526	
Net current assets		12,323		7,357
		56,947		42,838
Financed by:				
Share capital		5,164		52
Share premium		362		5,474
Retained profits		16,638		8,176
Shareholders' funds		22,164		13,702
Deferred taxation		5,825		2,600
Deferred liabilities		28,958		26,536
		56,947		42,838

Source: Reproduced by arrangement with Extel Statistical Services Limited, 37–45 Paul Street, London EC2A 4PB.

Appendix 4 Cosmos Air Holidays Ltd

PROFIT AND LOSS ACCOUNT (£000)

Year ended Nov. 30	*Turnover*	*Interest received*	*Profit before tax*
1975	37,886	192	588
1976	45,630	230	220
1977	50,789	159	507
1978	55,219	186	633
1979	75,954	457	727
1980	88,685	985	1,289
1981	91,318	1,027	955

BALANCE SHEETS (£000)

	1979	1980	1981
Current assets			
Cash	2,646	3,604	3,380
Tax recoverable	–	–	263
Stocks	527	468	294
Debtors	5,998	6,274	8,944
	9,173	10,347	12,933
Current liabilities			
Creditors	7,392	7,953	10,729
Bank overdraft	–	226	217
HP agreements	353	90	–
Taxation	213	48	–
Advances	2,790	2,677	2,843
	10,750	10,995	13,790
Net current assets	(1,577)	(647)	(857)
Fixed assets	3,944	3,796	4,260
Deferred revenue expenditure	1,118	1,249	1,309
Deferred asset	–	–	1,059
	3,485	4,397	5,771
Capital	100	100	100
Capital reserve	130	420	420
P & L A/c	941	2,222	3,337
Deferred loan	600	600	600
Minority interest	382	694	954
Deferred tax	1,240	360	360
HP agreements	90	–	–
	3,485	4,397	5,771

Source: Reproduced by arrangement with Extel Statistical Services Ltd, 37–45 St Paul Street, London EC2A 4PB

Appendix 5

ASSOCIATION OF BRITISH TRAVEL AGENTS (ABTA)

Operation Stabilizer was referred to the Office of Fair Trading (OFT) in December 1982 under the 1976 Restrictive Trade Practices Act. The main attack of the OFT on the ABTA agreement was directed against the exclusivity provisions which prohibited members from dealing with non-members; package tour operators could not sell foreign package tours through travel agents who were not members of ABTA, and travel agents could not sell foreign package tours organized by non-ABTA tour operators. The OFT argued that 'Stabilizer' was a fetter on competition, impeded innovation and was contrary to the public interest. ABTA claimed that removal of 'Stabilizer' would deprive the public of benefits such as protection against financial loss and collapse of holiday arrangements, and the availability of better trained staff, better premises and better travel insurance arrangements.

The court refused to declare 'Stabilizer' contrary to the public interest, but declared the staffing, premises and certain other restrictions including retail price maintenance to be so. These latter restrictions had prevented ABTA operations in banks, supermarkets, post offices, etc.

7 International Computers (A)

In May 1981 changes in the senior management of ICL were announced. These involved the appointment of Mr C. Laidlaw as chairman in place of Mr Philip Chappell who had become chairman in February 1980; the appointment of Mr R.W. Wilmot as managing director; and the appointment of an additional non-executive director, Mr J.A. Gardiner. These appointments were approved by the British Government which, although not a shareholder in ICL, had become involved when the company ran into difficulties in 1980. The government had decided in March 1981 to guarantee loans for the company of up to £200 million, which encouraged the company's four principal UK bankers to increase their facilities to a total of £270 million for a period of up to two years. The 'price' of the government guarantee was the right to make senior management changes.

DEVELOPMENT OF ICL

International Computers was created in 1968 by an amalgamation of International computers and Tabulators, and the computer interests of English Electric. These in their turn had comprised a variety of computer operations, including parts of Ferranti, Elliott Automation, Marconi, and EMI. The UK Government was a main sponsor of the formation of ICL in an attempt to create a 'national champion' of sufficient size to compete with the American multi-nationals such as IBM. In 1965 ICT (one of the companies which subsequently helped to form ICL) had a 30% market share in the UK, and a £55m turnover, based on its 1900 series of computers launched in 1964 at an estimated development cost of £50m. ICT sold its 1900 series computers at 10–15% below the equivalent IBM System 360 prices, but this depressed its return on capital in 1965 to 2%. The 1964 Labour Government soon saw the significance of the UK computer industry, and in 1965 offered ICT a £5m grant to further develop the 1900 series. The 1966 Industrial Reorganization Corporation

(IRC) selected the computer industry as a major target. In 1967 it started talks between English Electric, the main shareholder in English Electric Leo Marconi (EELM) and Elliott Automation. A merger was agreed and the IRC provided £15m cash. Later that year the Ministry of Technology initiated merger talks between English Electric Computers and ICT. In spite of the incompatibility of their products, negotiations continued until March 1968 when their merger was announced.

The government agreed to provide grants totalling £13½m over four years for research and development, and to purchase through the IRC £3½m of equity in the new company, International Computers Ltd (ICL). ICL was then the largest European computer company and ranked fifth in the world. In 1969 it held just under half of the UK computer market, with sales of £115m. The UK was maintaining its position as the only European country where IBM was denied more than 50% of the market.

Plessey, a major UK electronic components company, acquired its share for £18 million at the outset. Shortly after EELM and ICT merged, English Electric was acquired by GEC.

ICL AND THE COMPUTER MARKET

The public sector represented about 30% of the total UK market of which ICL held the major share in 1973 (approximately 60%) followed by IBM (approximately 30%).

ICL gradually concentrated on specific industry/market sectors such as central and local government, finance, retailing and distribution and manufacturing. This approach led to the recruitment of industry specialists and to the improved training of its salesmen in techniques and market requirements. ICL's stated objective over the five years 1973–8 was to double sales, to improve profitability and to increase exports up to 50% of turnover. (See Appendix 1.) Within its chosen market sectors, it aimed to win sales where mass data storage and remote access were vital and where the scope for communications development was considerable.

ICL's market shares in France and Germany were 3% and 1% respectively compared with IBM's 60%+ in both countries. In fact IBM's position within the European Economic Community had become so dominant that the EEC Commission decided to undertake a formal investigation in 1974. In traditional Commonwealth markets ICL was stronger. It also had a strong position in Eastern Europe where its share of imports into Comecon was 35–40% compared with IBM's 25%.

ICL had virtually no North American sales. Protective tariffs (typically 9%) discouraged imports generally, and the US Government Defence Agencies applied discriminatory preference factors loaded up to 50% against imported computers. The private sector was also firmly encouraged to buy American. Moreover, the indigenous competition was aggressive.

In Western Europe US companies were generally dominant. Using sales and installed capacity as measures of market share they had in 1972 nearly 85% of the French market and 78% of the West German market.

The US companies also encouraged computer exports from their European subsidiaries. Paradoxically, the French industry, which was the weakest in terms of indigeneous producers, had a good export position with a positive balance of trade of nearly £13m in 1970.

In the UK, ICL had an equal share of the market with IBM – 35%, whilst half of its sales were exports (25% of sales in continental Europe). In total, ICL's 3% share of the world market for large computers put the company into eighth place in the international sales league.

A feature of the computer industry was the importance of the 'customer base'. This arose because of the high cost of switching computer suppliers (associated mainly with software development), and the result that users become virtually 'locked in' to their computer supplier. (See Appendix 3 for an explanation of this problem). Replacement and expansion of installations accounted for nearly 80% of the market, and thus 'locking-in' was a significant market advantage.

PROBLEMS OF THE INITIAL ORGANIZATOIN

ICL's formation in 1968 inevitably created stresses and conflicts within the organization, particularly within engineering and technical groups where old allegiances were sustained. The widely differing systems that ICL became responsible for maintaining in the field stretched its facilities considerably. Besides the 1900 and System 4 series, ICL was committed to maintain fifteen other systems. It soon became a vulnerability, as existing users felt little obligation to renew obsolescent equipment with ICL computers.

Profitability suffered in 1971 and 1972, and there were rumours that Plessey and GEC would sell out. Burroughs announced that it was prepared to take over ICL, and for a while it seemed that the government (still wedded to a policy of 'no lame ducks') would agree. Before this happened, Mr Tom Hudson, a Plessey board member and the man who had built up IBM's UK operation, was appointed ICL chairman. He appointed Mr Cross from Univac as managing director in May 1972. Previously ICL was run by an executive board responsible to the main International Computers (Holdings) Board. Now the executive board was confined to statutory duties while the management of ICL was delegated to a three-man executive committee of the holding board, consisting of Mr Hudson, Mr Cross and Mr Humphries, the vice-chairman. The manufacturing and marketing divisions were completely reorganized, thereby integrating ICL's activities. ICL adopted a new marketing oriented posture in line with Mr Cross's board approach to the computer business. The quality of middle management was also strengthened by improving functional responsibility, by improving financial controls and by hiring able personnel, particularly from Univac.

During the period 1972 to 1979 ICL achieved growth rates well above the norm even for such a fast-expanding industry as computers and associated equipment. From a lowly £3m profit before tax on sales of £154m in 1972, the succeeding years to 1979 saw an average yearly sales growth of almost 25% and a corresponding growth in profits of 28%. This was even more remarkable considering that other sectors of the economy had been hit by recessions during this period.

By the end of 1979, however, ICL's competitive position in the world markets suffered a severe erosion due to the high level of UK inflation, and the strength of sterling. Combined with a significant increase in the group's fixed-cost base, the company were ill-prepared to react swiftly to the sudden halt in growth caused by the UK recession. The support of the British Government had, however, provided some breathing space for the radical new measures taken to put the company back on its feet.

ICL's PRODUCT RANGE

The 1900 series was ICL's most profitable system and over 1,500 had been installed world wide. It generated about 75% of the ICL's sales in 1973, with prices from £90,000 upwards. The 1900 series was the most popular computer of its type in Europe after IBM's 360 series and 1400 series. It compared well with IBM's 370 series, but existing 360 users who wished to upgrade to the 370 specification could not do so with ICL equipment. IBM, by contrast, developed certain parts of their 370 range to emulate the 1900 series, but the incompatibility of their respective data files was still a major problem. ICL deliberately protected the 1900 series from the IBM attack by a competitive price/performance policy intended to be 10–15% ahead of IBM and by strategies designed to lock in customers to ICL products.

The System 4 series had not been promoted since the 1968 merger. Market development was restricted to existing users who required an upgrade, to new customers attracted by the System 4's real time communications capability, and to Comecon customers attracted by its compatibility with Russian RIAD computers. System 4 compared well with IBM's System 360 and had compatible architecture, but little operating system compatibility.

1973

The 2903 series was introduced in April 1973 and in its first 15 months it won over 500 orders. It was compatible with the 1900 series, though ICL was keen to avoid 1900 users moving down to the smaller systems. Rather it was aiming at the first-time commercial users in the £1m turnover range. The 2903 was technically advanced, with a major selling and operating advantage in that it required no air conditioning. A typical 2903 installation was priced at £40,000. It competed with IBM's System 3, though IBM were expected to introduce a competitive new system within 18 months.

1974

The larger 2900 series computers were aimed at the market covered by the IBM 370 series, but offered a better price/performance. The conversion from 1900 series and 370 series to the 2900 series was designed to be straightforward.

By the end of 1974, ICL's range was:

Small Systems	2903
Medium Systems	1900 series
	System 4 series
Large Systems	2970 (P3)
	2980 (P4)

Its range covered most of the mainframe market. ICL also marketed a wide range of peripheral equipment, but it tended increasingly to purchase peripherals from specialist producers, rather than making them itself.

1976–1981

Developments within the product range continued with larger machines (2976) and smaller (2903/20), thus lengthening the product range. During 1976 the next major shift occurred with the takeover of Singer Business Machines, bringing with it System Ten (smaller than any existing ICL computer), the 1500 series of terminals and the Point of Sale terminal. This takeover also took ICL into markets in which it had not previously been involved (e.g. Italy, Spain, Norway and Finland), and also added 2,500 customers to ICL's customer base of 5,000. And in the following years there were continual modifications and developments around the wide product range offered (e.g. 1978 saw the introduction of the 9500 Retail Business Systems and the 9600 Factory Terminals). 1978 to 1980 brought major new product developments with the addition to the range of the 7700 Information Processor, 'Distributed Array Processor' (DAP) which gave ten times more power for 20 to 50% cost increase, and ME29 (successor to the 2903): a new range of systems offering more facilities, greater terminal connectivity and processing power. ME29 gained 100 orders within a month of its introduction. The cost of the ME29 (according to the number of workstations it supported) ranged from £35,000 to £250,000.

Thus by 1980 ICL was operating across the broad scale of the mainframe computer business in competition with IBM. The only area in which these two were not involved at the time was the home/personal computers market dominated by Commodore (PET), Apple and Tandy.

COMPETITION

IBM was the main competitor for most data-processing systems based on medium and large-sized computers. The company operated on a world-wide basis backed by a comprehensive range of models, extensive software support and aggressive marketing. After IBM, Sperry-Univac was ICL's major competitor in the UK middle market, which included Honeywell, Burroughs and NCR. The latter three companies also operated at the smaller end of the market along with Philips, the Dutch-based organization. The US-based Digital Equipment Corporation (DEC) had established itself in the UK market with its versatile PDP range of mini-computers, originally in process control and scientific applications, and more recently in the data processing field.

Historically, ICL's main competition both in the UK and world-wide was clearly identifiable. With the changing nature of the market, however, competition in the small computer sector had become much more fragmented and more difficult to identify. With the advances in technology and the increased entry of 'new' suppliers, cross competition occurred across a spectrum of data-processing applications, both large and small. These 'new' suppliers consisted of first-time entrants and existing companies capitalizing on the rapidly developing area of business communications and information processing. At least 30 different manufacturers were supplying a variety of mini-computers and small business systems to the UK market in 1981.

PERSONAL COMPUTER MARKET

In August 1981 IBM announced its new personal computer. The machine was said to have an edge over its competitors, not because of any complex electronics but because it put together for the first time a series of advanced and tested concepts into one machine. The strategy had backfired on IBM, however, because they completely underestimated the demand the low prices would create and they found themselves unable to meet the orders. Even worse for IBM were the repercussions this had on its leasing business with older machines, and the net result was IBM's first drop in profits since 1951. However, the lessons of the pricing error seemed to have been absorbed, and though the new personal computers were competitively priced there was no attempt to undercut the competition drastically. The IBM view seemed to be that with its resources it could be assured of capturing a large share of the business and the market itself was going to be so large that there would be room for all. The pressures in this market would show over the longer period as machines became more sophisticated and cheaper, whilst development costs continued to rise and would affect the weaker companies.

The strategic implications of the IBM move were very significant. The personal computer market was expected to grow to annual sales of 4m units by 1985 with a value of £2,200m. IBM did not reveal its proposed ouput level, but market expectations were a capacity in the first year of 100,000 units and rapid growth thereafter. This meant IBM was moving towards being a low price/high volume consumer electronics firm – a somewhat different business from the one in which it had traditionally excelled.

During 1981 IBM was expanding at the other extreme and involving itself in the data transmission market: global communications, in which computers and people anywhere in the world are linked together by satellite and 'talk' to each other. As a market for the following decade, personal computers would provide enormous potential but the development costs would be exceptionally high.

PROBLEMS LEADING TO THE REORGANIZATION OF ICL

In November 1980, despite a 10% rise in mid-year profits to £20.5 million, the company warned that rising costs, along with a fall in demand, would have a 'significant and adverse' effect on 1979/80's full results. Like the rest of British industry, ICL was battling against recession, inflation and high interest rates in the home market, while the strength of sterling was taking its toll overseas. Despite a sales increase to £715 million, ICL revealed a 1979/80 plunge in pretax profits of over 40% to £25 million, and cash balances of £16 million replaced by an overdraft of over £10 million. On the announcement of the news, the shares fell to 79 pence, having reached a peak of 196 pence in September 1980.

It had seemed that the government, after being involved in the formation of ICL in 1968, had finally allowed the company complete independence when the National Enterprise Board had sold its 25% shareholding in ICL in 1980 for £38 million, making a profit of £25 million.

At the end of 1980 when ICL ran into difficulties, the government was faced with a delicate situation. Having participated in the creation of ICL as a 'national champion', and subsequently returned the company to private enterprise, the possibility of its collapse was both embarrassing and could have posed strategic problems. ICL was the provider and service maintainer of most large UK government computers.

The options which seemed to be available were:

1 Allow the company to solve its own problems. This might have ended in liquidation or takeover by another company or perhaps survival on its own. Clearly there were political and strategic risks attached to these possible outcomes.
2 Arrange for an 'orderly' takeover by an approved British company or approved computer company.
3 Enable the company to be refinanced with loans and/or guarantees, and ensure that the management (if necessary a new team) solve its problems.

Eventually the government settled on option 3, but there was little doubt that attempts were made on variations of option 2 during the year. Even after the government guaranteed the £200 million loans for ICL, there was pressure to arrange a takeover. Within days of the announcement of the 1979/80 collapse, the Department of Industry had approached BP and Shell to see if they would be prepared to take a stake in the clearly ailing ICL. They, and GEC in turn, politely declined to mount a rescue. With net debt heading for £250 million, pressure mounted from ICL's bankers for a detailed recovery strategy.

In early May 1981 Sperry-Univac of USA was preparing a bid. Sperry hoped that it would be able to take over ICL's enviable list of customers in a world market stretching from Australia to South Africa and from Germany to Hong Kong. It also hoped that it would be able to take over ICL's 35% share of the UK computer market – much of it in profitable government contracts.

Sperry expected to pay ICL shareholders only a small return for the takeover, offering only pence above the current market price – and to have the right to close down major ICL factories, lay off more than half of the ICL workforce, and virtually to end primary computer research and production in Britain. The harsh terms of the bid shocked senior ICL managers, but it won the support of the Treasury and was given a tacit go-ahead by industry secretary, Sir Keith Joseph. Sperry was not, perhaps, the perfect choice, but it was the best under the circumstances.

Sperry and ICL had problems common to all competitors of IBM in attempting to stay in the same broad market as the American multinational whose R & D budget was about equal to the whole of ICL's sales turnover. ICL had attempted to compete with IBM across the wide span of the computer market, whereas Sperry had adopted the approach of specializing in certain market segments. Sperry was recognzied to be an efficient organization and its chairman had been influential in developing Sperry's specialized approach and tight financial control. In 1971 Sperry had taken over the customer base of RCA for a very small cash outlay and succeeded in persuading nearly 90% of the customers to stay with Sperry.

A good deal of pressure was brought to allow ICL to be saved from takeover, and part of the plan was to allow a new management team the opportunity of nursing ICL back to health. Supporters of the plan prepared a thick file of reasons in its favour, ranging from the protection of jobs to the protection of the government's computerized PAYE system, from the reputation of Britain in overseas markets to questions of national security. Proponents of the 'sell it off at any price' policy argued that this was one last chance for the government to show that it still believed in the free power of market forces.

The decision was taken finally by the Prime Minister after consultation with a ministerial committee on ICL made up of Sir Keith Joseph and Kenneth Baker from the Department of Industry, Nigel Lawson from the Treasury, and Barney Hayhoe, the Civil Service minister whose responsibility was to present the interests of ICL's government customers. The arguments were complex and finely balanced. And in the end the government decided on an independent ICL but with a new management team.

What was the right strategy for ICL, and the British computer industry? There were industrial, financial and political implications in the decision to be made between the Sperry bid and its alternative. The most politically sensitive aspect of ICL's position was the government's reliance on the company for its own computers. Sir Keith Joseph made this clear when he voiced his support to the House of Commons on the new loan guarantees to the company. He pointed to the fact that ICL computers, to a value of more than £300m, supported vital operations in some 20 departments, including defence, revenue assessment and collection, agriculture, health and social security.

Government ministers recognized that new management would be very likely to seek further government financial support. The risk remained that ICL would need more than the guarantee for loans of £200m already provided. There was also no certainty that ICL would be able to repay or reduce its loans by the time the guarantees ran out in 1983. (See Appendix 3 for financial information.)

NEW MANAGEMENT

Rob Wilmot (aged 36 years and an electronics engineer) was recruited from Texas Instruments, the world's biggest independent manufacturer of micro-electronic components, whose UK subsidiary he had been running since 1978.

For the second time in less than ten years, ICL turned for leadership to a young British executive who had gained his experience working for a large American electronics company. The government hoped that he would be able to repeat the successful recovery in the company's fortunes engineered in the mid-1970s by Mr Geoffrey Cross. Mr Cross was recruited from Sperry-Univac of the US to become ICL's managing director during its financial trouble in 1972. He is remembered for installing effective management controls and completing the development of ICL's 2900 series of bigger computers. One of the major challenges that faced Mr Wilmot was to chart a new product strategy, enabling ICL to diversify away from its heavy dependence on mainframe machines. Mr Cross left ICL in 1977 for personal/family reasons after having seen sales and profits rise from £154 million and £3.3 million to £419 million and £30 million whilst he was managing director (1972–7).

ORGANIZATION AND STRATEGY

The new chairman stated in the company's Interim Statement in June 1981 that

> it remains part of our strategy over time to pursue collaborative ventures aimed at improving our product range in the future, and we shall be looking particularly for associations which provide synergy to our own product range and markets. It must again emphasise that any associations which ICL may seek must fulfil the criteria of safeguarding customer investment, both current and future, in ICL products . . . the primary task of the Board and Management . . . is to restore profitability. In regaining profitability, we will exploit even more strongly our excellent product range.

Rob Wilmot's emphasis was on the need for faster reactions at ICL, and he stressed that the company had to shorten dramatically the time needed for products to be developed and brought to the market. The twin elements of the strategy would be to rationalize the existing product range so that upgrades between products could be made in the field, and to introduce an element of 'managed risk' to allow faster development from the latest technology. His clear emphasis on developing products with inherent reliability was a contrast to his encouragement of more risk in product development. With an urgent need to save money, but a similar need to maintain R & D, Wilmot directed development teams to use the latest technology, and to allow for an element of risk in bringing it into new products. He consequently split up ICL's Product Development Group (PDG) into manageable sections. Mr Wilmot argued that the 5,000 redundancies were necessary because with a payroll of 30,000 the company needed a growth rate of 25% in real terms to keep paying them.

The primary task became one of restoring the company to profitability and the new catch-phrase within the company became 'profits before growth'. Previously the company had enjoyed years of expansion, with growth often over 20% p.a., and in the expansionist period of 1972–7 this growth had been supported by a period of sterling depreciation. From

1977 to 1981 the company had striven to maintain its growth objectives, but this period had been one of sterling appreciation and this laid a heavy burden on the company.

ORGANIZATION

From 1981 onwards the long-range organizational goal was to introduce product-line accountability in order to ensure that the selling and manufacturing operations responded promptly to market and company needs. This involved

1 the establishment of a new product marketing division to increase emphasis on the formulation and implementation of marketing strategies;
2 the creation of a strong team to develop standard applications software to increase sales of ICL products to new customers;
3 the consolidation of product supply and inventory control functions within the manufacturing operation to provide a focal point for the reduction of worldwide inventory levels;
4 the creation of separate development divisions for distributed systems, for mainframe computers and also for networking strategy.

PRODUCT AND MARKETING STRATEGY

ICL's 1981 strategy was based on the concept of 'information technology' dependent on distributed computing and the convergence of telecommunications with information processing systems. These needs highlighted the concept of a Networked Product Line in which the products ICL offered would be increasingly capable of communicating both with each other and with equipment from other suppliers. The complexity of networking had prevented many organizations from enjoying the full benefits of the equipment at their disposal. The 1981 strategy of ICL was to solve this problem by offering a linked product line.

1 *Product Developments*

(a) June 1981: System 25 was launched (based on System 10 from Singer which had 9000 installations worldwide). System 25 was a small system capable of handling 20 jobs simultaneously and supporting up to 200 terminals. It could be linked to a mainframe computer (including non-ICL mainframes).
(b) October 1981: Series 20 was announced; this was ICL's new Distributed Resource System (DRS 20). The DRS 20 was a

range of multi-micro-based work stations for use in local area networks (LANS) and aimed at the growing market for office systems and distributed processing.

(c) November 1981: Major additions were announced to the 2900 series based on the same central processor technology as the successful 2966. Over 200 orders were taken for the 2966 between its first delivery in June 1981 and November 1981. (See Appendix 4 for information on product compatibility and comparability.)

2 *Marketing and Distribution Developments*

(a) 'Trader Point' was a new ICL-based organization established to help penetrate the market for products at the smaller end (e.g. System 25, DRS 20 and PERQ work stations). 'Trader Point' brought together up to eighty dealers in computers, software etc, and ICL supported them with publicity and in other ways. Such a move to using dealers as part of the marketing effort was unusual in the computer industry.

(b) Introduction to forty 'Computer Point' centres around the world to provide local demonstration and direct sales.

3 *Collaborative Ventures*

Of all the developments undertaken by ICL's new management, the joint ventures with Japanese and American manufacturers created most interest.

(a) Fijitsu: In October 1981 ICL announced that agreement had been reached with Fujitsu of Japan. Early access to Fujitsu mainframe advanced-chip technology would enable ICL to develop highly competitive mainframe products without massive investments in in-house specialist chip technology, allowing ICL development efforts to be focussed on creating ICL's Networked Product Line whilst providing an assured growth path for existing 2900 customers.

(b) In September 1981 ICL announced a collaborative agreement with the Three Rivers Computer Corporation of USA which enabled ICL to market the PERQ scientific graphics work-stations outside USA and Japan. Production would be in the UK with expected sales of around 1000 p.a. The PERQ provided the scientific and engineering user with an easy-to-use computer capable of linking into local area networks (LANS).

(c) In October 1981 ICL announced that they would market under the ICL label (DNX 2000) the new MITEL all-digital private telephone exchange (PABX) based on CMOS VLSI technology. The Mitel-ICL venture represented a further step on ICL's Networked Product Line concept and brought together into one product line the two competing approaches for office automation, that is, the PABX-based network and the computer-based IOM bit local area network (LAN).

(d) In March 1982 ICL announced they had concluded an agreement with the National Enterprise Board (NEB) transferring the assets relating to the NEXOS 2000 word processor to ICL (at book value). ICL would produce a variant of the NEXOS 2000 and market it alongside its own ICL 7700 Information Processing which provided both word and data processing. (Nexos came about as part of the NEB's electronics industry strategy in 1979 as the marketing arm for the electronic office of the future.)

NETWORKING STRATEGY

Rob Wilmot indicated that the focus for ICL would drive product activity in the direction of a Networked Product Line. ICL's traditional mainframes could already participate in advanced wide-area networks (WANS) and all future ICL products would fit into the network strategy. Also ICL could support local area networks (LANS) which can interconnect equipment on the same site. (see figure 7.1).

Thus, with the growth in office technology, hardware compatibility and inter-connectability across a range of devices represents a distinct competitive advantage, not only because of the expansion and udpate of facilities, but also due to the cost of ownership in terms of equipment and maintenance and support.

Networking encompasses the integration of whole product ranges based upon advanced systems architecture developments. IBM first launched its Systems Network Architecture (SNA) in 1974 and this was followed by ICL's Information Processing Architecture (IPA) introduced in 1980. In the words of Gordon Peake, business manager of IPA:

> We wanted this architecture to encompass developments which we don't even know of, including office-of-the-future technology. . . . By 1985 half ICL's total sales will be dependent on IPA.[1]

Part of ICL's strategy was to aim at the large IBM market, with the ability to 'talk' to IBM mainframes, to supply plug-compatible processors and to encircle an IBM site with ICL peripherals.

IPA already operated between ICL's UK head offices and its operations in South Africa and Australia. This was providing a relatively cheap form of data transfer and, with expansion to other parts of the international operation, unit data transfer costs would decrease signifi-

[1] *Computing*, 4 January 1982.

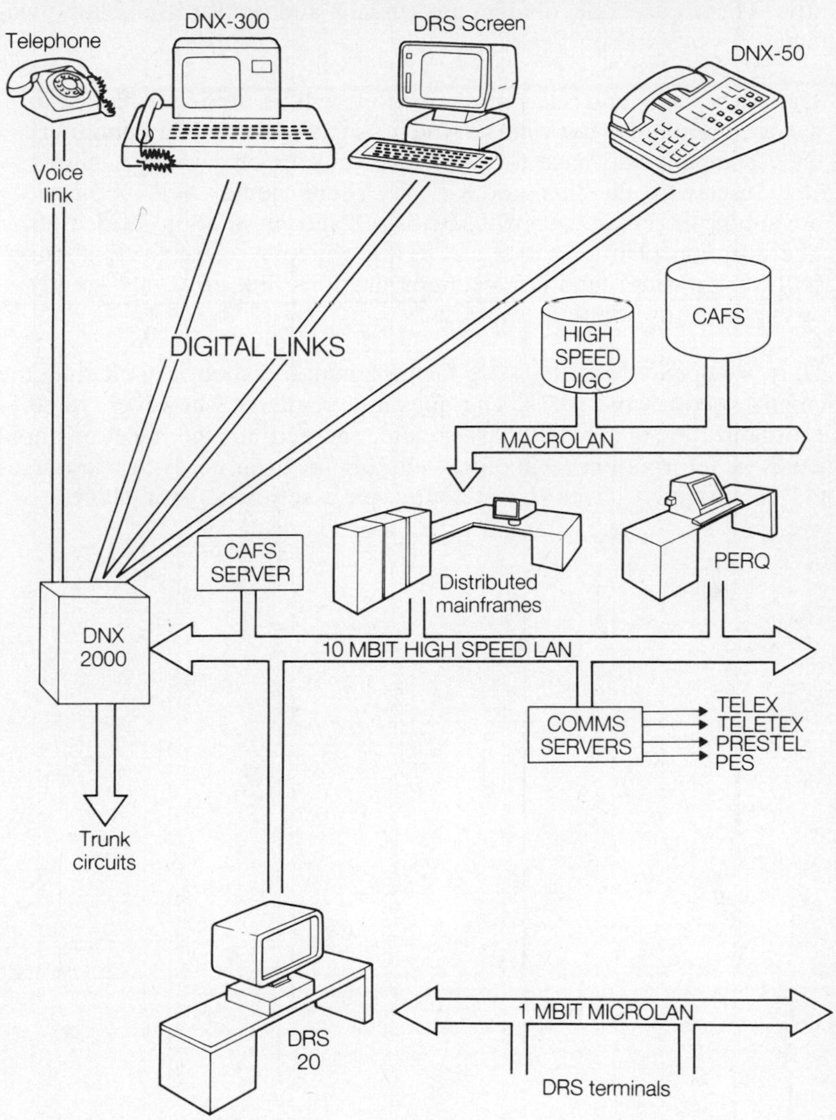

FIGURE 7.1 ICL DNX-2000 Distributed network exchange

cantly. The future role of data processing and transmission links was summed up by Gordon Peake,

> Data processing and telecommunications will be ultimately linked in a new discipline – telematics. And to succeed in selling computers each company will have to allow free transfer of data. IPA allows ICL users to do that today. . . . There could well be great advantage in linking up with British Telecom (BT) in 1983 after liberalisation of its services. . . . BT is thinking aggressively about its future position and a telecommunications link up would greatly strengthen our ability to sell IPA.[2]

Thus, it appeared that ICL was facing a major challenge in meeting the changing needs of the 1980s. The questions remained, however, whether the organization's new strategy would succeed in the face of rapid changes in information technology and whether the necessary resources could be sustained, given the pressures for a return to profitability.

[2] *Ibid.*

Appendix 1

EVIDENCE GIVEN TO THE SELECT COMMITTEE ON SCIENCE AND TECHNOLOGY OF THE HOUSE OF COMMONS – JANUARY 1983[1]

In a memorandum to the committee, ICL stated:

> It is the objective of ICL Group to double its turnover during the next five years, with half its business coming from outside of the UK. . . . The ICL Group is a total systems company that aims to meet all the data processing needs of its customers.
>
> It is now useful to restate a number of key determinants of ICL's marketing and product strategies.
>
> (i) the need to conserve the investment made by individual users of ICL systems
> (ii) the ability at the same time to offer continued freedom to upgrade, develop and extend their application
> (iii) the need to offer the economies made possible by improvements in technology
> (iv) the determination to provide in all respects a service of the highest standard
> (v) the ability to make choices in system design which allow continuous adaptation to the developing use of computers.
>
> It is frequently argued that in order to succeed in competition with IBM it is necessary to adopt a policy of new identity with current IBM systems (although the looser term "compatibility" is generally used). ICL considers that such a policy violates several of the criteria listed above. In particular, it involves such complete loss of free choice that (v) is totally unsatisfied.
>
> This is further supported by other arguments concerned with commercial viability of such a policy and the practical impossibility of following it with any success for more than a very limited time and at some distance behind IBM. "IBM compatibility" virtually precludes the offering of any significant price/performance advantage over IBM. Our policy is, therefore, to maintain such a degree of compatibility with IBM products as will permit reasonable ease of communication with or conversion from IBM systems while preserving the desired freedom of design choice necessary if we are to continue to compete successfully with IBM on the direct merits of our systems and support abilities.

[1] HMSO *Second Report on the UK Computer Industry* (First Part), 1983.

Appendix 2

RESULTS FOR THE YEAR TO 31 MARCH 1981 (£m)

	1981	*1980*
Turnover	711.1	715.8
Trading (loss)/profit	(18.7)	51.4
Interest	31.1	26.3
(Loss)/profit before taxation	(49.8)	25.1
Taxation	5.4	7.4
(Loss)/profit after taxation	(55.2)	17.7
Minority interests	0.2	–
(Loss)/profit before extraordinary item	(55.0)	17.7
Extraordinary item[a]	78.1	7.7
(Loss)/profit attributable to shareholders	(133.1)	10.0
Dividends	–	4.0
Net (loss)/profit	(133.1)	6.0
(Loss)/earnings per 25p share before extraordinary item	(41.22p)	13.26p

[a] Redundancy and rationalisation programme costs.
Source: Company Reports.

BALANCE SHEET AT 30 SEPTEMBER 1981 (£m)

	1981	*1980*
Employment of capital		
Equipment on rental to customers	63.6	56.5
Other fixed assets	63.1	72.3
Total fixed assets	126.7	128.8
Investments	21.4	17.3
Deferred assets	19.7	16.0
	167.8	162.1
Current assets		
Inventory	139.6	183.2
Less progress payments	7.6	10.5
	132.0	172.7
Receivables	170.5	155.5
Bank and cash balances	36.9	34.4
	339.4	362.6
Current liabilities		
Payables	132.1	132.7
Provisions	47.2	1.3
Taxation	5.2	4.5
Bank overdrafts and short-term loans	97.4	44.9
Credits for exports	11.6	23.4
Dividends	–	2.7
	293.5	209.5
Net current assets	45.9	153.1
	213.7	315.2
Capital invested		
Share capital	83.4	33.4
Reserves	(11.8)	108.0
Shareholders' funds	71.6	141.4
Minority interests in subsidiaries	1.5	2.1
Medium- and long-term loans	92.3	116.8
Deferred liabilities	48.3	54.9
	213.7	315.2

ICL

	1980 (£m)	*1979 (£m)*	*1978 (£m)*	*1977 (£m)*	*1976 (£m)*	*1975 (£m)*	*1974 (£m)*	*1973 (£m)*	*1972 (£m)*
Turnover	715.8	624.1	509.4	418.7	288.3	239.8	200.5	168.6	154.3
Trading profit	51.4	63.7	49.4	37.0	28.6	21.3	17.4	14.1	7.2
Profit before taxation	25.1	46.5	37.5	30.3	23.1	16.2	13.4	10.9	3.3
Taxation	7.4	11.2	10.7	11.7	8.3	9.0	6.4	4.9	2.3
Profit after taxation	17.7	35.3	26.8	18.6	14.8	9.4	7.0	6.0	1.0
Minority interests	–	0.2	0.3	0.5	0.3	0.2	0.2	0.3	–
Dividends	4.0	4.0	2.8	2.5	1.7	0.2	0.2	0.2	–
Net profit retained	6.0	31.1	23.7	15.6	12.8	9.0	6.6	6.3	1.0
Employment of capital									
Fixed assets	128.8	142.6	120.7	101.8	72.3	65.3	55.1	54.2	50.4
Investments	17.3	15.6	15.0	14.7	17.8	8.4	7.8	7.8	7.9
Deferred assets	16.0	14.4	17.5	18.9	17.3	11.1	6.9	6.0	4.4
Net current assets	153.1	140.3	132.0	111.6	101.2	88.1	75.0	68.0	60.9
	315.2	312.9	285.2	247.0	208.6	172.9	144.8	136.0	123.6
Capital invested									
Shareholders' funds	141.4	146.8	124.6	103.7	89.7	75.9	64.6	59.3	50.4
Minority interests in subsidiaries	2.1	2.2	2.1	2.1	1.8	1.9	1.7	1.7	1.4
Medium- and long-term loans	116.8	99.0	87.9	77.4	80.6	63.2	55.4	57.9	56.7
Deferred liabilities	54.9	64.9	70.6	63.8	36.5	31.9	23.1	17.1	15.1
	315.2	312.9	285.2	247.0	208.6	172.9	144.8	136.0	123.6

Number of employees at end of year	33,087	34,401	33,978	32,156	27,317	28,069	29,178	28,798	27,701
Ratios									
Earnings per 25p share	3.26p	26.30p	19.86p	13.56p	10.90p	6.05p	5.09p	4.92p	0.83p
Dividends per 25p share – net	2.98p	2.98p	2.07p	1.86p	1.30p	0.16p	0.17p	0.18p	–
Net assets per 25p share	1.06p	£1.10	£0.93	£0.78	£0.67	£0.57	£0.48	£0.44	£0.38
Turnover per employee	£21,600	£18,100	£15,000	£13,000	£10,600	£8,500	£6,900	£5,900	£5,600
	%	%	%	%	%	%	%	%	%
Profit before taxation as a	3.5	7.4	7.4	7.2	8.0	6.8	6.7	6.5	2.1
percentage turnover				15.0	13.7	12.3	12.0	10.4	5.8
Trading profit as a percentage of capital invested at end of year	16.3	20.4	17.3	29.2	25.8	21.3	20.7	20.9	6.5
Profit before taxation as a	17.8	31.7	30.1	N/A	N/A	N/A	N/A	N/A	N/A
percentage of shareholders'				N/A	N/A	N/A	N/A	N/A	N/A
funds at end of year				N/A	N/A	N/A	N/A	N/A	N/A

Appendix 3

PRODUCT COMPATIBILITY AND COMPARABILITY

A constant feature of the industry has been the dominance of IBM, and an understanding of this can be gained from the reaction of other manufacturers to IBM's introduction of their Series 360 and 370. These IBM computers which were first introduced in 1964 resulted in a situation whereby two out of every three computer installations were IBM products by 1970 and IBM outsold its nearest five competitors put together. Although much of IBM's success had always depended on its marketing strength and user support, when IBM introduced its Series 360 the technology was so far in advance of all others since then that the 360/370 range essentially defined the terms by which all IBM's competitors must compete.

The response of most manufacturers was to develop new products based on direct compatibility with the 360/370 designs. A major feature of the 360 Series was that it was a true range of computers which were software-compatible with each other. This meant that a program written for one machine in the series could be used on any of the others. Specifically the whole range was 'upwards-compatible' which means that a user could move up to a larger machine and still use the original software program. Also the range was 'forwards-compatible' which meant that users could be confident that when models were introduced they could change to them and continue using their original software.

This feature of software compatibility proved to be crucial in enabling a rapid expansion of computer sales in the UK (e.g. there were 220 computers in use in 1960 and this had grown to 6500 by 1970). This 'generation' of computer models formed a considerable advance on the machines of the 1950s with which they were software-incompatible. When software was simple and the cost of its production minute compared to the cost of the hardware this had not been important, but subsequently software became more complex (and hence expensive) and at the same time integrated circuit developments reduced the cost and increased the power of the hardware. This became the basis of a 'customer base' as users became reluctant to switch manufacturers when changing their computer models because of the costs of rewriting their software.

As an example of the high costs of software conversion, it is estimated that to convert all the software regularly run on a typical mainframe installation from one system to another could take 25 man-years of programming effort. So for a computer manufacturer not able to offer 'forward-compatibility' it has a worse effect than just placing a burden on the user of the machine, for when the time comes to change their machine the users are no longer 'locked in' to that computer manufacturer.

ICL, during the period of IBM's introduction of the 360/370 Series, was producing two different series. The 1900, introduced in 1964, was itself highly developed architecture with similar 'upwards' and 'forwards' compatibility to the 360, and ICL had sold over 1000 installations by 1968. Also ICL at this time had the System 4 range (inherited from English Electric) which, although it had sold very few, was in fact software-compatible with IBM's 360. Sysem 4 was therefore a forerunner of the large number of 360-compatible ranges produced in the late 1960s by manufacturers who had become convinced that the advantages of the IBM architecture were such that it was essential to copy it.

ICL faced a dilemma in that it was extremely expensive to support two systems and therefore it had to choose between continuing the development of the 1900 Series or maintaining System 4 as a potentially lucrative entry in the rapidly growing IBM-compatible market. IBM introduced a price-cutting policy which caused severe difficulties to its copiers and led to some of them leaving the industry (e.g. RCA). ICL's response was to decide to replace both its ranges with a new series. This meant enormous development costs and continuous marketing expenses for two series (1900 and System 4) until the new series arrived. A further potential difficulty was that in attempting to move to a new 'generation' of machines ICL would create a problem of 'software compatibility'.

The new series became known as 2900 Series and its introduction in late 1974 coincided with developments in the industry of mini-computers and small business systems. In the UK the first of these new mini-computer systems was Computer Technology Ltd (CTL) formed by Ian Barron, and it was followed by others including Ferranti and GEC. ICL's entry into this small systems market came about as a result of its takeover of Singer Business Machines in the mid 1970s. The System 10 from Singer became successful and later accounted for almost a third of ICL's turnover. Although the 2900 Series's incompatibility with the 1900 inevitably lost ICL a number of important users to other computer manufacturers, the new series eventually established itself as a technological success.

PART II

Growth

8 Bejam

Retailing traditionally offered opportunities for entrepreneurs to develop a business and achieve rapid growth, and often millionaire status, in a relatively short period of time. The important characteristics of those who succeeded seemed to include the ability to recognize a market opportunity and to take advantage of it by creating a retail image or format which appealed to the market. Examples of successes were Habitat and Mothercare in the 1970s and Tesco in the 1960s. The key to success in retailing differed from that in manufacturing industry for not only were cost control and productivity important, but location played a crucial role as well as the image/format. For a retailer this image was equivalent to the notion of product/market scope for a manufacturer, i.e. what products to sell and to which customers. For Habitat it was plain and simple, well-designed furniture to sell to the emerging young middle classes, whilst for Tesco it had been low-price/good-value groceries aimed at a poorer section of the population.

BACKGROUND

In 1968 John Apthorp founded Bejam as a retailer of bulk packs of frozen foods sold alongside freezers, and within ten years recorded sales turnover of nearly £100 million. (See Appendix 1.) Like many other retailers he had researched the American market but he felt that unlike America, the smaller size of British supermarkets would not enable bulk sales of frozen foods at that time. He was convinced, however, that frozen food sales would grow and that a speciality retailer would appeal to the public. He rejected the contemporary method of selling frozen foods by refrigerated vehicles for home delivery. He opened his first outlet in Edgware, London in 1968 with a limited product range of about 100 items, mostly staple products such as peas and fish fingers. The major frozen food manufacturers were reluctant to supply Bejam in the belief that such freezer centres were a short-term phenomenon and that it would damage the relationships they were then building with the emergent supermarket chains. This meant that Bejam had to make special arrangements with small manufacturers to produce bulk packs. The first freezer centre was successful and John Apthorp opened four more in the first year and a further ten in the second year. The success continued and by 1974 Bejam was a chain of 100 freezer centres and by 1982 had reached nearly 200.

Bejam's growth was closely related to the changes in society with more working housewives, more widespread ownership of cars and, especially, increasing ownership of freezers. In 1968 the annual sale of freezers in the UK was 50,000 and by 1973 over one million homes had a freezer, and with annual sales reaching 500,000 in 1980, over half of the homes then had a freezer. (See Appendix 2.)

Competition soon followed not only from (among others) the Co-operative Society and Cordon Bleu with chains of specialist freezer centres, but also from supermarket chains which, as their stores grew in size, were able to expand their product ranges to include bulk packs of frozen foods. (See Appendix 3 on frozen food sales.)

FINANCING GROWTH

The pace of growth which Bejam accomplished was difficult to finance from internal resources and, in order to assist, Bejam sold 20% of its equity to a bank in 1971, and in 1973 undertook a public flotation of its shares. In preparation for this flotation, Bejam recruited Laurence Don, a former finance director of Tesco, and he assisted in the clarification of the organizational structure and created a highly centralized multi-tiered hierarchy. Two joint managing directors undertook the day-to-day control of the chain, with each of them responsible for half of the outlets, and one in charge of buying and marketing and the other of property, distribution, finance and group services. John Apthorp became executive chairman and Abbie Goldblatt executive in charge of expansion.

The flotation was a great success with the shares being over-subscribed many times. Bejam then aimed to maintain tight central controls in order that it could maintain the flexibility of a small company facing the inevitable pressures of growth. Every week area managers (responsible for about ten of the freezer centres) were given breakdowns of costs as well as weekly sales figures.

COMPETITION AND PRICING

As Bejam grew to be the UK's biggest retailer of frozen foods the major manufacturers began to supply them, and Bejam also began to sell other non-frozen foodstuffs, although frozen foods represented 80% of all foods sold and they continued to sell freezers (160,000 in 1982). As they grew, their ability to negotiate prices with suppliers improved with the effect of an improvement in margins whilst being able to sell at prices at least as low as competitors (especially supermarkets which Bejam considered their biggest competitors). In 1980 Cordon Bleu was taken over by Argyll Foods which operated Presto Supermarkets, Liptons and Lo-Cost Discount Centres and with the further acquisition of 66 Freezer-Fare centres which it added to Cordon Bleu it formed a chain of 130 outlets. (See Appendix 4 for information on Cordon Bleu up to this point.)

Although Bejam considered the growth of supermarket chains and especially the development of the huge out-of-town superstores (see tables 8.1 and 8.2) as its main competition, it was not without advantages itself as it had huge cold-storage facilities which enabled cheaper buying, and its smaller product range enabled the production of a monthly price list for customers with consequent tight control at store level. Frequently supermarkets could not maintain this as, with many thousands of product items in stock, whilst pricing was theoretically established by head office, it was often practically decided by the supermarket manager. By 1983 Bejam was the equal market leader with Sainsbury in frozen foods, each having 11% share of the market, with the Co-operative Society and Tesco each on 10% and all other freezer centres combined with 12%. Bejam had achieved this position through bulk sales, for its retail-size pack share of the market was only 3%.

TABLE 8.1 Growth of superstores (over 25,000 sq ft) 1971–1982

Year	*Number*
1971	32
1972	44
1973	67
1974	81
1975	104
1976	124
1977	151
1978	186
1979	218
1980	241
1981	276
1982	318

Source: Mintel

TABLE 8.2 Principal operators (at 1982)

	Superstores (over 25,000 sq ft)	*Large supermarkets (10,000–25,000 sq ft)*
Allied Suppliers	11	75
Asda	65	14
FineFare	31	40
International	18	41
Key Markets	4	28
Linfood	8	10
Safeway	1	47
Sainsbury	10	171
Tesco	80	130
Waitrose	0	38
Co-operative Societies	43	N/A

Source: Mintel

INDUSTRY AND MARKET DEVELOPMENTS

The ten-year period between the Census of Distribution in 1971 and that in 1981 showed dramatic changes in UK food retailing. The number of grocery outlets fell by over 46%, and of these the largest share was in the multiple chain sector where a deliberate policy of closing small outlets in order to concentrate on opening large superstores led to a fall of over 50%. After allowing for inflation, real growth in sales by grocery outlets was about 1% per annum but the multiples had continued their growth at the expense of independents and co-operatives, with market share rising from 44% to 63%.

The demographic changes of the 1970s which affected retailing were:

1 growth of home ownership,
2 growth in car ownership,
3 increase in working wives,
4 increase in numbers of households with two incomes,
5 reduction in working week and increase in holiday time,
6 increase in numbers of unemployed,
7 increase in proportion of the population retired and also those at school.

As the food retailers moved towards larger out-of-town stores there was an increase in sales of non-food items (see table 8.3) which offered higher margins.

TABLE 8.3 Non-food sales in multiples/co-operatives in 1981

Product	*Proportion of outlets stocking* %	*Share of the market achieved* %
Household goods	27	46
Electrical goods	20	37
Gardening goods	14	35
Clothing/footwear	11	31
DIY products	9	29

Source: Trade estimates

However, the 1981 recession caused some retailers to reconsider their product ranges and a number began to withdraw from certain markets, e.g. Asda withdrew from the 'white-goods' market, i.e. refrigerators, freezers and cookers. Such reconsiderations led many retailers to turn to fresh foods and to own-label brands as areas of expansion.

A significant report to the industry was published in May 1981 when the Monopolies and Mergers Commission reported on 'Discounts to Retailers' which had investigated the allegation that the bigger discounts given to larger retailers by suppliers was unfair. In general the Commission did not find that the practice had an adverse effect on competition, and concluded that it was in the public interest as the benefits of bargaining power were frequently passed on to the public. However, the conclusions also commented that the practice could encourage a harmful level of concentration in the retail trade.

MAJOR FOOD RETAILERS

1 *Sainsbury* By 1981 Sainsbury was the leading food retailer with 260 stores (average size 21,000 square feet), 47,000 employees and profits of £65 million. (See table 8.4.) Sainsbury was noted for the efficiency it had brought to food retailing and particularly its stock ordering and stock replacement methods. Each product on Sainsbury shelves was coded by a label on the shelf front and the stock level read every day and sent to regional warehouses which then despatched the required number of items to bring stock levels up to pre-determined levels.

2 *Asda* Asda had concentrated from an early stage on superstores, having the advantage of entering the industry later than others in 1965. It was Leeds-based and started in the north, beginning its expansion in the south considerably later as it reported that each superstore needed ten-acre sites, eight of which were for car-parking, and a population of 100,000 to provide sufficient customers. Asda was

able to convert a higher proportion of each store's total area into sales area as opposed to warehousing or administration.

3 *Tesco* Tesco had for many years been the leading food retailer and, following a struggle for market share with Sainsbury in 1977, the company undertook a major re-organization, moving further into very large stores and closing smaller ones. Unlike its competitors, Tesco was generally represented all over the country, with a total sales area of 7.2 million square feet.

4 *Kwik Save* Kwik Save operated 300 stores of an average size 6,000 square feet over the north, Wales, and the midlands. It concentrated on a narrow product range of about 1,000 packaged branded products (compared with about 5,000 in the average supermarket) presented in a rather spartan atmosphere and, with no individual pricing of items, it saved on labour costs, which enabled Kwik Save to offer the lowest prices on these products in the industry.

TABLE 8.4 Major food retailers – 1981

Company	*Sales £m*	*Return on assets %*	*Gross profit margin %*	*Stock turnover*	*Debt/ Equity %*	*Current ratio*	*Acid test*	*Outlets*
Sainsbury	1531	20.6	3.8	12.8	5.1	0.8	0.1	260
Asda	1188[a]	28.5	4.3	15.1	–	0.9	0.5	79
Tesco	1820	14.7	2.7	12.1	25.6	0.7	0.04	554
Kwik Save	389	44.4	3.8	21.7	–	0.6	0.2	300

[a] Includes £128 million for furniture and carpet sales
Source: *Investor Chronicle*

With respect to growth, the Bejam executives considered the only two constraints to be locations for new outlets and management's ability to run a larger operation whilst maintaining flexibility. Over the years the average Bejam store had grown in size and by 1983 was 4,000 square feet. The stores were still located in the south-east and south midlands which were the areas where the ownership of freezers was at its highest.

Appendix 1 Bejam PLC

CONSOLIDATED PROFIT AND LOSS ACCOUNT, YEAR ENDING JUNE 30 (£000)

Year	*Turnover*	*Interest received*	*Profit before tax*	*Profit after tax*
1973	16,930	9	1,010	574
1974	24,589	31	1,215	584
1975	35,723	64	1,608	757
1976	52,811	77	2,641	1,198
1977	79,185	314	4,802	4,248
1978	90,975	340	4,418	3,986
1979	123,324	646	6,044	4,589
1980	164,072	965	8,273	7,503
1981	199,736	694	9,021	4,692

CONSOLIDATED BALANCE SHEETS (£000)

	1979	*1980*	*1981*
Current assets			
Stocks	12,117	20,986	22,586
Debtors	4,552	2,825	5,167
Cash	3,978	4,577	7,128
	20,647	28,388	34,881
Current liabilities			
Creditors	14,955	24,790	28,954
Overdraft	1,523	389	241
Corporation Tax	560	527	1,430
Advanced Corporation Tax	531	698	854
Dividend	759	905	1,087
Bills of exchange	1,500	–	–
Profit-sharing scheme	–	–	–
	19,828	27,309	32,860
Net current assets	819	1,079	2,021
Fixed assets	19,151	23,394	26,503
Capital work-in-progress	–	2,115	1,661
Associated companies	884	705	312
Account recoverable	–	–	–
	20,854	27,293	30,497
Capital	5,424	7,238	7,243
Share premium	19	–	9
Profit and loss account	12,411	17,055	18,355
Deferred tax	–	–	1,890
Loans	3,000	3,000	3,000
	20,854	27,293	30,497

ANALYSIS OF SALES (£000)

	Food	*Freezers etc.*	*Restaurants etc.*	*Total*
1978	83,914	7,061	–	90,975
1979	109,400	7,776	6,148	123,324
1980	142,691	8,368	13,013	164,072
1981	175,027	11,912	12,797	199,736

Source: Reproduced by arrangement with Extel Statistical Services Ltd, 37–45 Paul Street, London EC2A 4PB

Appendix 2 Freezer ownership

1 UK SALES OF FREEZERS AND FRIDGE/FREEZERS (THOUSANDS)

	Freezers	*Fridge/Freezers*
1974	714	295
1975	850	400
1976	835	430
1977	755	575
1978	600	565
1979	640	635
1980	570	560

Source: Birds Eye Frozen Foods

2 HOUSEHOLDS OWNING FREEZER OR FRIDGE/FREEZER (%)

1971	6
1972	9
1973	14
1974	19
1975	26
1976	32
1977	37
1978	41
1979	45
1980	50

Source: Birds Eye Frozen Foods

Appendix 3 Frozen food sales

1 CONSUMER EXPENDITURE ON FFROZEN FOODS

	£ millions (current prices)
1974	293
1975	365
1976	470
1977	550
1978	605
1979	700
1980	850

Source: Birds Eye Frozen Foods

2 OUTLETS SELLING FROZEN FOODS

	Freezer centres	*Others*
1974	1,100	116,000
1975	1,150	112,000
1976	1,100	104,000
1977	1,100	99,000
1978	1,100	92,000
1979	1,100	86,000
1980	1,050	78,000

Source: Birds Eye Frozen Foods

Appendix 4 Cordon Bleu Freezer Food Centres Ltd

PROFIT AND LOSS ACCOUNT, YEAR ENDING AUGUST 31 (£000)

Year	*Turnover*	*Interest paid*	*Profit before tax*	*Profit after tax*
1973	3,822	23	80	48
1974	5,405	81	103	51
1975	7,391	49	119	57
1976	9,048	32	198	103
1977	11,791	53	263	127
1978	12,797	73	175	79
1979	16,757	50	520	520
15 months ending March 1981	46,326	63	1,022	1,022

BALANCE SHEETS (£000)

	31 Dec. 1979	*28 Mar. 1981*
Current assets		
Stock	2,400	3,994
Debtors	271	744
Due from group companies	–	289
Assets held for disposal	–	165
Cash	444	17
	3,115	5,209
Current liabilities		
Overdraft	–	444
Creditors	3,377	7,676
Due to group companies	–	135
Loans	–	1,020
	3,377	9,271
Net current assets	(262)	(4,062)
Fixed assets	1,902	5,185
Goodwill	–	1,164
	1,640	2,287
Capital	158	158
Share premium	45	45
Retained earnings	1,437	1,684
Deed purchase consolidated	–	400
	1,640	2,287

Source: Reproduced by arrangement with Extel Statistical Services Limited, 37–45 Paul Street, London EC2A 4PB

9 John Crowther

In 1981 Mr Trevor Barker who was an accountant and businessman, but without any close experience of the textile industry, was invited to buy out the shareholding of Joe Hyman in John Crowther Plc and become the chairman. Joe Hyman was a well-known entrepreneur who in the 1960s had built up Viyella in Lancashire into one of the largest cotton and allied products companies in the world. John Crowther Plc was a small Huddersfield-based woollen fabric manufacturer which had survived the severe 1979–81 recession which had caused the closure of many British textile firms.

The company had been producing fine-quality woollen fabrics for the domestic and export markets since it was founded in 1840. After Mr Barker became chairman he instituted a programme of rationalization and reorganization. He modernized fabric production, which rose from 1.8 million square metres in 1981 to 5 million in 1985. He also expanded the company operations by acquiring Patsy Yarns – a knitting yarn producer – in 1982; Grantwear Ltd (trouser manufacturers); Lennox Knitwear (ladies' and men's knitwear) and Regina Fabrics (furnishing fabric merchant) in 1985.

In 1984 he closed down the company's producer of man-made fibre waste products. By 1985 the company was employing 470 people, and for its year ending December 1984 reported sales of over £10 million and profit before tax of £514,000. (Appendix 1 provides financial information on J. Crowther Plc.)

In late 1985 Mr Barker was considering making an offer for Carpets (UK) which was the UK carpet manufacturing side of Carpets International and for another carpet manufacturer, Weavercraft Industries Ltd, to form a carpets division which would then make J. Crowther Plc the major carpet manufacturer in the United Kingdom.

THE UNITED KINGDOM CARPET INDUSTRY

By 1984 the UK market for carpets was worth approximately £700 million at manufacturers' selling prices (msp) with imports taking about 22% of this. For many years the UK had been a net exporter of carpets, but in 1980 imports exceeded exports for the first time and had continued to grow. Table 9.1 provides information on UK production, imports and exports for the major carpet products.

TABLE 9.1 UK carpet market

	million square metres			
	UK production	*imports*	*exports*	*UK market*
1974	157	8	36	129
1975	161	8	28	141
1976	177	11	40	148
1977	169	10	45	133
1978	170	17	36	151
1979	164	23	29	158
1980	138	32	21	149
1981	131	40	15	156
1982	125	43	14	154
1983	138	51	13	176
1984	129	60	15	177

Source: *Business Monitor* and British Carpet Manufacturers Association

As Table 9.1 shows, UK output peaked in 1976 with exports reaching a peak in 1977, and imports climbed steadily over the period from 8 million square metres to 55 million square metres in 1985, such that by 1984, imports were achieving 32% of the UK market by volume (and 22% by value).

In general, the imports were largely from other EEC countries, for example, 93% of 1984 imports were from these countries, with the major share taken by Belgium which alone accounted for 38 million square metres. (Appendix 2 provides further information on the carpet market.)

The marked success of the Belgian carpet industry was attributed largely to the lower prices charged which, in turn, were associated with the real exchange rate of sterling. Between 1978 and 1984 the Belgian franc had effectively fallen by 34% against sterling. Coupled with this was the concentration by the Belgian industry on the more inexpensive tufted carpets. Table 9.2 over shows typical carpet prices.

During the late 1960s and early 1970s rising living standards in the UK and increased household formation had led to extensive growth in the

TABLE 9.2 Average price (cif) per square metre (1984)

Tufted carpet	*UK*	*EEC (excluding Belgium)*	*Belgium*
All types	£3.60	£3.72	£2.27
Printed	£3.30	£3.53	£3.57
All synthetic	£3.13	£3.54	£2.22

Source: British Carpet Manufacturers Association

carpet market, as more new houses were carpeted, previously uncarpeted areas of houses were covered, and fitted carpets, with greater area, replaced rugs and carpet squares.

As this growth slowed down, UK manufacturers increasingly turned their attention to exports, with the result that exports grew by 20% in the mid 1970s and represented up to a quarter of UK output. The UK market remained the major market, however, as sales in that market per capita were higher than most countries, and ranked fourth in Europe. The major export markets for UK manufacturers were the other EEC nations which, by 1984, accounted for 50% of exports sale, with Ireland alone responsible for 25%.

Up to about 1970 the traditional strength of the UK industry had been in the manufacture of high-quality woven carpets such as Axminster and Wilton, but the development of tufted carpeting and printing introduced largely in the mid 1950s took over the major share of the market and by 1973, tufted carpets represented 62% of all sales, rising to 84% by 1984. (See table 9.3.)

TABLE 9.3 UK carpet sales by type of construction

	Axminster	*Wilton*	*Tufted*	*Other*
	%	%	%	%
1973	23.7	8.6	62.3	5.4
1977	17.2	4.7	73.2	4.9
1981	12.8	3.9	80.0	3.3
1984	10.9	2.9	83.4	2.8

Source: British Carpet Manufacturers Association

The growth in sales of tufted carpets was not only a response to the lower price at which they could be offered, but also a consequence of a change in consumer tastes away from intricately patterned carpets towards plainer carpets in conjunction with patterned soft furnishings.

A further trend in carpet manufacturing was the proportion of wool used. (See table 9.4.)

TABLE 9.4 Percentage (by weight) of wool used by UK manufacturers by type of construction

	Tufted	*Woven*
1973	9	60
1974	8	58
1975	10	55
1976	13	52
1977	13	50
1978	12	48
1979	16	51
1980	15	52
1981	14	57
1982	15	57
1983	18	57
1984	18	65

Source: British Carpet Manufacturers Association

Traditionally wool was the most important fibre used in carpet construction but it was more expensive than other fibres, especially as the pile had to be extremely dense to achieve appropriate weaving qualities. With the introduction of man-made fibres, increasingly at lower costs and subsequently specially designed for carpet use, there was a trend towards mixtures of fibres. Generally speaking, wool remained the most important fibre used in woven carpets, whilst nylon was the major fibre in tufted carpets (58% of fibres).

UK CARPET MANUFACTURERS

Although the UK market had grown in volume terms by 27% between 1974 and 1984, the UK market manufacturers had not fared as well as their output was down by 27% over the period 1976 to 1984. As a consequence, there was considerable rationalization, including a fall in employment in the industry from 32,000 employees in 1976 to 16,000 in 1984, and in the depths of the 1979–80 recession a quarter of the manufacturers closed down. (See Table 9.5.)

Carpets International was the largest UK manufacturer, with carpet brands such as 'Crossley', 'Kosset' and 'Gilt-Edge', and held about a 20% share of the domestic market sales and was also involved in the industrial contract carpet market (e.g. Heathrow Airport, which was the area of eight football pitches, was carpeted by Carpets International). Associated Weavers of Bradford had a 10% share of the domestic market when it closed down in 1980. Some companies specialized in one construction of carpet only; examples of these were Shaw Carpets which produced tufted

TABLE 9.5 Employees

1979	31,000
1980	23,300
1981	20,200
1982	18,500
1983	17,900
1984	16,400

Source: British Carpet Manufacturers Association

carpets only and BondWorth, which produced only woven axminsters. BondWorth went into liquidation in 1979. Most of the major manufacturers, however, were involved in both types of carpet construction. By 1984 market shares of the major manufacturers were:

Carpets International	15%
Brinton	8%
Shaw Carpets	6%
Donaghadee[1]	6%

Source Casewriter's estimates

There were about 60 carpet manufacturers of various sizes in the UK, employing in 1985 16,000 people.

Background to some of the companies follows.

Gaskell Broadloom Plc

Employing 468 people, Gaskell manufactured a variety of types of carpet including berber and tufted, as well as underlays, with 82% of sales in the UK.

£000s	*1984*	*1983*	*1982*	*1981*	*1980*	*1979*
Sales	15,348	12,727	11,573	13,563	12,533	11,883
Profit/(loss) before tax	1,204	1,351	686	192	610	1,104
Capital employed	7,567	7,252	7,089	7,325	7,827	4,043
Debt/equity %	16	21	27	37	46	9

Stoddard Holdings Plc

Employing just over 1,000 people, Stoddard manufactured both woven and tufted carpets, selling to domestic and contract markets, with 92% of sales in the UK.

[1] A subsidiary of Vantona-Viyella

£000s	1985	1984	1983	1982	1981	1980	1979
Sales	33,371	33,173	32,637	34,997	22,822	23,853	23,101
Profit/(loss) before tax	(559)	76	(1,140)	(2,252)	(1,866)	86	765
Capital employed	6,886	8,417	8,902	9,532	14,129	10,324	10,811
Debt/equity %	5	5	4	5	5[a]	31	37
Employees	1,079	1,154	1,391	1,980	N/A	N/A	N/A

[a] Long-term debt converted to convertible, cumulative preference shares

Shaw Carpets Plc

Shaw Carpets concentrated on the manufacture of tufted carpets, employing 475 people with 84% of sales in the UK.

£000s	1985	1984	1983	1982	1981	1980	1979
Sales	41,533	40,737	36,500	33,448	36,210	34,493	30,831
Profit/(loss) before tax	346	1,494	962	(2,260)	465	1,050	1,645
Capital employed	5,484	6,036	4,895	4,413	6,512	6,751	6,374
Debt/equity %	27	36	31	24	30	32	38

Firth Carpets

Firth Carpets was a subsidiary of Readicut International Plc, manufacturing carpets for the domestic and contract markets at mills in Yorkshire and in the USA.

Sales and operating profits for the carpets division of Readicut were as follows:

£000s	1985	1984	1983	1982
Sales	33,445	30,862	27,186	27,220
Operating profits	2,276	2,500	1,688	970

Donaghadee Carpets

Donaghadee was a subsidiary of Vantona-Viyella Plc, manufacturing tufted carpets and wilton carpets in Northern Ireland.

£000s	1984	1983	1982	1981	1980	1979
Sales	39,000	32,200	na	na	29,195	27,013
Profit before tax	500	1,500	na	na	(505)	(1,095)

Information about Carpets (UK) and Weavercraft appears in the appendices.

In the UK the retailing of carpets was largely dominated by two large retail chains, Harris Queensway and Allied Carpets. Harris Queensway, with 205 outlets called variously 'Harris Carpets', 'Carpetland', 'Ross Carpets' and 'General George' and with arrangements to sell through other – largely department – stores, had about 12% of carpet sales. Allied Carpets (a subsidiary of ASDA) had 65 outlets and a market share of about 10%. Other significant retail outlets were departmental stores with about 12% and furniture stores with 15%.

Although carpets had brand names, the advertising expenditure in the industry did not reflect this. Indeed, advertising was likely to be by retailers rather than manufacturers. In 1984 manufacturers' advertising (both TV and press) totalled £1.56 million with a significant proportion of this supported by fibre producers, e.g. International Wool Seretariaat and ICI's new carpet yarn, 'Timbrelle', and the balance on individual brands such as 'Kosset' (Carpets International), 'Flotex' and 'Heuga' (both contract carpet suppliers). The retailers Harris and Allied spent between them in the same year about £16.5 million.

Carpets International manufactured carpets both in the UK, where it was known as Carpets (UK), and overseas and, as the largest manufacturer, was not insulated from the difficult period that the British industry went through at the time of the 1979–81 recession. The company produced a loss before tax for four consecutive years in 1980 to 1983 inclusive, before its 1984 results showed a small profit. (Appendix 3 gives financial information on Carpets (UK).) In 1982, following three poor years, the company undertook a reorganization of its corporate structure, involving the loss of senior management and the arrival of a new chairman in December 1982; the closure of a large carpet mill at 'Crossley's' in Halifax; and concentration of woven manufacture in Kidderminster and tufted manufacture at 'Kosset' in Brighouse, Yorkshire. Although the company had manufacturing interests outside of the UK, it was the UK operations which were the major loss-makers, so the new senior management applied its effort of cost reduction, production rationalization and marketing changes to those areas. The number of employees fell from 4,489 in 1982 to 2,893 in 1984.

As indicated above, the company was involved in both woven and tufted carpet manufacture, and in 1984 these represented 43% and 45% of sales respectively and the balance of 12% was sales of yarns and non-woven floor coverings. The company sold to both the retail/domestic market (70% of its sales) and the industrial contract market (19%). Retail sales were generally through departmental stores, and the multiple carpet chain outlets accounted for less than 15% of output.

The best-known brand names of the company were 'Crossley', 'Gilt-Edge' and 'Kosset' in the retail market and 'CIC' in the industrial contract market.

In 1984 an analysis of the 177 million square metres of carpeting sold in the UK was as shown in table 9.6.

TABLE 9.6 1984 UK carpet sales

	million sq metres	*£ million*
TYPE		
Tufted		
UK manufacturing	98	353
Imports	56	156
TOTAL	154	509
Woven		
UK manufacturing	16	180
Imports	2	13
TOTAL	18	193
Others		
UK manufacturing	3	23
Imports	2	8
TOTAL	5	31
GRAND TOTAL	177	733

Source: Listing particulars by J. Crowther plc, 9 October 1985

CROWTHER ACQUISITIONS IN 1985

In September 1985 John Crowther Plc announced its proposal to acquire the British carpet manufacturing facilities of Carpets International Plc which was known as Carpets (UK) and another carpet manufacturer called Weavercraft Industries. For Carpets (UK) the price offered was £6.34 million in cash plus 1.25 million Crowther shares (valued at 60 pence each), and in addition Crowther would assume responsibility for the £6 millions debt owed by Carpets (UK). For Weavercraft the price offered was to be 4.5 million Crowther shares. Weavercraft Industries was a Bradford-based carpet manufacturer which was privately owned and controlled by Mr Michael Abrahams with net assets of £5.4 million, employing about 750 people.

Mr Abrahams had many years' experience of the carpet industry and had previously built up Associated Weavers as a carpet manufacturer and sold the company in 1974 to an American firm. He bought back the assets in 1980 and changed the name to Weavercraft and concentrated on the manufacture of synthetic woven carpets which sold at the lower end of the price range. Following the introduction of new, cheaper, tufted carpeting, Weavercraft introduced more expensive wool-rich carpets for the industrial segment of the market such that by 1985, 25% of sales were wool-blend carpets and 40% of these sold to the contract carpet market. The remaining 75% were at the upper end of the synthetic woven carpet market. Sales and operating figures for Weavercraft are given in Appendix 4.

Mr Barker's proposal was that J. Crowther Plc should acquire Carpets (UK) and Weavercraft Industries to form a new, major force in the British carpet market. Mr Michael Abrahams would join the board of directors of J. Crowther Plc as deputy chairman and assume responsibility for the direction of a new carpets division. If the proposals were accepted, the company would be reorganized to form three divisions. These would be 'Cloth', 'Clothing' and 'Carpets'. The first two would essentially be the J. Crowther companies and the third would comprise Carpets (UK) and Weavercraft Industries put together.

The Cloth Division

This was one of the largest manufacturers of pure wool cloth in Europe with a vertically integrated unit converting raw wool into fine-quality wool fabric. About 80% of the division's sales was to domestic garment manufacturers, but the largest customer, taking 15% of output, was a West German company which sold finished garments to most major store groups in Europe. Crowther had concentrated on higher-quality fabrics used mainly in men's and women's outerwear. The division also spun yarn for the hand-knitting and machine-knitting markets and provided about 10% of its yarn output to fabric-makers in the division.

The Clothing Division

This consisted of three companies: Grantwear, Lennox and Regina.

1 Grantwear produced 640,000 pairs of men's trousers a year from three factores in Leeds and sold to ten retail groups such as BHS, ASDA, C & A and Tesco, who put their own private labels on the product.

2 Lennox produced fully fashioned sweaters from natural fibres such as wool and angora from two factories in Leicestershire, and sold to ten customers such as Laura Ashley, Next and BHS, for sale under own private labels.

3 Regina was a merchant for an extensive range of upholstery and curtain fabrics sold to retailers including Allied Curtains and the John Lewis Partnership.

The Carpet Division

The company would put together the facilities of Carpets (UK) and Weavercraft Industries to form a new carpets division with production concentrated on the most suitable plants rather than continuing to use existing facilities, and it was hoped by this to achieve reduced production costs through manufacturing efficiencies. The two companies were considered to have complementary product ranges and customer profiles; for example, Carpets (UK) had been strong in selling to department stores and independent retailers, whilst Weavercraft had concentrated on the multiple chain retailers and on wholesalers.

In presenting the proposal, Mr Barker indicated that a pro forma analysis of turnover by the proposed divisions for the year ending June 1985 would have been as set out in table 9.7.

TABLE 9.7 Sales turnover (£ thousands)

	UK	*Overseas*	*Total*
Cloth division	6,185	3,934	10,119
Clothing division	5,178	–	5,178
Carpet division	70,408	9,158	79,566
TOTAL	81,771	13,092	94,863

Appendix 1 John Crowther Plc

PROFIT AND LOSS ACCOUNTS, YEAR ENDED DECEMBER (£000)

	1980	*1981*	*1982*	*1983*	*1984*
Turnover	3,802	3,661	5,611	7,334	10,865
Operating costs	(4,438)	(3,729)	(5,340)	(6,911)	(10,098)
Operating profit/(loss)	(636)	(68)	271	423	767
Bank and short-term loan interest	(275)	(202)	(225)	(196)	(253)
Profit/(loss) on ordinary activities before taxation	(911)	(270)	46	227	514
Taxation	(5)	(4)	3	(35)	(57)
Profit/(loss) on ordinary activities after taxation	(916)	(274)	49	192	457
Preference dividends	(11)	(11)	(11)	(11)	(11)
Profit/(loss) before extraordinary items	(927)	(285)	38	181	446
Extraordinary items	–	–	–	(141)	(60)
Profit/(loss) attributable to ordinary shareholders	(927)	(285)	38	40	386
Ordinary dividends	–	–	–	(72)	(126)
Retained profit and loss for period	(927)	(285)	38	(32)	260

BALANCE SHEETS, YEAR ENDED DECEMBER (£000)

	1980	*1981*	*1982*	*1983*	*1984*
Fixed assets					
Tangible assets	1,803	1,817	2,079	2,301	2,792
Investment	–	–	–	4	9
	1,803	1,817	2,079	2,305	2,801
Current assets					
Stocks	1,003	1,257	1,368	1,825	2,946
Debtors	476	725	953	1,688	2,517
Cash at bank and in hand	2	3	3	3	5
	1,481	1,985	2,324	3,516	5,468
Creditors (due within one year)					
Borrowings	1,106	1,331	1,541	911	1,551
Other creditors	646	1,224	1,581	2,665	3,483
	1,752	2,555	3,122	3,576	5,034
Net current assets/ (liabilities)	(271)	(570)	(798)	(60)	434
Total assets less current liabilities	1,532	1,247	1,281	2,245	3,235
Creditors (due after one year)					
Borrowings	–	–	–	–	441
Provision for liabilities and charges	–	–	–	96	–
	1,532	1,247	1,281	2,149	2,794
Capital and reserves					
Cumulative Preference Shares of £1 each	300	300	300	300	300
Ordinary Shares of 25p each	900	900	900	1,800	2,108
Share premium account	–	–	–	–	37
Revaluation reserve	–	–	–	–	40
Profit and loss account	332	47	81	49	309
	1,532	1,247	1,281	2,149	2,794

ANALYSIS OF TURNOVER (£000)

Location of customer	*1980*	*1981*	*1982*	*1983*	*1984*	*6 months ended 30 June 1985*
United Kingdom	3,636	3,565	5,336	6,638	8,613	5,578
Europe			199	425	1,910	2,084
North America	166	96	28	197	290	449
Rest of the world			48	74	52	–
	3,802	3,661	5,611	7,334	10,865	8,111

Appendix 2 The UK carpet industry

(a) SALES BY TYPES OF CONSTRUCTION

		Total sales		*Export sales*	
Carpet type	*Year*	*msm*	*£m*	*msm*	*£m*
Axminster	1980	20.2	155.9	4.4	35.5
	1981	16.6	137.6	2.9	26.9
	1982	15.6	135.9	3.1	28.8
	1983	16.2	149.5	3.1	29.9
	1984	16.1	163.6	3.1	33.4
Wilton	1980	5.9	64.6	1.1	10.4
	1981	5.1	59.3	0.6	6.8
	1982	4.6	55.0	0.7	6.7
	1983	4.5	56.4	0.7	7.2
	1984	4.3	58.3	0.8	8.2
Tufted	1980	106.8	296.5	14.6	41.7
	1981	104.4	299.8	11.3	32.1
	1982	101.4	321.9	10.1	31.0
	1983	113.5	353.2	8.5	30.9
	1984	107.5	391.2	9.5	38.5

Source: Derived from *Business Monitor* PQ 4384/5

(b) MAJOR IMPORTS OF MACHINE-MADE CARPETS (£m)

	Axminster			*Wilton*			*Tufted*		
Origin	*1982*	*1983*	*1984*	*1982*	*1983*	*1984*	*1982*	*1983*	*1984*
EFTA	0.08	0.02	0.02	0.4	0.6	0.4	2.3	3.3	3.3
Eastern Europe	0.09	0.02	0.2	0.5	0.3	0.4	–	0.04	0.04
Far and Middle East	0.08	0.1	0.05	0.4	0.7	0.7	1.5	2.2	2.9
USA	0.09	0.1	0.03	0.2	0.5	0.5	4.3	3.8	1.7
Israel	–	–	–	1.0	1.2	0.6	4.2	3.8	4.2
EEC	4.6	3.3	2.5	6.6	7.4	7.6	94.5	116.9	142.9
of which Belgium	0.2	0.4	0.3	4.2	5.2	5.7	49.9	65.6	85.4

Source: Derived from *Business Monitor* PQ 4384/5

Appendix 3 Carpets (UK)

PROFIT AND LOSS ACCOUNT, YEAR ENDED DECEMBER (£000)

	1980	*1981*	*1982*	*1983*	*1984*	*6 months ended 30 June 1985*
Turnover	68,748	60,371	61,376	59,661	59,655	30,000
Operating Costs	(74,478)	(65,124)	(67,646)	(61,722)	(59,326)	(29,670)
Operating profit/(loss)	(5,730)	(4,753)	(6,270)	(2,061)	329	635
Interest	(3,497)	(2,154)	(2,124)	(1,393)	(1,257)	(663)
Loss on ordinary activities before taxation	(9,227)	(6,907)	(8,394)	(3,454)	(928)	(28)
Loss on activities after taxation	(9,227)	(6,907)	(8,394)	(3,454)	(928)	(28)
Extraordinary items	(1,713)	(466)	(2,455)	(446)	(81)	–
Loss for period	(10,940)	(7,373)	(10,849)	(3,900)	(1,009)	(28)

BALANCE SHEETS, YEAR ENDED DECEMBER (£000)

	1980	*1981*	*1982*	*1983*	*1984*	*Six months ended 30 June 1985*
Fixed assets						
Tangible assets	17,297	13,533	11,510	10,393	10,660	10,218
Current assets						
Stocks	13,179	15,031	13,048	13,630	13,977	15,404
Debtors	10,829	9,995	10,756	10,092	10,745	10,345
Cash at bank and in hand	31	20	25	20	21	36
	24,039	25,046	23,829	23,742	24,743	25,785
Creditors due within 1 year						
Bank overdraft	1,314	362	845	716	1,454	1,351
Assumed bank borrowings						6,127
Other creditors	8,146	10,410	10,796	9,152	8,611	8,431
	9,460	10,772	11,641	9,868	10,065	15,909
Net current assets	14,579	14,274	12,188	13,874	14,678	9,876
Total assets less current liabilities	31,876	27,807	23,698	24,267	25,338	20,094
Capital and reserves						
Called up share capital	1,750	1,750	1,750	1,750	1,750	1,750
Profit and loss account	(2,954)	(9,537)	(19,396)	(22,850)	(22,607)	(22,635)
	(1,204)	(7,787)	(17,646)	(21,100)	(20,857)	(20,885)
Amount due to Carpets International Plc[a]	33,080	35,594	41,344	45,367	46,195	40,979
	31,876	27,807	23,698	24,267	25,338	20,094

[a] Carpets International Plc was the ultimate holding company of Carpets (UK).

ANALYSIS OF TURNOVER (£000)

Location of customer	*1980*	*1981*	*1982*	*1983*	*1984*	*6 months ended 30 June 1985*
United Kingdom	60,709	54,029	54,446	54,521	54,302	27,161
Europe	5,099	3,452	3,990	2,604	2,695	1,601
America	1,750	1,700	1,300	1,418	2,505	1,266
Rest of the world	1,190	1,010	1,640	1,118	153	277
	68,748	60,371	61,376	59,661	59,655	30,305

Appendix 4 Weavercraft Industries Ltd

PROFIT AND LOSS ACCOUNTS, YEAR ENDED DECEMBER (£000)

	7 months ended 30 June 1981	*1982*	*1983*	*1984*	*1985*
Turnover	7,598	14,815	17,573	16,768	17,406
Operating costs	(7,342)	(14,387)	(16,557)	(17,006)	(16,885)
Operating profit/(loss)	256	428	1,016	(238)	521
Interest receivable and similar income	38	129	45	1	–
Interest payable and similar charges	(121)	(290)	(311)	(380)	(445)
Profit/(loss) on ordinary activities before taxation	173	267	750	(617)	76
Profit/(loss) before extraordinary items	173	267	750	(617)	76
Extraordinary items	–	–	–	(634)	1,119
Retained profit and loss for period	173	267	750	(1,251)	1,195

BALANCE SHEET, YEAR ENDED JUNE (£000)

	1981	*1982*	*1983*	*1984*	*1985*
Fixed assets					
Tangible assets	2,186	3,287	4,475	4,270	4,612
Current assets					
Stocks	1,676	2,344	3,252	3,158	3,874
Debtors	1,952	1,916	2,588	2,814	3,045
Cash at bank and in hand	1,161	1,635	1,059	–	2,369
	4,789	5,895	6,899	5,972	9,288
Creditors (due within one year)					
Borrowings	–	167	346	1,582	412
Other creditors	1,844	2,906	3,729	3,124	6,494
	1,844	3,073	4,075	4,706	6,906
Net current assets	2,945	2,822	2,824	1,266	2,382
Total assets less current liabilities	5,131	6,109	7,299	5,536	6,994
Creditors (due after one year)					
Borrowings	(1,500)	(2,211)	(2,651)	(2,139)	(1,594)
	3,631	3,898	4,648	3,397	5,400
Representing at 30 June 1985					
Capital and reserves					
Called up share capital					5,594
Capital reserve					273
Profit and loss account					(467)
					5,400

ANALYSIS OF TURNOVER (£000)

Location of customer	*7 months ended 30 June 1981*	*1982*	*1983*	*1984*	*1985*
United Kingdom	7,529	14,058	16,487	15,114	14,669
Europe	28	684	865	716	759
Middle East	41	73	166	305	175
North America	–	–	55	633	1,803
	7,598	14,815	17,573	16,768	17,406

10 Trusthouse Forte (A)

BACKGROUND

Trusthouse Forte Limited is the largest hotel, catering and leisure group in the world. It was formed in 1970 by the merger of the Trust Houses Group Limited and Forte Holdings Limited.

Trust Houses were formed in 1903 with the main objective of restoring the standards of the old coaching inns, many of which had fallen into decline following the development of the railways. Over the years the company grew into a nationwide group of hotels, with overeas hotel interests as well.

Sir Charles Forte, now executive chairman of Trusthouse Forte Ltd, founded Forte Holdings Limited in 1935. The major expansion of his company began in the post-war period and soon Forte activities spanned the whole range of catering: popular and exclusive restaurants, banqueting, airports and in-flight catering, duty-free shops, motorway service areas, and from 1958, hotels in Britain and overseas. By 1970 the company had 41 hotels, a number operating in partnership with BEA and BOAC, now British Airways. That association continues and has been enlarged.

The company's sales operations included the United States and Japan, with a turnover in 1980 of £772 million. (See Appendices 2 and 3.) THF is primarily an hotel company with almost three-quarters of its profits currently coming from this source. In 1980 THF had a total of 810 hotels throughout the world. These hotels ranged from exclusive hotels such as the Hotel George V in Paris to the Post Houses and Inns found in the UK.

The second most important profit centre to the THF organization is catering, which includes 15 high-class restaurants and goes down the scale to in-store catering. The Little Chef restaurants run by the group are particularly popular with tourists and travellers. The activities of Gardner Merchant can be included in this section. This company carries out industrial catering contracts using the facilities provided by the client firm.

THF Leisure Division contributed 5% of the profits in 1980 and has since been extended by acquisition. This division includes such things as theatre restaurants, sports and leisure centres and the recently acquired Blackpool Tower amusement complex. (See Appendix 4 for subsidiary profile.)

PHILOSOPHY AND POLICIES

Investment Policy and Growth

The THF board maintains a policy of keeping the company balance sheet strong to aid future investment. To this end the various company properties are revalued at regular intervals thus preventing understatement. The company looks ahead for investment opportunities that will provide good returns in the future. Profits representing an optimum return on capital employed are the hallmarks of Trusthouse Forte. THF's stated initial target return on investment is of the order of 15% to 20% per annum pretax and preinterest.

The company stated in 1980 that the heaviest investment programme in its history would be maintained and that the priority areas of expansion for THF were Britain, USA, Europe and the Middle East. It seemed likely that much of this investment would be spent in the hotel industry, but THF's other interests would not suffer any loss of investment as a result. A large proportion of THF's investment in the hotel industry was destined for refurbishing existing and recently acquired hotels.

The company believes in growth by profitable expansion. This has meant several past acquisitions and more recently several joint ventures. There is now some evidence that the more recent acquisitions are leading to diversification for THF, for example into printing. However, such diversification programmes are only undertaken if the board feel the acquisition will complement the existing operations.

The THF board believe that providing good customer service in its hotels can only be achieved by giving the staff extensive well-supervized training. To further this aim THF has invested £3m in providing full and comprehensive training programmes for its staff at all levels.

Marketing

In order to maintain good customer service and relations, each individual unit is made responsible for its own profitability. This includes involving the hotel management not only in their own regional marketing, but also in the total group marketing policies. THF have found that, overall, this approach reduces the impersonality of such a large organization whilst still providing all of the advantages of the large organization in terms of general business operation: for example, financial control, management techniques and standards of quality.

Trust House Forte is an international company competing in a world market. It must therefore sell its services in all the major markets in the world. However, since 70% of the company's business comes from its British hotel and catering operations, Britain remains a priority destination to be sold.

THF's marketing activities have been geared towards three company-set objectives:

1 Internationally to increase visitors to Britain from overseas.
2 To increase the number of visitors to THF worldwide.
3 Within Britain to gain a bigger share of the relatively static home business and holiday traffic particularly during weak or out-of-season trading periods.

THF's marketing problem can be defined in two stages; first the need to sell Britain as a destination, and second, to sell its own hotel and catering facilities.

To back up the work done by the overseas sales staff, who number 130 and operate in 37 countries, THF runs a full programme of promotional, advertising and PR activity, all designed to promote the name THF worldwide thus gaining customer awareness and respect.

In Britain customer awareness of the THF name is very high and considered to be better than any of its competitors, this being the conclusion of an independently commissioned report. Overseas, however, the company is less well known and for this reason the company launched an international corporate advertising campaign in 1980 to improve awareness of THF, its hotels and services among European and American audiences.

The major problem to the industry in general is to increase occupancy levels, thus giving a greater base over which to spread the high fixed costs which are inevitable in the hotel industry. THF's occupancy levels are 10% to 15% higher than those experienced by the rest of the industry. This situation has been brought about by three things:

1 THF's well-organized worldwide referral and advanced booking system,
2 effective marketing positioning, and
3 innovative sales effort.

Point 2 refers to the fact that in the UK, each THF hotel has its own character and well-defined position in the market. There are several types of provincial hotels including seven airport hotels, 30 Post Houses and 70

Inns. Although all of them appear in the upper quarter of the tariff range, and each possesses at least two stars on the AA/RAC scales, there is a considerable difference between, say, the Post Houses which the Price Commission defined as 'a modern hotel outside City Centre on a major road not offering room service or porterage' and an Inn, a small two-star hotel with food and drink facilities aimed both at residents and at the local trade. Each of these different types of outlet fills an identifiable niche in the market and complements the rest of the company's business.

Relating to point 3, the company has attempted to identify its problem areas and then produced packages aimed specifically at improving these areas. For example, the business trade for hotels tends to be Monday to Thursday which means rooms are unoccupied at weekends. If the occupancy can be increased during these 'slack' periods, then the high fixed cost structure, as stated above, can be spread over an increased 'output' and thus the marginal increase in occupancy will lead to a greater increase in profits.

The company's answer to this problem was to introduce, in 1980, the Weekend Bargain Breaks and Hightime Holiday packages, backed by a vigorous marketing campaign. This action resulted in an extra 120,000 sleeper nights being sold in a year when the English Tourist Board recorded a total market decline of 4%. In 1981 this market was estimated as being worth 750,000 sleeper nights to THF every year. Partly as a result of these special promotional schemes, perhaps 20% of the visitors to THF's UK hotels are British residents on holiday.

The company has also successfully introduced the Gold Card system, which is THF's own form of credit card. This is of particular benefit to the frequent traveller, notably the businessman, as the cardholder has access to the full range of facilities provided by THF.

THF has identified the credit operations as another way of increasing business and has introduced other measures aimed at both the individual traveller and the businessman.

One further growth area identified by THF is that of conference catering. The company has established a system whereby the conference organizer can ring a central function and be dealt with swiftly, also being given advice as necessary.

PAST GROWTH AND ACQUISITIONS

Since the formation of THF, as a result of a merger in 1970 between Trust Houses group and the Forte group, its growth has been considerable. The policy for growth was reflected in the building of new interests, notably the Post House operation, and also in the acquisition of existing properties as the result of takeovers. An example of the latter is the acquisition of some hotels previously owned by the Lyons group, which took place in early 1977.

The Allied Takeover

During 1971, not long after the formation of THF, an unsuccessful takeover bid was made by the Allied Breweries group. The result of this attempted takeover was that Allied Breweries were left with 22% of THF's voting shares, which was not enough to gain any control over the company. The effect for THF was that Sir Charles Forte was forced to take out expensive loans in order to buy up THF shares, thus ensuring that control of the company remained with him and the existing board.

There was a change of management at Allied Breweries in 1975, and the new chairman was of the opinion that a 22% holding in THF was of little use to Allied Breweries. The financial position of the THF group was sound and a takeover bid from a 22% voting position was considered very unlikely to succeed. Therefore in August 1978 the Allied Breweries group sold its 22% shareholding in THF under the supervision of the board.

The Lyons Takeover

The takeover of the Lyons hotel group began in November 1976 and involved THF acquiring 35 hotels in Britain and Eire in a deal worth £27.6 million. This increased THF's hotels to 800 in 1976. Sir Charles said at the time 'It is more or less a natural thing for us to get together for this deal. They want to dispose of their hotels and we want to expand our business.'

The payments for this deal were made in instalments, with the projected cash flows expected to cover these payments, except for the deposit which Sir Charles said the company could find.

The Lyons takeover meant an extra 5,500 rooms were added to the THF group, 3,500 of which were in London. At this time the rooms were to cost THF around £4,000 each, with no leases or associated contruction costs to be paid. The cost of construction during this period was estimated at £30,000 per room in London; this represented a considerable saving to THF.

The chain of hotels that was purchased excluded three of the prestigious Lyons hotels which left a group that, on their own, were profit-making. The omission of these profitable hotels meant the Lyons hotel division operated at a loss during 1976, with an increased deficit being forecast for 1977.

The general industry forecast for 1977 predicted an increase in the numbers of tourists and also increased margins. The latter was due to the ending of the price war over the package tourist by the hoteliers. This meant that the London acquisition would pay for itself in the foreseeable future.

By February 1978 THF had increased its representation in London, to a total of 14 hotels offering 6,600 rooms. Prior to this, although larger overall, it lagged behind its rivals such as Grand Metropolitan in the number of rooms offered in the capital.

Expansion in USA

In March 1978 THF began further expansion in the USA with the announcement that its wholly owned subsidiary Knott Hotels had agreed in principle to acquire Colony Foods including Colony Foods under the names of Colony Kitchen and Hobs Joe's, mainly in the Western United States.

THF said of the takeover, 'It is a good base for expansion in restaurants in America.' Its restaurant position in the USA at this time was quite strong with its trade through the Knotts Hotel group, which amongst its outside catering contracts, supplied all the meals for the UN building in New York.

In April 1980 THF withdrew from a further bid in America after an offer of £38.8 million was said to be insufficient to secure the deal. Eric Hartwell, the vice-chairman and chief executive, said at the time that THF still wanted to expand in the USA and were prepared to make a major acquisition. As a result of reduced gearing during the previous year, THF had cash resources of £60m available for such an acquisition and with this cash earning a healthy 20% interest they could afford to wait and be choosy.

Shortly after this Rocco Forte (the group deputy chief executive) made an announcement on behalf of the group that stated that a new expansion programme was planned for the USA. The programme, that was to take immediate effect, was to include operation of the new Plaza Hotel in Dallas, in which THF had an equity stake.

This highlighted THF's change in investment policy in the USA where it was now minimizing its investment costs by operating in the luxury-bracket hotels on long-term management contracts with as little as a 10% equity investment.

Rocco Forte also stated that the group's aim was to have around 15 to 20 hotels in the United States and the same number in other countries.

During February 1981 Grand Metropolitan, a rival of THF, acquired Liggetts hotel group in the USA in response to THF's gradual expansion in the United States. This represented a major move for Grand Metropolitan, as THF annual sales in the USA for 1980 were $175m compared with Liggetts quarterly sales of approximately $300m.

Recent UK Investments

During April 1980 THF made an announcement of its intention to invest a further £40m in its Post House operation. This was the first indication of a major new hotel investment by a British hotel group since 1974 although there had been some expansion in the USA during this period.

The estimated cost per room of the Post Houses was £27,000 (average). The first Post House was due to open in 1980, with three being planned for the 1981 financial year despite the forecast decline in the tourist trade.

In November 1980 THF stated that the building programme was to be accelerated and a fourth Post House was to be built in the 1981 financial year.

Also in November 1980, THF closed a deal which involved the purchase of the greater part of the Thorn-EMI leisure interests. This purchase included such things as the Prince Edward Theatre, the Empire Cinema and Ballroom, Leicester Square, the Blackpool Tower complex and the Chichester Yacht Marine. The takeover also provided for Lord Delfont to become chairman and chief executive of THF leisure division. The takeover dovetailed neatly with THF existing entertainment outlets; it owns the Talk of the Town in London which it has operated in partnership with Lord Delfont and the acquisition of premises with catering facilities enabled THF to employ its expertise in this field.

DIVERSIFICATION

In February 1981 the THF group made another acquisition, but this time into a seemingly unrelated field. The company involved was the publishers Sidgwick and Jackson Limited. This company originally belonged to Forte (Holdings) but was not included in the merger with Trust Houses in 1970 because it was deemed not to fit in with the new concern.

73.3% of Sidgwick and Jackson's 'A Capital' was controlled by three people, Sir Charles Forte, Eric Hartwell and Leonard Rocco who were all board members at THF. The publishers had made a loss in 1980 of £108,000 but were forecast to come into profit in 1981 at £211,000. However the major reason for the acquisition was that THF was about to embark on a number of publishing ventures associated with the tourist and catering business. Sir Charles did state that he wanted the publishers to remain independent, albeit within the THF group.

THF had, in the past, been unsuccessfully involved in publishing, notably its ventures in magazine publishing, for example *Time and Tide* and *Investors Review* both of which were discontinued, while the idea of a new magazine 'Panache' was shelved in its early stages.

Further diversification also took place in 1980 when the directors of THF felt they should apply to participate in the seventh round of oil exploration licences, particularly in view of the government's active encouragement for major non-oil companies to participate in consortium applications led by experienced oil-industry operators. In view of the enormous potential and importance of this national asset the company decided to join several consortia.

FUTURE DEVELOPMENT

Many of THF's future development policies and actions had already been predestined, i.e., much of 1980's and 1981s acquisitions are just the start of a much larger future development. During the course of the 1980 financial year more than £95m was spent worldwide to build new hotels, acquire others, to refurbish and redecorate properties, to buy new equipment and to develop new markets. THF had stated that its priority regions for expansion were Britain, USA, Europe and the Middle East.

The previously mentioned Post House programme was one example of a British investment; there are now 34 Post Houses offering accommodation for up to 8,500 people.

Further expansion of the Little Chef catering establishments was forecast for 1981, with the company expecting to open a further 30 new restaurants.

A catering innovation in 1979 was the Julie's pantry fast service hamburger restaurants. The first 'in town' operation of Julie's Pantry was in London's Knightsbridge and there were two others at Scratchwood (M1) and Corley (M6) motorway service stations. Five others were planned to open during 1980.

The Kardomah chain of restaurants which is aimed at shoppers was to be restyled during 1981 and there were plans to open or acquire further restaurants during the year. There are also plans for the catering partnership, which specializes in catering in departmental stores, to increase the number of its outlets by 50%.

In October 1980 THF took over the management of the Hotel des Bergues in Geneva, a 143-bedroomed hotel which is ranked highly among the world's most exclusive hotels. THF plans to spend in excess of £1m on refurbishing and redecorating this hotel.

THF has also put forward a broad plan for the United States, which is to have deluxe quality hotels in major cities across the USA and Canada. During 1981 THF hoped to be adding luxury hotels in Tulsa, Little Rock and Miami in the USA and Toronto in Canada to complement its existing properties in New York, Dallas and Philadelphia.

THE SAVOY TAKEOVER BID

Early in 1981 THF made a takeover bid for the Savoy group. (See Appendix 5 for list of Savoy operating subsidiaries.) The complex voting system of the Savoy group, which had evolved over the years as a result of repeated takeover attempts by various groups, meant that THF used a different approach to this bid.

THF tried to get High Court approval to hold two separate meetings of the 'A' and 'B' Savoy shareholders, in an attempt to gain 75% of the 'A' shareholders' backing which would have effectively given THF control of the group. The reason this approach was necessary in order to control 51% total equity was that the 'B' shares carry a greater voting strength than the 'A' shares (in the region of 4:1). Both parties had agreed that a High Court ruling was necessary and in the event the court ruled against THF, saying the court had no power to rule as a point of law in this respect and that the part of the Companies Act upon which THF had based its case was irrelevant.

The bid made by THF was thought to be £67m for the group. Sir Charles said at the time that a key factor behind the takeover move had been his dismay at plans to sell the east wing for development; 'we should be building hotel rooms, not closing them down' he said.

In the 1980 published accounts for the Savoy Group, the followng statement appeared in the director's reports:

> Interest received amounted to the comparatively small sum of £47,040 but interest paid on loans and bank overdrafts reached a record figure of £1,204,453, making it clear why the directors, with the knowledge of the British Tourist Authority and London Tourist Board, decided it was right to dispose of surplus accommodation in the Savoy building in The Strand, by realizing its potential for offices and permanent apartments, for which it was originally built and used. (See Appendix 6.)

The sale of this building would be of assistance in reducing the overhead expenditure of the group, and the proceeds of the sale would also bring about a substantial reduction in interest payable by the group.

In August 1981 the Ladbrook group finally secured a deal to take over the east wing of the Savoy which they planned to convert into offices.

As a result of the takeover move THF controlled more than 60% of the Savoy equity, but because of the above-mentioned voting structure it only held 37.47% of the votes.

Appendix 1 THF's business structure

Trusthouse Forte is primarily a hotel company, and almost three-quarters of its profits currently come from this source. The second most important profit centre is Catering, with Leisure and Miscellaneous Interests contributing 5% each to group profits. THF's own food and liquor supply companies account for the greater part of the Miscellaneous Interests.

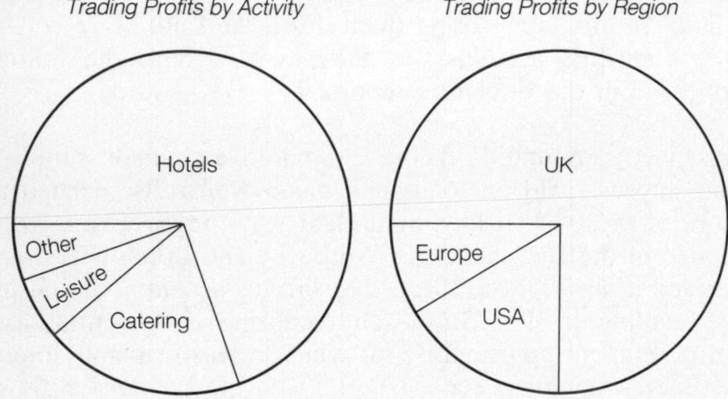

Source: Trust House Forte 1980.

The right-hand diagram shows clearly where in the world THF's profits arise. A total of 80% of THF's profits are earned in the UK, but notice should be taken of UK receipts from foreigners.

The domestic hotel trade is a staple part of THF's business, accounting for 52% of trading profits on 31% of the group turnover. The healthy margins which are achieved in the UK are partly due to THF's higher room occupancy levels in the UK, about 67% against 50% in the USA. The effect on profit of increasing occupancy levels can be seen in Table 10.1.

This relationship can be most simply put as follows: a 5% change in occupancy levels produces 7% change in the number of guests which causes a 25% movement in profits.

Table 10.2 gives a breakdown of the trading activities of THF's world hotels, its worldwide catering organisation, and its leisure and other interests for the year 1980.

TABLE 10.1 Operational gearing – THF UK hotels, 1980

(£m)	*Occupancy*		
	62%	*67%*	*72%*
Revenue	219	236	253
Fixed costs	97	97	97
Variable costs	89	96.5	103
Trading profit	33	42.5	53

Source: Trust House Forte 1980.

TABLE 10.2 THF's trading activities, 1980

(a) *Hotels outside Britain, 1980*

	Trading profit		*Sales*	
	£m	*% of THF*	*£m*	*% of THF*
USA	9.9	11	54.4	7
Europe etc.	7.8	9	61.2	8
TOTAL	17.7	20	115.5	15

(b) *THF catering profits analysis, 1980*

	Trading profit		*Sales*	
	£m	*% of total*	*£m*	*% of total*
UK	17.3	20	335.8	43
USA	(1.3)	–	17.3	2

(c) *Analysis of leisure and other interests*

	Trading profit		*Sales*	
	£m	*% THF*	*£m*	*% THF*
Leisure	4.1	5	33.9	4
Misc.	4.3	5	33.8	4

Source: Trust House Forte 1980.

Appendix 2 THF Ltd and Subsidiaries

BALANCE SHEET (£m)

	1980	*1979*
Assets employed		
Fixed assets	579.3	490.6
Investments	32.2	36.3
Subsidiary companies	–	–
Current assets		
Stocks	21.7	20.7
Debtors	94.0	86.0
Short-term deposits	34.8	52.8
Bank balances and cash	10.7	11.8
	161.2	171.3
	772.7	698.2
Current liabilities		
Creditors	123.8	102.0
Taxation	18.4	30.2
Dividends	13.9	12.2
Bank overdrafts	14.8	6.0
	170.9	150.4
	601.8	547.8
Financed by		
Ordinary and Trust Shareholders		
Share capital	51.5	50.6
Reserves	351.3	296.2
Shareholders' Invesment	402.8	346.8
Minority interest	10.7	9.7
Deferred taxation	0.7	1.0
Loan capital	187.6	190.3
	601.8	547.8

Appendix 3 Five-year Record

	1980	*1979*	*1978*	*1977*	*1976*
Trading receipts (£m)	772	721	614	531	452
Trading profit (£m)	82.0	81.6	70.1	54.3	40.6
Profit before taxation (£m)	66.0	68.2	55.5	38.0	23.7
Profit attributable to shareholders (£m)	47.7	40.3	31.7	24.5	10.6
Earnings per share (p)	23.3	20.0	15.7	12.2	5.9
Dividends (£m)	18.7	16.2	10.7	8.3	7.4
Dividends per share (p)	9.0	8.0	5.3	4.1	3.7
Dividend cover (times)	2.6	2.5	3.0	3.0	1.4
Net liquid funds (£m)	31	59	56	44	25
Assets employed (£m)	602	548	506	410	354
Shareholders' investment					
Total (£m)	403	347	294	193	140
Per share (£)	1.95	1.71	1.46	0.95	0.69
Loan capital (£m)	188	190	203	213	208
Ratio of loan capital to shareholders' investment	0.5:1	0.6:1	0.7:1	1.1:1	1.5:1
Depreciation (£m)	19.0	17.4	14.0	13.6	13.3

The above figures have been restated where necessary to reflect the current accounting policies of the group.

Profit attributable to shareholders and earnings per share are before extraordinary items. The earnings and dividends per share and shareholders' investment figures have been adjusted for the scrip issue in April 1979.

Appendix 4 Facts profile of Trusthouse Forte

HOTELS

	Number	Rooms	Beds
Great Britain			
London	19	6,431	10,093
Provinces	184	15,267	24,171
TraveLodge	6	502	980
Henekey	9	271	439
Total Great Britain	218	22,471	35,683
North America			
TraveLodge wholly owned and joint venture	302	18,591	31,948
TraveLodge franchise	244	20,858	34,772
Other hotels	6	2,184	3,680
Europe and rest of the world	31	6,089	11,408
Associate hotels	9	2,106	4,010
	810	72,299	121,501

CATERING

High-class restaurants	15
Henekey's Steak Houses	29
Henekey's Licensed Houses	8
Little Chefs	185
Motorway Service Areas	9
Kardomah/Speciality Restaurants	54
Parks Restaurants	10
Forte's Bournemouth Restaurants	5 multiple outlets
In-store catering	12
Colony Food Restaurants (USA)	108

LEISURE INTERESTS

Theatre restaurants	3
Piers	7
Amusement Parks (including Blackpool Tower complex)	6
Self-catering holiday villages	3
Restaurants/cafes in leisure complexes	11
Cinemas	3
Amusement Centres	49
Theatres/Concert Halls	9
Show bars/Bars/Bierkellers	78
Licensed Houses	5
Dolphinaria	2
Sports Centres with Squash and Ten-pin Bowling clubs	24
Function venues and ballrooms	26
Yacht Marina	1

AIRPORT SERVICES

Flight catering services for some 75 airlines from 20 airports, together with:

Airport cleaning services for 28 airlines
Airport catering on 20 airports, including
  30 restaurants
  40 buffets
  39 licensed bars
  8 VIP lounges
Shops on airports
  13 duty free
  22 duty paid
Shops on ships
  1 duty free

GARDNER MERCHANT

Caters to over 2,000 clients' establishments supplying over one million meals daily.

Appendix 5

PRINCIPAL SUBSIDIARY COMPANIES OF THE SAVOY GROUP

Claridge's Hotel Limited
The Berkeley Hotel Company Limited
The Connaught Hotel Limited
Hotel Lancaster, Société Anonyme
Simpson's-in-the-Strand Limited
Stone's Chop House Limited
Savoy Theatre Limited
Forest Mere Limited

Appendix 6 Savoy Hotel Ltd

CONSOLIDATED BALANCE SHEET AS AT 31 DECEMBER 1980

	£	£	*1979* £
Capital Employed			
Ordinary capital		2,834,096	2,834,096
Reserves		14,155,694	15,241,524
Debenture stocks, mortgages and loans		5,505,000	5,505,000
Minority shareholders' interest in subsidiaries		92,528	116,534
		£22,587,318	£23,697,154
Represented by:			
Fixed Assets			
Freehold properties		13,816,788	15,417,940
Long leasehold properties		7,197,507	7,041,794
Short leasehold properties		491,278	378,358
Motor vehicles and sundry plant		600,658	596,685
		22,106,231	23,434,777
Current Assets			
Stocks	3,677,508		3,237,903
Debtors and prepaid expenses	3,186,345		3,432,330
Investments	264,026		262,294
Advance corporation tax recoverable	239,126		425,000
Taxation recoverable	30,990		–
Deposits, bank balances and cash	676,495		815,470
	8,074,490		8,172,997
Current Liabilities			
Creditors and accrued charges	4,022,195		4,390,895
Current taxation	157,434		159,502
Deferred taxation	6,600		316,425
Proposed dividend	325,684		325,684
Bank overdrafts	3,081,490		2,718,114
	7,593,403		7,910,620
Net current assets		481,087	262,377
		£22,587,318	£23,697,154

CONSOLIDATED PROFIT AND LOSS ACCOUNT FOR THE YEAR ENDED 31 DECEMBER 1980

1979 £		£	£
5,223,936	Trading profit for the year		3,672,982
3,245,826	Deduct: Cost of general maintenance	3,565,372	
508,384	Depreciation and amortization	569,364	
3,754,210			4,134,736
1,469,726			(461,754)
79,006	Add: Dividends and interests receivable		47,040
1,548,732			(414,714)
1,029,236	Deduct: Interest payable		1,204,453
519,496	Loss for the year (1979: Profit)		(1,619,167)
–	Add: Provision for estimated liability of past years PAYE and national insurance		175,000
519,496	Loss before taxation (1979: Profit)		(1,794,167)
75,892	Taxation credit (1979: Charge)		(138,008)
443,604	Loss after taxation (1979: Profit)		(1,656,159)
17,724	Deduct: Minority interest		(24,006)
425,880	Balance for the year before extraordinary items		(1,632,153)
33,244	Add: Extraordinary items (including realization of a prior year revaluation surplus of £1.9m)		2,503,333
459,124	Balance for the year after extraordinary items		871,180
325,684	Dividend proposed A and B Ordinary Shares 11.49% (1979: 11.49%) gross equivalent 16.41% (1979: 16.41%)		325,684
133,440	Retained profit for the year		545,496
8,681,931	Retained profits at beginning of the year		8,815,371
£8,815,371	Retained profits at end of the year		£9,360,867

Net and Nil basis	Loss per share (1979: earnings)	Net basis	Nil basis
1.50p	A Ordinary Shares of 10p each	(5.76p)	(4.60p)
0.75p	B Ordinary Shares of 5p each	(2.88p)	(2.30p)

11 Grand Metropolitan

In 1980 Grand Metropolitan succeeded in taking over the US-based Liggett Group. The deal had taken six weeks to complete, from inception to culmination; a somewhat protracted time scale compared with previous acquisitions. In 1969 Grand Metropolitan had launched a takeover bid for Express Dairies, the UK national food and milk chain, within a day of hearing that the company was up for sale.

Grand Metropolitan's capital employed had risen from £138m in 1970 to almost £3 billion in 1981. The growth of the company had stemmed largely from an acquisition policy which in the early 1970s had been stated by the chairman as:

> . . . We only acquire companies which we consider are capable of expansion. We have made three major acquisitions during the past two years and in each, with guidance from Grand Metropolitan, the existing management and staff have increased profits substantially. We do not believe in interfering in day to day management but the financial resources and central managerial services of Grand Metropolitan are available to all our subsidiaries.[1]

Towards the end of 1981 Grand Metropolitan acquired Intercontinental Hotels from Pan Am, for $500m cash, against rumoured competition from the Hilton corporation and four major airlines. Early in 1982 the company sold off virtually all of its regional hotels for some £30m.

DEVELOPMENT OF GRAND METROPOLITAN

In 1961 Mount Royal Ltd became a public company and, following a number of acquisitions, changed its name to Grand Metropolitan Hotels Ltd; in 1973 the name was further adjusted to Grand Metropolitan Ltd.

[1] Statement to Truman shareholders in 1971 inviting them to accept Grand Metropolitan's, rather than Watney's, offer (company sources).

Originally the company had operated a number of hotels in the Mayfair district of London and subsequently broadened its activities into the industrial catering industry by acquiring Bateman (1967) and Midland Counties (1968).

Its bid in 1969 for Express Dairies, the second largest milk distributor and processor in the UK, was a significant move for the company as it meant involvement outside the catering field. The Express Dairies acquisition met with opposition both from within the company itself and from investors, many of whom felt that it was an area capable of only slow (if any) growth and that Grand Metropolitan lacked the expertise to manage it. 1970 saw the takeover of Berni Inns for £15m in shares and Mecca, the leisure group which owned betting shops, bingo and dance halls.

In 1971 Trumans the brewers, with nearly 1,000 public houses and off-license outlets, joined Grand Metropolitan. In 1972 Watney-Mann (owners of International Distillers and Vintners (IDV) and the third largest brewer in the UK) was acquired by Grand Metropolitan. This brought the group a further 6,000 public houses, 1,000 off-licenses and 34 hotels.

It was this takeover of Watney-Mann, at a cost of £400 million, which took Grand Metropolitan to the forefront of the European brewery industry and this move virtually doubled the company's size overnight.

By 1975 Grand Metropolitan's turnover of £1,201.4 million and profits of £93.3 million was as outlined in table 11.1.

TABLE 11.1 Turnover and profits by division in 1975.

Division	*External sales*	*Trading profits*
Hotels, entertainment, catering and public houses	33%	41%
Milk and food	23%	13%
Brewing and distribution	13%	21%
Wines and spirits	18%	17%
Betting and gaming	13%	8%

Source: Company Report, 1975

During this year the company entered into management agreement for the operation of three additional properties: the Europa Lodges at Newcastle and Gatwick and the Westmorland Hotel in London. On the industrial catering side, activity was extended in Europe, the Middle East and the Far East, in order to reduce dependency on a reduced UK market. The Bateman Catering subsidiary established regional offices in Bahrain, Teheran and Jakarta, while Midland Catering (the equipment design company) had gained valuable export orders from eastern Europe and the Middle East.

By 1976 the UK Brewing and Distribution operation which included Websters, Drybroughs and the Coca-Cola franchise, had undergone a major programme of regionalization. The main reasons for restructuring were to bring the company's activities nearer the marketplace and to stimulate greater involvement and participation both by company, personnel and licensed-house tenants.

1977 saw a variety of increased activities with the acquisition of the London International Hotel and the Grand Hotel (Birmingham), the expansion of bingo operations, the opening of four new Berni and Schooner Steak Houses in the south of England, and the acquisition of the Yeovil-based Cricket Matherbie Dairies.

DEVELOPMENTS BETWEEN 1978 AND 1980

Hotels and Catering The company's determination to provide higher standards of service and facilities for the 1980s was demonstrated by several development and improvement projects to existing sites. These included the opening of new coffee shops in a number of London hotels and the establishment of public areas at a number of regional hotels.

The Dubai Metropolitan was opened in January 1979 following on the heels of successful business gained by the Industrial Catering Division in Saudi Arabia, Kuwait and Libya. In April 1979 the Hotel d'Angleterre in Copenhagen was acquired and in the same year a management contract for the Algosaibi Metropolitan Hotel in Saudi Arabia was agreed.

The Berni and Schooner activities were expanded with the addition of eight new branches and in August 1979 Berni Inns signed a joint venture agreement with Wendy's International Inc of the USA, to operate 'Wendy Old Fashioned Hamburger Restaurants' in the UK. This partnership was dissolved at the end of 1980. The new fast-food concept was, however, further developed with the opening of two London-based 'Huckleberry's' fast food stores – a venture development in association with Burger Queen Enterprises of Louisville, Kentucky. By 1980 there were four Huckleberry Stores in the UK and three 'Barnaby's' (a new catering venture) in the south-east.

In 1980 Grand Metropolitan acquired three major hotels in Paris, the Meurice and the Prince de Galles in the luxury class and the Grand, a fine, four-star standard. During this year industrial catering activity was increased in the Middle East, Europe, the USA and Japan, and extended into Mexico and South America.

Milk and Foods The combined profits of Grand Metropolitan's Express Milk and Foods division made steady progress during 1979, mainly due to the benefits of past investments in modernizing production facilities. However, the surplus of milk production in the EEC gave rise to uncertainties in forecasting future profitability in spite of the

Community's attempt to balance supply with demand.

In 1980 negotiations were completed with the State of Vermont in the USA, for the leasing of a large cheese whey processing plant. During this year the US-based Dry Milks Inc was acquired to market the products subsequently produced from the Vermont plant.

Brewing and Retailing Following acquisition of the Cadbury Schweppes holding in Cantrell and Cochrane (Great Britain) Limited, a holding company was formed in 1978, to include the latter and Coca-Cola (Southern Bottlers) Limited. The immediate priority was to increase sales through the promotion of both product lines in the separate specialist markets. During this period £1 million was invested in a new bottling plant at Sunbury-on-Thames, to help meet the expanding market for 0.5 to 1 litre bottles across the product range.

The basic importance of the tied trade through pub ownership was recognized by Grand Metropolitan's acquisition of the public houses and taverns of EMI Limited in 1979, for the Chef and Brewer Limited retailing arm. During 1980 Chef and Brewer built or purchased fifteen new public houses and made major improvements at ninety-five others.

Wines and Spirits In 1978 the responsibilities of the executive directors of IDV were redefined and a new position of group marketing director was established. At the same time senior management appointments (many of them in the marketing area) were made in the UK, Canada, South Africa, Australia and Portugal.

Close trading relationships were set up in the USA with Glenmore Distilleries in 1979 and in the same period a joint venture, IDV-Dransfield & Co Ltd, was established with the Fung Ping Tan Co. of Hong Kong, for marketing of IDV products in the Far East.

During 1980 a new bottling and distribution facility was purchased in Maçon, France and building of a distillery was commenced in Sri Lanka. The major event of that year, however, was the acquisition of the American Liggett Group Inc, with its two liquor importing businesses (The Paddington Corporation and Carillon Importers Ltd), for a price of $590 million.

Leisure During 1978-9 the major developments in Grand Metropolitan's leisure activities included refurbishment in ballrooms and improvements in social clubs. Three new 'Cinderella Rockafella' twin-scene night spots were established and six new bingo operations were started in the north of England. During this period Mecca Promotions produced a number of programmes for television in conjunction with the BBC. These included the UK Dance Championships and the British Boy/Girl Disco Dancing Championships.

In September 1980 reconstruction was commenced on a former large-capacity ballroom in Purley. The development includes a 12-court Squash

Club and a Cinderella-Rockafella nightspot. During this year a number of less profitable leisure operations were disposed of.

External sales and trading profits for the periods 1979 and 1980 were represented by each division as shown in table 11.2.

TABLE 11.2 External sales and profits by division in 1979 and 1980.

Division	*External sales (£m)*	*Trading profit (£m)*	*External sales (£m)*	*Trading profit (£m)*
	1980		*1979*	
Hotels	360.1	27.3	308.3	27.8
Milk and Foods	539.7	32.6	471.8	27.2
Brewing and Retailing	671.4	65.7	615.1	64.3
Wines and Spirits	474.6	36.2	447.6	36.1
Leisure	381.9	28.7	328.0	23.8

Excludes Liggett's trading figures (4 months) and UK Milk and Foods
Source: Company Report, 1980

ORGANIZATION AND MANAGEMENT

In 1980 Grand Metropolitan underwent a major reorganization and six operating divisions were formed. (See Appendix 1.) The company chairman Sir Maxwell Joseph now heads a group comprising the managing director (Stanley Grinstead), finance director (Clifford Smith) and the six chief divisional executives. A small group of staff comprising 40 specialists handles matters concerning financial, tax and property affairs. The activities of the six divisions cover:

1 Hotels and Catering
2 Milk and Foods
3 Brewing and Retailing
4 Wines and Spirits
5 Leisure
6 Liggett (acquired in 1980)

Grand Metropolitan's divisional operations were run by six chief executives who had wide scope to carry out their own strategies provided they remained successful. These executives met once a month with the managing director to review profit and cash-flow performance.

There was some restriction as to the direction in which a division might grow, in that expansion had to be in a similar field. For example, the expansion of a brewery into hotels would be discouraged. This control of scope was demonstrated when IDV's desire to expand its product lines through acquisition of US distributors was superseded by the group's takeover of Liggett as a whole rather than merely bidding for its liquor distribution subsidiaries.

The highly decentralized structure of Grand Metropolitan seemed well suited to its operations. The group had concentrated its activities in consumer products and services where an early knowledge of, and fast response to, evolving tastes were considered vital to success. It was Grand Metropolitan, for example, which turned Watneys away from the disastrous standardized 'red pubs'.

SIR MAXWELL JOSEPH

Maxwell Joseph's career had been shrouded in publicity. After leaving school at the age of 16 he started work at 30 shillings (150p) a week for a Hampstead estate agent to learn the property business. After serving in the Royal Engineers during World War Two he moved into the hotel business and by 1953 he had joined Grand Hotels which owned the lavish Mayfair Hotel.

By 1955 he owned half-a-dozen London hotels, but it was the purchase of the Mount Royal for £1 million in 1957 that took him into the realms of big business. Following a spate of property deals, Grand Metropolitan materialized in 1962 and subsequently acquired Gordon Hotels in 1964. Some two years later Maxwell Joseph had bought banking interests (Lombards) and gaming clubs, branched out into European hotels, joined the board of Cunard and had taken over Bertram Mills's circus. The speed with which such decisions were taken is reflected in his own philosophy towards acquisitions:

> All I say is 'yes' or 'no'. Once you start delving into tremendous detail you are lost. . . . You have to look at business in a simple way and keep to the few vital questions.[2]

Maxwell Joseph sold off the property side of his business in 1970 to concentrate on Grand Metropolitan's activity within the hotel and catering industry. Personal motives played a part in this investment,

> One of the reasons I got out of the property business was because it is time-consuming and something you have to do yourself. . . . Unfortunately anyone can go out, do a deal in a week or two and can earn himself more than you can pay him for a year.[3]

[2] *Sunday Times*, 2 April 1972

[3] *Ibid*.

However, it is Maxwell Joseph's experience with property dealings that no doubt contributed to the successful management of hotels. Once described as the 'wizard of the property scene', his policies of buying freehold or long-leasehold property and the avoidance of tying up large sums in working capital had paid off handsomely.

With regard to overall control of the business Maxwell Joseph's style had been described as management by remote control. His method involved delegating of all operating authority to trusted subordinates:

> If you are going to take over a successful business run by men who believe in their ability to make a success of things, then you cannot expect them willingly to accept their orders from head office.[4]

This did not mean to say, of course, that acquisitions had merely been added to Grand Metropolitan and left entirely unchanged or that the benefits from synergy and subsequent management reorganization had been ignored. Indeed there were no less than eight divisional chief executives in 1972 with total sales standing at £434 million, compared with six (including the new Liggetts division) in 1980 on sales of over £1,200 million. The former organization comprised UK Hotels, Popular Catering, Mecca, Trumans, Berni Inns, Watneys, IDV and Express Dairies.

Nonetheless, such changes reflected corporate 'tuning' rather than direct interference with the strategic business unit *per se*. In the words of Stanley Grinstead, managing director of Grand Metropolitan:

> His (Maxwell Joseph's) management system is almost total delegation of all but the key strategic decisions, relying on his judgement of people to build up for himself a strong management team and his own business and entrepreneurial instincts to guide his company. Joseph has a philosophy akin to that of Charles Clore – he introduced the idea that a public house could and often should be valued as a property rather than just as a beer shop. . . . Joseph's motives are somewhat different from Clore's. He is now going for the industrial logic of supplying your own beer and food through your own outlets.
>
> . . . In the past the major force which has shaped Grand Metropolitan Hotels has been the stock market and the decisions of key institutions as to who should own and manage assets of companies like Trumans, Watneys, IDV and Samuel Webster.
>
> He (Maxwell Joseph) is supremely confident in Grand Metropolitan . . . he regards it as socially responsible, managerially efficient and financially sound. . . . He also argues that opportunities for rationalisation within his now diversified group have no

[4] Company Report (1971).

> tendency to reduce overall market competition.
>
> . . . Maxwell Joseph said in March 1972 'it is one of my objectives to get into the leisure industry as the standard of living rises and incomes grow'. He is however convinced and there is a good deal of evidence to support him, that the pursuit of leisure in its own right can be dangerous, i.e. Grand Metropolitan entertainment concerns are usually supported by bricks and mortar.[5]

During the aftermath of the Watney Mann takeover Grand Metropolitan suffered a temporary setback when the share price collapsed from a 1972 high of 276p, to 18.5p three years later. Commenting on the situation Sir Maxwell Joseph had remarked: 'I wasn't quite insolvent but if the shares had gone down another penny or penny ha'penny I would have been'.[6] Yet this period was to prove the resilience of the chairman who's key strengths were considered to comprise a rarely flexible instinct for the work of both property and people and an unrivalled eye for the hotel business on which Grand Metropolitan was founded.

In an era of workaholics Sir Maxwell Joseph had been remarkable for his professed four-day, 16-hour week. He prided himself on his ability to concentrate only on important decisions without getting bogged down in details. The result was that despite Grand Metropolitan's size, it retained the agility to make opportunistic strikes like the purchase of Liggett, the US liquor and tobacco group, in 1980, and the Intercontinental Hotels group in 1981. Each cost over £250m.

Perhaps the best example of Sir Maxwell Joseph's ability to turn on a sixpence is the Watney Mann bid in 1972. On the morning of 27 August 1971, he sat in his office dismissing suggestions that – in the wake of his successful bid for Truman's – he might buy a national brewery chain. In mid-afternoon came a chance to buy a strategic stake in Watney. He took it.

That bid set a new British takeover record – not only for price but probably for acrimony, too. Sir Maxwell Joseph had said through the 1960s that he had no appetite for contested bids. But at Watney, and at Truman's before it, he proved that he could win the fiercest of fights.

THE LIGGETT TAKEOVER

In December 1979 Grand Metropolitan announced that it had made an official filing in connection with the US anti-trust regulations for the purchase of shares in the US-based Liggett Group.

Grand Metropolitan indicated that it intended to acquire from time to time, depending upon market conditions and other factors, additional

[5] A.M. Sewell, Paper delivered at the University of Bradford, August 1973.

[6] Ibid.

shares of Liggett which together with present holdings, would result in ownership in excess of $15m of Liggett's outstanding voting securities. At that time Grand Metropolitan owned approximaely 4.4 per cent of the ordinary shares of Liggett at a cost approaching $15m.

In March 1980 the Liggett group was granted a temporary injunction to block Grand Metropolitan's attempt at increasing its shareholding, although on 24 March Grand Metropolitan had increased its shareholding to 9.5%. The injunction froze Grand Metropolitan's bid for ten days until a court hearing which was scheduled for 2 April. This hearing led to Liggett winning a further injunction barring Grand Metropolitan from acquiring more shares and disposing of its current Liggett shares except in a manner approved by the court.

On expiration of the injunction Grand Metropolitan made its full intentions clear when in mid April it announced an all-out bid for 90.5% of Liggett shares. The proposed tender of $50 for every ordinary share represented an outlay of approximately £190m. Managing director of Grand Metropolitan, Stanley Grinstead commented:

> We estimate that although we will come to borrow money, clearly we will still increase earnings per share at the indicated bid price. The bid will obviously raise borrowings as a proportion of shareholders funds to around 50 per cent but we do not envisage this enduring.
>
> We will keep an open mind about what interests of Liggetts we keep and what we will eventually sell.[7]

Apart from the legal troubles and difficulty of foreign companies winning contested bids in the US, many institutions considered that Grand Metropolitan could end up with a deal safeguarding distribution of J & B Whisky in that market without necessarily taking over Liggett. (IDV's J & B Whisky had been distributed in the US by Liggett's Paddington Corporation since 1937.)

Despite further legal problems, including temporary injunctions, Grand Metropolitan proceeded with its bid for Liggett, through its registered subsidiary in the US, Grand Metropolitan Sub Corporation. Liggett's shares, which had been suspended temporarily, continued trading on 21 April but remained unchanged at $44¼ at the close on 22 April.

On 23 April Liggett announced the sale of its drink and wines subsidiary Austin Nichols, to French drinks group, Pernod Ricard for a price of $95.5m. Austin Nichols accounted for about one-third of the $13m drinks division's profit which meant that it would be sold on a price earnings ratio of 14 or more – almost twice the valuation Grand Metropolitan had put on the group as a whole.

This move threw a shadow over Grand Metropolitan's bid because

[7] *The Times*, 15 April 1980.

Austin Nichols was a main factor in the company's original interest.[8] Not only did Austin Nichols import Pernod and Campari, but also it manufactured one of the leading brands of bourbon – 'Wild Turkey' – and had built up a highly respected nationwide marketing network.

Stanley Grinstead, on hearing of the proposed sale, put forward a counterbid for Austin Nichols but this failed to get even consideration from the Liggett board. As a consequence he wrote to the Liggett board indicating that this sale of a major asset to Pernod Ricard would be viewed as improper in view of Grand Metropolitan's outstanding bid and that they could be sued if Grand Metropolitan's counter-offer was denied at least the opportunity of consideration. Subsequently, Grand Metropolitan advised its American lawyers to take all necessary legal steps to prevent the sale of Austin Nichols to Pernod Ricard.

On 29 April a Delaware court rejected Grand Metropolitan's request for an order to stop Liggett from selling Austin Nichols to Pernod Ricard. However, a Liggett shareholder had also filed suit, but against Liggett to stop its opposition to Grand Metropolitan's offer.

Grand Metropolitan announced its intention to sue Liggett for the sale of Austin Nichols on 1 May. Stanley Grinstead accused Liggett of asset stripping and deliberate obstruction to Grand Metropolitan's offer. He also accused Liggett of trying to sell Paddington, the subsidiary which handled J & B Whisky, which was the best-selling American brand. Grand Metropolitan threatened to cease supply of J & B and also to revoke other contracts it had with Liggett. Ironically, this time the Delaware Supreme Court reversed its previous decision on Grand Metropolitan and allowed the original bid to proceed.

On 7 May the US-based Standard Brands stepped in with a bid for Liggett for up to 45% of shareholding at $65 a share, including an offer for all of Liggett's 7% preferred stock at $70 per share. The two groups also announced a merger once the deal was completed. Standard Brands had long been mooted a possible bidder for Liggett. Its operations included margarine, yeast, nut products, wines and spirits and confectionery. The mainstay of its operations in the UK included Walkers Crisps and Planters Peanuts.

Liggett had contended that Grand Metropolitan's offer was too low and that its own financial advisors had valued the liquidation of assets at over $50 per share. The Standard Brand's merger offer had been valued by Wall Street at around $62 per share. On 10 May Grand Metropolitan threatened to withdraw the J & B Whisky franchise – a move which Liggett was prepared to drag through the courts.

On 15 May Grand Metropolitan announced an increase in its offer for Liggett from $415m to $570m representing a valuation of $69 per share.

[8] Indeed, Grand Metropolitan had for two years made unsuccessful attempts to purchase Austin Nichols, before launching its full-scale bid for Liggett.

(The bid also included an offer of $158.62 per share for the $5.25 cumulative convertible preference stock and $70 per share for the 7% cumulative preference stock.) On 16 May a joint statement from the two companies announced the acceptance of Grand Metropolitan's offer by Liggett.

Including its initial stake in Liggett, Grand Metropolitan spent almost $600m to complete the deal, but the acquisition also picked up $97.5m in cash from the previous Austin Nichols sale.

THE LIGGETT DIVISION ACTIVITIES

The acquisition of Liggett Group Inc by Grand Metropolitan was a logical extension of a productive long-term relationship between the wines and spirits activities of the two companies. The acquisition gave IDV, which is responsible for the operations of the Liggett wines and spirits companies, a much larger base for marketing wines and spirits in the important US market.

Wines and Spirits The Paddington Corporation had distributed IDV's principal brand, J & B Rare Scotch Whisky, in the United States since 1937. By 1970 it had become the best-selling Scotch in America. Paddington also distributes two other IDV whiskys – Royal Ages and Catto's Gold Label. Following Grand Metropolitan's acquisition of Liggett, Paddington was appointed the distributor of three additional IDV brands – Baileys Original Irish Cream, Croft Original Sherry and Croft Distinction Port.

Liggett's other wines and spirits subsidiary is Carillon Importers Ltd, the US importer of Grand Marnier, Bombay English Gin, Absolut Swedish Vodka and Italian, French and Greek table wines.

Soft Drinks Liggett owned two leading soft-drink bottling companies. Each is the sales leader in its franchise territory with approximately half the total soft drink.

With headquarters in Columbia, South Carolina, Atlantic Soft Drink Company distributes its products in most of that state and parts of three contiguous south-eastern states – Tennessee, Georgia and North Carolina. Atlantic is the fourth largest franchise bottler of Pepsi-Cola and also markets Mountain Dew, 7-Up, Dr Pepper, Schweppes and other brands.

Liggett's other soft-drink bottler is Pepsi-Cola Bottling Co of Fresno, which markets Pepsi-Cola, Mountain Dew, and other brands in ten counties of the San Joaquin Valley region of California.

Physical Fitness Products and Sporting Goods Liggett's Diversified Products Corporation led the United States market in sales of physical fitness products, basketball equipment and table-tennis tables.

In March 1980, Diversified acquired Leach Industries, Inc, the major US manufacturer of racquet-ball racquets and a leading distributor of racquet-ball and other accessories.

Diversified's physical fitness products include bar-bells, exercise bicycles, exercise benches, weight-lifting belts, tension hand grips, chest pulls, jump ropes, exercise wheels, and ankle and wrist weights. It provides a full range of basketball and table tennis equipment. Indoor and outdoor recreational games include badminton, volleyball, tetherball, horseshoes and darts.

Pet Foods Allen Products was the fifth largest manufacturer of pet food in the United States. Alpo, its principal product, was the largest-selling canned dog food in the US and has 18% of the total canned market.

Allen's new dry dog food plant in Allentown, Pennsylvania, was completed in late 1979 and produced almost one-fifth of the company's dry dog food in 1980.

Cigarettes and Tobaccos Liggett & Myers Tobacco Company makes L & M, Chesterfield, Lark and other brands of cigarette for sale in the United States.

The Pinkerton Tobacco Company was the largest manufacturer of loose-leaf chewing tobacco in the United States and a producer of other smokeless tobaccos and pipe tobaccos. Pinkerton's principal brand, Red Man, was the largest selling loose-leaf chewing tobacco in the US. Its pipe tobacco included Velvet, Granger and Black Clipper, as well as Edgeworth and several other brands manufactured under licence. Liggett's subsidiary in Brazil, Liggett & Myers do Brasil Cigarros Limitada purchased, processed, and sold Brazilian leaf tobacco in the world market.

LIGGETT'S TRADING FIGURES

For the last four months of the 1980 financial year, Liggett's contribution to Grand Metropolitan sales and trading profits were £155m and £22.4m respectively.

Liggett's overall performance in 1980 amounted to a trading profit of $105m., broken down by industry segment as shown in table 11.3.

INTERCONTINENTAL HOTELS TAKEOVER

On 21 August 1981 Grand Metropolitan revealed that agreement had been reached to purchase Intercontinental Hotels from the US-based Pan-Am Group. The latter had announced its intention to sell only three days previously.

TABLE 11.3 Liggett's performance in 1980, by segment.

Segment	*$m*
Cigarettes	24.0
Tobacco	10.4
Wines and Spirits	24.8
Pet Foods	12.0
Soft Drinks	21.1
Sporting Goods	12.7
	105.0

Source: Company Report 1980

By moving so fast the Grand Metropolitan takeover team led by Mr Stanley Grinstead was able to beat off a host of rival contenders rumoured to have included the giant Holiday Inns group, the Hilton Corporation and four major airlines.

Intercontinental had net assets of only $116m, although this figure did not include anything for management and lease agreements. It owned only six hotels outright and had a minority stake in the London Intercontinental Hotel. But it operated another 76 through management lease and franchise arrangements.

As a result of the deal Grand Metropolitan, which had grown to be Britain's twelfth biggest company partly through a series of massive takeover deals, moved into the top echelon of international hotel operators. Its own 66-strong hotels division, including the London International and Europa, currently ranked second in Britain behind the 800-strong Trusthouse Forte chain.

Stanely Grinstead (the managing director) explained how his group made a head start in the race for Intercontinental. Spurred by thoughts that all international airline operators could be running into fincancial difficulties, his management team began looking for sale possibilities at the beginning of the year.

In July the group was put in touch with Pan-Am by United States investment bankers. As a result Mr Grinstead put in an offer for the hotels division on 9 July but was told by Pan-Am that the division was not for sale. From then on, however, Pan-Am's financial difficulties began to mount and Stanley Grinstead, Mr Orr and deputy managing director Mr Clifford Smith flew out for fact-finding talks with the Pan-Am board.

The talks were only expected to last over the weekend but on Sunday Mr Grinstead made a formal offer.

Mr Grinstead said that Grand Metropolitan had also been helped in discussions because of Pan-Am's fears that rival contenders in the United States could run foul of American anti-trust regulations.

In October 1981 a decision was taken in principle for Grand Metropolitan to merge the Grandmet International and Metropolitan Hotel companies into Intercontinental Hotels Corporation, with effect from 1 April 1982.

The merger of the two companies under a single management would facilitate the development of an integrated marketing approach and increase the ready availability of a larger geographical coverage of hotels for guests.

It was intended to maintain and, wherever possible, to improve the standards of all hotels in the context of their categories and their locations.

DIVESTMENT

In January 1982 Grand Metropolitan announced its intention to sell off almost all of its 26 regionally based hotels – among them the Elizabethan Falcon at Stratford on Avon – to the Queens Moat Houses chain for £30m. The deal was substantially in cash, with Grand Metropolitan getting a Queens Moat stake of around 7% in growth stock.

The company had already announced a programme of rationalization involving the sale of ten of its 18 London hotels, which included the Europa and Britannia in Grosvenor Square, package-tour properties such as the Mount Royal and the Piccadilly, the St Ermin's in Victoria and the Mayfair.

Grand Metropolitan had originally contemplated expanding its provincial chain but the cost of some £30m spread over a time-scale of three to four years was considered inappropriate to the group's plans. The purchase of the Intercontinental Hotels had led to a combined group that was considered to have too large a representation in London compared with the rest of the world.

FINANCE

On 30 September 1975 Grand Metropolitan announced the underwriting of a right's issue of ordinary shares at 50p each which was subsequently 91% subscribed. The proceeds of the issue were used to reduce borrowings, which had risen by £79m from 1973 to 1974. The £37.6m raised by the rights issue and the sale of Grand Metropolitan's interest in the Carlsberg brewery was used to reduce bank overdrafts and short-term borrowings totalling almost £125m.

One of Grand Metropolitan's financial objectives was stated to be the improvement of the 'relationship between borrowing and assets by developing a positive cash flow until conditions are right for further judicious expansion.'[9] Capital spending amounted to £41m in 1976, while cash-flow was held positive at £32m. During this year the relationship of total borrowings to shareholders' funds and deferred taxation was 152 per cent. By the end of 1977 financial gearing had improved to 127 per cent and, after allowing for capital investments of over £58m, net cash surplus was £12.8m.

During 1978 profits attributable to ordinary shareholders increased by over 56% to approximately £81m (after adjustments) and earnings per share to 18.5p. During this year interest charges were substantially reduced by the conversion of 10% convertible unsecured loan stock and by reduced borrowings. The ratio of total borrowings to shareholders' funds (less goodwill) had fallen to about 66% and a cash surplus of £10m remained after investments in fixed assets of £80m. In 1979 a further rights issue raised £49.6m (including premiums) and retained profits amounted to £72.6m. Capital expenditure, however, was increased to nearly £125m and, consequently, short-term borrowings increased by £16m.

After revaluation of the group's assets in 1980 the surplus over previous book values amounted to approximately £565m. This surplus enabled the company to write off all goodwill from the consolidated balance sheet. Following the valuations and including the full effect of the Liggett acquisition, the net borrowings of Grand Metropolitan were equivalent to approximately 46% of shareholders' funds. During 1981 profits from overseas business represented approximately 35% of total profits as against 26% in 1980. This shift in the geographical balance of business was largely attributable to the organization of Liggett and Inter-continental, but at the expense of increasing the ratio of total borrowings to shareholders' funds. In spite of the increase in borrowings, the group generated a cash surplus from its operations after investing more than £160m in new property, plant and equipment.

[9] Company Report, 1976.

Appendix 1 Grant Metropolitan organization (1981) – board structure

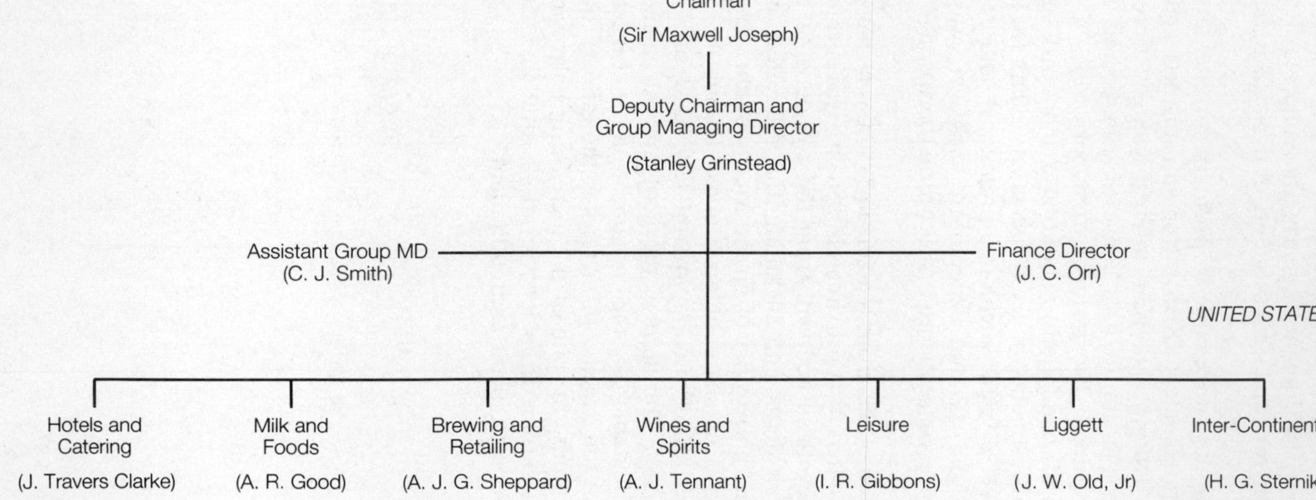

Appendix 2

CONSOLIDATED PROFIT AND LOSS ACCOUNT (£m)

		1981		*1980*
External sales		3,221.2		2,582.6
Trading profit		276.6		212.9
Interest		90.0		60.8
Profit before taxation		186.6		152.1
Taxation		445.2		29.7
Profit after taxation		141.4		122.4
Minority shareholders' interests	4.3		2.4	
Parent company preference dividends	0.5		0.5	
		4.8		2.9
Profit attributable to ordinary shareholders before extraordinary items		136.6		119.5
Extraordinary items		13.2		2.5
		149.8		122.0
Ordinary dividends		38.7		34.0
Transferred to reserves		111.1		88.0

	1981	*1980*
Earnings per share	26.2p	23.3p

	1981	*1980*
Movements in reserves		
Reserves at beginning of year	981.8	432.8
Retained profits for year	111.1	88.0
Adjustments to property revaluation surpluses (1980 surplus on revaluation)	3.7	565.6
Premiums on share issues, less expenses	7.7	0.5
Goodwill and other intangibles acquired during the year	(152.1)	(105.1)
Reserves at end of year	952.2	981.8

CONSOLIDATED BALANCE SHEET (£m)

		1981		1980
Sources of finance				
Ordinary shareholders				
Issued share capital		260.6		256.6
Reserves		952.2		981.8
		1,212.8		1,238.4
Preference shareholders		12.7		12.7
Minority shareholders in subsidiaries		37.2		33.3
Loan capital		910.7		566.5
Taxation				
Deferred	2.0		7.8	
Payable after 30 September 1982	10.5		9.7	
		12.5		17.5
		2,185.9		1,868.4
Invested in				
Fixed assets				
Properties (including freehold and long leasehold of £1,388.4m, 1980 – £1,224.8m)		1,480.1		1,306.5
Plant, equipment and vehicles		411.8		352.6
		1,891.9		1,659.1
Associated companies		48.1		9.5
Investments and long term loans		41.6		34.8
Deferred ACT		21.1		16.3
Currentt Assets	462.5		376.9	
Stocks	451.1		367.4	
Debtors	61.8		46.3	
Short-term deposits and cash and bank balances		975.4		790.6
		2,978.1		2,510.3
Current liabilities				
Short term borrowings (secured – £1.3m, 1980 – (£2.3m)	94.4		73.7	
Creditors (secured – £46.7m, 1980 – (£47.3m)	592.1		502.4	
Taxation payable within one year	83.5		46.6	
Proposed final dividend	22.2		19.2	
		792.2		641.9
		2,185.9		1,868.4

FIVE-YEAR RECORD (£m)

	1977	*1978*	*1979*	*1980*	*1981*
Sources of finance					
Ordinary shareholders' funds	366.4	536.0	688.7	1,238.4	1,212.8
Preference shareholders and minorities	30.1	32.1	40.4	46.0	49.9
	396.5	568.1	729.1	1,284.4	1,262.7
10% convertible unsecured loan stock	122.3	–	–	–	–
Loan capital	353.2	342.9	266.9	566.5	910.7
Deferred and future taxatation	13.9	28.6	21.0	17.5	12.5
	885.9	939.6	1,017.0	1,868.4	2,185.9
Invested in					
Fixed assets	811.3	856.8	937.3	1,719.7	2,002.7
Net current assets	74.6	82.8	79.7	148.7	183.2
	885.9	939.6	1,017.0	1,868.4	2,185.9
External sales	1,640.7	1,850.3	2,170.8	2,582.6	3,221.2
Profits					
Profits before interest	129.6	151.7	179.2	212.9	276.6
Interest	52.0	35.7	43.2	60.8	90.0
Profit before tax	77.6	116.0	136.0	152.1	186.6
Tax	23.8	32.9	30.4	29.7	45.2
Profit after tax	53.8	83.1	105.6	122.4	141.4
Minorities and preference dividends	1.6	1.3	3.5	2.9	4.8
Profit attributable to ordinary shareholders	52.2	81.8	102.1	119.5	136.6
Earnings per share[a]	12.9p	18.2p	21.8p	23.3p	26.2p
Dividends[a]					
Time covered	3.1	3.9	3.5	3.5	3.5
Ordinary dividend per share	4.25p	4.74p	5.75p	6.625p	7.425p

[a] For comparative purposes the figures of earnings per share and times covered in 1977 have been adjusted to show the position had the conversion of the convertible loan stock been effective in that year. In addition, adjustment has been made to take account of the bonus element in the 1979 rights issue.

12 Hanson Trust and Berec

The years 1971–81 were a period of rapid and sustained growth for Hanson Trust in which profits before tax grew from £2.9m (1971) to £49.7m (1981) based upon a programme of aggressive expansion, especially in the US.

At the end of 1981 the company was involved in a takeover bid, this time for Berec Group Ltd, well known for its 'Ever-Ready' Batteries.

Hanson Trust PLC began in 1964 when Wiles Group Ltd, a company then based in Yorkshire, obtained a quotation on the London Stock Exchange, and in that year added to its existing business in the agricultural services industries by acquiring a commercial vehicle distributor, Oswald Tillotson Ltd, of which James Hanson was a director. He had run successful companies in North America and the UK, his family having had important business interests in Yorkshire since the middle of the nineteenth century. During the next three years a number of relatively small private company acquisitions were made, and profit before tax grew from £138,000 in 1964 to £1,218,000 in 1968.

The name of Wiles Group Ltd was changed to Hanson Trust Ltd in 1969 (James Hanson had become chairman in 1965), and in the period up to 1973 a number of UK acquisitions were made of publicly quoted companies (see the section below on acquisitions). Internal development also continued, with a substantial investment programme resulting in profit before tax increasing to £8.2m in 1973.

Hanson's activities were principally based in the UK until 1973, when a major policy decision was taken to commence activities in the United States, and the deputy chairman left the Hanson board and moved abroad to guide the development of the group's overseas interests. From an initial equity investment by Hanson in North America of $3,000 in 1973, a business was built up with annual sales in excess of $1 billion for the year ending September 1981. By 1981 Hanson Trust had become the fourth largest UK investor in North America.

In June 1981 the shares of Berec Group Ltd previously known as Ever-Ready Battery were trading on the London Stock Exchange at 53 pence each. By December 1981 the price had risen to 150 pence as the result of competing takeover bids for Berec from Hanson Trust PLC and Thomas Tilling Ltd.

This case-study traces the developments of these takeover bids and gives further information on the three companies involved. It ends at the point when the board of directors make their final decision between the two rival bidders in their recommendation to their shareholders.

On 8 July following the AGM of Berec the price of Berec shares started to rise rapidly, and on 10 July Hanson made a 'dawn raid' for Berec shares with the share price ending at 94 pence. A 'dawn raid' in 1981 became the jargon used when a company selects shareholders of a company in whose shares it is interested, and makes an offer to buy them direct to the shareholder. Usually, such shareholders are easily identifiable, large institutions such as the insurance companies or pension funds, and often such a raid presages a full takeover bid. The 'dawn raid' of 10 July enabled Hanson to buy just under 15% of the Berec shares. Under the Stock Exchange takeover code, 15% is the limit for such a 'raid'.

Hanson said at the time that no bid for Berec was contemplated and they were merely making an investment. Two weeks later Hanson raised £44m with a rights issue. (In order to make a rights issue a company has to give appropriate notice and join a queue to prevent a number of large issues flooding the market at one time.)

On 4 September 1981, Hanson announced a full bid for Berec. The terms of the offer were:

Berec shareholders would be offered three Hanson shares for every eight Berec shares. As Hanson shares were valued in the market at 294½p on 4 September, this valued the bid at 110p per Berec share, compared to the value in the market on 4 September of 93p. As an alternative, Hanson was willing to make a cash offer for Berec shares of 105p. This put a total value on Berec of £73 million.

The directors of Berec responded rapidly and within two days had announced that they considered the terms of the takeover as totally inadequate, and strongly advised their shareholders not to sell their shares. Mr Stapleton, the Berec chairman, in a letter to shareholders said that the company's assets were worth 194 pence per share, or 225 pence per share in current cost terms. Such proximity between these two levels, he said, demonstrated the recent heavy investment programme undertaken by Berec, and both figures were greater than the Hanson offer of 105 pence. The reason the company's profits had been depressed in the past four years was because of this heavy re-investment programme and the recession, he argued. Berec profits had fallen from a peak of £29m before tax in 1977 to £10.5m in 1980, when the final dividend was halved and lower profits were forecast for the first half of 1981. Mr Stapleton considered, however, that '. . . Berec was at a low point in September 1981, and expected a positive cash-flow within the next twelve months'.

Sir James Hanson, chairman of Hanson Trust, responded with his own letter which pursued the Hanson case to buy Berec. He claimed that the present management of the battery group had not earned an adequate return on its assets, and that it was time for a change. He added that the bid represented an opportunity for the shareholders to benefit, and pointed out that before the Hanson bid the shares had been only 53 pence. His letter to shareholders ended by asking them to consider 'what will be the price if Hanson's offer lapses?'

LETTERS TO THE *FINANCIAL TIMES*:

From L.W. Orchard *29 October 1981*

Sir, – The time is fast approaching when the shareholders of one of the largest and most successful battery companies in the world have to make a decision either to stick with their investment or sell out at a "catsmeat" price to a financial group whose success to date has been achieved by buying companies the brainchild of other people and moulding them into a financial conglomerate. I refer to the Hanson offer to Berec shareholders.

In the highly technical field of electro-chemical systems, the Berec Group has one of the best research teams in the world which has enabled it technically not only to keep up with rapidly advancing technology, but also to initiate new and improved products.

Research, as we all know, costs money. Berec has always had a further problem in that the scale of its manufacturing operations needs support from a substantial engineering division, whose function it is to design plant unobtainable elsewhere, to put together very accurately battery systems at speeds of many hundreds per minute – such developments take several years. In the last few years, no fewer than four new primary systems have been developed, namely alkaline-manganese, silver oxide, zinc air and lithium, which has put considerable strain upon the Berec research development teams.

But that work is now more or less concluded, and as the economies of the world pick up, Berec is ready to take full advantage of increasing markets and further advances in the development and use of battery operated products.

Both its markets in the 110 different countries in which it trades, and its profits should show substantial increases without any assistance from Hanson.

Hanson recognizes this, and that is why it is trying to acquire Berec while Berec's share price is low – depressed by poor financial results in the last two years, and by the depressed state of the London Stock Exchange.

Having spent more than 40 years in the battery industry, I know it better than most, and I also know its great potential. I, therefore, say to my fellow shareholders in Berec, "What can Hanson do for Berec that Berec cannot do for itself?". Answer – nothing.

We are being pressured to relinquish our interest in future Berec profitability in favour of sharing it with existing Hanson shareholders, without Hanson making any contribution whatsoever to that future prosperity.

Through the courtesy of your columns, Sir, I wish to alert Berec shareholders so that they do not fall into the Hanson trap of parting with a very good asset on account of vague assurances from the chairman of Hanson. Do what I am doing. Drop the Hanson paper in the wastepaper basket where it belongs.

From John H. Pattisson *30 October 1981*

Sir – Mr L.W. Orchard, whose letter on the subject of Berec Group appeared on October 29, tells us that for more than 40 years he was in the battery industry and knows it better than most. That letter does not mention that for 24 years Mr Orchard was a director of Berec, which was of course formerly the Ever Ready Company, and that he was its chairman for over 10 years until his retirement in 1979. I should disclose that I am an executive director of Hanson Trust.

First of all Mr Orchards's exposition of Hanson's business philosophy in the first paragraph of his letter must be utterly refuted. Hanson can be unashamedly proud of its record of developing the companies it has acquired over the years, as any examination of its published accounts will show.

In a different capacity I met Mr Orchard in 1972 when the company of which I was then managing director was acting for Crabtree Electrical Industries, which Ever Ready acquired in September that year. In a circular issued then by the board of Ever Ready, under the chairmanship of Mr Orchard, Crabtree shareholders were promised an "exciting future." When the acquisition was completed the price of Ever Ready (Berec) shares, appropriately adjusted for a subsequent rights issue, was 147p. Only a few months ago it was as low as 53p.

In Mr Orchard's letter to you he talks of the "highly technical field of electro-chemical systems" in which Berec is involved and asserts that Berec has kept up with the rapidly advancing technology in the industry. In his chairman's statement in June 1978, Mr Orchard told the Ever Ready shareholders that "in spite of both City and government department references to so-called 'new high technology' batteries, there is neither anything 'new' nor anything 'high' in the context to which they refer, apart from higher costs in using such systems." At the same time, although reporting pre-tax profits £3.7m down for the year at £25.3m, Mr Orchard assured his shareholders that the company was "in good shape." Its reported profits have continued to decline ever since.

The Ever Ready accounts in 1977 showed Mr Orchard as having an interest in 5,737 unrestricted ordinary shares, 75,000 incentive scheme shares and 55,000 share options, i.e. an interest in a total of 135,737 shares. The share register of Berec as at September 11th 1981, shows that he is the registered holder of 3,000 ordinary shares; it does not disclose whether Mr Orchard still has an interest in any Berec incentive scheme shares. Would Mr Orchard, who has offered investment advice gratuitously to your readers, like to let them know what share interest he retains in Berec, and whether he has sold any shares, and if so at what prices, over the past four years?

From L.W. Orchard *2 November 1981*

Sir – Relying on your magnanimity, may I reply to Mr Pattisson's letter to you of October 30th. His letter is, alas, a rather poor example of the art of sidetracking the issue.

Instead of answering my question "What can Hanson do for Berec that Berec cannot do for itself?" he lets himself down by descending to the arena of personal attack on me which begins to look as though this form of behaviour is an agreed Hanson board tactic against anybody who disagrees.

Hanson seems to pay a great deal of attention to the volume of shares that a director or ex-director holds, and appears to judge management by such absurd criteria. Really, Mr Pattisson, you will have to do better than this – if you don't want to give a straight answer why pile your opponent with abuse?

And finally, don't be impertinent – my shareholding in Berec is my affair and I am under no obligation whatsoever to reveal it to anybody – including Hanson.

BACKGROUND INFORMATION ON THE COMPANIES

Berec Group Ltd

Berec is best known for its Ever Ready Batteries which comprise its main area of interest, although the company does have interests in toolmaking, and, of course, cycle lamps. The company has had continuous problems since 1977 when PBT reached £29 million, and the market capitalization of the shares was £140m. In 1980 profits fell and the market capitalization went down to £40m. (See Appendix 1 for financial data on Berec.)

The main problem had been the advance of battery technology involving mercuric and silver oxide and alkaline manganese which offered both smaller battery size and longer life than the Ever Ready traditional zinc oxide product. The group in response began spending heavily on developments, including £51m on fixed assets in the years 1977–80. However, it was still behind with the new technology compared to the major US competitors (e.g. Mallory).

Following the bid from Hanson, the Berec board of directors prepared their defence and circulated a second letter to their shareholders with the publication of their half-year (interim) figures (ending 29 August).

Berec's pre-tax profits of £2.21m for the first half of the 1981–2 year compare with £3.25m for the first half of 1980–1. Revenue had risen slightly from £110m to £118m, but trading profits had fallen from £5.77m to £5.2m. The Berec board commented that the second quarter had shown some improvement and forecast profits of £14m for 1981/2 (£10m in 1980/1), and promised shareholders restoration of the dividend in 1982 to at least the 1980 level of 5.5 pence (1981 saw it cut to 3.4p).

This second letter to shareholders reviewed the 'important structural changes in Berec's business, and in particular the company's adjustment to the impact on its market of new battery technology.' Berec's response to the Hanson charge (in the Hanson document) that Berec management had been taking their time while others forged ahead was that they had invested heavily in new systems and foreign markets.

On 29 October 1981, Berec placed the following quarter-page advertisement in the *Financial Times*:

> With profits improving, markets growing and major investment and cost-saving programmes being completed this year, how can accepting Hanson's offer make any sense?
>
> Berec's profits are now improving. Berec's directors are forecasting attributable profit before taxation of about £14 million in the current year. In the first half of the year such profit was higher than last year's, and the upward trend evident in the second quarter has continued through September when management accounts showed profits fully up to expectations.
>
> Berec is a leader in growing markets. Berec is the market leader in Europe and Africa and the second largest manufacturer of dry batteries worldwide. The markets for zinc carbon batteries and new battery systems, particularly alkaline manganese, are expected to grow in real terms over the next few years – alkaline manganese is expected to grow by 24% per annum in Europe.
>
> Berec's recent investments are about to show returns. Berec's demonstrably superior range of alkaline manganese batteries is to be launched in early 1982. Cost-saving measures have resulted in a

> 10% improvement in productivity in the United Kingdom battery companies, and further benefits are expected next year as start-up losses are eliminated, particularly in Hong Kong.
>
> Berec shareholders should not give away their company at the very moment when the tide is beginning to turn.
>
> That would make no sense at all.

The *Financial Times* made the following comments on the Hanson bid for Berec:

> Although share prices have fallen sharply since Hanson made its bid, Berec's forecast of £14m pre-tax is much better than the market had been anticipating. And the prospective yield at the offer price is over 7%. Despite all that, the odds are that unless Berec can come up with a white knight, Hanson is going to win the day with little or no improvement to its present terms.
>
> This is a reflection of Berec's performance over the last decade. Until the rise in sterling exposed the weakness of its traditional business in the late 1970s, its annual spending on research and development had been running at way under 1% of sales. This effort has been substantially increased, but the group now faces formidable competition in the new systems. It says that by 1985 these products will be producing extra sales of £50m at today's prices, which does not sound like a sensational return on an investment which has already absorbed £40m in the last four years. On a short-term view, the Berec forecast looks quite ambitious – it requires a 53% profits improvement in the current half year. And in the last year or two Berec has had more than its share of "exceptional" problems. (*Financial Times*, 16 October 1981).
>
> Berec arguments for continued independence have centred on the pay-off that should come through from the large investment of the last few years. Unfortunately, there is nothing in the company's record to lend conviction to the promise it now holds out of future success. (*Financial Times*, 29 October 1981).

The Hanson offer was due to close on 31 October 1981, but on the previous day Thomas Tilling Ltd unveiled an agreed last-minute package intended to rescue Berec. The Berec board had agreed with Tilling a one-for-one share offer from Tilling which represented a 20% increase on the price offered by Hanson. Tilling's bid valued Berec at £89.45m, but there was no cash alternative to the share offer (unlike Hanson). Mr Stapleton (Berec chairman) welcomed the Tilling offer, and indicated that the Tilling management style would enable the existing Berec management to get on with their job. In contrast, Hanson criticized the Berec management, calling it 'inept' and promised sweeping management changes. The Hanson response to the Tilling bid was to reply that they would consider it carefully and take their time in deciding what to do.

Thomas Tilling Ltd

Thomas Tilling was a holding company owning a broadly based group of 20 companies operating in diverse trades throughout the world. The pattern of group activities had been developed since 1949, when sales were less than £10m, and growth had been augmented by acquisitions both in the UK and internationally. In the year ending December 1980, Tilling reported profits before tax of £70m on sales of £1,700m. (See Appendix 2 for further details on Thomas Tilling Ltd).

Amongst the companies owned by Tilling, the better-known were Heinemann's the publisher, Pretty Polly (ladies tights manufacturer), and the Cornhill Insurance Company. The management philosophy proclaimed by Tilling was to encourage its companies to manage their own affairs, subject only to central guidance on corporate policy, planning, investment and finance.

The bid by Tilling, agreed with the Berec directors and announced on 30 October 1981, was nearly 30% higher than the Hanson bid. Yet the chairman of Tilling did not regard the price as too generous, and pointed out that Tilling (like Hanson) prided itself on not paying over the odds. He said that the fact that the acquisition would result in a dilution of Tilling's earnings per share would only be temporary.

By the end of 1980 about 35% of Tilling assets of £423m were invested in the USA following £30m of acquisitions and capital expenditures there in 1980. 10% of assets were in continental Europe, and 40% in the UK. Berec as a UK company would represent nearly 25% of the group's enlarged assets, and could thus upset the careful international balance Tilling had built up. The Tilling case for taking over Berec was that Tilling had been looking for a new UK acquisition, and Berec could be used to build up business which could exploit the Ever Ready brand name, and these strategic prospects had tempted it to make its biggest ever bid and also to enter a bid battle for only the second time.

Hanson Trust PLC

Like Tilling, Hanson Trust was a diversified conglomerate and had grown, with record sales and profits each year for the previous seventeen years, on the basis of acquiring basic staple businesses such as foods, basic engineering, textiles and building bricks. (Appendix 3 gives financial information on Hanson.)

Table 12.1 indicates the major acquisitions Hanson had made since 1967 when it acquired Scottish Land Development Limited ('SLD'), a company engaged in the distribution of earth-moving and construction equipment. Two years later the business of Jack Olding, another leading distributor of similar equipment, was purchased, and merged with SLD to become the largest multi-franchise distributor in the UK.

West of England Sack Holdings Limited, a public company, was acquired in 1968 and became, with the later addition of certain milling

TABLE 12.1 Major acquisitions, 1967–1981

	Date acquired	*Cost (£m)*	*Industry*
UK			
Scottish Land Development	February 1967	0.7	Construction equipment distribution
West of England Sack Holdings	June 1968	3.1	Agricultural sack hirers
The Butterley Company	December 1968	4.7	Brick manufacturers, quarriers and engineers
Jack Olding	April 1969	1.7	Construction equipment distribution
National Star Brick and Tile	February 1971	1.4	Brick manufacturers
Castle Brick Company	April 1972	2.7	Brick manufacturers
BHD Engineers	February 1973	12.2	Engineers
Henry Campbell Group	December 1978	4.9	Linen and synthetic yarns and threads
Lindustries	September 1979	27	Linen and synthetic yarns and threads, engineering and polymers
USA		*$m*	
J. Howard Smith	December 1973	32	Animal feedstuffs and edible oil production from menhaden fish
Carisbrook Industries	September 1975	36	Speciality textiles and textile finishing machinery
Hygrade Food Products	April 1976	32	Meat processing and packing
Interstate United	December 1977	30	Food service and vending
Templon Spinning Mill	November 1978	7.25	Speciality textiles
McDonough Co	January 1981	180	Footwear, building materials and hand tools

interests, the Agriproducts Division in the UK.

In 1968 a leading producer of facing bricks, The Butterley Company Limited, provided an important diversification into a basic industry. Its own growth and positive cash-flow eventually led to further acquisitions in this field, including National Star Brick and Tile Holdings in 1971 and, in the next three years, brick-making interests of the British Steel Corporation and the National Coal Board.

In 1973, after Hanson's successful development in the UK which increased profit before tax from £138,000 in 1964 to £8.2 million, a major policy decision was made to invest also in the United States. The first major acquisition was J. Howard Smith, now Seacoast Products Inc, one of the two major companies engaged in the production of animal feedstuffs and edible oils from Menhaden, a fish primarily caught in the Gulf of Mexico.

Seacoast produced profit before tax of $13 million in its first full year of ownership, and, since much of the purchase price was on a deferred basis, with its good cash flow it became a source of funds for further development in North America. In 1975 the speciality textile business of Indian Head Inc was acquired, and is now managed by Carisbrook Industries Inc. In the following two years Hygrade Food Products Corporation, a publicly quoted company and one of the leading US meat processors, was purchased and a successful public tender offer was made for Interstate United Corporation, a professional food service management company. In each of these cases the purchase price was less than the book value of the underlying assets acquired, and the companies have continued to earn significant profits.

In 1979 the successful takeover of Lindustries Limited, a diversified UK industrial company, brought with it Barbour Threads Limited, a natural partner in Northern Ireland to the thread business of the Henry Campbell Group acquired by Hanson in November 1978. In addition, Lindustries had a number of engineering and polymer companies mainly in the United Kingdom which tied in well with existing businesses of Hanson. Lindustries was acquired at a material discount to net asset value.

In January 1981 McDonough Co was acquired at a total cost of $180 million. McDonough operated in the USA in three industries: footwear, building materials and hand tools. It employed approximately 8,000 people.

McDonough Co

Footwear Endicott Johnson manufactured, imported, wholesaled and retailed footwear, principally in the popular price range. A full range of men's, boys' and infants' footwear was produced in ten factories. In addition, Endicott contracted with overseas and United States suppliers for the production of footwear designed to its specifications for re-sale through its own distribution system. Its 689 retail stores and leased departments in 39 states sold footwear for the entire family.

Over 50% of Endicott's net sales were made through its retail outlets. Some 40% of Endicott's sales were represented by sales to approximately 18,000 independent retailers, whilst the balance related to footwear manufactured to customers' specifications and sold under private brand names. The majority of the manufacturing facilities were located in New York State, with other plants located in Illinois, Missouri and Pennsylvania. These plants had an annual capacity to produce approximately 12 million pairs of shoes. The distribution of footwear was co-ordinated through eight distribution warehouses in Missouri, New York and Ohio, with a combined storage capacity of approximately six million pairs of shoes.

Building Materials The building materials group constituted Gulf Coast Portland Cement and Houston Shell and Concrete based in Texas which produced cement and ready-mixed concrete.

The Portland Cement plant in Houston had an annual capacity of approximately 1,000,000 tons of finished cement. Portland cement is produced by grinding gypsum with semi-finished cement clinker. The annual production of clinker was approximately 330,000 tons, and the balance of the clinker used for finished cement production was purchased from domestic and foreign sources. Just over a third of the finished cement produced by Gulf was used by Houston Concrete in the production of ready-mixed concrete and road base materials. Substantially all the cement, ready-mixed concrete and related products manufactured by Gulf and by Houston Concrete were sold within a 120-mile radius of the city of Houston. There were 12 ready-mixed concrete batch plants with capacities ranging from 90–400 cubic yards of ready-mixed concrete per hour.

Hand Tools The hand-tool group had its headquarters in Parkersburg, West Virginia, and manufactured a broad line of lawn, garden and industrial hand tools under the brand names of 'Ames' and 'Douglas'. Founded in 1774, Ames was the world's leading shovel manufacturer, and other products included hose reels, rakes, forks, hoes, garden shears and pruning tools. In addition, Ames was a major manufacturer of a complete line of winter tools, such as snow shovels and snow pushers.

Products were sold nationally to approximately 2,200 customers, including independent distributors of hardware, garden supplies and industrial products and also to large national and regional retailing operations.

In the financial year ended 31 January 1980, McDonough earned a pre-tax profit of $36.3 million on sales of $450.6 million. McDonough, which accounted for stocks on a 'LIFO' basis, disclosed net tangible assets at 31 January 1980 of $144.5 million. If stocks had been valued on a 'FIFO' basis, net tangible assets would have totalled $186.1 million.

PRINCIPAL ACTIVITIES OF HANSON

Industrial Services: USA

The industrial services business of Hanson in the USA was conducted through Carisbrook Industries Inc and Interstate United Corporation. McDonough was also included in this division.

Carisbrook Industries Inc was engaged in the manufacture of speciality textiles through 11 trading companies. These included Native Textiles, the leading US manufacturer of fine-quality lace; Woven Goods, one of the two leading US producers of typewriter and computer impression tapes; and Crawford, America's second largest manufacturer of cushions and soft furnishings. The speciality nature of Carisbrook's products, which were outside the mainstream of the textile industry, enabled it to continue to produce an improvement in profit in 1980 despite difficult trading conditions.

Interstate United Corporation served over three million meals a day to Americans in schools, hospitals, factories, offices, recreational centres and sports arenas, both through food vending machines and cafeteria meals. Supply of foodstuffs and management of contracts were largely administered on a local basis at 2,500 customer locations spread over 40 states. Although certain foods were supplied by Hygrade, the majority were purchased from third parties. Interstate were the fifth largest food management concern in the USA, with more than 2,300 customers. During 1980, Interstate largely succeeded in offsetting the effects of the recession in the automotive industry through continuing development of its recreational feeding interests.

Industrial Services: UK

The industrial services business in the UK was organized in five main operating groups, Butterley Building Materials Ltd, SLD, Barbour Campbell, Northern Amalgamated Industries Limited and Lindustries Limited.

Butterley Building Materials Limited was one of the largest brick-making companies in the UK. It was engaged in the manufacture of high-quality facing bricks and light-weight aggregates. Facing bricks are primarily utilized for the exterior of buildings because of their durability and appearance. Current production was nearly three hundred million bricks per annum at eleven locations. Butterley had achieved considerable success in exporting its products to Europe while at the same time increasing its domestic market share. Reduced energy costs were also achieved through the introduction in one of its plants of Butterley's own design suspended-ceiling Hoffman Kiln, believed to be the most thermally efficient brick-firing system currently in use.

SLD provided products and services to the construction industry through six principal companies. It was the largest multi-franchise distributor of earth-moving and construction equipment in the UK, supplying the Clark Michigan range, Bobcat, Demag excavators, Barber-Greene asphalt plant and pavers, Euclid dumptrucks, Galion-BJD road planers and Rexnord compactors. It also manufactured and hired site amenity units and, through 40 depots nationwide in the UK and nine depots in Australia, hired out pumps and de-watering equipment. By far the most important contribution to SLD's earnings was the pump-hire business, and SLD was the leading company engaged in this business in the UK.

Barbour Campbell was the principal manufacturer of linen and synthetic yarns, threads and allied products in Northern Ireland and was formed by merging Barbour Threads Limited, a part of the recently acquired Lindustries business, with Henry Campbell & Company Limited. The division also had subsidiaries engaged in motor car distribution, builders' merchanting and carton manufacturing.

Northern Amalgamated Industries Limited was principally engaged in the manufacture of industrial honeycomb and building panels and in the distribution of laboratory glassware and vehicle building supplies.

Lindustries was engaged in engineering and polymer activities. Included amongst Lindustries' subsidiaries were Robert Morton DG Limited, a leading UK manufacturer of brewhouse equipment, and Delanair Limited, manufacturers of heat exchange equipment for automobiles. Its polymer business included wet-suit sheeting and specialized plastic mouldings. In 1980, its first year in its present form, profit before taxation was £5.4 million on sales of £65.3 million.

Agriproducts: USA

Hanson's Agriproducts business in the USA was conducted through two companies, Hygrade Food Products Corporation and American Farm Products Inc, which owned Seacoast Products Inc.

Hygrade Food Products Corporation was one of the USA's largest meat processors with nine processing plants and one hog slaughtering plant. Hygrade was concentrating its future development on processed meats such as frankfurters and hams which provide higher margins than fresh meat. Hygrade's brand names included Ball Park and Hygrade frankfurters and West Virginia hams and bacon. Its products were sold mainly to large retail chains.

Seacoast Products Inc was engaged in the production of animal feedstuffs and edible oils derived from menhaden fish rich in protein. Seacoast had a fleet of 31 carrier vessels, 62 purse seiners and 21 spotter planes to locate and catch menhaden, primarily in the Gulf of Mexico and to a lesser extent off the eastern seaboard. Its catch represented approximately 11% of all fish landed in the USA.

Seacoast's five processing plants extract the oil from the mehaden, dry and grind the solids into fish meal which is sold as a protein additive to fast-growth diets for poultry, weaning pigs and other livestock. The fish oil, which is relatively low in saturated fats, is used to make margarine and in the manufacture of cosmetics, paint and linoleum.

Agriproducts: UK

The Agriproducts division of Hanson in the UK was based on British Agricultural Services Ltd, which included the original business of Hanson, agricultural sack hire and milling and agricultural merchanting. The company also sold agricultural and light earth-moving equipment, in particular Massey Ferguson farm equipment.

The investment philosophy of Hanson was to search out basic industries and to apply close financial control whilst allowing free management right down to the local level. Management was motivated on the basis of its own planned objectives and consequent performance, with the emphasis on increasing earnings, positive cash flow and strict control of capital employed.

Hanson had been a conglomerate well known for its acquisitions. In October 1980 Hanson announced the purchase of McDonough of USA, a company with interests in footwear, building materials and hand tools, for $180m. In November 1980 Hanson made an offer for Central Manufacturing and Trading Group Ltd, and in May 1981 had made a £12m offer for G.H. Downing, a building materials manufacturer, but was outbid.

Seven months after buying McDonough, Hanson Trust recouped $50m by selling the cement operation which contributed only 10% of McDonough group profits. It is said that Hanson has an unfailing touch with acquisitions, and over eighteen years Hanson sales and profits have consistently risen.

The Hanson search for prospective acquisitions was in the hands of two men. Gregory Hutchings, a 34-year-old MBA with both industrial and investment experience, handled the whole of the UK market, and monitored virtually all the publicly quoted companies other than those which eliminate themselves under the Hanson acquisition criteria, i.e. the Hanson objective of increased earnings per share, and net worth year after year, eliminates all but low-risk, non-fashion areas where demand for the product is considered constant. Thus Hanson was unlikely to invest in micro-chips. In the USA the same monitoring was undertaken by 35-year-old Eric Hanson (no relation to Sir James), who was a Cambridge graduate with a diploma from INSEAD, and had been with Hanson since 1976.

Some insight into Hanson investment in the USA was given by an interview, reported in a Company Report, of David Clark, President of Hanson Industries Inc (USA) by David Frost.

> FROST You're well qualified to answer this question, David. In the time that I have commuted across the Atlantic, I have seen a lot of British firms come to America and brave a very competitive market over here and many have failed. Why do you think that Hanson Trust has succeeded?
>
> CLARKE It seems to me that there are a variety of reasons for

Hanson's success. I think it probably goes back to Sir James Hanson himself and his early business experience over here – before Hanson Trust – and the fact that both he and Sir Gordon White had travelled extensively in the United States and were very familiar with American ways. Hanson Trust planned its move by buying companies that had co-operative people and not people who resisted them.

FROST And why did they pick you first and why did you say yes to them?

CLARKE Over here, Hanson tends to be interested in companies which are looking to be bought. They don't, as a rule, like unfriendly takeovers. Our business was owned by my family who, for tax reasons, wanted to diversify their holdings. Hanson was interested because we were in a basic industry – the fish meal business – and it fitted well with the type of companies Hanson owned in the UK.

FROST It must have been an interesting, maybe even painful adjustment to make – was it very different to go from being the family proprietor to part of an industrial management company – was that an adjustment?

CLARKE Yes, but I expected that, so it didn't come as a surprise. The difference between a publicly held company and one privately held, is the degree of accountability which the management has to have. In a private business, you don't have to justify the money you spend or what you're doing, except to yourself. Whereas, in a publicly held company you do have to be extra responsible because you're not the owner. Hanson has thousands of shareholders and all of the management feels a strong fiduciary responsibility towards them.

FROST When running Seacoast, after Hanson acquired it, and now as president of Hanson Industries over here, how does the relationship work with head office, how much freedom of decision do you have?

CLARKE The day-to-day decisions are made by the line management because they are the people closest to the action and on the firing line.

FROST If their decisions are wrong. . . ?

CLARKE Well, it just so happens that we've been lucky enough to make a few right decisions in a row. Seriously though, 99% are made by the local divisional management. This is the only sensible way to run a company because these people are the most qualified to make the decisions. Besides, most people enjoy running their own show. Decisions pertaining to acquisitions or capital investments, which involve laying down permanent company money have to flow up to the very top of the company. Sir James would get involved in a large expenditure of capital or even for that matter a small one because that's permanent money.

FROST In your observation, are American business methods different from British, do they require slightly different skills? Would you do the job the same way if you were doing it in England?
CLARKE They're basically the same. Both are capitalistic societies. Hanson has been successful over here, as they have in the UK, because they understand what motivates people and I don't think that there is a difference between the UK and US, as to what motivates them. You may run into some instances where things are different, our legal system is vastly different to the legal system in the UK.
FROST More demanding, more complicated?
CLARKE I think it's more complicated, yes.
FROST David, what's the common thread between your companies, between Seacoast, Hygrade, the speciality textile businesses and Interstate?
CLARKE There are several common threads. The first is that they are all basic businesses; there's a minimum of high technology involved; they are fairly easy to understand. Also, they all have to do with either food or industrial services in some way or another. Seacoast supplying to the chicken business; Hygrade supplying hot dogs and hams; Interstate being a food service management business; and the speciality textile businesses. If you look at Hanson's acquisitions they tend to be in the food, clothing, building materials and service sectors.
FROST And assimilating all of those companies? If an attractive proposition came up tomorrow, could Hanson assimilate something more or do you have to have a period of consolidation now?
CLARKE I think very definitely we could take on something now. Our last acquisition, Interstate, is well into the group and over the past two years we have increased the management strength of Hanson Industries and we have shown we are ready for something new with our recent offer for McDonough.
FROST So how do you see the future – it's been a big growth from Hanson's original acquisition of Seacoast and you? Can it go on growing in proportion, is it possible to continue growing in size?
CLARKE While Hanson in the US is over a billion dollar company in sales, it is not necessarily large by United States standards. Exxon reports quarterly profits of over a billion dollars, so I think there are plenty of people standing in front of us.
FROST Do you get people coming up to you and if so how do you reply, saying here is a large American company now under "foreign" ownership, British control and this is the life blood of America seeping away into Britain. When people say that how do you reply?
CLARKE The undeniable fact is that US industry, as well as farm land and houses are being acquired at a greater rate by foreigners than ever before, but that's only demonstrating that the American is

becoming a global citizen. I'm sure most of us realize that it's a two-way street because the larger US companies have been buying into Western European companies and assets for a long time. Indeed, the USA owns more overseas than is foreign-owned here.

FROST What would you say, if you had to try to sum it up, will decide the future success of (a) Hanson Industries and (b) your own management in the USA?

CLARKE Well, I think that Hanson Industries has developed into a proven company over the past five or six years. It began with a very nominal investment. To be successful, all we had to do was stay with the original concept and maintain it. We now have the base and this is a favourable environment in which to expand. The opportunities are out there and it's a question of being patient and working hard enough to find them. Then make sure that they operate successfully after we buy them.

FROST And given that, what does Hanson Industries demand from you?

CLARKE I think it demands from us, everybody over here, a great deal of patience and perseverance. We must be very selective and make sure that every investment meets all Hanson's criteria – there must be no growth just for the sake of size. And then to persevere, to make sure that each of the companies purchased is operating at its most efficient capability because this is a game of efficiency. Here in the United States, if one is not efficient one gets pushed out of business by someone who is a little bit more so. One has to keep that edge sharp as well.

FROST Patience, perseverance plus a bit of luck.

CLARKE Plus a bit of luck, it always takes a bit of luck.

One reason why Hanson may not be popular as a takeover bidder is that it is never over-generous with its terms. Inevitably, bluff can play a role in a bid, and it often suits Hanson to be thought of as being quite capable of just dropping the offer if it is not accepted early. Also, the Hanson management are not noted for trying to win over the victim's board with sweet words. The directors of Berec had no illusions about what the Hanson management thought of them or about their likely position if the bid went through. They had no doubt remembered the Lindustries Company taken over by Hanson after a bid battle in 1979, where not one of the original directors remains on the board. By contrast, however, the takeovers by Hanson in the USA have been agreed bids, and the existing directors have invariably remained to manage the subsidiary. A Hanson director says 'This is possibly because of the different priorities of managers in the two countries. US managers often have large lumps of stock in their own business, whereas in the UK managers seem more concerned to protect their position. We sometimes find when we take over a company in the UK it doesn't really know why it is in business. We seek to instil an increased sense of profit responsibility.'

The Hanson management method is a system of decentralization, which means that the group employs only 18 people at its London HQ. The role of the HQ is confined to broad policy, financial control and allocation of finance. There are no frills like marketing, legal, pensions, industrial relations or purchasing services.

These jobs are the responsibility of the chief executives out in the various businesses, each of whom will have his own financial controller. In the UK four of the five divisional chief executives have been with Hanson for at least ten years, and the fifth had been running the Barbour Campbell Group for years before it was bought by Hanson in 1978.

Only one of the five has spent any time in any of the other divisions, and all have risen to the top through their own division. Such decentralization leaves little room for central HQ trappings that sometimes arrive with a new acquisition. Lindustries had a head office of 50 people, which has now disappeared, and the division is run by the chief executive and two accountants.

The objective is to ensure that responsibility for profit performance belongs to the operators in the field, and the financial performance of each is closely monitored from the centre (a parallel operation takes place in the USA with the six Hanson divisions there). Throughout the year, the divisions are checked for performance against profit targets, cash-flow targets and capital expenditure (the chief executives require approval for any capital expenditure down to the last £500). The pay-off for the managers for accepting and achieving these targets comes in the form of an incentive scheme related to profit performance, and a business making profits of £1 million could have up to five managers on incentive payments. Incentives of 20% of annual salary are not uncommon, and 50% not unknown. Performance is related to the return on capital and the incentive payments depends on an improvement over the previous year. This ensures some reliability as inflated returns within one year will come through, and make the following year's target more difficult to achieve. It has been argued that such attention to short-term profits is against the long-term profits interests of the group, but the Hanson directors reply that as Hanson is not involved in high technology (demanding high R & D investments), then it can expect rapid payback from its investment. To demonstrate this, Mr Martin Taylor (a director of Hanson) says,

> Butterley, a building materials manufacturer, was making profits of less than £400,000 when Hanson acquired it in 1969. Acquisitions and internal growth took the figure up to £1.75 million by 1972, and without any further acquisition of significance up to £5.5 million in 1981 (which was not a good year in UK for house building materials). Butterley has not attempted aggressively to increase its

market share of the UK brick market, but it has steadily pushed into higher-quality ranges and developed specialized strengths in particular sectors. Without the need for major new investment, the business has developed successfully under its own steam, and has thrown up cash to help develop other parts of the Hanson Group.

FURTHER DEVELOPMENTS

At the beginning of November 1981 following the Tilling bid for Berec (agreed with the Berec directors), Hanson had to decide whether to continue by increasing its offer or to sell the Berec shares it had acquired. If Hanson chose the latter course, then they would make a profit of £4½m, and it wouldn't be the first time that they had adopted that course, when as opening bidders they had driven a share price up and then sold at a profit. However, by agreeing the Tilling bid, the Berec directors had declared their hand and put a price tag on their company.

On 4 December Hanson responded to the Tilling offer by increasing its bid for Berec, and also bought a further 5% of the Berec shares at 150 pence to bring its holding to 21%. The new Hanson offer was 150 pence per Berec share, valuing the company at £95m, whereas the Tilling offer of one for one valued each Berec share at 144 pence.

Berec responded by advising shareholders to take no action pending further communications from the board. Mr Martin Taylor said that 'Hanson had been convinced that a higher bid was justified now that they had been given access to additional information from Berec which had been exclusive to Tilling, but now under the City takeover rules had been made available to Hanson.' The *Financial Times* of 5 December 1981 commented

> On the basis of the known facts, Tilling will be hard pressed to offer a lot more. Its original terms would have diluted its profits per share by upwards of 5%. It will have to seek its own shareholders' approval if it wants to offer more shares, and its balance sheet is already beginning to look quite highly geared with debt representing over two-thirds of shareholders' funds. But tiresome financial considerations sometimes take second place in a corporate slugging match. Berec shareholders should hold on tight – and trustees of those pension funds which sold out at 95p in Hanson's dawn raid last July might care to make a note in their diary.

On 16 December 1981 the Berec board withdrew its support for the Tilling bid, and advised shareholders to take up the Hanson offer. Berec said that they had received assurances about the future of the company's management and employees. The Tilling finance director said that they had been informed of the announcement, but were 'reserving their position' and their offer was still open, having been extended to 31 December 1981. Merchant bankers S.G. Warburg who had been advising the Berec board said that the company might still accept an improved offer from Tilling.

Three days later, on 19 December 1981, the Berec board placed the following quarter-page advertisement in the *Financial Times*:

Revised Offers from Hanson Trust PLC

The board of Berec has written to Berec shareholders recommending acceptance of the Hanson offers, whose first closing date is on 22 December 1981. However, in view of the likely Christmas postal delays, there is set below a press announcement issued on 16 December, which includes the text of the board's recommendation.

Berec Group Limited ("Berec") recommends offers by Hanson Trust PLS ("Hanson")

The directors of Berec announce that they have written to the shareholders of Berec recommending the offers by Hanson and withdrawing their recommendation of the offers from Thomas Tilling Ltd ("Tilling").

Members of the Berec board have had two meetings with Sir James Hanson and some of his board colleagues, during which assurances have been given to the Berec board regarding the future of Berec, its management and other employees. Sir James Hanson has reaffirmed his belief in the future and has stated that Hanson does not intend to make major changes to the Berec Group.

The Berec board believes that the revised Hanson offers are more advantageous than the Tilling offers, particularly because Berec ordinary shareholders have the choice of a cash offer in addition to an offer of Hanson convertible loan stock. Tilling has not indicated that it will increase its offer for the ordinary shares of Berec. The Berec directors and their advisers, S.G. Warburg & Co Ltd, consider the terms of the revised Hanson offer to be fair and reasonable, and the Berec directors unanimously recommend all shareholders to accept the revised Hanson offers, as they intend to do in respect of their own holdings. Before deciding whether to accept the cash offer of 150p or the offer of convertible loan stock of Hanson, the directors advise shareholders to consider their own tax position and, if they are in any doubt, to consult their own professional adviser.

Appendix 1 Berec Group Ltd

INTERIM RESULTS – HALF-YEAR ENDING 29 AUGUST 1981 (£m)

	Half-year 1981	*Half-year ending 29 August 1980*
Revenue	118.79	110.12
Trading profit	5.2	5.77
Interest	(2.99)	(2.49)
PBT	2.21	3.25

GROUP PROFIT AND LOSS ACCOUNT – 52 WEEKS ENDED 28 FEBRUARY 1981 (£000)

		1981		*1980*
Turnover				
United Kingdom Companies		129,893		118,961
Overseas Companies		111,396		110,751
		241,289		229,712
Trading profit		17,066		19,475
Net interest payable		6,529		2,290
Profit before taxation		10,537		17,185
Taxation		2,993		6,176
Profit after taxation		7,544		11,009
Minority interests		199		1,023
Profit before extraordinary items		7,345		9,986
Extraordinary items (net)		(1,455)		186
Profit attributable to shareholders		5,890		10,172
Dividends:				
Preference shares	14		14	
Ordinary shares	2,245		3,728	
		2,259		3,742
Profit retained		3,631		6,430
Earnings per share		11.10p		15.12p

BALANCE SHEETS AT 28 FEBRUARY (£000)

	1981	*1980*
Source of capital		
Share capital	16,715	16,694
Reserves	111,473	111,035
	128,188	127,729
Minority interests in subsidiaries	4,465	5,677
Loan capital	20,714	8,600
Deferred liabilities and credits	13,855	17,272
	167,222	159,338
Employment of capital		
Fixed assets[a]	93,820	89,096
Subsidiary companies	–	–
Investments	1,344	717
Current assets		
Stock	87,048	81,531
Debtors	48,176	46,351
Cash and deposits	12,054	10,336
	147,278	138,218
Current liabilities		
Creditors	37,912	39,029
Taxation	4,211	3,377
Bank loans and advances	31,704	23,515
Dividends	1,393	2,772
	75,220	68,693
Net current assets	72,058	69,525
	167,222	159,338

[a] Of which: Plant and equipment £36m; land and buildings: Freehold £43m, Long leasehold £11m, Short leasehold £3.6m.

TEN-YEAR RECORD (£m)

	1981	*1980*	*1979*	*1978*
Sale to third parties				
UK companies	129.9	119.0	114.3	109.6
Overseas companies	111.4	110.7	100.6	84.4
	241.3	229.7	214.9	194.0
Gross exports	62.3	50.8	53.3	53.3
Profit before tax	10.5	17.2	20.3	25.3
Tax	3.0	6.2	7.5	9.5
Profit after tax	7.5	11.0	12.8	15.8
Minority interests	0.2	1.0	2.0	1.5
Dividends	2.3	3.7	3.2	2.8
Profit retained before extraordinary items	5.0	6.3	7.6	11.5
Source of capital				
Share capital	16.7	16.7	16.7	16.6
Reserves	111.5	111.0	85.8	80.4
	128.2	127.7	102.5	97.0
Minority interests	4.5	5.7	10.4	8.5
Loan capital	20.7	8.7	11.2	14.0
Deferred liabilities and credits	13.8	17.2	16.4	11.4
	167.2	159.3	140.5	130.9
Employment of capital				
Fixed assets	93.8	89.1	55.1	49.8
Goodwill	–	–	–	–
Investments	1.3	0.7	0.7	0.8
Net current assets	72.1	69.5	84.7	80.3
	167.2	159.3	140.5	130.9

	1972	*1973*	*1984*
Profit before tax as % of sales:	14.1	17.0	14.3
Profit before loan capital interest and tax as % of capital employed:	26.9	31.2	24.3
Dividend per share (gross) in pence:	3.8	3.9	4.1
Earnings per share in pence:	8.6	11.6	10.3

1977	*1976*	*1975*	*1974*	*1973*	*1972*
96.4	72.9	61.0	51.4	40.5	34.4
75.9	56.8	42.9	37.8	30.5	25.7
172.3	129.7	103.9	89.2	71.0	60.1
41.9	29.5	22.6	16.3	12.4	10.9
29.0	16.4	12.4	12.9	12.2	8.6
10.5	8.0	6.0	6.3	5.2	3.5
18.5	8.4	6.4	6.6	7.0	5.1
2.1	1.3	1.0	1.0	0.7	0.5
2.5	2.3	1.7	1.5	1.7	2.0
13.9	4.8	3.7	4.1	4.6	2.6
16.5	16.5	13.1	13.1	13.1	8.6
73.8	38.0	28.2	24.2	18.3	16.0
90.3	54.5	4.13	37.3	31.4	24.6
8.2	6.0	5.2	5.0	4.6	3.4
15.3	16.6	16.9	12.3	4.1	1.3
9.0	14.4	11.8	8.0	4.9	4.6
122.8	91.5	75.2	62.6	45.0	33.9
47.9	39.5	39.2	36.7	29.5	26.9
7.4	7.7	7.7	7.7	7.7	–
6.5	1.9	1.7	1.2	1.1	1.1
61.0	42.4	26.6	17.0	6.7	5.9
122.8	91.5	75.2	62.6	45.0	33.9

1975	*1976*	*1977*	*1978*	*1979*	*1980*	*1981*
11.3	12.0	16.0	12.5	9.4	7.5	4.25
20.4	21.9	34.5	21.4	16.3	12.1	7.8
4.6	5.4	5.9	6.5	7.1	7.8	4.9
9.8	11.5	25.2	21.9	16.4	15.1	11.1

	Turnover (net) %	Profits (£000)
Principal activities		
Battery and allied activities	83	7,122
Other activities[a]	17	3,142
Associated companies	–	273
	100	10,537
Geographical analysis		
UK	40	11,024
Rest of Europe	25	(1,462)
Africa	28	9,147
Rest of world[b]	7	(1,916)
Associated companies	–	273
	100	17,066
Net interest payable		6,527
		10,527

[a] e.g. manufacture of electrical plugs and cables.

[b] The 'Ever-Ready' brand name was owned by Union-Carbide in USA and could not be used by Berec.

Employees

Weekly average number of employees: 15,499 of whom 9,592 were in UK.

Appendix 2 Thomas Tilling Ltd

PROFIT AND LOSS ACCOUNT FOR THE YEAR TO 31 DECEMBER 1980 (£m)

		1980		*1979*
Group sales		1696.6		1416.2
Group profit before interest and tax		98.7		103.6
Interest		28.0		22.5
Group profit before tax		70.7		81.1
Tax		14.1		10.5
Group profit after tax		56.6		70.6
Deduct:				
Amount attributable to minority shareholders	0.3		0.4	
Extraordinary items	4.3		3.1	
		4.6		3.5
		52.0		67.1
Dividends:				
Preference dividends	0.5		0.5	
Ordinary dividend	19.8		18.1	
		20.3		18.6
Retained profits transferred to reserves		31.7		48.5
Earnings per ordinary share		21.5p		29.4p

BALANCE SHEETS AT 31 DECEMBER 1980 (£m)

	1980	*1979*
Capital employed		
Tilling ordinary shareholders' interests		
Ordinary shares issued	52.7	51.6
Premiums on issues of shares	118.7	110.8
Reserves	303.8	272.5
	475.2	434.9
Preference shares issued	10.5	10.5
Total share capital and reserves	485.7	445.4
Deduct: Goodwill – premiums less discounts on acquisitions	62.3	58.5
	423.4	386.9
Minority shareholders' interests	3.2	4.1
Debenture and other loan capital	203.9	202.5
	630.5	593.5
Use of capital		
Fixed assets	277.6	251.4
Cornhill Insurance Co. Ltd – Net assets	35.7	30.1
Associated companies	5.9	4.0
Investments	92.1	99.4
	411.3	384.9
Current assets		
Stocks and work-in-progress	254.8	242.2
Debtors	289.5	285.9
Certificates of tax deposit	4.7	2.1
Bank balances and cash	40.6	27.9
	589.6	558.1
Current liabilities		
Creditors	255.0	254.1
Bank overdrafts and short-term loans	91.1	78.8
Tax	4.3	6.0
Dividends – Thomas Tilling Ltd	20.0	10.6
	370.4	349.5
Net current assets	219.2	208.6
	630.5	593.5

FIVE-YEAR RECORD (£m)

	1976	*1977*	*1978*	*1979*	*1980*
Group sales	671.3	811.2	1026.4	1416.2	1696.6
Group profit before interest and tax	52.1	63.1	74.7	103.6	98.7
Group profit before tax	41.9	53.9	64.9	81.1	70.7
Net profit available for distribution	27.2	35.3	52.5	67.1	52.0
Retained profits transferred to reserves	20.9	25.7	41.7	48.5	31.7
Earnings per ordinary share	16.3p	18.3p	24.6p	29.4p	21.5p
Dividend per ordinary share	3.485p	4.315p	4.818p	7.0p	7.5p
Dividend cover-times	4.8	3.9	5.1	3.9	2.8
Group funds employed					
Fixed assets	117.6	129.3	158.8	251.4	277.6
Net assets of Cornhill Insurance Company	17.2	22.1	24.4	30.1	35.7
Associated companies	2.2	2.0	4.2	4.0	5.9
Net trading assets	117.3	132.2	176.3	257.4	265.0
Goodwill	37.7	40.7	45.4	58.5	62.3
Total funds employed at the year-end	292.0	326.3	409.1	601.4	646.5
Represented by:					
Ordinary capital and reserves	196.1	255.6	303.3	434.9	475.2
Preference capital and minority interests	14.4	15.0	14.9	14.6	13.7
	210.5	270.6	318.2	449.5	488.9
Debenture and other loan capital	61.0	71.3	83.9	202.5	203.9
Bank overdrafts and short-term loans	27.6	31.2	67.2	78.8	91.1
Investments, bank balances,etc.	(7.1)	(46.8)	(60.2)	(129.4)	(137.4)
Net borrowings	81.5	55.7	90.9	151.9	157.6
Return on average funds employed[a]	18.8%	20.4%	20.3%	20.5%	15.8%
Gearing[b]	32.0%	19.5%	25.0%	28.0%	27.0%
Net tangible assets per ordinary share[c]	95.2p	102.5p	120.2p	145.8p	156.6p

[a] The return on average funds employed is the group profit before interest and tax as a percentage of average funds employed, being the mean of the funds at the beginning and end of each year.

[b] Gearing is the net borrowings as a percentage of total funds employed, less goodwill.

[c] Net tangible assets per ordinary share are represented by ordinary capital and reserves, less goodwill.

Appendix 3 Hanson Trust PLC

FINANCIAL YEAR ENDING 30 SEPTEMBER 1981 (£m)

	1981		1980	
Sales		855.9		684.3
US Industrial Services	453.6		242.9	
US Agriproducts	213.9		222.4	
UK Industrial Services	188.4		219.0	
Trading profit		54.1		40.2
US Industrial Services	32.1		12.1	
US Agriproducts	7.2		8.8	
UK Industrial Services	14.8		19.3	
Interest and expenses		4.4		1.1
Pre-tax profit		49.7		39.1
Tax	14.9		13.7	
Net profit		34.8		25.4
Minority interests		0.8		0.5
Extraordinary credit		0.3		0.6
Available to shareholders		34.3		25.5
Dividends	10.9		9.1	
Retained earnings		23.4		16.4
Earnings per share (25p ordinary)		31.2p		23.2p

PROFITS (£m)

	Year ending	
	1981	*1980*
USA		
Carisbrooks (speciality textiles)	13.0	7.8
Interstate (catering)	6.1	4.3
Endicott Johnson (footwear)	7.8[a]	na
Ames (handtools	5.2[a]	na
Hygrade (meat processing)	5.4	4.7
Seacoast (fishmeal)	1.8	4.1
	39.3	20.9

UK		
Butterley (building materials)	5.5	5.8
Lindustries (engineering, polymer)	4.9	6.6
Barbour Campbell (yarn and thread)	1.9	3.0
SLD (pumps and construction equipment)	1.9	3.1
British Agricultural	0.6	0.8
UK total	14.8	19.3
Less interest, etc.	4.4	1.1
Total profits before tax	49.7	39.1

[a] Eight months only.

BALANCE SHEET AT 30 SEPTEMBER (£m)

	1980		*1981*	
Assets less liabilities				
Fixed assets		91.8		128.7
Investments		6.1		3.7
Current assets				
Stocks	73.7		154.7	
Debtors	74.7		106.0	
Listed securities	6.1		22.6	
Proceeds receivable from bond issue	10.4		–	
Cash and short term deposits	51.2		175.3	
	216.1		458.6	
Deduct				
Current liabilities				
Bank overdrafts	28.7		36.0	
Current loan instalments	3.8		11.9	
Creditors	91.0		146.7	
Taxation	10.9		15.3	
Dividend	5.1		6.3	
	139.5		216.2	
Net current assets		76.6		242.4
		174.5		374.8
Financed by				
Ordinary share capital		26.8		27.4
Reserves		93.7		137.7
		120.5		165.1
Preference share capital		0.2		–
Minority interests		2.4		2.8
Loans		42.5		191.2
Deferred liabilities		8.9		15.7
		174.5		374.8

TEN-YEAR STATEMENT (£m)

	1980	*1979*	*1978*
Sales	684.3	658.0	604.6
Profit before taxation	39.1	31.2	26.1
Earnings per ordinary share	23p	18p	16p
Assets less liabilities			
Fixed assets			
Land and buildings	41.4	44.1	30.8
Other	50.4	47.4	39.6
	91.8	91.5	70.4
Investments	6.1	6.7	1.2
Current assets	216.1	209.9	160.9
	314.0	308.1	232.5
Deduct current liabilities	139.5	148.0	98.4
	174.5	160.1	134.1
Financed by			
Ordinary share capital	26.8	26.8	16.8
Reserves	93.7	80.0	57.9
Ordinary shareholders interests	120.5	106.8	74.7
Preference share capital	0.2	0.2	0.2
Minority interests	2.4	2.2	4.1
Loans	42.5	40.0	42.4
Deferred liabilities	8.9	10.9	12.7
	174.5	160.1	134.1
Assets per ordinary share	112p	100p	82p

1977	*1976*	*1975*	*1974*	*1973*	*1972*	*1971*
477.4	322.2	75.7	71.1	51.7	36.4	28.8
24.4	19.2	12.1	10.4	8.2	4.5	2.9
14p	11p	7p	7p	6p	4p	3p
29.6	30.8	19.3	13.6	5.2	4.4	3.4
27.0	25.5	17.4	11.6	7.9	6.8	4.5
56.6	56.3	36.7	25.2	13.1	11.2	7.9
0.9	1.4	1.5	3.4	3.4	0.8	–
135.1	132.1	77.4	49.7	45.1	28.7	17.1
192.6	189.8	115.6	78.3	61.6	40.7	25.0
63.4	65.2	48.2	32.9	20.4	17.7	11.7
129.2	124.6	67.4	45.4	41.2	23.0	13.3
16.8	16.8	16.8	7.9	7.5	6.3	3.7
50.2	40.5	31.6	25.4	23.4	10.1	3.8
67.0	57.3	48.4	33.3	30.9	16.4	7.5
0.2	0.2	0.2	0.2	0.2	0.2	0.2
3.5	3.6	1.5	0.4	0.2	0.1	0.1
40.7	48.4	11.1	8.8	9.2	4.8	4.8
17.8	15.1	6.2	2.7	0.7	1.5	0.7
129.2	124.6	67.4	45.4	41.2	23.0	13.3
77p	66p	55p	47p	46p	28p	17p

Appendix 4 The Battery Market

BACKGROUND

Technological developments in consumer products have caused the demand for compatible battery performance, with the result that the market has greatly altered its profile. More battery-powered appliances have been introduced, e.g. toys, TV games, electronic watches, clocks, calculators and cameras in addition to the traditional torches and radios.

The most widely used battery is the zinc carbon system which on the surface has changed little in appearance since its invention in 1868. However, significant changes in construction have taken place which have given this battery a significant improvement in performance and leak-proof qualities. The advantage of this battery system over others is its ability to recover between periods of usage and it has been further developed to meet the differing power requirements from the ever-widening range of battery-using equipment available today. Zinc carbon batteries are the most cost-effective system available.

Alkaline manganese batteries are more expensive than zinc carbon and are particularly suitable for sustained high-rate power discharge requirements such as cine cameras and cassette recorders. They also perform well at extremes of temperature.

The third variety are miniature batteries such as silver oxide, mercuric oxide and zinc air batteries. These are used in electronic watches and calculators as well as hearing aids where there is a demand for a minaiture battery giving low voltage power.

The popularity of sizes of batteries depends upon the popularity of equipment which uses them, and the trend is towards smaller size batteries such as the R6. Other popular sizes are the R20 and R14 size, although in the UK there is still a significant market for the power pack sizes such as the PP9.

Battery prices vary according to grades and in August 1982 the price of a zinc carbon HP7 made by the market leader, Ever Ready, was 16½p including VAT, while the Power Plus grade sold at 24½p and the alkaline manganese at 43½p. Similar differentials by grade applied to the other battery sizes.

MARKET SIZE

The total market for dry batteries in 1982 was estimated to be approximately £100m at manufacturers' selling prices. The growth from

£50m in 1974 could be attributed mainly to inflation and changes to expensive type of batteries rather than volume growth.

Ever Ready is the major UK dry battery manufacturer producing all systems, namely, zinc carbon, alkaline manganese, silver oxide, mercuric oxide, zinc air, lithium and rechargeable batteries. Vidor Limited, a subsidiary of Crompton Parkinson, also manufactures zinc carbon batteries. Duracell manufacture mercuric oxide and silver oxide batteries in the UK and import their alkaline manganese range. Ray-O-Vac, USA, withdrew from the zinc carbon battery market in 1976 and now market only a range of mercury and silver oxide batteries in the UK. Imports take about 14% of the UK zinc carbon market and come chiefly from Hong Kong and Germany, while the majority of the alkaline market is imported from Europe, Japan and the USA. The estimated total dry battery market in 1982 is divided as shown in table 12.2, with brand shares as shown in table 12.3.

TABLE 12.2 1982 Dry battery market by type: volume

Zinc Carbon	79%
Alkaline	14%
Mercury, silver, zinc air & rechargeable	7%
	100%

TABLE 12.3 Market shares

<table>
<tr><th></th><th>Zinc carbon</th><th>Mercury, silver & zinc air</th><th>Alkaline</th></tr>
<tr><td>Ever Ready</td><td>71%</td><td>8%</td><td>7%</td></tr>
<tr><td>Duracell</td><td>–</td><td>36%</td><td>82%</td></tr>
<tr><td>Vidor</td><td>6%</td><td>–</td><td rowspan="4">11%</td></tr>
<tr><td>Varta</td><td>8%</td><td>14%</td></tr>
<tr><td>Imports</td><td>6%</td><td rowspan="2">42%</td></tr>
<tr><td>Others</td><td>9%</td></tr>
<tr><td></td><td>100%</td><td>100%</td><td>100%</td></tr>
</table>

PART III

Management styles

13 Ariel Industries

The Ariel Group had its origins in a small company established in 1920 to supply accessories to the foundation garment industry. The company was associated with an American manufacturer from whom it purchased machinery of advanced design for the manufacture of these products.

Largely as a result of this technological advantage, the company enjoyed a period of high profitability and growth. By the mid-1950s, however, with the post-war boom over and no new products available, the company began to feel the effects of much stiffer competition, and earnings declined.

Consultants were called in and at intervals over a period of several years they introduced work study, production planning, sales forecasting and other schemes, but these had little lasting effect.

Early in 1962, the family directors were advised to go to the market for a professional manager. Acting on consultants' advice, they invited Mr Kenneth Edwards to join Ariel as general manager of the main operating company. This he did, in the belief that Ariel was a company big enough to do something with, but small enough to enable his style of management to be applied.

MR EDWARDS'S BACKGROUND

Mr Edwards grew up on his parents' farm where business in general buying, selling, and the affairs of the farm in particular were topics of family conversation in which the Edwards children were immersed from an early age. He was encouraged by his father to take initiatives and follow them through to their conclusion.

These started in a small way, but at all times a high degree of realism was achieved by the father insisting that the children use their own money. Whether they were buying and selling produce or rearing cattle, they were responsible for the initial outlay and for all subsequent decisions right through to eventual marketing.

Kenneth Edwards's association with manufacturing industry was originally intended to be of strictly limited duration. On leaving Cambridge University in 1952, he decided to take a job in industry for six months to see what it was like. After all, family longevity was such that this would still leave seventy years or so for farming!

Joseph Lucas Ltd was chosen from his list of potential employers as the company he would least mind embarrassing by resigning after only six months. In the event, however, he felt compelled on his first day with the company, to confess his short-term intentions to the education officer who had recruited him. It was suggested that it would be helpful to all concerned if these limited objectives were not widely circulated.

However, at the end of six months when he finally explained his position he was offered a series of interesting assignments which induced him each time to delay his resignation.

Ten years passed, punctuated by a succession of challenging appointments at Lucas, but his inherent interest in farming remained strong. Eventually, at Leicester a satisfying compromise was found; a new challenge with Ariel, but close enough to his farming interests to offer something of both worlds.

THE PROBLEMS OF BEING THE NEW GENERAL MANAGER

At this time Ariel's management was facing severe labour relations problems, and their products were in the last few years of their life.

Earning power was totally in the areas which were about to collapse, and other areas which had a future just had not been developed.

Mr Edwards soon saw that for a rescue operation to succeed he would first of all have to get management back into control of the company, and then quickly diversify into product areas with growth potential. To provide the wherewithall to fund the diversification he would have to find ways of releasing capital from the declining areas of the business. To shore up the operation until the new ventures paid off, he would need to squeeze the last drop of earnings out of the older products.

The company was in an overdraft position at this time, and although asset-heavy, considerable reorganization would be necessary before under-utilized assets could be released. The business was still under family control and decision-making was highly centralized. For example, even quite minor items of expenditure in both domestic and overseas operations required approval of the managing director. There was some reluctance to come to terms with the major decisions that needed to be taken if the company was to be re-established on a profitable basis. It had to be made very plain that unless firm action was taken in a number of areas, there would be no future for the company.

During the difficult few years following Mr Edwards's appointment there was pressure from some shareholders to sell off certain areas of the business in which the break-up value was considered to be greater than that of a going concern. This suggestion was resisted by Mr Edwards, who began to buy shares heavily in the company himself at this time to strengthen his opposition to such a move.

During this period he set up an employee share bank as a trustee company, through which employees had an indirect, risk-free stake in the equity of the group. Interest on these investments was related to dividends declared on Ariel shares.

By the end of 1973 Mr Edwards's shareholding was approximately 20% and the share bank held some 14% of the equity. No other shareholder held 10% or more.

PLANNING AND DIVERSIFICATION

In February 1969 Mr Edwards was appointed chairman of the holding company and in presenting his first report, for the year ending 30 November 1968, he noted the considerable cost of the company's diversification programme, and the continuing decline in demand for the traditional range of foundation garment accessories, which together had resulted in a fall in pre-tax profits of 30% compared with the previous year.

However, by the end of 1970 the chairman was able to report that the company had completed the re-organization programme it had set itself, and that he was pleased with the way new product lines were developing. He stated:

> The main ones are industrial fasteners, light engineered products including automatic assembly equipment and polyurethane formulations and components. These give us a product range which is wide enough to insulate us from the fluctuations in fortune in any particular industry, without losing for us the flexibility and good communications which a company of this size can enjoy.
>
> What is equally important is that the products themselves are to some large extent complementary, and the management skills required to run them are very similar. We are in the happy position where we have adequate cash resources to take every opportunity which presents itself to supplement these lines with profitable additions.[1]

In 1974, formal planning was based upon a requirement that there should be 15% growth in net assets in real terms each year, so that capital employed doubled approximately every five years. This objective was coupled with a wish to pay dividend of 5% on capital employed each

[1] This quotation and those which follow are from company sources, 1974.

year. Under 1973–4 tax arrangements these goals required pre-tax earnings of about 35% on capital employed.

In discussing his company's future, Mr Edwards explained that it was his intention to obtain separate stock market quotations for each operating subsidiary as soon as it had a satisfactory five-year track record.

> I do not believe in large companies, and I am not convinced that economies of scale are as clearly defined as is often believed. A turnover of, say, £3,000,000 from 300 people, turning in about half a million pounds a year, is a meaningful company. I believe that a company of that size is, in terms of performance and employee relations, an optimum unit.

In reorganizing Ariel, a number of people had developed certain talents for this type of operation, which made it important in Mr Edwards's view to adopt a strategy which would allow the company to capitalize on these reorganizational skills. It was also considered that the company had considerable management expertise in making simple products in very large quantities, and selling these to industry. Everything the company touched was said to fit precisely into that pattern.

Mr Edwards emphasized that in his opinion the key to corporate planning was not so much in setting objectives, but getting the necessary action to achieve those objectives: 'We put stress on making sure we have action going, consistent with what we want to achieve, but do not bother too much about the decimal points of the objective.'

There were considered to be very few technical factors limiting company achievement: a more significant constraint on growth was felt to be the amount of disruption that people can stand: 'Generally, you come up against the fact that if you push very hard you have to make a great many changes, and there is a limit to what you can do without making people unhappy.'

EMPLOYEE RELATIONS

Mr Edwards expressed his strong belief in free enterprise, but had certain reservations about the way in which the rewards of free enterprise were distributed. He had sought, and felt that he had to some extent succeeded in achieving, a system whereby salary increases were determined solely by performance and were not left to the subjective judgement of himself or any other member of the company. By developing a mathematical model which clearly showed the economic outcomes of each of the main strategies open to the company, he was able to develop and agree with the workpeople and their unions a wages policy which guaranteed automatic awards as the 'value added' within the company increased.

At Ariel, suggestions were invited from all sections of the company regarding future programmes, which were then jointly determined. It was agreed in advance what proportion of value added should be paid out, taking into consideration the need to plough back sufficient earnings to support the company's desired level of growth.

Programmes were measured in advance to determine expected yields, and employees knew in advance their salary expectations for that year. Rewards were paid month by month, according to value added, as the programme was achieved.

The scheme was seen as an important break-through by Mr Edwards, and had fundamentally altered a situation from one in which the company simply reacted to trade union demands, to one in which the company took the initiative in developing its reward system.

ORGANIZATION

In 1972 the group was enlarged by acquisition, and the possibility of future acquisitions was causing the company to review its management structure. It was hoped to organize the company in such a way that Ariel's direct management style and excellent employee relationships were not endangered. Within the group it was hoped that subsidiaries could grow independently until they reached a stage where some part of their equity could be given a separate stock market quotation. Reorganization would make each major subsidiary an operationally autonomous unit. Mr Edwards explained the company's organization in March 1974 as follows:

> Ariel Industries Ltd is the Public Holding Company. In line beneath this, but not in importance, we have Ariel Management Services Ltd employing a small number of people who are the central team: myself, our data processing and central accounting staff; altogether about 20 people.
>
> Everyone else is employed in subsidiary companies under a chief executive with his own structure. We have developed a style of management where we have effort all the way down the line. I think we have harnessed our people's imagination better than most. I do not see management as brilliance. The need for the genius is totally overrated. Our success is due to depth of interest rather than brilliance at any one level. Every operation is organized on such a scale that we get intelligence all the way down.
>
> The emphasis on the all-rounder by Business Schools is wrong. Management is a matter of getting together a team of people each with a particular cutting edge that is well honed. One of the things I have to do is to stop my people who have been on business courses from trying to dabble in things they are not good at. It is important to realize the business you are in and not to think that you can do

everything. There is a world of difference between knowing the management techniques and being able to make things happen. The problem is to find people in the market place with any entrepreneurial streak. We are after people whose instincts are right, who in a business situation can make things happen – these are the sort of men I want, not the smart Alecs.

We do have failures of course, perhaps one out of three. Some want to sit in the office and apply theory, but that does not make things happen. I bring people in at a lower level, and give them project work, throw them in and even let them make a mess of it at times. A man in his late twenties or early thrities may be put in as a general manager of something small, but something that is his. If he makes a success of that he moves onto something bigger and we are away. That is how I think managers are bred.

FINANCE

In April 1973, Ariel increased its authorized share capital from £750,000 to £1,750,000 in order to achieve three objectives:

1 To provide for a one-for-one scrip issue to shareholders as a step towards creating a freer market in the company's shares
2 To provide a block of unissued shares which could be used as part of the consideration in any future acquisitions
3 To qualify the company for trustee status.

With regard to the second of these objectives, whilst the company was primarily interested in cash acquisitions, it was recognized that cases could arise where equity was required as part of the consideration, and for this reason unissued shares should be available. There was little merit, in Mr Edwards's opinion in 'throwing paper around'. If one company issued shares to buy another, a larger company resulted, but what contribution did that make to the economy?: 'To finance our acquisitions we release cash from existing operations. If I had to issue equity to do it, who would I be fooling?'

Gearing had not been used by the company in its expansion programme, but it was anticipated that this would become necessary in the future. To this end the company would be prepared to accept one pound of debt capital for every two pounds of equity assets.

THOMAS HUNTER LTD AND GRETONE LTD

In July 1972 the shareholders of Thomas Hunter Ltd accepted a £1.8 million cash offer from Ariel for the whole of the issued share capital of their company. Hunter's was a long established private company manufacturing and marketing metal closures for the food industry, and equipment for applying those closures.

The company had a good profit record, but recently a change in marketing policy by some major food manufacturers had caused a swing away from closures of the type produced by Hunter. This change in demand, coupled with a totally inadequate investment programme, had caused a marked decline in earnings.

It was Ariel's intention to make whatever revenue and capital expenditure was necessary in order to regain business lost over the previous two years, and reverse the downward trend in profits. At the time of the acquisition, Hunter had approximately £900,000 in cash, surplus to requirements of the existing business.

On completion of the sale, Hunter's previous board of two directors retired and Mr Edwards and Mr George Beebee, a fellow director of Ariel, were appointed to the Hunter board. It was their intention to make as few changes as possible in the staffing of Hunter's and build the new management team substantially from existing executives. Reorganization at Hunter's was expected to be completed during the second half of 1974.

Although cash resources were used to purchase Hunter, Ariel, was able to free enough cash from subsidiaries to clear its overdraft and leave a substantial amount of cash in hand by the end of 1972, which it was considered would put the company in a good position in its search for further acquisitions during 1973. However, it was stated Ariel policy not to become involved in asset stripping, but to find a company complementary to its own and which would benefit from joining the group. An acquisition would only be of interest to Ariel if it could be left operationally intact, and given positive help in its development.

Gretone, Ariel's engineering subsidiary, was located in north-west England, at St Anne's-on-Sea, about 150 miles from its parent company's Leicester base.

In addition to mould and die manufacture, the company also produced test pieces and other components on a batch production basis for the aircraft and atomic energy industries. In 1973, about 25% of Gretone's output was for the aircraft industry.

The company occupied a new freehold factory, purchased in 1972, and with adequate space for a threefold expansion if required. Manufacturing facilities included jig borers, profile grinding machines, lathes, milling machines, cylindrical and surface grinding machines. There were also fabricating and some heat-treatment facilities.

Gretone operated as an autonomous unit under its managing director, Mr Alan Armitage, earning a pre-tax profit of £86,000 in 1973, on a turnover of £360,000, from its 70-strong, skilled work force.

At the end of 1973, Ariel acquired S O B Engineering Co Ltd, a somewhat smaller company then Gretone, and situated at Blackpool, a few miles north of St Anne's. This business was acquired as a result of a legal action by Ariel against its former owner who had also been an executive of Gretone. The value of this acquisition to Gretone was considered to be primarily its skilled labour force of 40 men.

Mr Armitage had transferred one of his own staff to S O B as works manager, but it was also occupying his own time to a significant extent in March 1974. Gretone had a full order book for the whole of 1974 with sufficient work for both factories. There was no intention at this time of combining operations at one site. It was considered doubtful, in any case, whether many of the men would be prepared to travel the few miles involved if operations were centralized at St Anne's. Because of the demand for skilled labour in the area, S O B employees would have little difficulty in finding alternative employment close to their present workplace.

Mr Armitage's main activity was in developing new business and negotiating with existing customers. Although located in the north-west of England, Gretone's work was also obtained from firms in other parts of the UK. The Republic of Ireland, too, was an important outlet, accounting for about 10% of Gretone's sales in 1973.

Both Mr Armitage and his planner/estimator considered it was necessary for Gretone's to have its own product. In common with other sub-contractors in the engineering industry, the company was considered to be vulnerable to the economic fluctuations of that sector, and would be among the early sufferers of a down-turn in business.

Nevertheless, in early 1974, subcontract toolmaking was a very profitable activity for Gretone.

Mr Armitage considered that about 35 people was probably an ideal size for a toolmaking business, providing rather more flexibility than Gretone enjoyed, especially when work was less plentiful. However, by careful planning and estimating, Gretone was able to compete successfully with smaller companies, especially on delivery, even though they might be undercut on price from time to time, by their competitors.

Gretone required a product of its own to provide some insulation from the economic fluctuations of its industry, and also to provide the basis for growth. Mr Edwards considered this so important that he devoted much of his time in the spring of 1974 to analysing how this might be achieved.

'Gretone is a very successful unit, but not yet large enough to be totally independent', he commented. 'We need to buy something to put with Gretone to achieve two things. Firstly, to build up the company to the right size, and secondly, to give it an "own product" content it its sales.' Mr Armitage did not envisage this to be a mass-produced product, but rather one which would utilize the company's precision engineering skills.

DEVELOPMENTS, 1980–1986

Ariel's fortunes began to decline rapidly from 1980 and by 1982, group trading profit before tax had slumped to just over £27,000 compared with over £137,000 in the previous year. (See Appendix 1.)

During this difficult period Mr Edwards strove to maintain the viability of the employees' share trust and in a letter to shareholders (Appendix 2) he put forward a proposition to outside shareholders which involved an invitation to sell their shares to the trust at a price of 30p (which was well above the 'low' of that year). Although dividends were held constant over this period, the chairman was pessimistic regarding the prospects for 1983 and thus anxious that shareholders should have the opportunity to cut their own 'losses' in the short term.

In 1985 only about 10% of Ariel's shares were held by outside shareholders, the rest being held jointly by the share trust and the directors. No dividends were paid in 1983 and 1984 although some of the profits made during 1980–3 were ploughed into new product development; the latter represented a diversification away from the traditional manufacturing business and into chemicals and soil-less crop-growing techniques.

The company ran into losses at the end of 1983 and these rose heavily through the years to 1986. (See Appendix 3.) In September of that year the employee trusts – of which there were now three, owning in total, 75% of the equity – were considering buying the company's older engineering businesses, Steels and Busks and S & D Rivet (industrial fasteners). This was a move basically to protect jobs and although neither business was particularly profitable, S & D Rivet was considered to have firmer long-term prospects.

Appendix 1 Ariel Industries Plc and subsidiaries

COMPARATIVE RESULTS, 1978–82 (£000)

	1982	*1981*	*1980*	*1979*	*1978*
Fixed assets	6,350	6,146	4,120	3,694	3,036
Net current assets (including advance corporation tax)	1,592	1,876	2,247	1,880	1,861
Capital employed	7,942	8,022	6,367	5,574	4,897
Turnover	7,702	7,175	8,506	6,778	6,229
Profit before taxation	27	137	1,028	813	717
Return on capital employed (after deducting taxation payable)	0.0 %	1.7 %	16.1 %	13.4 %	12.9 %
Earnings per share after diluted tax charge	0.02 p	2.29 p	17.13 p	12.40 p	10.55 p
Net dividend per share	1.352p	1.352p	2.704p	2.384p	2.134p

Appendix 2 Chairman's letter to shareholders, 11 August 1982

TO THE MEMBERS OF ARIEL INDUSTRIES plc

Dear Member,

In my statement contained in this year's Report & Accounts I mention that the directors have decided that there is a need for them to extend the application of the employees' share trusts so that these trusts can resume their long-standing role as 'last resort' buyers of the company's shares. The purpose of this letter is to explain the background to this decision, the steps which are being taken to implement it, and exactly how shareholders can take advantage of it if they so wish.

The initiative stems from our awareness that the future for the manufacturing sector of industry in this country is far from bright and consequently that there is a need for us to embark upon a major diversification programme. To do this, without recourse to shareholders for more capital, we shall need to reinvest the bulk of our earnings for the next four or five years, and this will inevitably restrict the amounts available for dividends. Being aware that a number of our shareholders rely upon dividend income and so will not be happy to accept a reduced payout for some years, we feel under an obligation to ensure that there is a ready market for their shares at some reasonable price should they wish to sell.

As you can see from the resolution to be put to members at the forthcoming Annual General Meeting, the directors are asking for authority to make available to the trustees of the employees' share trusts financial assistance not exceeding £1 million to enable the trustees to continue to operate as 'last resort' buyers of the company's shares. The intention is that the share trusts will, through their stockbrokers, undertake to buy at 30 pence any shares that are offered to them for a period of one calendar month commencing on Monday 23 August 1982. As the purchases will be made through the Stock Exchange shareholders can expect to receive 29.15/16 pence less the normal commissions. It is necessary for the purchases to be made in this way because the employees' share trusts cannot offer to purchase the shares direct without making a formal bid, and this would be expensive due to the professional fees involved.

The sum of £1 million has been arrived at to cover the possibility that all outside shareholders may wish to sell. To keep funds of this magnitude available is expensive, and so it is the present intention of your directors to limit the offer to one month. However, should the number of acceptances be such that the residual outside holdings are not sufficient to maintain a listing on the Stock Exchange, the offer will be automatically extended and I shall write to all remaining shareholders explaining the position as it then stands.

As shown in the latest Report & Accounts I have an interest in 1,208,899 shares which represent 20.1% of the issued capital of the company. This includes 100,000 shares held by my wife and 206,000 shares in my family trusts. My fellow directors hold a total of 7,900 shares (.1%), and the trustees of the Ariel Industries Employees' Share Trust (previously known as S & B Employees' Share Bank) hold a total of 1,794,000 (29.9%). In addition, the trusts established for overseas employees currently hold 12,022 shares.

I have been informed by the trustees of each of the employee trusts that it is not their intention to take advantage of this offer and furthermore, to minimize the funding required, your directors have agreed not to sell any of the shares they hold personally. However in my capacity as trustee of family trusts I must reserve the right to recommend acceptance for the shares held in those trusts.

The trustees' offer is at a price considered to be a fair one by Messrs Thomas May & Co, the company's auditors. It is being made so that existing shareholders who wish to sell can dispose of their holdings, in whole or in part without any concern that the size of the market will not be sufficiently large to take all the shares offered. Sadly the market in our shares has for many years been a narrow one, as was shown in April and May of this year when the price dropped below 20 pence. It recovered only when we announced the current initiative. Since then uninformed press comment has caused a further rise which your directors feel is not likely to be sustained.

Current trading levels still reflect the continuing recession and it is likely that the group as a whole will break even in the six months to 30 September 1982. I feel duty bound to point out that dividend prospects are uncertain and consequently that it is likely that when the current offer lapses the share price will drift to significantly lower levels.

I wish to emphasize that the company will endeavour to maintain its listing on the Stock Exchange and that members wishing to retain their holdings on a long-term basis are free to do so. As early indications are that the resolution will be approved at the Annual General Meeting, it is important that those who wish to sell should instruct their stockbrokers accordingly. The present offer is for a limited time and it is by no means certain that there will be any subsequent offers, and so I strongly recommend those shareholders who are unsure as to whether or not they should take advantage of it to consult their professional advisers. Those, who have no professional advisers are free to contact the company brokers, Messrs Smith Keen Cutler, Exchange Buildings, Stephenson Place, Birmingham B2 4NN, Telephone No. 021-643 9977, who will give them all necessary help and advice.

Appendix 3 Ariel Industries Plc and subsidiaries

COMPARATIVE RESULTS, 1983–86

	1986	*1985*	*1984*	*1983*
	£000s	*£000s*	*£000s*	*£000s*
Fixed assets	5,301	5,752	6,195	6,250
Net current assets	1,778	1,739	1,517	1,467
Capital employed	7,079	7,491	7,712	7,717
Turnover	9,837	9,995	8,481	8,906
Net profit (loss) before tax	(370)	(198)	(120)	35
Earnings per share (p)	(4.91)	(2.34)	(0.56)	0.04
High	38[a]	30	30	30
Low	28[a]	23	18	19

[a] To 15 August.

14 Habitat-Mothercare

BACKGROUND

The history of the Habitat-Mothercare group is one of explosive growth by merger and acquisition in recent years, and the dynamism and vision of one man – Terence Conran.

Terence Conran, Habitat's founder, was born in London in 1931, educated in Dorset and trained as a textile designer at the Central School of Art in London. He worked at the Rayor Design Centre and was one of a team of young designers to work on the 1951 'Festival of Britain'.

In 1952 he set up as a freelance designer making furniture in a London basement studio. As the business grew, a larger workshop was opened, a catalogue published and a small showroom added. The business continued to expand, and after a spell as a café owner, Conran moved his factory to Norfolk.

In 1956, the design group, Conran Associates was added, soon to become one of the foremost design groups in Europe, handling retail, office, product and graphic design contracts for leading companies worldwide. It has offices in London and Paris.

In 1964, he opened the first 'Habitat' shop in London's Fulham Road. The store's concept, stock and retailing style was very much part of the 'swinging sixties'. It used design as a marketing medium integrated into the new look being pioneered by Quant, Hockney, Bailey, Biba and others of that era. It soon became the place to be seen at. The Habitat look had started to be noticed.

Conran moved slowly, getting the concept right in a single shop before opening others. His expansion of the business was slow in coming, progress was methodical and highly researched. By 1978 Habitat had 25 stores in the UK, with trading profits at a modest £2m.

Having secured the UK base, Conran turned to expansion, first in Europe, then to the USA. The record of British retailers abroad is a mixed one. The British retailer is often shunned as an intruder in the European market and often outshone in the United States by far more stylish and aggressive groups. Conran's record is patchy but improving.

In the United States in 1977, he opened the first Habitat-type store. He was prevented from using the Habitat name as another organization controlled that trade mark. He chose instead, Conran Stores. Success was slow, and losses continued until 1982 when at last 'Conrans' reached breakeven and started to become profitable the following year. The group now has plans for more expansion in the USA.

Habitat's European adventure was more successful than the US expedition. Habitat was warmly embraced in France and then expanded into Belgium.

1981 was an important year for the company. Habitat was launched on the stock market, but the investors were at first not impressed. The reason for going public was a need to raise funds for expansion. Conran held 20% of the equity personally.

The next development in the Habitat saga saw Conran's most daring move yet. The newly public company bid for and formed a merger with the Mothercare Group in January 1982. At that time Habitat's market capitalization was around £50m, with assets of £15.4 million, sales of £67.2 million and net profits after interest of £4.4 million. Mothercare was more than twice the size of Habitat, controlling net assets four times greater than Habitat.

The new group, now called Habitat-Mothercare plc, continued its expansion in Europe, the USA, and lately in Iceland and Japan.

In the 1983 New Year's Honours List Terence Conran was given a knighthood.

In April 1983 the Habitat-Mothercare group completed the takeover of Heal and Son plc, the London furniture retailers.

In October 1983 the group took a 48% share in the sprawling Richard Shops chain which it acquired from Hanson Trust, in partnership with the Richard Shops management and the merchant bankers, Morgan Grenfell. Richard Shops is treated as an associated company in the accounts.

The number of stores owned by the group in 1985 was:

Habitat, Heals, Conran's	84
Mothercare and 'Now'	462
Richard Shops	204
	750

Total sq footage controlled 2,842,000 sq ft by Habitat-Mothercare plc.
Source: Company Accounts

STRUCTURE AND PHILOSOPHY

The Habitat-Mothercare Group is organized around three main divisions – Habitat, Mothercare and Richard Shops, each a semi-autonomous unit.

TABLE 14.1 Highlights of financial performance

	1985	*1984*	*% change*
Turnover	446.7	375.4	+19
Trading profit	43.9	35.2	+25
Profit before taxation	36.5	30.6	+19
Basic earnings per share	22.3p	18.2p	+23
Dividend per share	8.0p	6.5p	+23

Source Company Accounts (for 53 weeks ended 31 March 1985) (1984 – 52 weeks)

In addition to these major divisions, Heals, Octopus Books and Conran Associates are fitted. A separate functional group – The Design Group – is represented as a major functional department responsible for implementing design and merchandizing policy initiated by the operating divisions, across the whole group. Figure 14.1 gives the partial organization for the group, as at January 1985.

The Habitat-Mothercare philosophy of business is best summed up in Conran's own words: 'To build a group of autonomous, design-led enterprises mainly involved in speciality retailing, that benefit from being related to a strong central organization which provides a unique design, marketing, retail systems and financial service.'

The key term in the Conran lexicon is 'Design and Marketing'. The management of the group is firmly established around those words. Conran's style of leadership is quiet, but involved. Consultation is an important factor in Conran's success. The Mothercare takeover and its absorption were successful because of that process. Habitat was a lot smaller than Mothercare, yet the larger company was brought into the Habitat fold fairly painlessly.

The management conceded that the merger changed the character of the company considerably. At the time, Chris Turner believed: 'The priorities have changed, we used to be entrepreneurial, now we are big business worried about our shareholders.'

The group's explosive growth in the 1980s has had management problems, as Ian Peacock describes: 'The takeover of Heals and the expansion in France have stretched management resources to its limits. We still have to get Mothercare sorted out.'

The problems that Ian Peacock alluded to in late 1983 have not gone away. The organization structure is simple, with a functional-divisionalized format that works well, centred around the Design Group. The Design Group implements the design and marketing briefs that originate from the various operating companies. The design prowess of the organization is supported by a very professional management team, both at the centre and in the operating division.

When Mothercare was merged into Habitat's operation, a clash of

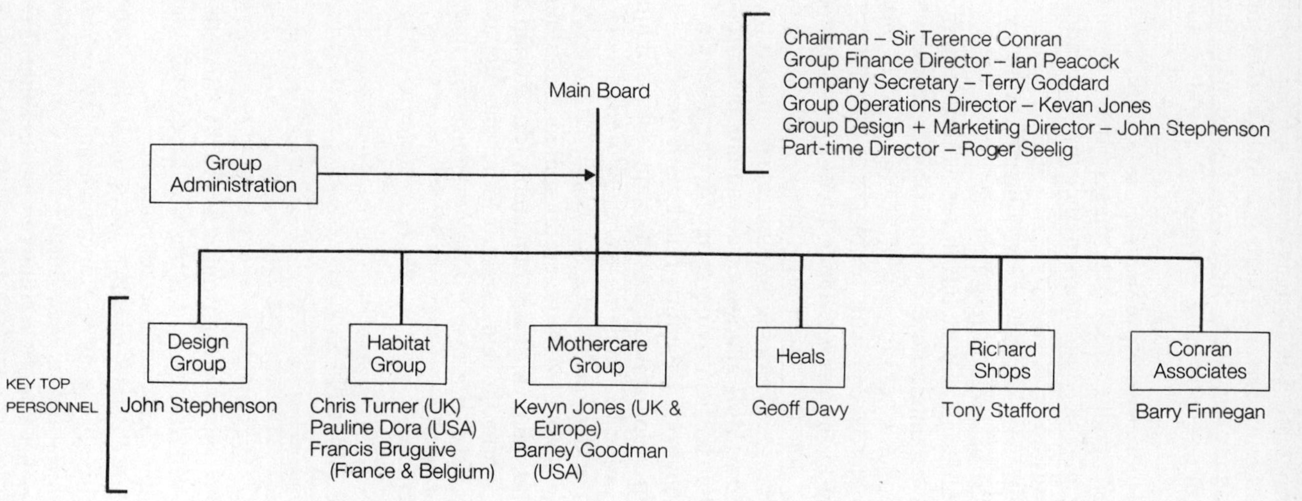

FIGURE 14.1 Partial organization chart of Habitat-Mothercare Plc as at January 1985

styles was evident. Mothercare was systems-driven, a legacy from Zilkha, and Habitat design-marketing driven. There was little early contact. 'We didn't force them together', says John Stephenson, design and marketing director, 'They were different trading entities. We built teams appropriate to each.'

'These problems at Habitat were predictable', says Turner, 'but new to us. As companies go public and get bigger they become more bureaucratic. I believe they become more inefficient. And saddest of all, the fun of the thing goes away.'

Are 'design' and 'business' difficult to reconcile? Are they different animals? Can designers run large corporations?

Conran does not see design and management as different animals: 'A designer uses a lot of common sense in analysing a problem and then bringing his creative talents to bear on it. Dealing with problems in business is very similar to dealing with problems in design.'

For Conran, the key to success is 'Management by Design'. Although not directly designing for the group, he does play a large part in approving designs, layouts, developing product ideas and prototypes and even talking to suppliers. This is in addition to running the corporation. It is this design sense that is the driving force for the company. Conran believes that 'store environment' integrated with product and merchandizing is crucial in helping to make shopping into a major leisure activity to be enjoyed rather than a chore to be endured. The High Street in Britain has discovered design.

1984–5 saw major developments in the group, aimed at consolidation of its existing strengths and the laying of a foundation for substantial growth and expansion. For Conran the fun has not gone out of business. He realizes his role as the head of a fast-growing organization that wants to be in the big league of retailing.

MAIN OPERATING COMPANIES

The Habitat Group

Habitat, started in 1964, has grown from strength to strength. Habitat sold good, well-designed furniture and furnishing accessories that had an appeal to a largely young and middle-class market.

The Habitat image has changed in subtle ways since the 1960s and has taken on a more quality appeal using 'functionalism' as its main design theme. The Habitat philosophy is best outlined by Conran himself. 'As creative retailers, our policy simply accounts to a belief that if reasonable and intelligent people are offered products for their home that are well designed, work well and are of decent quality and at a price they can afford, then they will like them and buy them.'

Conran believes that this philosophy has universal applications.

This credo has stayed with Habitat over the years, constantly being reinterpreted. The company has changed from a one-store operation in 1964 to 84 Habitat outlets in the UK, USA, Europe and Japan, by 1985. The image has remained untarnished, after a sticky patch in the early seventies when the group had quality problems. It remains the core of the new group.

TABLE 14.2 Sales profit for the Habitat operation

	1981	*1982*	*1983*[a]	*1984*
Habitat Retail Sales (£000's)				
Habitat UK	37,172	42,841	52,515	73,353
Habitat France & Belgium	22,119	28,916	38,164	41,003
Habitat USA	6,635	9,497	12,952	21,525
Total	65,926	81,254	103,631	135,880
	1981	*1982*	*1983*	*1984*
Habitat Retail Trading Profits (£000's)				
Habitat UK	4,094	3,847	5,598	8,026
Habitat France & Belgium	1,196	2,253	2,063	585
Habitat USA	(493)	(278)	177	732
Total	4,797	5,822	7,838	9,343

[a] Adjusted for a 52-week trading period.
The 1985 figures are shown in Exhibit 1.
Source: Company Accounts.

United Kingdom Over the years Habitat has changed the face of British retailing in the home and housewares market. Habitat caters almost exclusively to the young and newly married couples in the young executive market segment, with a higher than average disposable income. It was the Habitat design-led marketing strategy that proved attractive to this sector. Habitat offered an integration across the range of furniture and furnishing accessories all harmonized by colour, design and style – a 'total look'. Habitat's strategy was soon to become the bench mark for its imitators.

Conran has reinterpreted Shakespeare's seven ages of man, to three. In stage one, the couple set up home and buy their first set of furniture and look for value for money. In stage two, the family arrives, and comfort and the ability to survive the knocks of family life become paramount. In stage three, the children have left, and the couple re-furnish as they want, which tends to be towards a traditional style.

These three stages match the Habitat customer profile rather well. The archetypal Habitat customer is under thirty and in a professional occupation. However, clearly there exists a market for furniture and furnishing that do not fall into this segment: the childless couple, the older more traditional family that want 'style', but don't want 'stripped pine' or wish to buy from Waring & Gillow. Design and style are important pre-requisites. About 40% of the present UK population falls between the ages 30–40 years. Habitat, despite its high profile, only accounts for about 5% of the UK market for home furnishings.

The United Kingdom operation is by far the biggest in the Habitat Group. In the UK, Habitat continues to open new stores or re-site stores in new shopping areas as town landscapes change. Both merchandizing and marketing, along with design, are the key factors of success in the UK, as is the retailing skill of its staff. Other key indicators of success are stockholding, quality and distribution efficiency. A new Hi-Tech warehouse was opened recently in Wallingford to help achieve distribution economies and efficiency, along with new investment in automated re-ordering and EPOS terminals.

Habitat UK operates three levels of store size, each with its appropriate merchandise and product range tailored to suit the store's catchment area. The store's stock is supplemented by the mail-order catalogue side. The store sizes Habitat operates are large, midi and mini.

The mini-store concept was a new idea and is used in towns that would not support a full-sized branch. The variation of the mini-store is the midi-store: a larger unit, but with a small catchment area – examples are Worcester and Aylesbury. As Habitat further develop this store concept in their experimental sites, more such stores will be created. The idea is to find a formula to trade in areas whose catchment area precludes a full-scale operation, but redundant small Mothercare sites offer a small but profitable market potential. The experiment began in Lincoln.

France and Belgium Habitat's first foreign investment was in France, back in 1976. By 1985, the operation amounted to 25 outlets including three superstores in France and one in Belgium. The superstores trade under the name 'Grand H'. The sites were acquired when Habitat took over Maison de la Redoute.

Profits and turnover from the French and Belgium operation have been consistently good, with profits and turnover always rising. 1982 saw this growth peak. Trading conditions in the European markets changed dramatically with changing economic conditions. Habitat France was particularly badly affected.

The early expansionist policy of the Mitterand government proved profitable to Habitat France with 1982 profits rising by 21% and turnover growing by 23% over the 1981 figures. This expansion-led boom didn't last. The French Government changed its economic policy and the 'Delores Plan' was implemented. The franc was devalued, new taxes devised, and other taxes raised; the middle classes were particularly affected. The French furniture market suffered a 12% fall in volume in 1983–4 and this sluggish rate was to continue into 1984. Habitat sales and profits were badly affected. Profit in 1984 fell to £585,000. Additionally, a newly nationalized furniture retailers' group was liquidated by the government and their stock was heavily discounted in the market, adding to Habitat France's problems. This has now worked through the system.

Habitat France responded to this cut in volume by a major cost-cutting exercise. The newly opened Hi-tech warehouse at Cergy, designed to handle the Grand H operation, was to have its role modified. A series of dramatic stock-level reductions were implemented, HQ overheads were reduced dramatically, and salaries were to be linked, not to the retail prices index, but to performance. The operational objective was to be *selling*.

For Habitat France, salvation was seen in the new concepts behind the Grand H operation. The French management believe that the older stores in Central Paris need a major face-lift. With Grand H in place, Habitat France enters a new era. However, with trading conditions uncertain, the managment concede that their role in the operation has to be more precisely defined. The Grand H shops must, in their early trading days, be 'structured by efficient management, with subtle display methods, and a carefully balanced emphasis on our strong points.'

In addition to the Grand H operation, Habitat France also operated conventionally sized and ranged stores. for Habitat France 1983–4 was the year of reorganization, 1984–5 the year to make the new structure work.

Progress, however, is still hampered by a weak economic outlook, but second-half profits look to be improving in 1984–5 as retail sales in the economy as a whole begin to pick up.

Iceland and Japan In 1983–4 Habitat began an operation in Iceland in partnership with an Icelandic group. The operation is small at present, but plans are well advanced to build a very large store on the outskirts of Reykjavik. The Iceland operation will be sourced from the UK.

The Japanese operation has expanded fairly fast and now retails the Habitat range as developed for the Japanese market for 11 store sites in and around Tokyo. In addition Habitat has a franchise agreement with Seibu for sales in other stores around Japan. Sales are promising and in the last twelve months surpassed management expectations.

United States of America Habitat USA trades as Conran Stores Inc or more commonly 'Conran's'. The American operation began in 1977 with the first shop, and Habitat now has ten retailing units in the USA. Conran's USA has had a difficult early life. British retailers are often outshone in the UK markets, particularly in sectors like the household and housewares market. Conran's was no exception. The company became profitable only in 1983. Since then the company has begun to consolidate its trading base in the USA, opening new stores in Philadelphia and at White Plains in upstate New York. In order to support this operation, Conran's USA has invested in new warehousing and new management. It is hoped that once consolidation has been achieved, further expansion away from the north-eastern coast of the USA can become possible.

THE MOTHERCARE GROUP

Background – pre 1981–2 Mothercare was developed and founded by Selim Zilkha in 1961, as a specialist retail chain for marketing products for the mother and her baby. Zilkha's name for the group was brilliant – Mothercare; it was soon to become an indispensable part of family life. Over the years the product mix has altered as Mothercare has expanded its range of merchandise. It also handled a mail order operation, with catalogues published twice yearly. Its stores were clean, vibrant and run efficiently. The retail environment matched the social period very well.

Mothercare's strength in the UK market, was its name, its reputation, its range of products and, in its early days, its innovativeness. The Mothercare concept was, and still is, the only truly ranged specialist store of its type in the UK market. The backbone to the operation was Selim Zilkha's autocratic leadership. It was Zilkha who first pioneered an automatic computerized stock control and reorder system. Stock levels were recorded automatically using punched cards returned to the Watford head office and processed; stock could be reordered and be in the shops by Tuesday, after processing on Saturday. It was this computerized system that made Mothercare a formidable retailer through the late 1960s and early to mid-1970s. Mothercare's success in the UK market soon waned, as major retailers came into its market segment to compete head-on with it – Littlewoods, Babyboots, BHS and Marks & Spencer. Mothercare was not alone any more. Profits dived by the late seventies.

Mothercare, having developed its retailing concept in the UK, tried to export it abroad, in the European market and in the United States of America. In Europe, Mothercare's development was piecemeal, one shop at a time here and there. In America, this didn't happen. Mothercare bought a 110-strong chain of stores – Mother-to-be and Maternity Modes boutiques, and hoped to reach profitability by 1980. This objective was never reached.

Mothercare in Europe and the USA found trading difficult. Stores were closed in Europe in an attempt to stem European losses. In the United States its problems were more acute.

The US market is not as homogeneous as the UK market. Mothercare's stores in the USA were spread thinly across the country, making centralized buying and control difficult. By 1980, Mothercare was competing in a market where the top five US retailers had a combined annual turnover of $50 billion.

The Mothercare operation in the late seventies controlled stores whose average size was around 600 sq ft, small by any standard, particularly in the USA. The company found it difficult to find new sites, as the property boom in the US was forcing prices up. Mothercare was forced to purchase sites wherever it could. This led to a string of purchases dotted around the USA. By 1980, it had 200 stores, as far west as Los Angeles and as far south as New Mexico.

Added to this overstretched network of stores, Mothercare was faced with a squeeze on its trading margins. Nursery products formed a heavily discounted market where margins were very low. Meanwhile, children's garments had become 'high fashion'. Mothercare had to make its money where its US strengths were weakest – fashion clothes for children and pregnant women. The average lie of a product in this 'fashion' market was eight weeks. Mothercare's two catalogues a year meant outdated stock and poor choice.

In 1981 Mothercare's turnover was £170 million with profits of £17.9 million. This compared with profits in 1980 of £21.8 million. The profit trend was downwards. Mothercare looked jaded and tired in the UK market and had severe trouble in the US market

The Habitat-Mothercare Merger The newly public company Habitat merged with Mothercare in January 1982.

Zilkha and Conran have very similar management styles – both autocratic and approachable. Conran and Zilkha were at the centres of their organizations, shaping, moulding and creating very distinctive businesses. Both men are generalists rather than specialists: Conran a designer, Zilkha a banker. Both could look at the business as a whole and creatively apply novel solutions to potential problems. Zilkha was the systems man, Conran the entrepreneur. The Habitat-Mothercare union was agreed and the new group was born.

The way it happened didn't get the full approval of the City. In the words of one critic: 'Habitat and Mothercare are getting together for no better reason than Mr Zilkha has had enough, and cannot find a suitable successor in-house, and is looking outside for somebody to revive his rather jaded business. There are other ways of achieving this.'

The final plan turned out to be a 'reverse' takeover, known politely in Habitat circles as a 'merger'. The City's response was cool. Investors, who had earlier in the year subscribed to Habitat's share issue when the company went public, had to dig into their pockets once again. The committee of the National Association of Pension Funds called Terence Conran to a meeting to explain the rationale of the merger. One prominent underwriter, who turned down the underwriting said that the deal was 'too messy to understand. We don't believe that Habitat will be able to do well in the American market. It is a tough market and an uphill struggle all the way.'

Despite these problems Terence Conran managed to patch up a deal worth £110 million to clinch the merger. Habitat's share price suffered. It fell from 140p to around 120p and continued to fall to 105p by 14 January, when the Mothercare shares had to be tendered in acceptance. By June 1982, after the results of the new group were announced, the shares went up to 280p. The company management soon got to work to 'turn the Mothercare operation around'.

TABLE 14.3 Sales and profits for the Mothercare operations

	1982[a]	*1983*[b]	*1984*
Mothercare retail sales (£000's)			
Mothercare UK	56,680	157,967	185,417
Mothercare USA	10,334	29,982	36,977
Mothercare Europe	6,440	16,265	15,070
Totals	74,454	204,214	237,464
Mothercare trading profits (£000's)			
Mothercare UK	5,908	19,871	25,567
Mothercare USA	(1,064)	(1,061)	(170)
Mothercare Europe	100	267	(112)
Totals	4,944	19,077	25,285

[a] 5 months only.
[b] Unaudited and adjusted for a March year end; actually the final figures in the accounts are for a nine-month period.
The 1985 figures are found in Appendix 1.
Source: Company Accounts.

Mothercare 1982–5 One of the first problems that Habitat had when it took over Mothercare was to consolidate and harmonize year end dates. It was decided that Habitat would change its accounting year to that of Mothercare. For Mothercare to change from March to Habitat's June would have taken 12 months and cost around £100,000. To do it the other way allowed Habitat to change over in a week at around £250 in cost. Habitat is the more flexible of the two companies.

Mothercare's business had to be reappraised, the business had to be repositioned, revamped and restyled. Shops had to close in the UK and in Europe and the US operation to be looked at afresh. All this formed a formidable task for the management. The management did the following things to help boost the Mothercare business.

1 The Mothercare orange-and-white corporate colours were scrapped and replaced with less vibrant and softer blue, and there was an addition of gentle greens and pinks to the interior decor. This cost the new owners some £10 per square foot.
2 The Mothercare clothes perceived as 'shiny nylon' were redesigned

and given a fashion look. New designers and buyers were appointed.
3 Clothes for pregnant women and for children were redesigned and given the 'fashion treatment'.
4 The image of Mothercare was taken up-market, and a range of baby-food lines introduced. Mothercare nursery products, particularly furniture were given the 'Habitat' design treatment.
5 Small stores were closed, and some stores were resited in new shopping areas. New stores were opened in the UK.
6 Mothercare UK also opened a chain of 'Now' clothing and fashion accessories stores for the teenage market. Great things are expected of this venture.
7 Mothercare Europe reviewed its pricing policy, closed stores in Norway, Denmark and Sweden, and planned an expansion programme in Germany.
8 Mothercare USA had placed an overreliance on the sale of leading brands at a huge discount. A stock clearance programme was ordered and a 'new' Mothercare look planned, with the view to making the group a 'leading retailer in its field'. The old centralized system, was scrapped in favour of a regional one. Regional vice-presidents reported to Barney Goodman, the Mothercare USA chief. New designers, merchandisers and management were appointed to take Mothercare into profit in the USA.

The Mothercare division received an injection of new investment in the shape of new warehouse and centralized distribution facilities due to be operational in 1986.

Heals

Heals was a small privately owned family firm in the furniture and furnishing market, catering for the older, upper-middle class discriminating market. The company had a fine reputation for style, design and quality. Its furniture was both traditional and contemporary, covered in traditional fabrics and leathers. It traded from a prime-site location on London's Tottenham Court Road. The company had been making losses for some years.

TABLE 14.4 Selected financial information for Heal and Son Plc

	1981	*1982*	*1983*
Sales turnover (£m)	11.27	11.91	12.62
Profits (£m)	(0.77)	(0.92)	(0.95)
Shareholders' funds (£m)	7.15	6.58	5.64
Return on capital (%)	(10.7)	(14.0)	(16.7)

Source: Data Stream

Heal and Son Plc was taken over by Habitat-Mothercare Plc in April 1983 for around £5 million. The purchase was funded partly by cash and partly by an issue of preference shares, which diluted the group's final EPS in 1984 from 18.2p a share to 15.2p a share.

Habitat-Mothercare drew up plans for the Heals site. Part of the site was to become the new corporate headquarters for the group.

Redesign work commenced as soon as the takeover was completed. The refurbishment of Heals included the following major items: (a) reduce footage by 47%; (b) reduce merchandise options by 60%; (c) 35% of the range was to be 'new'; (d) establish retail management of Heals as a separate line to board level; (e) refit the entire store in London; (f) rationalize the staff wage and salary structure; (g) introduce new computer technology; (h) develop a coordinated design image from shopfitting through to stationery and vehicle livery.

Slowly sales are picking up. The store site now reflects Conran's design image and theme, consistent with Heals' image. Conran also now has an excellent head office building in Central London.

To quote Geoff Davy, chief executive of Heals: 'It soon became obvious that drastic treatment was needed and, provided the "patient" would withstand the shock, it could be carried out as quickly as possible.'

The Heals operation is consolidated within the Habitat group of companies, with its own managing director/chief executive. Sales are now responding to the new store environment and merchandise selection.

Related Companies

Richard Shops Richard Shops was an old-established retail chain of womenswear shops, founded in 1936 and formerly owned by Charles Clore in 1941, and then by the United Drapery Stores Group from 1949 onwards. UDS was taken over in 1983 by Hanson Trust, which proceeded to strip the group down. It sold Richard Shops to Habitat-Mothercare and its former management team, helped by Morgan Grenfell, the merchant bank. Habitat-Mothercare Plc holds 48% of the equity of Richard Shops and has incorporated the Richard Shops operation as an 'associated company' in its balance sheet. Richard Shops cost Habitat-Mothercare around £18 million.

Richard Shops are being redesigned and repositioned in the women's fashion market to compete with Hepworth's Next and Burton's Principles. The Design Group under John Stephenson is heading the review. A new three-year corporate plan has been drawn up and is now in place. The objective is to 'become the foremost women's fashion retailer in the British High Street'. The Richard Shops acquisition was financed by the sale and lease-back of a small number of stores at sums above the value placed on them at the time of the acquisition.

Conran Associates Conran Associates is an associated company in the

Habitat-Mothercare group. It is headed by Barry Finnegan, and the company acts as a design consultancy. It has been involved in a number of projects in recent years. Its most visible and prestigous project was the interior design of the Quatre Temps Shopping Centre in the La Defence complex in Paris, in 1981.

Conran Associates have been involved with Boots in France designing their chain of retail cosmetic shops called 'Sephora', with Marks and Spencer's home and wares range, with Hepworth's 'Next' stores, and most recently in the BHS new look. Conran Associates also advises the group on design and layout, although that is the purview of the Design Group. This small part of Habitat-Mothercare Plc is a highly profitable operation.

Conran Octopus A new joint venture with the publishers 'Octopus Publishing Plc' was completed in 1984 with the stated objective to sell 'well-designed books'. The Octopus company is also associated with other major store groups. The book company will tap Habitat-Mothercare's design expertise to jointly publish books for sale in Habitat-Mothercare stores as well as in the general book trade.

Events of 1985

Links with the Burton Group During the early part of 1985, the Burton Group of Companies, a major High Street fashion retailer, bid for the large Debenhams Group, a major department store chain. Mr Ralph Halpern, the chairman of Burton's persuaded Sir Terence Conran of Habitat-Mothercare to participate in the Debenhams takeover. Both men had plans for the Debenhams store sites, often in prime city-centre locations. Halpern and Conran had a new retailing concept called Galleria to use in the Debenhams store setting. It meant a totally coordinated and integrated retailing package from design of products to layout and store environment. Habitat-Mothercare were to get, through Conran Associates, the contract for all the design work on the new concept, as well as a 20% option to purchase the Debenham equity exercisable between 1 September 1986 and 31 December 1986. In addition the company would get 20% of the Debenhams floor space for its own products.

Conran's belief in store environment and shopping as an experience would now be allowed to be fully developed.

The Debenhams group was finally taken over by Burton's, after an acrimonious takeover battle involving accusation and counter-accusation, often in public, for around £550m.

The BHS Merger Habitat-Mothercare had been having talks with British Home Stores (BHS) management on a possible merger of the two companies. In April 1985 the talks broke down. However, the companies surprised the City by announcing a merger in November 1985. A new holding company would be set up and an equity swop would take place between the two sets of shareholders for shares in the new group. The deal is worth £1.52 billion on paper. The new holding company would be chaired by Conran, and the BHS head would be deputy chairman. The new group would have a combined sales turnover of just over £1 billion and a market capitalization of £1.52 billion, and would together control 800 stores and a combined retail space of 6.15 million square feet. The new group is now in the top 12 retailers by turnover in the UK.

(Appendix 1 has details of the background to the merger).

TABLE 14.5 The two groups compared

	Habitat-Mothercare	*BHS*
	Figures to 31.3.85	
Turnover	£447m	£550m
Pre-tax profits	£36.5m	£ 61m
Market capitalization	£670m	£851m
Number of stores	750	128
Sales area (sq ft)	2.9m	3.25m
Employees	10,959	24,354
Store names	Habitat	BHS
	Mothercare	Sava-Centres[a]
	Conrans	
	Richards	
	Now	

[a] Joint venture with J. Sainsbury
Source: *Financial Times*, 26 November 1985

TABLE 14.6 Top UK retailers by turnover

	Turnover £m	*Year-end date*
Marks and Spencer	3,194	31.3.85
Tesco	3,000	23.2.85
J. Sainsbury	2,998	23.3.85
Dee Corporation	2,434	27.4.85
Great Universal Stores	2,175	31.3.85
Boots	2,033	31.3.85
Sears Holdings	2,019	31.1.85
Argyll Group	1,677	30.3.85
Woolworths	1,166	2.2.85
W H Smith	1,067	1.6.85
Habitat-Mothercare/BHS[a]	997	31.3.85

[a] Indicates what combined turnover would have been at last year-end.
Source: *Financial Times*, 26 November 1985

Exhibit 1 Habitat-Mothercare Plc

SUMMARY OF RESULTS FOR THE 53 WEEKS ENDED 31 MARCH 1985 (1985 – FIFTY-TWO WEEKS ENDED 25 MARCH 1984)

	1985 *£000*	*1984* *£000*	*Change* *(%)*
Turnover			
Habitat, Heal's and Conran's	167,367	137,946	+21
Mothercare and 'Now'	279,366	237,464	+18
	446,733	375,410	+19
Trading profit			
Habitat, Heal's and Conran's	11,209	9,888	+13
Mothercare and 'Now'	32,678	25,285	+29
	43,887	35,173	+25
Profit on ordinary activities before taxation	36,501	30,617	+19
Basic earnings per share	22.3p	18.2p	+23
Dividend per share	8.0p	6.5p	+23

Geographical analysis (£000)

	1985	*1984*
Turnover		
UK	307,001	260,835
Europe	64,630	56,073
USA	75,102	58,502
	446,733	375,410
Trading profit	41,958	34,138
Europe	1,792	473
USA	137	562
	43,887	355,173

Exhibit 2 Habitat-Mothercare Plc

CONSOLIDATED PROFIT AND LOSS ACCOUNT FOR THE 53 WEEKS ENDED 31 MARCH 1985 (1984 – FIFTY TWO WEEKS ENDED 25 MARCH 1984) (£000)

	1985	*1984*
turnover, excluding sales taxes	446,733	375,410
Cost of sales	(372,543)	(314,246)
Gross profit	74,190	61,164
Distribution costs	(11,095)	(8,726)
Administrative expenses	(19,208)	(17,265)
Trading profit	43,887	35,173
Interest and other items	(7,386)	(4,556)
Profit on ordinary activities before taxation	36,501	30,617
Tax on profit on ordinary activities	(12,896)	(11,393)
Profit on ordinary activities after taxation	23,605	19,224
Extraordinary item	–	(4,500)
Profit for the financial year	23,605	14,724
Translation adjustments	1,145	(858)
Dividends paid and proposed	(8,463)	(6,877)
Profit retained	16,287	6,989
Earnings per share		
Basic	22.3p	18.2p
Fully diluted	19.2p	15.7p

CONSOLIDATED BALANCE SHEET AS AT 31 MARCH 1985 (£000)

	1985	*1984*
Fixed assets		
Tangible assets	151,486	127,277
Investments	15,583	16,682
	167,069	143,959
Current Assets		
Stocks	82,352	68,690
Debtors	17,917	13,941
Cash at bank and in hand	8,008	9,867
	108,277	92,498
Creditors (amounts falling due within one year)		
Bank loans and overdrafts	16,266	12,414
Proposed dividend	5,924	4,760
Current taxation	15,857	12,410
Other creditors	61,246	55,644
	99,293	85,228
Net current assets	8,984	7,270
Total assets less current liabilities	176,053	151,229
Creditors (amounts falling due after more than one year)		
Convertible unsecured loan stock	(39,088)	(39,088)
Long-term loans	(32,123)	(22,394)
	(71,211)	(61,482)
Provisions for liabilities and charges		
Deferred taxation	(3,285)	(4,265)
	101,557	85,482
Capital reserves		
Called-up share capital	10,579	10,579
Share premium account	8,603	8,603
Other reserves	38,422	38,634
Profit and loss account	43,953	27,666
	101,557	85,482
Total share and stock holders' interests		
Capital and reserves	101,557	85,482
Convertible unsecured loan stock	39,088	39,088
	140,645	124,570

Exhibit 3 Habitat-Mothercare Plc

ANALYSIS OF PRINCIPAL ACTIVITIES, 1981–4 FOR THE FIFTY-TWO WEEKS ENDED 25 MARCH 1984 (1983 – THIRTY-NINE WEEKS ENDED 27 MARCH 1983) (1982 – MOTHERCARE – 5 MONTHS ONLY)

	1984 *£000*	*1983* *£000*	*1982* *£000*	*1981* *£000*
Turnover				
Habitat, Heal's and Conran's				
UK	73,352	42,453	42,841	37,172
Europe	41,003	31,584	28,916	22,119
USA	21,525	10,857	9,497	6,635
	135,880	84,894	81,254	65,926
Mothercare and 'Now'				
UK	185,417	122,112	57,680	–
Europe	15,070	12,191	6,440	–
USA	36,977	23,516	10,334	–
	237,464	157,819	74,454	–
Conran Associates	2,066	1,261	1,439	1,239
Total turnover	375,410	243,974	157,14	67,165
Trading profits (losses)				
Habitat, Heal's and Conran's				
UK	8,026	4,984	3,847	4,094
Europe	585	1,828	2,253	1,196
USA	732	169	(278)	(493)
	9,343	6,981	5,822	4,797
Mothercare and 'Now'				
UK		25,567	16,022	
Europe	(112)	68	100	–
USA	(170)	(563)	(1,064)	–
	25,285	15,527	4,944	–
Conran Associates	545	363	521	467
Total trading profit	35,173	22,871	11,287	5,264

Exhibit 4 Five-year record (£000)

	1985	*1984*	*1983*[a]	*1982*[b,c]	*1981*[b]
Turnover, excluding sales taxes	446,733	375,410	243,974	157,147	67,165
Trading profit	43,887	35,173	22,871	11,287	5,264
Profit on ordinary activities before taxation	36,501	30,617	19,333	10,014	4,402
Profit on ordinary activities after taxation	23,605	19,224	12,006	6,823	2,862
Share and stock holders' interests	140,645	124,570	117,502	107,542	10,583
Capital and reserves	101,557	85,482	79,999	70,039	10,583
Earnings per share	23.3p	18.2p	11.3p	9.9p	8.6p
Dividend per share	8.0p	6.5p	4.0p	4.0p	2.7p
Trading profit to turnover	9.8%	9.4%	9.4%	7.2%	7.8%
Profit on ordinary activities before taxation to avera; capital and reserves	39.0%	37.0%	25.8%	24.9%	45.3%
Number of stores	546	521	506	481	52
Net selling space in '000 sq ft	2,454	2,318	2,120	1,864	709
Average number of employees	10,959	10,418	9,148	5,245	2,106
Number of full-time equivalents	7,436	7,068	6,306	3,806	1,701

[a] 1983 figures cover the nine-month period ended 27 March 1983.

[b] Figures for years prior to 1983 cover the twelve months to June in each case.

[c] 1982 figures reflect the inclusion of Mothercare as from 14 January 1982 to 25 June 1982.

Exhibit 5 BHS

CONSOLIDATED PROFIT AND LOSS ACCOUNT (FOR THE 52 WEEKS TO 30 MARCH 1985) (£000)

	Group	
	1985	*1984*
Turnover (including Value Added Tax)	608,581	546,850
Value Added Tax	58,137	52,456
Turnover (excluding Value Added Tax)	550,444	494,394
Cost of sales	484,219	435,640
Gross profit	66,225	58,754
Administrative expenses	12,199	10,668
Trading profit	54,026	48,086
Share of profit of related companies	4,855	4,390
Interest receivable	4,675	5,340
Interest payable	(2,575)	(2,623)
Profit on ordinary activities before taxation and extraordinary items	60,981	55,193
Tax on profit on ordinary activities	23,334	21,184
Profit on ordinary activities after taxation and before extraordinary items	37,647	34,009
Extraordinary items	–	(2,734)
Profit for the financial year	37,647	31,275
Dividends	14,045	12,436
Retained profit for the year	23,602	18,839
Earnings per ordinary share	18.1p	16.4p

CONSOLIDATED BALANCE SHEET (AT 30 MARCH 1985) (£000)

	Group 1985	1984
Fixed assets		
Tangible assets	215,622	170,848
Investments	32,497	23,199
	248,119	194,047
Current assets		
Stocks	60,594	57,281
Debtors	9,448	8,682
Cash at bank and in hand	46,583	72,886
	116,625	138,849
Creditors: amounts falling due within one year	87,067	79,695
Net current assets	29,558	59,154
Total assets less current liabilities	277,677	253,201
Creditors: amounts falling due after more than one year		
Loan capital	28,236	28,674
Corporation tax	16,686	15,913
Provision for liabilities and charges		
Deferred taxation	1,634	2,662
	231,121	205,592
Capital reserves		
Called-up share capital	52,346	52,137
Share premium account	4,024	2,666
Revaluation reserve	2,463	2,502
Other reserves	3,861	3,861
Profit and loss account	168,427	144,786
	231,121	205,952

Exhibit 6

FIVE-YEAR SUMMARY (£000)

	1981	1982	1983	1984	1985
Turnover (including value added tax)					
Merchandise	350,653	366,198	394,301	434,762	486,124
Food	74,929	78,134	78,884	81,099	88,277
Restaurant	26,643	27,308	29,544	30,989	34,180
Total	452,225	471,640	502,729	546,850	608,581
Turnover (excluding value added tax)	410,099	427,563	455,684	494,394	550,444
Trading profit	40,549	39,669	42,783	48,086	54,026
Share profit of related companies	229	1,506	4,001	4,390	4,855
Interest receivable	1,916	4,182	4,730	5,340	4,675
Interest payable	(3,036)	(2,795)	(2,640)	(2,623)	(2,575)
	39,658	42,562	48,874	55,193	60,981
Tax on profit on ordinary activities	12,052	15,765	21,711	21,184	23,334
Profit on ordinary activities after taxation and before extra-ordinary items	27,606	26,797	27,163	34,009	37,647
Extraordinary items	–	311	–	(2,734)	–
Profit for the financial year	27.606	27,108	27,163	31,275	37,647
Dividend per ordinary share	4.5p	4.75p	5.25p	6.0p	6.75p
Earnings per ordinary share	13.5p	13.0p	13.2p	16.4p	18.1p

Exhibit 7 BHS

RETAIL STATISTICS

£000	*1981*	*1982 £000*	*1983 £000*	*1984 £000*	*1985 £000*
Sales area at year-end (000 square feet)					
Merchandise	2,392	2,451	2,505	2,535	2,613
Food	208	211	211	209	226
Restaurant	259	264	276	289	309
Total	2,859	2,926	2,992	3,033	3,148
Stores opened in the year	Eastbourne	Reddith Peterborough Motherwell Guildford[a]	Fareham Harlow Woking	Bexleyheath	Ayr Carlisle Cheltenham Canterbury
Number of stores at year-end	116	120	123	124	128
Average number of employees					
Stores	24,791	23,444	23,489	22,310	22,613
Head Office & Atherstone	1,826	1,795	1,771	1,775	1,741
Total	26,617	25,239	25,260	24,085	24,354
Store full-time equivalents	13,612	12,860	13,120	12,516	12,555

[a] Lighting shop.

Appendix 1 Habitat-Mothercare/BHS Merger Details*

UK RETAILING AND THE BHS MERGER: CONRAN GOES SHOPPING AGAIN

By David Churchill, Consumer Affairs Correspondent

The re-shaping of UK retailing in the 1980s found a fresh and surprising impetus yesterday with the agreed £1.6bn merger between Sir Terence Conran's Habitat-Mothercare retail empire and British Home Stores, often described as the 'poor man's Marks and Spencer' of Britain's High Streets.

The move thrusts the merged group firmly into the top dozen of British retailers, based on sales, and is the latest in a series of mergers and take-overs (see table) which are radically changing the face of retailing in Britain.

Sir Terence Conran and a clutch of other leading retail entrepreneurs such as Burton's Ralph Halpern, Alec Monk of the Dee Corporation, and Sir Phil Harris of Harris Queensway, are taking advantage of the changed retail conditions of the 1980s to put together new combinations of store groupings which they believe will give British consumers what they want from shopping in the late 1980s and beyond.

Such merger moves, moreover, may only be a foretaste of what is to come. City analysts, who have been predicting a takeover of BHS for some time, are now turning their attention to other likely candidates such as Boots and W.H. Smith. 'We've only seen the tip of the iceberg as far as retail re-structuring goes,' argues John Richards, a senior stores analyst with stockbrokers Wood Mackenzie.

Those retailers who have not yet joined the takeover trail – for fear the government merger policy would prevent them doing so – have not been idle. Marks and Spencer, for example, is spending almost £500m over the next two years on a massive programme of store refurbishment and re-design. Other retailers are spending billions in total on similar new corporate identities in an attempt to woo the fickle consumer into their shops.

Why is British retailing being re-vamped in this way? The moves over the past five years have been prompted by several factors:

- The inefficiences of retailers in the 1970s were hidden by high

Source: *Financial Times*, 26 November 1985. Used with permission.

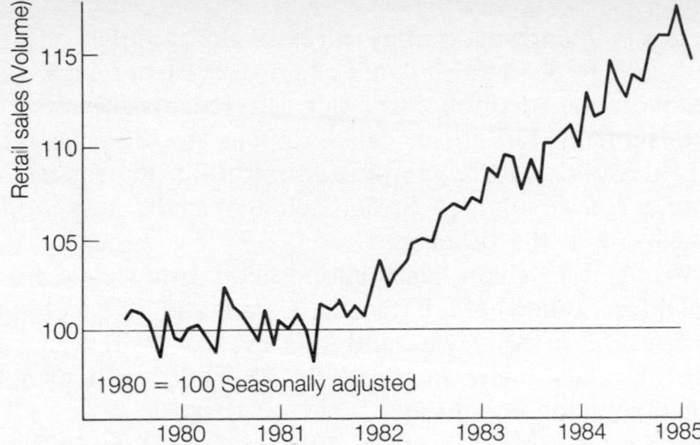

inflation – it was easier to pass on a price rise then try to improve productivity. But the low inflation rates of the 1980s have exposed the weaknesses of some store groups, who have been swallowed up by more efficient rivals.

- The onset of the recession from late 1979 onwards forced retailers to fight harder for an increased share of the retail 'cake' as consumer spending declined.
- Traditional retailing came under pressure from other types of spending – such as holidays abroad, eating out, and private health. Retail expenditure last year fell to about 39 per cent of all consumer spending – down from 43 per cent in 1980 and 53 per cent in 1950.
- Consumer attitudes and lifestyles are changing. As Edward Whitefield of the Management Horizons research company points out: 'Consumers have moved beyond the basic survival needs to the fulfilment of psychological aspirations.'

Product design, quality, and style have become more important to consumers in the 1980s. 'They not only want an improved standard of living, but also a better quality of life,' suggests Rodney Fitch of Fitch and Co, one of the design consultancies which has provided much of the impetus for the rejuvenated look of many stores and High Streets.

Design, in fact, has become the vehicle for the re-shaping of British retailing. Fitch and three or four other major designers have capitalized on the needs of retail entrepreneurs, not only to become more competitive by offering a distinctive retailing formula but also to help identify and implement new trading strategies. A survey carried out by the Mintel market research company found that almost nine out of ten major retailers had embarked on a design re-vamp during the past three years – and for many it was a continuing process.

Yet the design bandwagon may already be running out of steam. Already it is hard to distinguish some chain stores from each other, since the consultants involved often carry out assignments for more than one retailer. Consumers, moreover, also appear to be becoming more sceptical. Littlewoods, for example, found that its redesigned store trading at one end of Oxford Street actually trades less well than an unmodernized one at the other end.

The 125-strong BHS chain has for long been sandwiched in consumer and City opinion somewhere between Marks and Spencer and Littlewoods in terms of price, style, and quality. Its trading performance, however, became lack-lustre in the early 80s as a result of a failure to grasp changed retailing conditions.

Pre-tax profits fell from £41.8m in 1980 to £39.6m in 1981 on a sales increase that barely kept pace with inflation. Since then profits growth has been steady rather than spectacular, rising to £60.9m in the 12 months ending the beginning of April this year on sales of £608.6m.

Just at the time as new retailing formulae were emerging – such as Next in womenswear – and Marks and Spencer was pulling ahead of the pack, BHS lacked style and appeared down-market to the consumer. Nobody aspires to shop at BHS in the way that they, arguably, do to buy food at M&S or clothes at Next.

BHS, moreover, found itself in stiff competition for the middle market, which has emerged in the 1980s as the key consumer group with spending power. Adults aged between 25 and 45 with children and in the C1 and C2 socio-economic classes, with their high discretionary spending power, are the prize that stores such as Woolworths, Marks and Spencer, Debenhams, and so on are chasing.

The strategy adopted by BHS about three years ago, therefore, was two-fold: to improve the quality of its products and improve the look of its stores.

The design changes began in the Essex town of Harlow and so far over 40 stores have been refurbished at a cost of more than £150m. In addition, four new stores have been opened. The new design is loosely based on the American department store look of wider aisles, subtle lighting, and more relaxing colour schemes designed to appeal to BHS's predominantly women customers.

While BHS has publicly appeared to be happy with the way its design approach has gone others are not so sure. 'BHS must increasingly be asking the question about whether its design strategy is going to work,' suggests Wood Mackenzie's Mr Richards. 'It is difficult to see if the return so far is adequate for their expenditure.'

The second thrust of BHS's new marketing strategy was to upgrade its produce quality and appearance. Ironically, it retained last year Conran Associates, the design consultancy arm of Conran's empire, to help rejuvenate its product design

Conran and his management team based in the Heal's furniture store in

London's Tottenham Court Road are understood to have analysed BHS closely.

The merger is almost an exact replay of Conran's merger with Mothercare in 1982 – a deal that gave Conran the entry into the first division of UK retailing after two decades when Habitat was his main retail venture. Since then, Conran has launched an upmarket women's fashion chain called Now aimed at 25–45-year-olds (based on his experience at J. Hepworth where he was chairman when Next was created) as well as buying Richard Shops and the Heal's furniture store.

What Conran has brought to British retailing is a design flair and a sense of style that is lacking in so many other retailers. Habitat's initial success was based on providing stylish furniture to a new generation of young consumers brought up in the changing society of the swinging 1960s. In the 1980s, Conran has identified that same consumer desire for a certain style in a wide range of goods. Conran's success in the 1980s appears to be based as much on reputation as on anything concrete. The stores he has taken over have all had one thing in common: they have all been relatively sound operations but had lost their way in the retail world of the 1980s. 'Conran actually does very little with the store groups he acquires other than motivate the management and give them the leadership they seem to seek,' points out Richards.

One Mothercare senior manager points out that following the 1982 takeover, change came about by consultation rather than dictat.

Conran has not always had the magic touch: his early ventures in the US and France with Habitat took a long time to become established although they are now trading profitably. The Now and Heal's ventures, moreover, still have to prove themselves as retail formula in their own right.

But with the BHS merger, Conran has firmly established himself as the leading influence of British retailing in the 1980s. The question remaining, however, is: who next?

STORES IN SEARCH OF A MARKET

The small revolution which has occurred in the British High Street over the past five years primarily the result of retailers seeking sharper marketing profiles in an increasingly competitive business.

These forces have produced a spate of mergers, as well as a major re-think in shop design.

Woolworth, with 850 stores, has undergone one of the most dramatic transformations. Since the £310m take-over by a financial consortium in 1983, the group has employed design consultants such as Fitch to complement its research on selecting the right merchandise.

Currently the group is experimenting with a series of pilot schemes. Traditionally the group had 64 departments within each store.

In the pilot schemes these have been reduced to eight trial 'week-end stores' which are aimed at matching prices of major competitors in sensitive locations. Six other trial 'general stores' are in quieter High Streets and specialise in records, confectionery, children's clothes, and toys.

This idea of carfully defining target audiences was fine-tuned by Burton, the clothing group whose specialist outlets include the Next womens' chain and Top Shop which caters for a younger woman. Mr Ralph Halpern, chairman of Burton, already has something to show for these changes. In the 26 weeks to March 2 this year, the group raised lifted pre-tax profits by £8.6m with turnover up by 33 per cent.

Mr Halpern, whose group acquired Debenhams for £566m earlier this year after a fierce fight, intends to use the same approach there. The Debenhams Galleria concept offers a number of shops under one roof, aiming at the whole family.

The belief that the future of retailing is out of town was a major element in the £615m merger between MFI, the furniture group and Associated Dairies, the Asda and Allied Carpets group. Both companies believed there were considerable advantages to be had by combining their knowledge of site acquisitions and developments. The agreed bid created Britain's fourth largest retailer after Marks and Spencer, J. Sainsbury and Great Universal Stores.

Lisa Wood

MAJOR RETAILING MERGERS

Woolworth F.W./Dodge City DIY	£20.1m	1981
Habitat/Mothercare	£117.6m	"
Argyll Foods/Allied Supplies	£101m	1982
Paternoster Stores/F.W. Woolworth	£310m	"
Hanson Trust/UDS	£265m	1983
Argyll Group/Amalgamated Distilled Products	£233m	"
H. Samuel/James Walker	£29m	1984
Woolworth/Comet	£177	"
A. Guinness/Martin the Newsagent	£48.6m	"
Halfords/Ward White	£52m	"
Dee/International Stores	£180m	"
Dixons/Currys	£248m	"
Dee/Lennons	£23.2m	"
Sears/Foster Bros	£115m	1985
Asda/MFI	£615m	"
The Al Fayedh family/House of Fraser	£615m	"
Burton/Debenhams	£566m	"

Source: FT estimates.

Appendix 2 Habitat-Mothercare Plc and BHS Plc

ADDITIONAL INFORMATION

Shares in Issue at Case Date

Habitat-Mothercare	105,790,000	10p ordinary shares
British Home Stores	209,384,000	25p ordinary shares

Share Prices After the Announcement of the Agreed Merger between the Two Companies

Habitat-Mothercare	556p
British Home Stores	409p

Merger Terms

A new company would acquire all the assets and liabilities of the two companies. British Home Stores' shareholders would receive 1 share in the new company for 1 BHS share. Habitat-Mothercare's shareholders would receive 138 shares in the new company for 100 H-M shares.

15 House of Fraser

House of Fraser was the largest department store group in the UK, even though it had 120 stores nationwide and over 16,000 full-time and 10,000 part-time employees, it was probably best known for its world-famous Harrods in London.

The group had been built over the years following its foundation in 1873 by acquiring other departmental store groups, and until 1972 it had been House of Fraser policy to allow these groups to continue trading in their traditional manner. In 1972, however, the company installed regional groupings with common buying management and trading methods. During the 1970s the company continued to expand and continued investment in its well-known stores such as 'D.H. Evans', 'Dickens and Jones', 'Army & Navy Stores' and 'Harrods' in London, 'Kendal Milne' in Manchester and 'Rackhams' and 'Binns' throughout the country. In 1980 House of Fraser moved to a more centralized organization and instead of having seven regional groups it formed one company (House of Fraser (Stores) Ltd) which would own all the property and employ all the staff with the single exception of the Harrods group. (Appendix 1 shows the management structure of the House of Fraser).

Over the period 1979 to 1983 the pre-tax profits of House of Fraser declined, although sales turnover rose by nearly 30%. (Appendix 2 gives financial information for the House of Fraser). During the 1970s House of Fraser became involved with Lonrho plc.

By 1979 Lonrho, which was an international conglomerate with extensive interests around the world, but especially in Africa, as part of its policy to expand its interests in the UK had bought a 22% shareholding in House of Fraser, and when it acquired a 70% holding in Scottish and Universal Investments Ltd, which itself held 10% of Fraser shares it brought Lonrho's holding in Fraser up to 29%. Consequently the purchase of Scottish and Universal Investments Ltd was referred to the Monopolies and Mergers Commission which allowed it to proceed, taking the view that although a 29% holding in House of Fraser would give

Lonrho considerable influence its greater interest would be in the profitability of its investment, and therefore in the continuing success of the department store chain, and it would not be likely to interfere in the management of the stores group.

Subsequently in 1981 Lonrho made an offer of 150 pence a share for the balance of the shares in the House of Fraser, valuing the latter at £226 million.

The bid was referred to the Monopolies and Mergers Commission which reported in December 1981, and in refusing approval for the merger said:

> Relations between them (i.e. Lonrho and House of Fraser) have been severely tested by the acrimonious disputes of the last two years and growth of mutual confidence has been prevented by Lonrho's public criticism of the competence of House of Fraser's management and by its attempt to replace four House of Fraser directors at the 1980 annual general meeting. . .
>
> We consider it probable, therefore, that if the merger took place Lonrho would be faced with the departure, or at least the disaffection of some of the most experienced directors and senior executives of House of Fraser. While it would be possible for Lonrho to fill any vacancies, by promotion from within House of Fraser or by recruitment from outside the company, there can be no certainty that persons so appointed would possess the experience and independence of judgement of the present senior management of House of Fraser. We believe therefore that in view of the lack of depth of relevant experience in Lonrho, temporary and perhaps more permanent damage to House of Fraser's efficiency would result from the merger. . .
>
> We consider that House of Fraser is generally an efficient group and that its performance and management have been improving. It is the largest departmental store group in the United Kingdom and plays an important role in the country's retail trade. We see a clear public interest in the efficiency of the House of Fraser. We believe that because of House of Fraser's size, and the importance of its assets to Lonrho, its autonomy would be considerably limited, and that the merger would result in the transfer of major decisions affecting it to Lonrho. We have referred to (i) the likely effect of the merger on the directors and senior executives of House of Fraser, (ii) the difficulties inherent in a merger between two very large companies with different histories, character and type of business, and (iii) the strain on Lonrho's management of undertaking the further responsiblities involved. . . .
>
> As regards Lonrho, we have commented in previous reports on the extent to which it is dependent on its chief executive, Mr Rowland, and we believe the events illustrate yet again the

> degree to which his personal style of management is firmly imprinted on the company and his views tend to dominate its policies. . . . Mr Rowland's dislike and suspicion of Warburgs,[1] arising out of its previous connection with Lonrho, appear also to have had considerable influence on Lonrho's actions. . .
>
> . . . We have no doubt that he (Mr Rowland) still plays the major role in its affairs, particularly in regard to its acquisitions, and that the group in which he is the largest single shareholder, remains highly dependent upon his abilities. He is now 64 years old and told us at the time of *The Observer* reference[2] that he was contemplating retirement. During the present reference, however, he said that he now hopes to remain as chief executive of Lonrho for some time, but to put in fewer hours, perhaps spending more time on group business in America. The chairman[3] and deputy chairman of the group are well past normal retiring age. In these circumstances, and in the absence of a fully developed system of corporate management or of any established succession we think that the further major expansion of Lonrho by acquisition of House of Fraser at this time involves uncertainty and risk for the latter. . . .
>
> . . . We consider that there is at least a very real and substantial risk that the efficiency of House of Fraser would deteriorate seriously as a result of the merger, and that it would be detrimental to the public interest that it should be exposed by the merger to such a risk. We believe, indeed, that the merger, if it takes place, may be expected to result in such a deterioration which would be adverse to the public interest.[4]

Mr Tiny Rowland had not usually been defeated when he had wanted some acquisition, and he did not immediately withdraw following the recommendations of the Monopolies and Mergers Commission report. Mr Rowland had joined Lonrho in 1961 when pre-tax profits were £160,000, and was the major force in the expansion of the company throughout Rhodesia, Uganda, Tanzania, Malawi, South Africa and other African emerging nations. (See Appendix 3 for financial information on Lonrho). His reputation had grown over the years until in the early 1970s he faced a setback when, following a management consultant's report on the company, he was faced with a revolution by eight of his co-directors who demanded his resignation by putting a

[1] S.G. Warburg were the merchant bankers advising House of Fraser in their defence against Lonrho. Warburg's had formerly acted for Lonrho prior to 1972 but resigned after arguments with Mr Rowland.

2 In February 1981 Lonrho bought the *Observer* for £6 million. This acquisition was referred to the Monopolies and Mergers Commission which agreed it could proceed.

[3] Mr Duncan Sandys became chairman of Lonrho in 1972.

[4] *The Monopolies and Mergers Commission* report on the proposed merger between Lonrho Ltd and House of Fraser Ltd, HMSO, 9 Dec. 1981.

resolution to the board of directors. Mr Rowland responded by seeking a court injunction to prevent the resolution being put to the board and claimed that only the shareholders could make such a decision.

During the court hearing many accusations were made and in gauging British public opinion the Prime Minister (Mr Edward Heath) called the affair 'the unpleasant and unacceptable face of capitalism'. The dispute was referred to an extraordinary meeting of shareholders who supported Mr Rowland and achieved the resignations of the opposing eight directors. This was followed by an inquiry by inspectors appointed by the Secretary of State for Trade and Industry, and when they reported three years later in July 1976 they were severely critical of some of the actions of Mr Rowland and of other directors. It was clear, however, that Mr Rowland was supported by the many private individuals who held shares in Lonrho rather than the institutional shareholders. Mr Rowland himself was a major shareholder in Lonrho with a holding of 17% of the ordinary shares.

To continue his pursuit of House of Fraser, Mr Rowland announced that he intended to remove the objections made by the Monopolies and Mergers Commission report of 1981. However, in September 1982 Mr Rowland caused a surprise when he wrote an article in *The Times* which suggested that the House of Fraser and Harrods should be separated:

> The House of Fraser falls easily into two halves. Harrods is separately run, does not share a career structure with Fraser, contributes an astonishing near 50% group profits, and owns considerable property and assets, not the least of which are its famous name, reputation and trademarks. We are particularly concerned that Harrods as a whole should remain free of loans and contractual obligations which may otherwise spill over from the remainder of Fraser as it struggles on.
>
> The Board, *in loco parentis*, is asked to entail these irreplaceable assets for the benefit of shareholders, by demerging. Harrods on its own would be a most attractive stock in the market, carrying a substantail price earnings ratio. I believe that any bid for Harrods Limited would bring several counter bids, and apart from the improved value and likelihood of returns which all shareholders would enjoy, there would be no tactical gain to Lonrho.
>
> The remaining bulk of 110 plus stores, representing substantial property and current assets, debtors and stocks earning a lower return on investment would then be exposed to market review, and to concentrated management effort and policy in producing better results. The recovery prospects of this half, plus the asset strength of the balance sheet could support a market valuation of I think, 80p to 100p per share, or £120m to £150m.
>
> I do not mean to be unkind when I say that the present part-time

> chairman[5] is suited for neither of these tasks, although he has been an enjoyable adversary in the fight to prevent us making a bid direct to shareholders, as we would have preferred. Shareholders deserve a full-time man to forward the complicated demerger with good will, and for Part Two of House of Fraser a young and enthusiastic team of retail experts is needed to revitalize the stores and so protect jobs and incomes.
>
> It has been suggestd by the present board that a property company should be formed within the stores group, but I look on that as wrong and destructive. The stores and their properties form natural units, just as Harrods does, and House of Fraser should remain a department store group whose properties are an integral part of their business.[6]

Mr Rowland put forward two resolutions, the first that the 'demerger of Harrods' should be considered by an independent investigation, and second that Professor Smith be replaced as chairman of the House of Fraser. Lonrho supported these resolutions with circulars issued to employees of the stores group as they arrived for work.

The issues were presented to an extraordinary meeting of Fraser shareholders (Appendix 4 shows a shareholder profile for the House of Fraser as at January 1981) in November 1982 which supported the principle of a Harrods demerger, but rejected the demand for Professor Smith's dismissal. The proposition for demerger was referred to the board for consideration and not to independent investigators, and the meeting requested a report before February 1983. Finally in March 1983 the Fraser board of directors met to consider the report which presented the arguments both for and against splitting Harrods from the House of Fraser, but the opposing parties on the board (which included Lonrho representatives) could not agree and a majority vote recommended no action be taken, but the issue should be referred once again to the shareholders. The meeting was scheduled for May 1983.

On 13 April 1983 Lonrho put forward a resolution for the meeting: 'That this meeting approves the proposal to demerge Harrods, first considered by shareholders in general meeting on November 4, 1982'. Lonrho also added: 'If for any reason House of Fraser should persist in denying shareholders the possibility of voting on the resolution as put by Lonrho at that meeting then Lonrho will seek to adjourn the meeting until such times as both resolutions can be considered together'.

House of Fraser also issued a circular to shareholders on the 13 April 1983. The Fraser resolution read: 'That this meeting accepts the recommendation of the board of directors to shareholders that Harrods

[5] The chairman was Professor Roland Smith who was engaged on a two-day a week contract in February 1982.

[6] *The Times*, 20 September 1981.

remains within the House of Fraser group and expresses confidence in the board'.

Lonrho replied that: 'It deeply regrets that in an apparent effort to frustrate the free expression of shareholders' opinion through a straight forward vote on the issue of demerger, the board majority at House of Fraser have chosen to present to shareholders a resolution linking the issue of demerger with a vote of confidence.'

The weeks before the meeting enabled a great deal of campaigning to be undertaken by both sides in the dispute. Lonrho employed advertisements in the financial press (see Appendix 5). Fifteen senior managers of Harrods wrote to Fraser shareholders supporting the board's contention that Harrods should remain within Fraser, and pointed out that Harrods' uniqueness must be maintained and that using the Harrods name indiscriminately would damage the store. They pointed out that Harrods gained from House of Fraser market information, trading generally and shared economies of scale in buying, etc.

Mr Rowland of Lonrho wrote an open letter of reply to the 15 senior managers of Harrods disputing that they had sufficient evidence to come to their decision, and saying that if they were not privy to the confidential documents they were in no position to advise shareholders how to vote. He disputed the point about market information and suggested that a store like Harrods had no need of Fraser services.

House of Fraser issued a circular to its shareholders pointing out that they were unable to publish the confidential information contained in the demerger report as it could be commercially damaging to House of Fraser in competitors' hands, but that the board of directors had come to their decision on the basis of that information.

The shareholders meeting took place on 6 May 1983, and they had to decide on the two resolutions. Lonrho proposed 'That this meeting approves the proposal to demerge Harrods first considered by shareholders in general meeting on 4 November 1982'. House of Fraser proposed 'That this meeting accepts the recommendation of the board of directors to shareholders that Harrods should remain within the House of Fraser group and express confidence in the board'.

Appendix 1 House of Fraser Limited

MANAGEMENT STRUCTURE

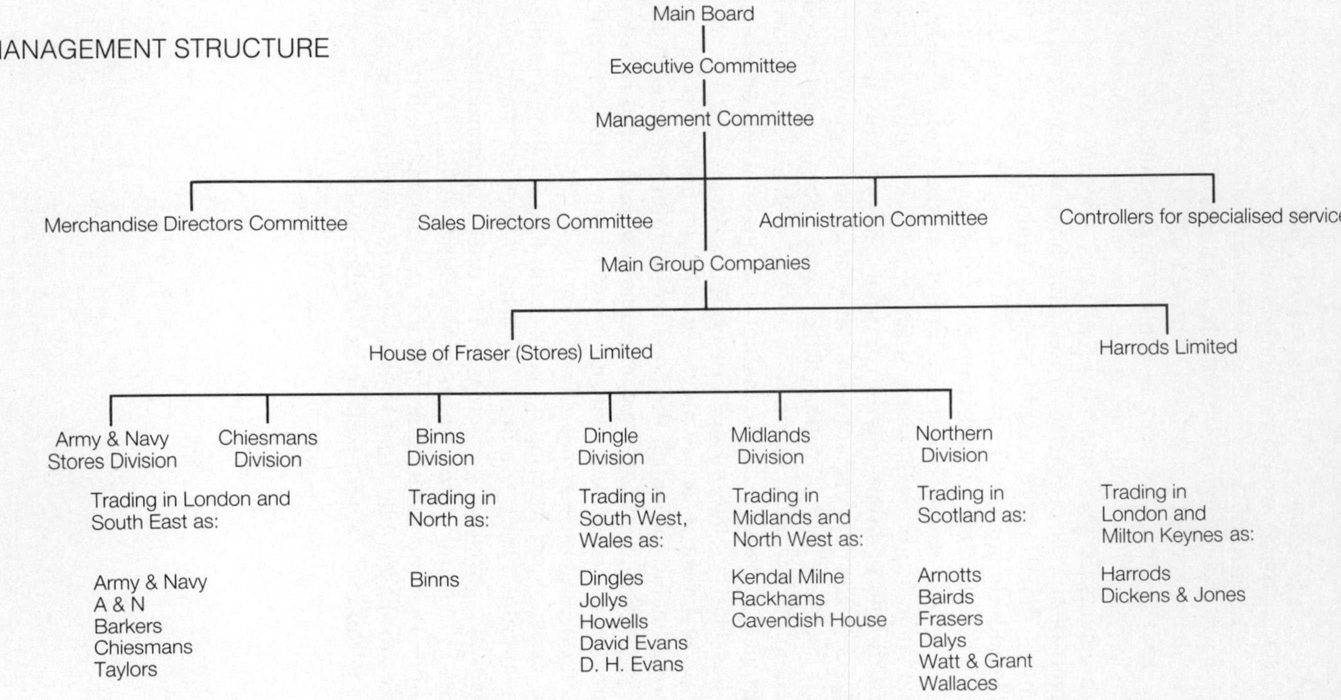

Each of the divisions is managed by a separate local management company.

Appendix 2 House of Fraser Financial Data

PROFIT AND LOSS ACCOUNT FOR THE 52 WEEKS ENDED 29 JANUARY 1983

	1983 *£000*	*1982* *£000*
Total turnover	876,726	826,638
Less: Value Added Tax	105,946	98,964
Turnover	770,780	727,674
Cost of Sales	503,349	477,287
Gross profit	267,431	250,387
Distribution costs	209,465	199,988
Administrative expenses	18,926	16,591
Trading profits	39,040	33,808
Other operating income	3,300	2,175
Share of profits of related companies	607	539
	42,947	36,522
Investment income	101	131
Investment receivable	1,224	1,837
Interest payable	(9,826)	(9,349)
Allocation to profit-linked share plan	(1,258)	(1,113)
Profit on ordinary activities before taxation	33,188	28,028
Taxation thereon	10,243	3,377
Profit on ordinary activities after taxation	22,945	22,651
Extraordinary items	(365)	1,555
Profit for the financial period	22,580	26,206
Dividends	11,453	10,641
Profit retained	11,127	15,565
whereof:		
Retained in related companies	337	298
Retained in Group	10,790	15,267
	11,127	15,565
Earnings per ordinary share	15.1p	16.3p
Dividend per ordinary share	7.5p	7.0p

BALANCE SHEET AT 29 JANUARY 1983 (£000)

	1983	*1982*
Fixed assets		
Tangible assets	393,230	369,163
Investments	6,365	5,456
	399,595	374,619
Current assets		
Stocks	113,682	107,272
Debtors	177,135	152,525
Investments	1,711	1,329
Deposits at short call	4,071	5,416
Cash and bank balances	11,871	17,373
	308,470	283,915
Current liabilities – Creditors: amounts falling due within one year		
Trade creditors	62,647	55,225
Debentures, loans and overdrafts	32,536	30,540
Other liabilities	58,392	49,730
	153,575	135,495
Net current assets	154,895	148,420
Total assets less current liabilities	554,490	523,039
Creditors: amounts falling due after more than one year	57,885	40,785
	496,605	482,254
Capital and reserves		
Called up share capital	38,828	38,649
Share premium account	24,135	23,201
Revaluation reserve	212,298	215,452
Profit and loss account	214,998	199,521
Related companies reserves	6,346	5,431
	496,605	482,254

FINANCIAL RECORD, YEARS ENDED JANUARY (£000)

	1979	*1980*	*1981*	*1982*	*1983*
Total turnover	614,073	699,813	777,387	826,638	876,726
Profit before taxation	40,492	37,147	34,408	28,028	33,188
Taxation	14,788	14,729	9,901	3,377	10,243
Net profit attributable to members	25,704	22,418	24,507	24,651	22,945
Extraordinary items	–	–	17,608	1,555	(365)
Dividends	6,612	9,004	9,974	10,641	11,453
Profit retained	19,092	13,414	32,141	15,565	11,127
Depreciation	7,537	8,479	9,563	12,454	13,921
Reinvested in the business	26,629	21,893	41,704	28,019	25,048
Earnings per ordinary share – before extraordinary items	17.4p	15.0p	16.3p	16.3p	15.1p
Dividend per ordinary share	4.4p	6.0p	6.6p	7.0p	7.5p

CONTRIBUTION OF 'HARRODS' TO GROUP TURNOVER AND PROFITS (£m)

	1980	*1981*	*1982*	*1983*
Gross turnover				
Harrods	145.1	157.2	172.8	183.3
Rest of House of Fraser	554.7	620.2	653.8	693.4
	699.8	777.4	826.6	876.7
Trading profits				
Harrods	15.6	13.6	13.6	16.2
Rest of House of Fraser	27.8	31.7	20.2	22.8
	43.4	45.3	33.8	39.0

Profits stated are before interest, other operating income or results of related companies.

A proportion of overhead or central costs were charged to Harrods, and the basis of allocation used was in proportion to stocks and debtors.

Appendix 3 Lonrho Plc – Financial Data

CONSOLIDATED PROFIT AND LOSS ACCOUNT FOR THE YEAR ENDED 30 SEPTEMBER 1982 (£m)

	1982	*1981*
Turnover	3,008.94	2,415.41
Profit before tax and interest	149.67	169.50
Net Interest Payable	74.56	57.86
Profit after tax		
Group	54.47	83.62
Associates	20.64	28.02
	75.11	111.64
Tax	38.75	50.92
	36.36	60.72
Minority Interests	16.40	25.43
Profit attributable to shareholders before extraordinary items	19.96	35.29
Extraordinary items	10.78	11.67
Profit attributable to shareholders after extraordinary items	9.18	23.62
Balance at 30 September, 1981	114.78	107.70
Dividends	23.70	23.70
Other reserve movements	11.36	7.16
Balance at 30 September 1982	88.90	114.78
Earnings per share		
Net basis	7.62p	13.50p

BALANCE SHEET, 30 SEPTEMBER 1982 (£m)

	1982		*1981*	
Fixed assets				
Land and buildings	488.66		428.36	
Mining assets	93.08		105.73	
Equipment	136.53		118.72	
Capital work in progress	40.71		16.67	
Associates	197.56		189.09	
Investments	43.41		43.38	
			999.95	901.95
Current assets				
Stock and work in progress	398.81		328.35	
Debtors	326.35		321.86	
Cash and deposits in bank	56.28		136.25	
	781.44		781.46	
Current liabilities				
Creditors	415.67		336.52	
Tax	48.06		56.29	
Bank loans and overdrafts	242.08		222.01	
Dividend	21.09		23.70	
	726.90		638.52	
Net current assets		54.54		142.94
Total assets employed		1054.49		1044.89
Funds employed				
Share capital		65.50		65.46
Reserves		471.51		422.71
Equity interest		537.01		488.17
Minority interests		111.09		213.10
Deferred tax		2.94		.75
		651.04		702.02
Loans		403.45		342.87
		1054.49		1044.89

EIGHT-YEAR FINANCIAL RECORD, YEAR ENDED 30 SEPTEMBER (£m)

	1982	*1981*	*1980*
Turnover	3,008.94	2,415.41	2,100.66
Group profit before interest	129.03	141.48	148.11
Profit before tax	75.11	111.64	119.10
Profit after tax, minorities and excluding extra-ordinary items	19.96	35.29	45.04
Cost of dividend	23.70 (net)	23.70 (net)	24.41 (net)
Fixed assets	758.98	669.48	539.86
Net current assets and investments	295.51	375.41	308.45
Total funds employed	1,054.49	1,044.89	848.31
Total equity interest	537.01	488.17	446.66
Net assets per share (pence)	205	186	171
Earnings per share (pence)	7.62	13.50	19.42

1979	1978	1977	1976	1975
1,565.45	1,491.37	1,257.25	1,083.42	606.00
98.01	93.33	98.39	98.10	65.39
78.23	78.72	83.60	91.99	62.71
33.23	35.15	42.85	38.58	22.86
15.82	12.58	12.37	7.51	3.86
(net)	(net)	(net)	(net)	(net)
385.84	358.18	325.63	219.86	166.24
218.62	134.62	132.33	161.21	113.75
604.46	492.80	457.96	381.07	279.99
378.48	330.42	296.31	251.26	183.41
171	166	150	113	107
16.11	17.67	22.85	24.08	17.90

Appendix 4 House of Fraser

SHARE CAPITAL

The major part of House of Fraser's share capital at 31 January 1981 consisted of 150.6 million ordinary shares of 25 pence each (£37.65 million). In addition, there was £0.75 million preference capital outstanding in three different classes of preference share. The ordinary share capital was held as follows:

	million	%
Lonrho	45.1	29.9
N C Head Office Nominees Ltd (including 4.15 million Fraser family holdings)	4.3	2.8
National Coal Board Pension Fund	3.6	2.4
Legal and General Assurance Society Ltd	2.9	1.9
British Railways (Wages Grade) Pension Fund	2.5	1.7
Trustees of House of Fraser profit-linked share plan	2.3	1.5
Post Office Staff Superannuation Fund	2.1	1.4
Robert Fleming Nominees Ltd	1.3	0.9
Robert Fleming Nominees Ltd ZZ Account	0.4	0.3
	64.5	42.8
Holders of less than 1 per cent of the issued ordinary share capital (including 1.73 million Fraser family holding)	86.1	57.2
	150.6	100.0

Appendix 5 Lonrho Advertising in the Financial Press

On Sunday, 24 April 1983, Lonrho placed a quarter-page advertisement in the *Sunday Times* addressed to all House of Fraser shareholders incorporating the following points:

SEPARATING HARRODS IS THE WAY TO GET HOUSE OF FRASER TOGETHER

The House of Fraser Board have called an Extra-ordinary General Meeting on 6 May 1983. They have presented a resolution which links the demerger of Harrods with a vote of confidence in the Board. We, the minority directors, strongly disagree with this resolution which we consider is contrary to the spirit and intent of the resolution passed in November 1982. We wish shareholders to consider the demerger on its own merits, and to be in no doubt about the advantages of separating Harrods from House of Fraser. The vote of no confidence should not have been coupled with a resolution for or against demerger. We urge the shareholders to vote against the Board's resolution and not to be distracted by the expression of confidence. The Board has left shareholders who favour demerger with no other choice.

Let Harrods Grow

By owning a direct stake in Harrods shareholders would have an investment in the finest store in the world, which now generates well over half the profits of the whole group. Unfortunately, propping up sick relations has now begun to have detrimental effects. The world's leading departmental store is short of funds for its own refurbishment. At present it is not even fully air-conditioned.

Increased Dividends?

Over the last five years, Harrods alone has paid more in dividends to House of Fraser than the shareholders have received from the entire group! Is it not possible that by owning a direct stake in Harrods, shareholders would receive increasing dividends?

Exploit the True Potential

The release of Harrods would allow you to have an investment stake in Harrods which will then be free to use the profits which it generates each year. Great improvements could be made to the store and better service could be afforded.

Long Term Potential

The shareholders will retain their investment in 102 House of Fraser stores, which would have long term potential.

Forced to Perform

The rest of the group will be forced to perform. With the loss of their source of 'easy money', the management of House of Fraser will be compelled to deal with those parts of the group which do not produce a return, and will in the end provide a more secure future for staff.

SHAREHOLDERS ARE URGED TO SUPPORT DEMERGER BY VOTING AGAINST THE RESOLUTION

From Lord Duncan Sandys and R.W. Rowland expressing a contrary view to the Board.

On Monday, 25 April 1983, Lonrho placed a quarter-page advertisement in the *Financial Times* addressed to House of Fraser shareholders incorporating the following points:

SEPARATING HARRODS IS THE WAY TO GET HOUSE OF FRASER TOGETHER

At the Extra-ordinary General Meeting of the House of Fraser plc to be held 6 May 1983, every vote cast will be critical in ensuring the successful future of Harrods and the rest of the House of Fraser stores.

Resolution: Accepting the recommendation of the Board that Harrods should remain within the House of Fraser and expressing confidence in the Board.

Vote AGAINST the resolution as shown and post your proxy card today.

By voting against the resolution you will be voting in favour of a demerger of Harrods.

As a shareholder you should consider:

1 The advantages of owning shares in two public companies
2 The advantages of receiving dividends from both companies
3 The possibility of an increased value on your shares
4 What you could possibly lose by a demerger
5 What you will probably gain.

From Lord Duncan Sandys and R.W. Rowland Directors of House of Fraser.

PART IV

Strategies for Declining Environments

16 F Pratt Engineering

By late 1983 the engineering companies of Britain were beginning to show signs of recovery from the recession which had begun several years before. Those which had survived had done so by concentrating on slimming down their workforces, cost-cutting and as a result raising productivity across the industry generally by 12% in the period 1979–83. During this period the volume of engineering output had fallen by 16%, direct employment by 25% and capacity by aproximately 30%. The large engineering companies depended upon the manufacturing companies which purchased 75% of all mechanical engineering output as their own capital investment, and the latter had plenty of spare capacity themselves. Internationally the UK had always been net exporters of engineering products, but the difference had declined from a surplus on the balance of trade in 1979 of £3 billion to a surplus of £500 million in 1983.

COMPANY BACKGROUND

F Pratt was an engineering company which manufactured products used in the machine tool industry and process plant industry as well as in general engineering. At one time the range of equipment supplied by the company had been very closely tied to machine tools, but it had expanded the range, for example, into hydraulics, in order to lessen its dependence on one sector.

The original company which came to bear the name F Pratt was incorporated as a limited company in 1897. As a firm it was just over 100 years old when F Pratt & Co Ltd became a public company in 1953. The first operations could be traced back to a date a little earlier than 1850, but there were no firm records to fix a precise date.

At that time, the company manufactured and factored certain machine tools and, prior to the outbreak of the First World War, it added both independent and universal chucks[1] to its product range. Following on the First World War, Pratt continued to manufacture these two types of chuck and also carried on the business they had developed in manufacturing machine tools. This manufacture was gradually dropped, however, although the company continued to factor machine tools almost up to the outbreak of the Second World War.

During the period between the two wars, the company added to the range of chucks. The variety of both Independent and Scroll Chucks was greatly increased and notably the latter part of the inter-war period saw the development and production of compressed air equipment. Following the end of the Second World War the company began manufacturing the Woodworth range of workholding equipment which was designed for companies specializing in high mass production, such as the automobile industry.

In the summer of 1953, F Pratt & Company became a public company with shares quoted on the open market and remained as a single unit for only a short time. Within 15 months negotiations were started which led to the acquiring of F Burnerd & Co Ltd, who were then situated at Kidbrooke in London. For some time Burnerd had been a major competitor in the Independent and Universal Chucks market, and the merging of that company with F Pratt ensured their being the largest supplier in the world of the particular product range.

In 1961 Pratt became a holding company, having diversified into a range of activities which, by 1980, included forgings and stampings, tooling equipment and gauges, optical and medical equipment and process plant, in addition to the original business. By this time the company had a turnover of over £22 million, with profits before taxation of nearly £1 million on net assets of approximately £15.5 million.

For the financial year ending 1981, the company suffered a loss, before taxation, of over £1 million. However, the profit available for distribution amounted to over £500,000, due to the disposal of the group's optical business, Hamblin and Wingate (Holdings), for around £4.5 million. After costs attributable to factory closure and redundancies as a result of losses in the traditional workholding division, the net contribution of extraordinary items to profits was £1.65 million. (Appendix 1 gives financial information on F Pratt Plc.)

Pratt had done extremely well on the Hamblin sale as it had only acquired the company seven months previously and had paid only £850,000 for the acquisition. During 1981, trading conditions in the United Kingdom had deteriorated, hitting the engineering industry particularly hard and forcing the closure of Pratt's Winchester-based factory, which manufactured lathe chucks and collets. Overall the year

[1] A chuck is a piece of equipment which is fitted to a machine tool either to hold the cutting tool or the piece to be cut (e.g. rather like the drill-holder on a domestic drill but, of course, much larger).

had been one of retrenchment during which time lathe chuck production had been amalgamated into one factory (Halifax) and the forging activities had also undergone significant reorganization.

At the beginning of 1982, a new chairman, Mr James Hendin, was appointed. Mr Hendin was a non-executive director of the 600 Group,[2] an engineering company which owned a 27% stake in Pratt, and for many years had been an important customer. The appointment followed closely on the heels of a boardroom dispute concerning head office expenses, which was finally resolved, but only after a good deal of adverse publicity. To the company's credit overall net debt had been cut from £6.48 million to £2.29 million, and with the reorganization completed, Pratt appeared to be in line for recovery. Indeed, the company was recommended by the *Investors Chronicle* as a possible speculation. (Appendix 2 shows the organization chart for F Pratt Plc.)

Although Pratt's had survived the 1980/81 engineering recessions there were still problem areas within the whole business. For example, in the Workholding Division the inflow of orders was still low, and in attempting to cut costs the company had closed down one factory in the south of the country, and transferred the work to Halifax in Yorkshire, but a number of key employees had been loathe to move. This resulted in higher retraining costs than expected and timelag before the move became productive. But they had taken the opportunity to modernize production methods and introduced new models of numerical controlled machine tools. Nevertheless, the Workholding Division was not producing profits.

The Forging Division supplied the car industry, general engineers and aerospace and defence contractors, all of whom had suffered throughout the recession, and although the division was able to maintain its sales levels, profit margins had been eroded due to competition.

The company was attempting to diversify its interests, for example via a purchase of a 40% interest in Pratt Burnerd America in partnership with an American company, and also with the introduction of new products. These new products included an automatic dairy system,[3] an opthalmic chair (which would be used in eye hospitals), a co-rotating twin screw compounder and pipe cutting equipment which the company had not invented, but for which it had secured manufacturing and distribution rights from the American inventor. This provided a simple and accurate method of cutting and end preparation of pipework installed in various areas including naval vessels, nuclear power stations and process plants.

An additional diversification was an 80% acquisition of Trojan Structures Ltd which manufactured a unique form of container which

[2] 600 Group was a large UK engineering company with interests in the machine tool sector.

[3] The 'Bratlan' automatic dairy system came within the definition of 'process plant equipment'.

could expand to five times its own size to form a building, and could hold up to four tonnes of equipment. It could be used in a wide variety of situations including emergency use, additional facilities and exhibition displays.

The continuing losses allied with new product development costs led the company to a further divestment in October 1982, when it sold its forging division as represented by the Omes-Faulkners subsidiary company for £2.7 million, although it was at a book value of £6.3 million in the Pratt accounts. Omes-Faulkner had been responsible for £1.09 million of Pratt's £1.57 million pre-tax losses in 1982 on its sales of £4.59 million. (Appendix 3 shows financial information for the Omes-Faulkner subsidiary.)

Just before October 1984 when its financial year ended it was expected that F Pratt Plc would be announcing pre-tax profits of about £300,000 on sales turnover of £9.5 million which would enable the company to resume dividend payments which had not been paid since 1981. As a consequence the company share price rose slightly to 52 pence.

THE MACHINE TOOLS INDUSTRY

The engineering industry can be sub-divided into many sectors, and traditionally one of the most important sectors was that of 'machine tools'. Machine tools range in size from one ton to five hundred tons, and in price from £1,000 to £300,000. The British Standard defined a machine tool as 'a power driven machine not portable by hand, which in operation works metal by cutting, forming, physico-chemical processing or a combination of the techniques'.[4]

Machine tools are a vital part of industrial progress, and virtually every product at some stage in its manufacturing process involves a machine tool. On average there are approximately 3,000 different types of machine tools, ranging from relatively simple boring machines to numerically controlled lathes, although the vast majority are adaptations or refinements of three basic types, i.e. the lathe, the drilling machine and the grinding machine.

Machining is done to previously forged or cast metals by tools with sharp cutting edges made of materials harder than the metal being cut. Whilst the process is under way, lubricants or coolants are applied such as compressed air, water, or an emulsion of oils/water.

The performance of the UK machine industry had been declining for some years, and from a base of 100 in 1975, the index of production had fallen to 45 by 1982. In the decade ending in 1982 imports of machine tools had achieved a penetration of the UK market of 61% compared to 30% in 1972.

[4] British Standard 4640 (1970).

In 1966 the first commercially available electronic integrated micro-circuits entered the market, and by 1967 there were fourteen manufacturers worldwide incorporating them in machine tools. Development of such numerically controlled machine tools was very rapid although it did not account for more than 5% of UK production by value, and discouraged many manufacturers through fear of product obsolescence. It was at this time that many British machine-tool manufacturers failed to grasp the opportunities from that technological revolution. The most famous name in British machine tools was that of the Alfred Herbert company which had a 20% share of the UK market in the 1960s, and whose commercial director stated, 'To maintain our current prominence in the industry, we have strong research, design and manufacturing groups and a powerful marketing organization. With the start we've got, I don't think there's any doubt that 25 years from now we'll still be relatively as strong as we are today.'[5] Herbert's profits peaked in 1967 but by 1975 it had to be taken over by the National Enterprise Board to preserve it from liquidation, and by 1980 the company had to be dismembered with debts of £57 million.

By the beginning of 1983 orders taken by the British machine-tools industry, facing competition from cheaper innovative Japanese imports, had sunk to about £333m, slightly more than half the total in 1979.

Orders for the first three months of 1984 were 19% higher than the last quarter of 1983 and 35% higher than the same period in 1983, although overall orders were some 40% down on 1979. It was evident that a number of firms were ready to come to the rescue of British machine tool companies. Tube Investments took over Alfred Herbert, John Brown Engineering found a buyer for its Wickman multi-spindle lathes business, and the Webster and Bennett vertical boring machines, and another for the Halifax-based Kitchen Walker boring machine operation.

Penetration of the UK market by Japanese producers, particularly in computer numerically controlled (CNC) machining centres and lathes had been quite spectacular. The Japanese share of imports rose overall from 4% in 1976 to 13% in 1982. The Japanese machining-centre share of imports, however, rose from 2% to 70% with CNC lathes doubling their share to 38%.

A number of factors combined to slow down that performance, however. A poor home market had weakened volumes in Japanese plants and consequently, their ability to export competitively. The UK lathe market had declined substantially anyway, and complaints by local manufacturers at the level of Japanese imports resulted in agreement with Japanese manufacturers and the Ministry of Trade and Industry in Tokyo to cut back on machining centre sales in the UK, by about 20% in 1984.

Agreement among UK producers to ask for an extension of that

[5] *Management Today*, September 1983.

agreement angered machine tool importers in Britain, and threatened to divide the industry's representative body, the Machine Tool Trades Association which acts for both local manufacturers and importers.

A number of UK manufacturers had also threatened the position of importers by concluding licensing agreements with Japanese manufacturers, particularly for small CNC machining centres which could perform a wide range of cutting tasks in both large and small machine shops.

Judging by the strength of home market orders, the industry was on the verge of an upswing in its traditional cycle. Analysts were guarded about forecasting just how strong the recovery would be, but there was general agreement that orders were unlikely to return, this time at least, to the £600m of 1979.

PROCESS PLANT[6]

Process plant covers a multitude of industries from food and drink manufacture to extracting oil from the North Sea. However, despite its wide spread of uses, the sector had taken a heavy battering during the recession as companies cut back on capital investment.

There had been substantial redundancies in the process plant industry during the period 1979–83. A number of manufacturers had been forced out of business. The most recent company to be overtaken was Capper Neill, which called in receivers at the end of February 1984.

Nonetheless, there were signs of recovery in other industries that were starting to affect parts of the process plant industry. Food and drink manufacturers which had been at the sharp end of the boom in consumer spending – even if a lower proportion of household budgets was spent on eating and drinking – had been modernizing and rationalizing production by investing in new plant and machinery.

Tax concessions to boost North Sea Oil exploration, announced in the 1983 Budget, were now likely to work their way through to process plant manufacturers making platforms and other equipment for rig operations. The oil industry estimated that expenditure on North Sea Oil exploration and development was likely to total at least £60bn between 1984 and the end of the century.

There was also a resurgence in capital expenditure on process plant by the chemical industry in 1983, and it was forecast that capital expenditure by the industry could rise by more than 25% by 1985. Investment was likely to be aimed at improving productivity of older plants and continuing the industry's diversification into speciality chemicals. New projects would be concentrated in the £1m to £10m range rather than the £100m-plus range of the 1970s.

[6] Defined by its manufacturers as 'all that range of plant equipment and machinery used to convert material from one form into another and pack it for sale to industry or the public at large.'

Appendix 1 F Pratt Plc

CONSOLIDATED PROFIT AND LOSS ACCOUNT – OCTOBER 1983 (£000)

	1983	*1982*
Turnover	7,231	13,379
Less cost of sales	5,471	11,274
Gross profit	1,760	2,105
Less distribution costs	727	954
Less administrative expenses	998	2,307
Plus other operating income	14	62
Operating profit (loss)	49	(1,094)
Interest payable less receivable	(306)	(447)
Loss on ordinary activities before taxation	(257)	(1,541)
Taxation on ordinary activities	(33)	(65)
Loss on ordinary activities after taxation	(290)	(1,606)
Extraordinary items	(276)	(3,764)
Loss attributable to shareholders – Transfer from reserves	(566)	(5,370)
Statement of retained profits/reserves		
Balance at 31 October 1982, as previously reported	5,608	10,975
Prior year adjustment	(220)	(245)
As restated	5,388	10,730
Loss for the year	(566)	(5,370)
Exchange adjustments	44	28
Balance at 31 October 1983	4,866	5,388

CONSOLIDATED BALANCE SHEET – OCTOBER 1983 (£000)

	1983	*1982*
Assets less liabilities		
Fixed assets		
Tangible assets	3,912	4,061
Investments	372	344
	4,284	4,405
Current assets		
Stocks and long-term contracts	3,771	4,201
Debtors	2,108	1,948
Cash at bank and in hand	23	302
	5,902	6,451
Current liabilities		
Creditors: amounts falling due within 1 year	3,055	3,078
Net current assets	2,847	3,373
Total assets less current liabilities	7,131	7,778
Creditors: amounts falling due after more than 1 year – loans	895	1,020
Net assets	6,236	6,758
Capital and reserves		
Called-up share capital (25 pence par value)	1,369	1,369
Share premium	222	222
Revaluation reserve	1,401	1,431
Other reserves	1,714	1,714
Profit and loss account	1,529	2,021
Shareholders' equity	6,235	6,757
Minority interests	1	1
	6,236	6,758

FIVE-YEAR RECORD (£000)

	1983	*1982*	*1981*	*1980*	*1979*
Turnover	7,231	13,379	18,855	22,129	19,413
Profit/(loss) before taxation	(257)	(1,541)	(1,006)	1,070	493
Taxation	33	65	79	14	(338)
Profit/(loss) after taxation	(290)	(1,606)	(1,085)	1,056	831
Extraordinary items	276	3,764	1,651	(232)	(8)
Profit/(loss) attributable to shareholders	(566)	(5,370)	566	824	823
Dividends	–	–	240	326	323
Retained/(borne) by the group	(566)	(5,370)	326	498	500
Net assets employed –					
Tangible fixed assets	3,912	4,061	7,814	9,580	8,611
Fixed asset Investments	372	344	553	672	652
Net current assets	2,847	3,373	7,041	5,384	5,820
	7,131	7,778	15,408	15,636	15,083
Financed by –					
Shareholders' equity	6,235	6,757	12,095	12,062	11,182
Minority interest	1	1	1	1	1
Creditors falling due after more than one year	895	1,020	3,312	3,569	3,569
Deferred taxation	–	–	–	–	324
Deferred investment grant credit	–	–	–	4	7
	7,131	7,778	15,408	15,636	15,083
Per ordinary share –					
Profit/(loss) after taxation	(5.3p)	(29.3p)	(19.9p)	19.5p	15.4p
Dividends	–	–	4.4p	6.0p	6.0p

In 1980 prior years were restated to reflect the change in accounting policy for deferred taxation.

In 1983 the figures for 1982 and 1981 were restated to reflect the change in basis of stock valuation.

SUBSTANTIAL SHAREHOLDERS ORDINARY SHARE OF 25p EACH

	Number	*Percentage*
The 600 Group Plc	1,467,725	26.8
Prudential Corporation Plc	367,892	6.7
Drayton Consolidated Trust Ltd	325,875	6.9
Norwich Union Insurance Group	299,000	5.5
Maurice James Industries Plc	274,000	5.0
Directors (and their families)	54,700	1.0

Appendix 2 F Pratt Engineering Corporation

GROUP STRUCTURE – 1981

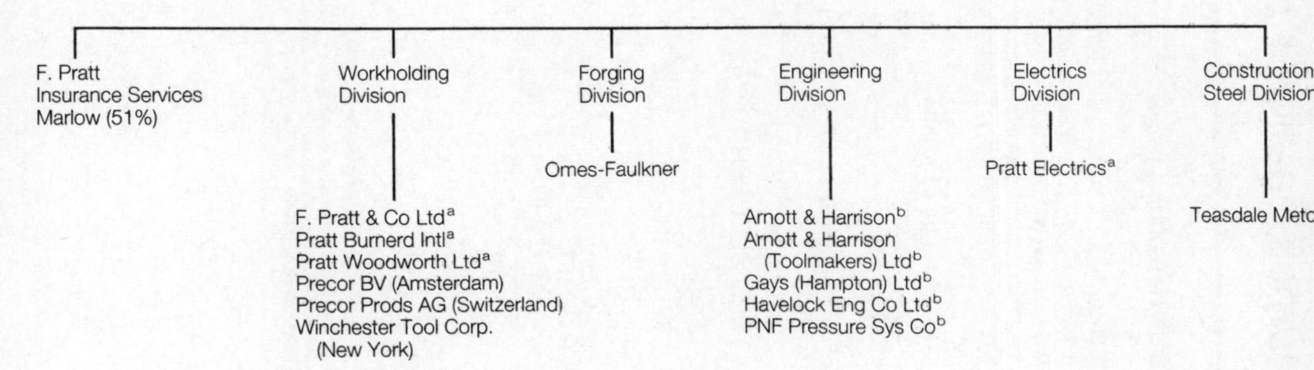

[a]Located at Halifax, West Yorkshire.

[b]Located at Hampton.

Appendix 3 Omes-Faulkner Ltd

PROFIT AND LOSS ACCOUNTS (£000)

	6 months to April 1982	*£'000 Year ending October*				
	1982	*1981*	*1980*	*1979*	*1978*	*1977*
Sales	3,203	7,467	7,391	6,815	6,365	6,404
Profit/(Loss) before tax	(631)	(387)	100	296	215	284
Tax	–	(78)	439	303	(102)	(137)
Profit/(Loss) after tax	(631)	(465)	539	599	113	147

BALANCE SHEET AT YEAR END OCTOBER 1981 (£000)

Fixed assets		1,271
Current assets		
Stocks	1,778	
Debtors	1,545	
Tax recoverable	153	
Cash	4	
	3,480	
Current Liabilities		
Creditors	720	
Short-term loans	120	
	840	
Net current assets		2,640
Net tangible assets	3,911	

17 Silentnight

The UK Bedding Industry

THE MARKET FOR BEDS AND MATTRESSES

Over the 1970s, the bed and mattress market was one of the most stable, and changes in sales levels rarely upset the equilibrium of manufacturers' profitability. However, by 1980 the situation had changed, sales began to decline, profitability began to fall and several companies went into liquidation.

TABLE 17.1 UK manufacturers' sales of beds and mattresses

Year	*Value £m*	*Volume M. Units*
1975	95.7	4.9
1976	109.0	6.3
1977	117.9	6.0
1978	143.1	6.7
1979	154.1	6.6
1980	153.2	6.2
1981	162.0	5.5
1982	176.27	5.3[a]
1983	189.47	5.4[a]
1984	198.21	5.6[a]

[a] estimated

Value and share volume figures are calculated on different bases and it is not possible to determine the unit price of a bed by dividing value by volume.

Source: *Business Monitor*

The market for beds is unique in the furniture market in the sense that domestic manufacturers have retained and built upon their long-established reputation for quality products and, so far, overseas competition has been largely repelled.

TABLE 17.2 Overseas trade in beds (£)m

	1979	*1980*	*1981*	*1982*	*1983*	*1984*
Exports	3.03	2.75	2.30	2.76	2.22	2.04
Imports	0.54	0.56	1.00	1.45	2.35	1.86
Balance	2.49	2.19	1.30	1.31	−.13	0.18

Source: *Business Monitor*

The three main submarkets in the beds sector are: bases, mattresses and bed ends. The majority of beds are made from wood and upholstery, but there is still a small market for metal mattress supports and bed ends.

TABLE 17.3 Structure of the bed products market – % of MSP value

	1979	*1980*	*1981*	*1982*	*1983*	*1984*
Mattresses	54	54	52	52	52	52
Upholstered bases	37	36	37	37	36	37
Bed ends, headboards, bunk beds	9	10	11	11	12	11

Source: *Business Monitor*

MARKET SIZE AND TRENDS

Sales of beds and bases became static in the late 1970s after a steady growth. At the same time, consumers have been trading down in terms of quality and the value of sales has not been keeping pace with inflation.

Some sectors of the bed market have been relatively bouyant as there has been a trend towards storage bases and bunk beds in the late 1970s. Specialist retailers claim that storage beds accounted for 60% of sales whilst non-specialists claimed they accounted for 40%.

There has been a shift away from double beds to single beds, with lower unit values, in 1979, the market was divided approximately evenly between single and double beds. By 1984, however, the single beds were outselling double beds in a ratio of 53:47.

Through the 1970s unit sales of spring mattresses declined each year, and the unit sales of foam mattresses have increased. The trend to cheaper foam mattresses has been helped by a fashion for wooden beds and bunk beds with a foam mattress which are suitable for children. Foam is not important in the double-bed sector but accounts for a large proportion of single-bed mattress sales. The majority of purchasers of single beds are not buying for themselves, but for children or guests and so may not be as concerned about quality as they might otherwise be.

People buy beds and mattresses when they set up home, when children need them and for guest rooms. This is largely between the ages of 25–34. There is also a large replacement market. In the replacement market which takes place in the 55–64-year-old group of the population, sales of mattresses are higher than those of bases for economic reasons. If the bed is not distorted, then it is cheaper to replace only the mattress.

Growth areas in the market are luxury beds and storage beds. Although orthopaedic beds remain the most popular, consumers are moving away from them towards those which offer more comfort as well as a firm core for spinal support. These premium-priced luxury beds are also more profitable for manufacturers.

Space utilization has increased in importance as more people buy flats and newer houses with smaller rooms. Storage beds, bunk beds and convertibles have increased in popularity. Drawer divans are the most popular, accounting for 75% to 80% of storage beds, and divans and over 80% of all bed sales.

Convertible sofas can look good for seating and also provide a spare bed for guests. As this has been realized, so the market has grown, although convertible sofas have been available for many years. UK manufacturers' sales of convertibles have been steadily increasing since late 1982.

TABLE 17.4 UK manufacturers' sales of convertibles

Year	*£m MSP*
1981	8.3
1982	7.6
1983	13.1
1984	14.9

Source: *Business Monitor*

The buying of a bed is not on the whole considered to be an exciting purchase as it is not generally on view to visitors. Bed purchases compete with electrical and durable goods for discretionary spending.

MANUFACTURERS AND MARKET SHARE

By 1982 the number of manufacturers involved in the bedding industry was 80, compared to a total of 460 after the Second World War. This gives an indication of the nature of concentration in the bedding market.

There are a number of important manufacturers and brands in this market, each with between 4% and 9% market share, the exception being Silentnight who overtook Slumberland as brand leader by the late 1970s. The fortunes of other brands have been variable.

TABLE 17.5 Market share by volume

	1979 %	*1982* %	*1984* %
Silentnight Group	20	30	28–30
Airsprung	3–5	9	12
Sykes (Dorlux)	–	8	9–10
Rest Assured	5–6	4–5	6–7
Reylon	3–5	3–4	5–6
Myers	5	6	4–5
Sleepezee	5	5–6	4–5
Dunlopillo	5–6	4–5	4
Others	38–42	17–21	13–21

Source: Mintel/Trade estimates

There has been a large increase in own-label manufacturing of beds and mattresses in the 1980s. These products are now thought to account for 20 to 25% of sales. Most of the major manufacturers produce own-label products for retailers, but labels usually state the name of the manufacturers to give an assurance of quality.

Silentnight Holdings plc is the leading UK manufacturer of beds and mattresses. In addition to the Silentnight name, the company is also responsible for Sealy Sleep products, Layezee beds and Perfecta bedding. Silentnight has achieved its strong position by cultivation of the retail trade, and an emphasis on the right product at the right price. Silentnight has spent very little on promoting its products to the public, except for selected advertising in particular areas, and as a result, brand awareness is low even though in the past few years efforts have been made to rectify the situation. However, most effort is still below the line to the retailer. In July 1984 the company launched the 'Super Sleeper' into the luxury bed sector with a £500,000 launch budget. It is being produced under licence from the American firm Serta.

The Airsprung group, selling middle-range beds, is second in the market after significantly bettering distribution in all retail areas since the late 1970s. Their share has increased from 4% to 12% in ten years. It supplies MFI with an estimated 20% of its volume going through this retailer.

Slumberland, one of the loss-making concerns of Dupont, was sold to Melatex, a privately owned company, in February 1983 for £470,000, and Silentnight recently backed out of an opportunity to purchase it. The upmarket trade marks include Somnus and Posture springing. The operation has been very much slimmed down since the takeover of Melatex, and it is reported to be profitable once again.

Relyon and Rest Assured have maintained their market share despite their products being higher priced. In value terms their market shares are higher than in volume terms. Relyon in particular have reported better turnover and profits in 1983 and 1984 compared with earlier years. Sykes (Dorlux), a manufacturer positioned very much at the lower end of the price range, has done very well and gained a significant market share, as consumers have become increasingly price sensitive. Due to the aggressive stance of MFI and Queensway, consumer preferences have shifted towards a premium price segment and a larger low-priced segment, with the middle-range sector declining significantly. Sykes (Dorlux) were well positioned to take advantage of this shift, and those companies aiming at the middle range (for example, Silentnight) have had to rethink their marketing strategies.

RETAILERS AND DISTRIBUTION

The distribution profile for beds is significantly different from that for furniture as a whole. In all other sectors of the furniture market, one outlet or another has a position of some dominance; for example MFI dominates the kitchen furniture and multiple retailers dominate the upholstery sector. Sales of beds, on the other hand, are very well spread across a wide range of outlets.

TABLE 17.6 Bed purchases by type and outlet

Outlet	*1981*	*1982*	*1984*
	%	%	%
Bedding and furniture shops	43–45	42–43	43–44
Department stores	15–17	14–15	15–16
Discount warehouses	11–13	15–17	20–22
Mail order	8–10	7–8	5–6
Co-ops	6–7	5–6	5–6
Other	10–14	11–17	6–12

Source: Price Commission/Trade estimates

Harris Queensway and MFI are the two largest firms in the discount warehouse business in the country, with Harris Queensway alone accounting for 7% of all bed sales. Allied Carpets have now entered the bed retailing market, and the importance of discounters is likely to continue.

ADVERTISING AND PROMOTION

From Table 17.7 it can be seen that the main media efforts have been fairly modest. Many major manufacturers spend very little on above-the-line advertising. In fact most of the promotional expenditure by manufacturers is through the retail trade.

TABLE 17.7 Advertising expenditure

	1982 *£000*	*1983* *£000*	*1984* *£000*
Orthopaedic Bed Advisory Service	403	905	1187
Sealy Beds	155	198	132
Dunlopillo Beds	–	–	113
Silentnight Divans	334	1131	79
Sleepezee	175	38	53
Slumberland	106	–	–
Other brands	172	296	400
TOTAL	1345	2568	1964

Source: Meal/Mintel

From previous national advertising campaigns Slumberland has the highest brand awareness, and also appeared near the top in the share of recall.

SILENTNIGHT HOLDINGS PLC

Introduction

Founded by Tom Clarke after the war, Silentnight is the largest bed manufacturer in the UK. Additionally, a small proportion of group turnover is accounted for by manufacture and sale of bedroom, lounge and kitchen furniture. The family still has a majority (approximately 52 per cent) of the issued ordinary shares which are held in a private investment company which is wholly owned and controlled by them. At the age of 65, Tom Clarke is chairman. The company went public in 1973 and the profit record was excellent until the late 1970s. In 1978 the chairman reported increased sales (up 50% to £38m) and profits (up 34% to £3.5m), and he emphasized that Silentnight was a growth business and the EPS had more than trebled in 5 years. In 1979 sales (£50.9m) and profits (£4.21m) reached record levels.

1980–1985

In 1980 Silentnight experienced a fall in profits which was caused by a general recession in the UK economy and specifically by very competitive conditions in the furniture market and substantial de-stocking by retailers. During the year there were various sales and closures estimated to result in an after-tax loss of approximately £1m. In 1981 profits continued to fall, and factory closure and reorganization costs totalled £1.32m. However, profits increased in 1982, helped by a switch from £402,000 interest charges to an interest credit of £335,000. For the three years to 1984, pre-tax profits and sales remained fairly static.

In the period 1981–5, Silentnight had the largest investment programme in the industry, of approximately £5 million per annum. Early investment was on capacity extension, and latterly expenditure has been directed towards new manufacturing technology. Most recently a new manufacturing plant has been built to produce the new Super Sleeper bed. This bed is constructed on the basis of a completely new system of springs made under licence from a company in the USA where it is reputed to have gained market share since its introduction a few years ago. Silentnight have sole UK manufacturing rights for the Super Sleeper. The basic benefits are that it has a longer life and is more comfortable. Also, there has been greater investment in distribution in order to provide retailers with a better service and reduce delivery times. To this end, delivery route planning has been computerized (£2.5m) and £1.4m spent on vehicles. Also a new exhibition centre has been opened near Barnoldswick, which is the location of the head office, displaying a wide range of company products.

Recently, two plants have been closed and a Scottish timber mill sold, and the disposal of a leasing company has raised £2.75m in cash. In an effort to reduce costs and improve efficiency, the group has used its increasing size to introduce economies of scale based on vertical integration. Parkinsons, a separate Yorkshire-based company within the group, supplies woollen felt. Another company exists solely as a buying arm for the manufacturing divisions. The group also handles its own soft wood imports at Hartlepool and makes some spring units and timber frames. It is now moving towards direct importation of hardwoods.

Products and marketing

Most of Silentnight's promotion and advertising expenditure is to retailers, which is thought more cost-effective than a television advertising campaign. Silentnight have made efforts to improve their marketing with the launching of the Merchandise Development Service unit (MDS). This provides a design service aimed at increasing the sales productivity of floor space and improving retailers' profitability. The MDS is an attempt to gain competitive edge though superiority of merchandise and differentation from competitors through creating and projecting a new Silentnight image.

Silentnight's marketing effort has in the past been aimed at some 7,000 high street stores and mail order houses. In recent years, they have begun to sell to the discount and specialist retailers including Queensway.

Also, Silentnight made a contribution of £65,000 to support Olympic gymnasts in 1984 as 'there's a strong marketing link between beds, good health and fitness-building activities', and it is considered particularly appropriate as Silentnight pioneered 'firmer beds for your good health'.

Several new products have been produced which indicate an increased awareness of changing consumer preferences and environmental conditions, such as the move to single beds, space-saving furniture and home-assembly furniture.

Appendix 1

INDEX OF RETAIL PRICES – ANNUAL AVERAGE

1974	108.5
1975	134.8
1976	157.1
1977	182.0
1978	197.1
1979	223.5
1980	263.7
1981	295.0
1982	320.4
1983	335.1
1984	351.8

Source: *Annual Abstract of Statistics*, 1985.

Appendix 2

HOUSING – PERMANENT DWELLINGS COMPLETED (thousands)

1974	280
1975	322
1976	325
1977	314
1978	289
1979	252
1980	240
1981	204
1982	177
1983	198
1984	212

Source: *Abstract of Statistics*, 1985.

Appendix 3

CONSUMERS' EXPENDITURE AT 1980 PRICES (£m)

	Furniture & floor coverings	*Cars, motorcycles & other vehicles*	*Electrical, radio, TV & other durables*	*Total consumer expenditure*	*GNP*
1974	3151	4855	1497	125,630	216,430
1975	3278	5152	1774	124,748	213,234
1976	3417	5325	2044	125,175	222,144
1977	3155	4725	2305	124,564	222,235
1978	3322	5804	2750	131,373	231,033
1979	3696	6668	3348	137,256	236,357
1980	3429	6307	3584	136,789	230,036
1981	3354	6366	3861	136,429	227,042
1982	3424	6570	4403	137,581	231,111
1983	3724	7909	5018	143,011	238,406
1984	3754	7294	5372	145,241	242,267

Source: *Annual Abstract of Statistics*, 1985.

Appendix 4 Silentnight Holdings Plc

FIVE-YEAR SUMMARY YEAR END 31 JAN (approx) (£000)

	1985	*1984*	*1983*	*1982*	*1981*
Turnover	79,788	76,667	77,270	72,794	65,926
Profit before taxation	2,233	5,239	5,225	5,110	3,038
Taxation	(598)	30	730	334	829
Profit after taxation	2,831	5,209	4,495	4,776	2,209
Extraordinary items	1,325	–	–	–	1,319
Profit attributable to shareholders	1,506	5,209	4,495	4,776	890
Dividends	1,238	1,238	1,125	1,125	788
Retained earnings	268	3,971	3,370	3,651	102
Earnings per 10p share:					
Before taxation	5.0p	11.6p	11.6p	11.4p	6.7p
After taxation	6.3p	11.6p	10.0p	10.6p	4.9p
Net dividend per share	2.8p	2.8p	2.5p	2.5p	1.8p
Fixed assets	21,770	19,991	18,296	16,260	12,411
Net current assets	7,190	9,264	6,227	4,272	2,983
Long term liabilities	(6,848)	(7,536)	(2,774)	(2,196)	(762)
Capital and reserves	22,112	21,719	21,749	18,336	14,632
Net tangible asset value per 10p share	49.1p	48.3p	48.3p	40.7p	32.5p
Total borrowings including bank overdrafts to shareholders' funds	24.2%	22.1%	13.9%	13.3%	10.6%

Appendix 5

Silentnight Holdings Plc
CONSOLIDATED BALANCE SHEET, 2 FEBRUARY 1985 (£000)

	1985	*1984*
Fixed assets		
Tangible assets	21,770	19,991
Current assets		
Stocks	6,647	7,688
Debtors	12,671	17,210
Investments	750	1,616
Cash at bank and in hand	2,559	630
	22,627	27,144
Creditors: amounts falling due within one year	15,437	17,880
Net current assets	7,190	9,264
Total assets less current liabilities	28,960	29,255
Creditors: amounts falling due after more than one year	3,947	3,817
Provision for liabilities and charges	2,697	32,557
Minority interests	204	162
	6,848	7,536
	22,112	21,719
Capital and reserves		
Called-up share capital	4,500	4,500
Profit and loss account	17,612	17,219
	22,112	21,719

Appendix 6

Silentnight Holdings Plc
CONSOLIDATED PROFIT & LOSS ACCOUNT, 2 FEBRUARY 1985

	1985	*1984*
Turnover	79,788	76,667
Cost of sales	56,469	52,172
Gross profit	23,319	24,495
Distribution costs	14,942	13,905
Administrative expenses	5,500	5,030
	20,442	18,935
Trading profit	2,877	5,560
Interest receivable	273	272
Interest payable	(917)	(593)
Profit on ordinary activities before taxation	2,233	5,239
Taxation on profit on ordinary activities	(598)	30
Profit for the financial year	2,831	5,209
Extraordinary items	1,325	–
Profit attributable to shareholders	1,506	5,209
Dividends	1,238	1,238
Profit transferred to reserves	268	3,971
Earnings per ordinary 10p share		
Before taxation	5.0p	11.6p
After taxation	6.3p	11.6p
Statement of retained profits and reserves	*1985* *£000*	*1984* *£000*
Reserves at 28 January 1984	17,219	17,249
Profit retained for the year	268	3,971
Foreign exchange adjustments	125	(1)
Adjustment to deferred taxation account	–	(4,000)
Reserves at 2 February 1985	17,612	17,219

Appendix 7

CHAIRMAN'S REVIEW 1985 – AN EXTRACT

At our Annual General Meeting last year I was disappointed to have to forecast the results for the year would be half those of the year before. Unfortunately, our financial results for the year confirmed my worst fears with the final profit coming out at £2.2 million before taxation.

The intense competition in the furniture, upholstery and bedding industry at both retailer and manufacturer level continues unabated.

The retailer is, of course, himself subject to immense competition and consumer pressures, but a continuation of the current trend of buying on price alone can be to no-one's benefit. As major retailers win a larger and larger share of the trade at the expense of the independents, so purchasing power is concentrated in fewer and fewer hands. The squeezing of manufacturers' margins, as a result of being forced to give discounts unrelated to savings, only puts British jobs at risk. It is often overlooked that consumers are also earners, and the price of inadequate investment is ultimately unemployment.

Having seen the damaging effect on other industries of under-investment, we have decided on a policy of continuing to give the consumer quality, choice and value, as we believe this to be the medium-term answer to our present problems. Our fixed assets reflect investment in high-quality equipment and commercial vehicles, continuing our progress towards a more efficient operation. Improved efficiencies, particularly through product innovation linked with quality, will I am sure restore our former profitability.

The amount of money being expended on research and development in the market place, product development and machinery development is now reaching substantial proportions. That which justifies further research and development encourages your directors to re-double their efforts in order to secure a more stable medium-term development of our business.

With regard to our Super Sleeper products, we remain convinced of the superiority of these products over their competitors. Unfortunately, because of the programmed delivery of the machinery, it will be the second half of 1985 before the benefits of this investment begin to show through to the bottom line. We are encouraged by the development of Super Sleeper in the market place, where it has achieved spectacular results for retailers who have supported our marketing effort.

Our investment during 1984 continued at the level of £5 million-plus, principally in the Super Sleeper installation which, when complete in its new building, will be a very fine spring-making investment capable of carrying us into the 21st century.

Five years ago, in the year ended 2 February, 1980, the group employed 3,479 people to produce a turnover of £64 million. You will see from these accounts that the number employed is now 2,787, a drop of approximately 20%, for a turnover of £79 million which is a substantial increase in productivity, so that our merchandise is sold in 1985 at very similar prices to 1979, hence my remarks on the need for product innovation and the strengthening of our marketing.

Mr Christopher Burnett will be joining the board of the company as chief executive. He is currently a director of Whitecroft plc and chief executive of the Building Supplies division. Prior to joining Whitecrofts Mr Burnett was managing director of the Fertilizer Division of Fisons plc which he joined from McKinsey & Co. He holds a Master's degree in Business Administration from the Harvard Business School and is aged 44.

Appendix 8

PUBLIC & PRIVATE SECTOR HOUSING FORECAST, 1970–1988

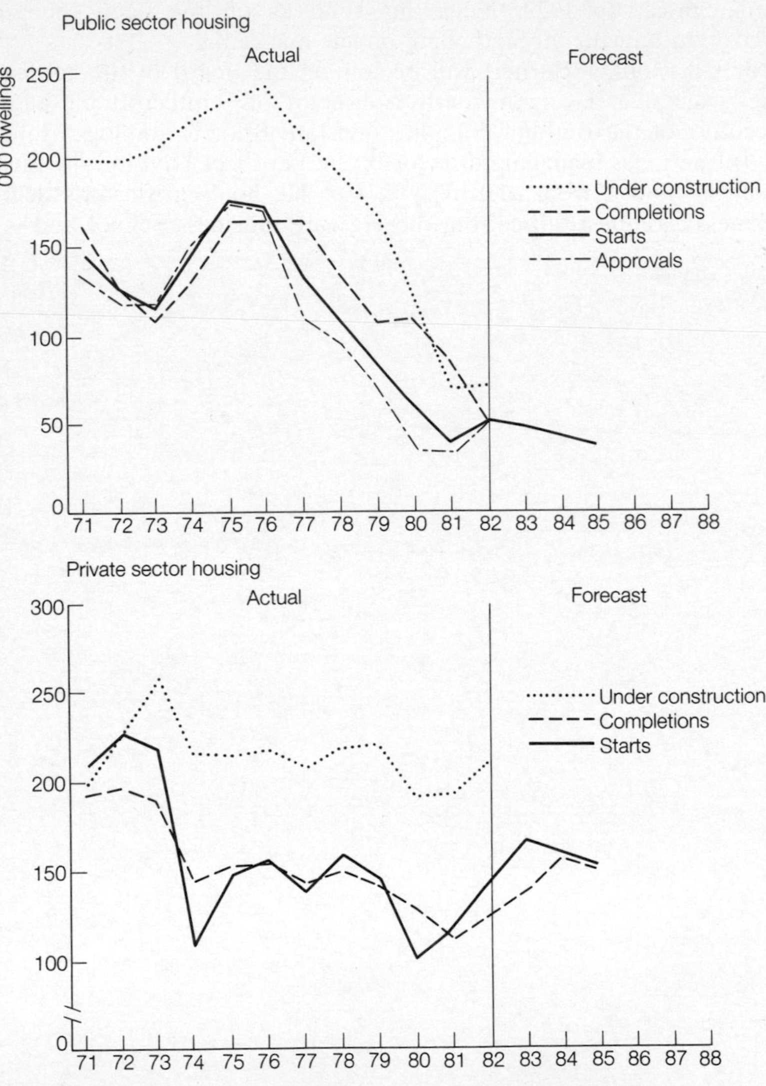

Source: Dept. of Environment Housing and Construction Statistics

Appendix 9

PROJECTED POPULATION TO 2003

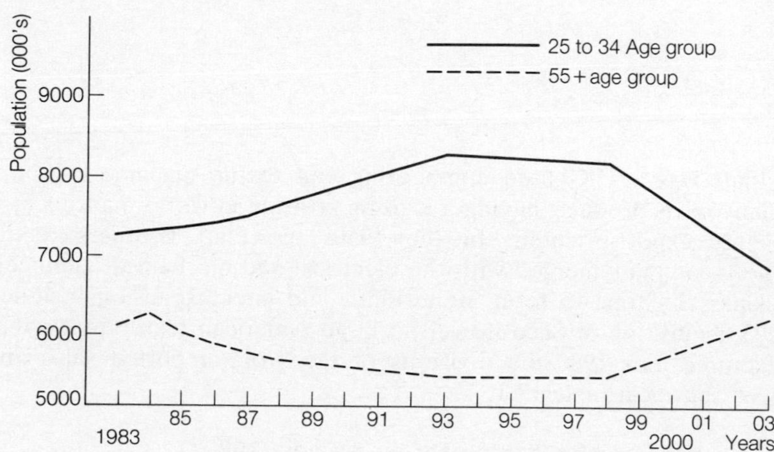

Source: Population Census and Surveys

18 Stone-Platt Industries

Stone-Platt was a UK-based engineering and textile machinery group, with many of its products having a leading position in world markets as it was highly export-oriented. In the 1950s the Platt Brothers textile machinery company merged with the electrical and mechanical engineering business J. Stone to form Stone-Platt, and later expansion included the 1973 acquisition of Saco-Lowell, a large American textile machinery manufacturer. For 1980 the divisions of the group reported sales and profits as shown in table 18.1.

TABLE 18.1 Group sales and profits by division, 1980

Division	*Sales*	*Trading profit (loss)*
	£m	*£m*
Electrical	47.5	4.28
Textile Machinery	79.2	(2.67)
Marine and Mechanical	40.8	(0.13)
Pumps	18.1	1.2

In 1978 the pre-tax earnings per share of the group were 24.3 pence, but following losses in 1979 and 1980 a new chairman took over and, after reviewing the operations of the group, its management structures, markets, financial position, manufacturing units and the outlook for the future, he announced in early 1981 the sale of the Pump Division, some disposals from the Marine and Mechanical Division, and a major capital reconstruction of the financing of the group agreed by the shareholders at an extraordinary general meeting. (See Appendix 1 for financial information on the group).

The group was largely engaged in the manufacture of capital equipment for sale in world markets, and although there was some overseas manufacturing capacity, the UK operations depended largely on export sales. Consequently, they had been forced to adjust not only to the very severe world recession of the late 1970s, but also to the strength of the £ sterling and the high UK interest rates. These pressures were felt particularly in Platt Saco Lowell (PSL) which as a company within the textile machine division was reliant on export business, and its over-capacity led to the decision to close down part of its operations in early 1980 at a considerable reduction in the group's net worth.

Despite the recession, group sales for 1980 had totalled £193.5m (which included only ten months' contribution by the Pump Division before its sale), and exports from the UK were £75m and accounted for 62% of UK output. At the end of the financial year the group had an order book of orders outstanding of £87m. For the 1980 financial year the divisions had performed as follows:

ELECTRICAL DIVISION

This had continued to improve its position in:

1 Equipment for railways and mass transit systems throughout the world, including passenger car air-conditioning, power generation, heating and ventilation.
2 Energy systems including incinerators, furnaces, boilers (burning a variety of fuels including waste products).
3 Power handling equipment such as variable speed drives, electronic controllers and switches.

Sales in 1980 had improved by 13% over 1979 and profits by 44% over 1979, largely as a result of a return to profitability of the Australian subsidiary company.

TEXTILE MACHINERY DIVISION

1 Platt Saco Lowell manufactured a wide range of machinery for processing natural and man-made fibres, with factories in Oldham UK, USA and Spain. Marketing and product developments were co-ordinated between the three countries. Its 1980 results reflected the recession in the textile industry and PSL's sales had declined 20% from 1978 to £59.6m. In 1980, although the American and Spanish operations had remained profitable, serious losses were incurred on UK manufacture which was virtually wholly dependent on export sales. The 1980 trading loss (before interest/taxes) was £2.8m compared to £3.0m in 1979. The depth of the worldwide textile industries' recession was reflected in the results of the UK textile industry where yarn production had fallen by 47% between December 1979 and December 1980, and employment in the UK textile industry had fallen by one-third.

2 Scragg manufactured machinery for processing continuous filament[1] fibres and reported 1980 sales of £19.6m (34% lower than 1979) and profit (before interest and tax) of £100,000 compared with £1.4m for 1979. The 1980 market for such texturizing machinery[2] was severely depresed due to a number of factors – the world economic recession, excess capacity in developed countries, slowing down of expansion in developing countries and growing consumer resistance to textured polyester[3]. To some extent these trends were offset by the demand for nylon hosiery machines which showed a sales increase. Texturizing machinery had been one of the growth points of the textile machinery market and the processing speeds of draw-texturing machinery had increased fourfold between 1971 and 1979.

Product development was an important part of the Textile Division as it constantly strove to manufacture up-to-date machinery incorporating the latest technical developments to improve product quality, reduce customer operational and maintenance costs, and increase flexibility.

MARINE AND MECHANICAL DIVISION

This comprised two propellor businesses (fixed and variable pitch propellors) for shipping and the associated specialized foundries which also supplied the motor vehicle industry. In 1980 the division produced an overall loss of £130,000 (before interest and tax) which was slightly worse than 1979.

PUMP DIVISION

Two months before the end of the 1980 financial year this division which made specialized pumps used in a variety of growth industries was sold for £11.7m after producing a ten-month profit (before interest and tax) of £1.2m compared with £1.1m for a full financial year in 1979. It had been considered that to support the division's growth would have required investments in the business which the group could not afford.

Through most of the 1970s Stone-Platt had been one of the engineering industry's success stories with exports accounting for two-thirds of its sales, and return on capital employed equal to more than 20% for most of the years and reaching 25% in 1975. It was noted world wide for its

1 Man-made fibre of indefinite length.

2 Texturizing machinery was used to make textured yarns, i.e. to crimp, coil, loop or form other desirable distortions.

3 Polyester was a generic name for man-made fibres made from a specific type of polymer.

product developments especially in the high speed open-end spinning[4] frames within its textile machinery business. But the times had been changing and an indication of some difficulties arrived in early 1979 when, unexpectedly, the group warned that profits for financial year 1978 were going to be much worse than expected and the announcement was followed by a fall in the share price from 120 pence to less than 50 pence within six months. Soon after the profits announcement it was confirmed that the director responsible for textile machinery was leaving for personal reasons, and there followed a string of management changes in the Stone-Platt Lancashire textile machinery businesses.

The market for textile machinery had been changing and it became clear that Stone-Platt had not adapted in time, for whilst the home market had been dwindling for years the group had been compensating by selling large turnkey[5] products to the developing world. As the 1970s proceeded, those large one-off contracts had become harder and harder to get as textile companies increasingly specified particular pieces of equipment instead of taking the large integrated package. Whilst Stone-Platt continued to search for the huge contracts, their competitors had been turning to the smaller deals. Also the technological lead the group had developed in open-end spinning frames was cut back. As the international textile industries entered recession and the strong sterling exchange compounded Stone-Platt's problems, its textile machinery companies' profitability dropped dramatically from its record year of 1976 when they recorded over £11m profits on sales of £113m, and by 1979 it was clear that the group had serious overcapacity in its textile machinery divisions.

A decision to close down a large factory in Oldham, Lancashire, created a write-down of reserves of £17.5m, and this fall in shareholders' funds brought the company in breach of some medium-term loan agreements. (The creditor had a fixed charge, or prior claim, on company assets which had suddenly fallen dramatically.) As a consequence the group had to renegotiate with its creditors (largely the clearing banks) in order to agree a capital reconstruction. The problem facing the company was reasonably clear: it had some healthy/profit-making businesses but its major business (textile machinery) was continuing to lose, which meant it could not trade its way out of trouble. The option of a conventional rights issue of its shares was not available, as the share price had fallen so low and had reduced the group's stock-market value to less than £12m. In a standard rights issue a company could reckon on raising roughly a fifth of its market capitalization and Stone-Platt needed far more than that.

[4] Open-end spinning was the production of spun yarns by a process designed to separate and subsequently reassemble individual fibres.

[5] In a 'turnkey' project a major supplier undertook a complete installation and arranged for the contributions of sub-contractors.

The only remaining avenues of escape were sales of parts of the business (of which the profit-makers would be the easiest to sell) and new loan or financing agreements. The first part of the rescue package was put under way, and disposals of the Pump Division and parts of the Marine and Mechanical Division raised £16m which enabled borrowings to be reduced, but the second part of the package took over twelve months to negotiate but was ready by early 1981. Under the terms of the deal, which received shareholders' approval, Stone-Platt doubled its outstanding share capital by issuing 40 million of a special new class of share which would have priority in terms of income and capital over the existing equity. Twelve million of the new shares were taken up by Equity Capital for Industry (ECI) and Finance Corporation for Industry (FCI)[6] and with merchant bankers Hill Samuel they provided underwriting for any remainder after offering the balance of £28m to existing shareholders. In addition four clearing banks agreed to provide a ceiling of £40m in borrowing facilities for the UK operations, including £25m on a five-year loan. This included strict borrowing conditions, among them a 1:1 limit on the ratio of borrowings to shareholders' funds (see figure 18.1).

At the extraordinary shareholders' meeting on 6 April 1981 shareholders approved the issue of 40 million convertible Cumulative Preference Shares at 25 pence each for cash at par. In consequence the issued equity capital of the group became £20,099,815 made up by £10,099,815 of ordinary stock units of 25p each and £10,000,000 of the new shares. In recommending that shareholders should approve the package, the board's statement said that the package 'still carries a health warning. In particular shareholders should make their own judgements whether to take the risk of investing further by applying for the new shares offered.' The offer was not a rights issue but was open to shareholders, who could apply for any number of shares. Those who did not apply would have their stake in the company diluted by 50%, and even those who did apply in proportion to their existing holdings (e.g. one new share at 25 pence for every existing share held) would still suffer a dilution of their stake in the company of 15% because of the new capital injected by ECI and FCI for the 12m new shares. Early in 1981 the market price of the shares was hovering around 25 pence.

The outcome was a much healthier balance sheet after the capital reconstruction, with shareholders' funds of nearly £50m supporting loans of approximately £30m. A new chairman and a new chief executive had been installed and their objective for financial year 1981 was to 'break even before tax' and they had quickly reduced employees to 8,000 in 27 locations from 13,000 employees in 52 locations a year previously.

At the end of financial year 1981 Stone Platt's balance sheet was forecast to show shareholders' funds at £40m and borrowings at £34m,

[6] FCI is a subsidiary of Finance for Industry and owned by the clearing banks and the bank of England, whilst ECI was owned by insurance companies and pension funds.

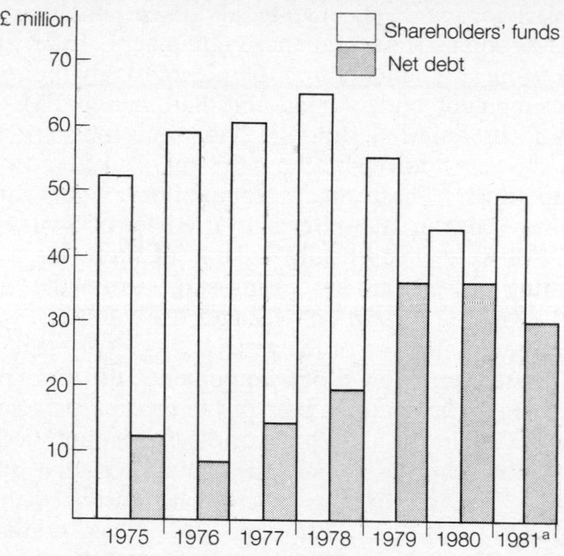

FIGURE 18.1 **Shareholders' funds/net debt**

[a]After equity injection and reorganization costs

and the board of directors were searching for a solution to a problem. This was

> that the UK textile industry was in decline, few of our products had a home market unlike the company's American plant employing 1,250 and sited in the centre of the USA textile industry and the Lancashire factories were forced to rely on exports to developing countries like Taiwan and Korea. And although the quality of PSL's machinery was high, competition against the mainly German and Swiss rivals in a declining market became cut-throat. In the summer of 1981 the recession in demand had taken a further turn for the worse and prices were tumbling to the lowest level ever quoted for a spindle in living memory.[7]

Apart from the price fall for spindles, the annual sales of spindles had halved following the energy crisis of the mid 1970s, but to win business in both the developed and developing countries the big European manufacturers had had to offer very low prices and generous financial packages and this had left little margin for error if contracts were delayed or other problems arose. Customers around the world had become reluctant to

Statement by the Chairman of Stone-Platt in March 1982.

pay a premium price for extra refinements, and in certain areas could opt for cheaper and less sophisticated Japanese equipment. In an attempt to lower costs the European manufacturers had increasingly looked at their research and development budgets and this had caused PSL delays in modernization, and its financial shortage had often meant it had been unable to match the very thorough after-sales service offered by leading continental competitors. These main competitors were Zinzer and Schubert and Salzer (both in West Germany), Rieter of Switzerland and Marzoli of Italy. All were theoretically capable of supplying a complete system incorporating the various processing stages from the opening of the cotton bales to winding of yarn on packages ready for use. In addition other firms concentrated on parts of the process, e.g. Trutzschler of West Germany concentrated on blow-room equipment (the first processing stage) and on carding.[8] The spinning part of the process attracted others, including Investa of Czechoslovakia, the world's biggest producer of rotor spinning equipment which had become the main alternative to conventional ring spinning. The winding process, which transferred the yarn to appropriate package size for customers' use, was dominated by Schlafhorst of West Germany and Savio of Italy. Winding was the one part of the process for which PSL did not produce equipment, although there were alternative methods to winding such as friction-twisting systems which PSL had been developing. Overall West Germany accounted for 30% of the world's exports of spinning machinery and exported 90% of its output largely to advanced, high-income countries.

[8] Carding was aligning the fibres into straight lines.

Appendix 1 Stone-Platt Industries

PROFIT AND LOSS ACCOUNT, YEAR ENDING 31 DECEMBER (£000)

	1980	*1979*
Sales	193,498	211,467
Profit before interest and tax	2,055	2,535
Interest payable	(7,590)	(5,473)
Loss before tax	(5,535)	(2,938)
Tax	(1,919)	(2,592)
Loss after tax	(7,454)	(5,530)
Minority interests	338	(285)
Preference dividends	(120)	(113)
Loss attributable to ordinary stockholders	(7,236)	(5,928)
Ordinary dividends	(40)	(565)
Loss before currency translation and extraordinary losses	(7,276)	(6,493)
Currency translation losses	(2,914)	(1,482)
Extraordinary losses	(4,794)	(9,535)
Withdrawal from reserves	(14,984)	(17,510)

BALANCE SHEETS (£000)

	Balance sheet at Dec. 1979	*Balance sheet at Dec. 1980*	*Effect of[a] disposals/ financing*	*Proforma[b] balance sheet*
Assets employed				
Current assets				
Inventories	64,683	61,589	(6,836)	54,753
Debtors	60,540	40,920	(6,767)	34,153
Cash and short-term deposits	4,185	3,375	(359)	3,016
	129,408	105,884	(13,962)	91,922
Current liabilities				
Creditors	67,015	55,492	(12,849)	42,643
Overdrafts and short-term loans	2,978	1,770	(413)	1,357
Customer pre-payments	6,445	5,119	(1,195)	3,924
Tax	2,433	2,077	93	2,170
	78,871	64,458	(14,364)	50,094
Net current assets	50,537	41,426	402	41,828
Investments	2,884	2,671	347	3,018
Fixed assets	43,163	33,566	(3,515)	30,051
	96,584	77,663	(2,766)	74,897
Capital employed				
Ordinary share capital[c]	10,000	10,100	10,000	20,100
Reserves	44,866	29,882	(500)	29,382
Ordinary stock-holders' equity	54,966	39,982	9,500	49,482
Preference capital	2,929	2,929	–	2,929
Minority interests	1,804	1,002	(190)	812
	59,699	43,913	9,310	53,223
Debentures and other borrowings	36,885	33,750	(12,076)	21,674
	96,584	77,663	(2,766)	74,897

[a] Agreed capital reconstruction.

[b] Balance sheet at 31 December represented to show the position at that date with the following items recognized: (1) The proceeds, net of £0.5m expenses, of the new convertible cumulative preferred ordinary shares received April 1981. (2) Proceeds from the disposal of the group's 55% interest in Barry-Wehmiller Ltd sold in March 1981. (3) Projected proceeds and costs of the disposal from and reorganization within the Marine and Mechanical Division.

[c] Shares at par value of 25 pence.

SOURCE AND APPLICATION OF FUNDS (£000)

	Changes due to disposals	*1980*	*1979*
Results of operations and sources of funds			
Loss before tax	–	(5,535)	(2,938)
Adjustment for items not involving movement of funds			
Unrealized exchange movements	–	(2,914)	(1,482)
Depreciation	–	5,093	5,103
Losses retained in associates	–	153	(34)
Net costs and provisions for disposals			
Reorganizations and refinancing	1,346	(4,794)	(7,500)
Exchange on fixed assets	–	1,518	1,015
Sale of fixed assets and investments	5,091	7,428	1,222
Total funds generated/(absorbed)	6,437	949	(4,614)
Application of funds			
Purchase of fixed assets	–	4,442	9,220
Effect of acquisitions	–	–	2,035
Investments in associate	–	–	1,500
Dividends paid	–	160	1,215
Tax paid	370	2,275	2,646
Increase/(decrease) in debtors	(6,898)	(19,620)	2,115
Increase/(decrease) in inventories	(9,158)	(3,094)	6,782
(Increase)/decrease in creditors and prepayments	8,991	12,849	(14,237)
Other	132	404	(337)
Total funds applied	(6,563)	(2,584)	10,939
Movement of funds	13,000	3,533	(15,553)
Represented by:			
(Decrease)/increase in cash	(1,538)	(810)	(1,945)
Decrease/(increase) in loans and overdrafts	14,538	4,343	(13,608)
	13,000	3,533	(15,553)

ANALYSIS OF SALES AND PROFITS (£000)

Divisions	*1980*		*1979*		*1978*		*1977*		*1976*		*1975*	
	Sales	*Profit (loss) before interest & tax*	*Sales*	*Profit*	*Sales*	*Profit*	*Sales*	*Profit*	*Sales*	*Profit*	*Sales*	*Profit*
Electrical	47,500	4,284	41,900	2,975	36,400	4,601	33,000	3,847	26,800	3,150	19,900	1,115
Textile machinery												
PSL	59,600	(2,819)	70,400	(2,969) }	96,800	3.701	91,900	8,711	117,300	11,327	93,500[c]	8,328
Scragg	19,600	149	29,900	1,385 }							5,300	331
Marine	40,800	(130)	40,600	(83)	34,100	2,319	31,000	3,390	33,000	3,110	27,500	2,587
Pump	18,100[a]	1,188	22,600	1,082	23,700	1,883	20,100	1,308	17,600	729	12,500	1,261
Barry Wehmiller[b]	7,900	(617)	6,100	145	–	–	–	–	–	–	–	–

[a] 10 months' figures only.
[b] Stone-Platt held 55% equity.
[c] First year that Ernest Scragg & Sons figures included (information not available for years 1976 to 1978).

FIVE-YEAR REVIEW (£m)

	1976[a]	*1977*[a]	*1978*	*1979*	*1980*
Sales	194.7	176.0	192.8	211.5	193.5
Profit before interest and tax	18.5	17.6	12.5	2.5	2.1
Profit/(loss) before tax	15.8	14.8	9.5	(2.9)	(5.5)
Profit/(loss) after tax	8.7	8.7	7.0	(5.5)	(7.5)
Ordinary stockholders' earnings	8.5	8.6	6.8	(5.9)	(7.2)
Retained profit/(withdrawal from reserves	7.3	1.0	3.6	(17.5)	(15.0)
Current assets	114.9	113.5	122.4	129.4	105.9
Current liabilities	58.7	56.8	65.7	78.9	64.5
Net current assets	56.2	56.7	56.7	50.5	41.4
Investments	2.1	2.4	1.4	2.9	2.7
Fixed assets[b]	30.0	30.0	33.3	43.2	33.6
Assets employed	88.3	89.1	91.4	96.6	77.7
Ordinary stockholders' equity	59.7	60.9	64.5	55.0	40.0
Preference and minority interests	4.2	3.8	4.4	4.7	3.9
Debentures and other borrowings	24.4	24.4	22.5	36.9	33.8
Capital employed	88.3	89.1	91.4	96.6	77.7
Capital expenditure	£6.8m	£6.9m	£8.5m	£6.8m	£4.4m
Product development expenditure	£4.4m	£4.5m	£5.1m	£7.8m	£7.8m
Gross dividend per share	4.98p	5.48p	6.05p	2.0p	0.14p

[a] Published figures for the years 1976 and 1977 have been adjusted to reflect the current accounting policies for deferred tax and inventory valuation.

[b] Fixed assets for the years 1979 and 1980 include the effect of the property revaluation carried out in 1979.

ANALYSES OF SHAREHOLDINGS AT 31 DECEMBER 1980

	Ordinary shares		Preference shares	
	Number of holdings	Shares held (%)	Number of holdings	Shares held (%)
Size of holding				
1 – 500	9,890	4.0	367	2.2
501 – 2,500	3,259	8.9	100	3.3
2,501 – 10,00	504	5.7	16	3.2
10,000 – 25,000	56	2.2	7	4.1
25,001 – 50,000	21	2.0	10	14.8
50,001 – 100,000	12	2.2	9	22.9
100,000 and over	59	75.0	6	49.5
	13,801	100.0	515	100.0
Holding by category				
Individuals	13,238	18.5	458	6.1
Insurance companies investment trusts, pension funds and other corporate holders	381	56.7	45	66.9
Nominees	182	24.8	12	27.0
	13,801	100.0	515	100.0

GEOGRAPHICAL SALES ANALYSIS

	1980		*1979*	
	£m	%	*£m*	%
United Kingdom	46.7	24	47.7	22
Other EEC	18.5	10	20.4	10
Other Europe	22.8	12	20.4	10
Total Europe	88.0	46	88.5	42
Asia	24.1	12	30.3	14
North America	54.2	28	53.0	25
Africa	14.7	8	22.6	11
South America	8.4	4	12.6	6
Australasia	4.1	2	4.5	2
Total	193.5	100	211.5	100

19 Dunlop Holdings

INTRODUCTION

In 1888 John Boyd Dunlop invented the first usable pneumatic tyre and Dunlop came into being. By the turn of the century the Dunlop Rubber Co., as it became known, had two factories in Birmingham, then the centre of the UK car and bicycle industry.

The next twenty years were a period of growth and expansion. Investments were made in rubber estates in Malaya, and tyre factories were opened in Japan and the USA. The product range expanded through the acquisition of a wheel manufacturer and the addition of golf balls and aircraft tyres. Also textiles used in the tyres were now manufactured in mills owned by Dunlop.

As with many other companies, the collapse in world trade in 1929 was almost fatal for Dunlop. The dramatic fall in commodity prices and in particular the price of rubber was the major cause of the problem. Under new management the company recovered slowly, widening its range of products which usually included components based on rubber technology.

World War Two offered the company considerable opportunity to increase sales of existing products and to develop and manufacture new products for military use. However, on the negative side, plantations were seized in Malaya, and German and French factories were bombed. The end of the war saw another period of expansion. The experience and expertise developed in the war were now used to develop civil applications from the knowledge gained. At the same time military spending remained at a high level for several years, providing a profit base for such expansion. The range of sports goods expanded to include footwear. Rubber belting and hose had many new applications, and flooring materials provided a further extension to the product range. The company continued its policy of expansion largely by selling to new geographical markets in the 1960s.

TECHNOLOGICAL CHANGE IN THE 1960s

In the 1960s a change took place in tyre technology with the development of the radial tyre which was expected to replace some or all of the sales of the cross-ply tyre. The radial could be steel- or textile-based, with the steel-based tyre giving greater durability (over twice the mileage of a cross-ply tyre) but the textile tyre providing greater adhesion to the road in wet conditions. Michelin was the first company to make a significant commitment to the radial tyre and it chose the steel-based version. Dunlop opted for the textile-based tyre, which was the wrong choice, and by the time they had changed to the steel-based version Michelin were market leaders.

THE 1970s AND THE DUNLOP-PIRELLI UNION

The vicious price war which developed in the early seventies forced companies such as Uniroyal to withdraw from Europe. In an attempt to combat the threat of Michelin, Dunlop and Pirelli entered into an unusual form of agreement whereby a union would result through the exchange of minority interests; maybe this was seen as a prelude to a full merger of the two companies.

The balance of the union suffered in the first year, when Pirelli made huge losses and Dunlop were obliged to make a £41.5 million provision against their original investment.

As part of the deal, shares held by Pirelli in Dunlop Limited were redesignated to 'preferred' shares; any losses suffered by Dunlop Limited in the future would be borne 100% by UK shareholders. Thereby, Pirelli would not be entitled to any of the profits of Dunlop Limited until Industrie Pirelli returned to profit.

In the early 1970s, Dunlop consequently refused to invest money in Pirelli until it returned to the black. As a result of this, Dunlop's stake was eventually reduced to 19%.

The agreement was terminated in October 1981. A statement showing the effect of the Union between 1970 and 1976 is shown in table 19.1.

TABLE 19.1 Attributable profit of the Dunlop-Pirelli union, 1970–1976

£m	*1970*	*1971*	*1972*	*1973*	*1974*	*1975*	*1976*
Union-attributable profit	10	1.3	3.7	17.3	20	20	40
Dunlop share of union-attributable profit	7	10.4	12.7	10.5	11	14	19
Pirelli share of union-attributable profit	3	(9.1)	(9)	6.8	9	14	21

The history of Dunlop through the 1970s can be seen through the following extracts from company reports.

1972 UK TYRE MARKET

The level of business in the replacement market was sustained for the greater part of the year. Then, to end a discount war which was confusing to the public, recommended retail prices were discontinued. There are signs that the policy is proving effective.

Some progress was achieved in volume and market share, but increased costs were not fully recovered and profits were slightly reduced.

Preparations for the launch of the Dunlop 'Denovo' – the 'Total Mobility Tyre' – are well advanced. Vehicle manufacturers are showing increasing interest and two models fitted with this revolutionary new safety tyre are expected to appear at the London Motor Show. The Department of Trade and Industry and safety organizations in Britain and abroad are well aware of its unique qualities.

Germany

Although the German economy grew slightly faster than in 1971, the demand for tyres was below industry expectations. However, demand for steel-braced radial-ply car tyres continued to rise and capacity is being extended. An independent survey of tyres of this type available in the German market gave an exceptionally high rating to the Dunlop SP4 tyre.

Turnover of Dunlop A.G. was a little below the 1971 level, but the fall in profits was rather greater, owing to intensive price competition coupled with rising costs.

1973 TYRE MARKET IN EUROPE

The second half of the year was adversely affected by rising raw material and other costs, which were not fully recoverable and then only with some delay. In addition, industrial disruption in our own and customers' factories in the United Kingdom lost the company an estimated £3¾ million and the employees £1½ million.

In the European Economic Community, the problem of over-capacity in the car tyre business was aggravated by the effects of the energy crisis in the latter part of the year, and profits were depressed, especially in France and Germany. In product areas outside the automotive industry, however, results were better than in 1972.

Rubber market losses

As explained more fully in the Directors' Report, contrary to company policy, certain forward sales of latex and dry rubber were left unhedged. With rising prices, this failure to hedge gave rise to losses of £4.8 million,

£3.2 million after tax. Of this latter amount £1.9 million was attributable to Dunlop Holdings.

Denovo launched

Denovo, the total mobility tyre, was launched at the London Motor Show and fitment to two models (Rover 3500S and Mini 1275GT) was announced. During the year, development work continued with car manufacturers in the UK and overseas. The Denovo development team was honoured by being chosen for the MacRobert Award from the Council of Engineering Institutions to mark the outstanding engineering achievement of the year.

1974 CHAIRMAN'S REPORT – EXTRACT

It was clear from the start that 1974 would be uncertain and difficult, imposing considerable strains on private-sector companies. The energy crisis, inflation, price controls, politics, currency instability, industrial unrest, and recession all combined to ensure this.

So the management had four objectives – to control the use of funds tightly and to safeguard the liquidity of the business; to maintain profitable growth as far as possible; to be highly selective in the use of resources; and to seek additional savings, particularly in oil-based materials and energy.

In the United Kingdom, trading activity recovered well after the three-day week and, as a result of increased operating efficiency and cost savings, UK operations contributed a larger share of the group's profit than in the previous year. This improvement would have been greater but for price control which bore heavily on a number of operations.

In continental Europe, the car tyre business continued to be depressed, with fierce competition from imports in Germany which resulted in a trading loss; France and Spain were unable to recover costs quickly enough because of price restraints.

1975 CHAIRMAN'S REPORT – EXTRACT

Recession, or high inflation, or both, were experienced in almost every area in which we operate. Indeed many of the countries experienced the worst recession for decades. All product groups were affected, not least the motor industries in developed countries with car manufacture particularly hard hit.

However, Dunlop achieved record attributable profits of £15 million, nearly 50% more than in 1974 (before an 'extraordinary item'). The improvement owes much to careful control of resources – as well as to gains in efficiency, particularly in the United Kingdom. There was a strong performance by our Engineering and Industrial Groups, a good growth in exports, and a useful upturn in Germany.

Our interests in overseas Pirelli activities also contributed significantly to the improved profits.

Changes in world markets have created opportunities as well as problems. Technical innovation in products for the off-shore oil industry, for irrigation, for fire protection, and for conveyor belting already yield good results and again illustrate the renewal and widening of the group's product range. The carbon fibre brakes for Concorde, now in service, were another 'Dunlop first' and are already being developed for other advanced aircraft, military and civil.

1976 CHAIRMAN'S REPORT – EXTRACT

1976 saw the end of the post-OPEC recession and Dunlop has emerged a stronger company than when we first began grappling with the severe problems of 'stagflation' brought about by the oil crisis.

For the third successive year, there was a significant improvement in group profits and the sharp increase in 1976 owed much to our broad international spread. Both Dunlop and Pirelli activities outside continental Europe contributed substantial increases in earnings; operating profits in the UK also showed a marked increase, although when adjusted for inflation, they are still less than is required for the expansion of the home businesses.

During the past year we have re-appraised the group's objectives and set new and stretching targets, basing them on a longer-term view of our world markets, as should be expected of a multinational group. We are now moving into a period when greater emphasis will be given to the faster development of certain of our businesses. In a phrase, we have changed from selective containment to selective expansion.

1977 CHAIRMAN'S REPORT – EXTRACT

A year ago, we reported a change in general policy 'from selective containment to selective expansion'. This was based on improving results and a financial position which was strengthening internally and could then be supported by the rights issue of May 1977. These encouraging conditions persisted with improved results for the first half-year. Towards the end of the year, however, results were disappointing though the financial position remained satisfactory.

Attributable profits for the year 1977 fell by 20% from the previous year, but it is encouraging that the profits from activities other than tyres increased. They now represent approximately two-thirds of total profits compared with 55% last year.

What happened? The greater general growth in demand which governments were seeking, without renewed inflation, was not realized. In the industrialized countries particularly, excess production capacity or price controls or both, depressed margins, particularly for tyres. In the

United Kingdom, the so-called 're-entry' from precise wage control towards more general guidelines caused frustration and more industrial disruption than I can ever remember in Dunlop factories. This was supplemented by stoppages among customers. Fortunately, resultant losses were partly offset by more satisfactory results in other parts of the group, but then the rise in the general value of sterling between June and the year-end reduced the apparent profits accruing both in Dunlop and associated Pirelli international operations.

This is the last Annual Report which I shall have the privilege to present to you. Accordingly, I take this opportunity to express sincere appreciation to all my colleagues on the Board and fellow employees in Dunlop for the encouragement, co-operation and support which they have given in fair and rough weather.

Sir Campbell Fraser, whom the Board have selected as their new Chairman, has served the Company since 1956 and has been Managing Director since 1971. During these eight years he has built round him a team which represents not only a deep knowledge of the business but a mixture of talent and experience well suited to present conditions and the political and social environment in which business is carried on at home and abroad. Times are not easy but objectives are clear, the management team is in good heart and I wish every success to them and all who are concerned with the future of Dunlop worldwide. – REAY GEDDES.

At this point in Dunlop history it will be useful to take a more detailed look at Dunlop operations. The detail appears in the Appendices (10 and 11) in order to avoid interruption to the general flow.

1978 CHAIRMAN'S REPORT – EXTRACTS

Tyres in Europe

It is generally accepted that the companies making tyres for the European market have more capacity than is needed. The major reasons for this over-capacity are: widespread factory construction in the late 1960s; the halt in the growth of motoring mileage following the oil price increases of 1973–4, and its aftermath; and the growing use of the steel-radial tyre which provides the motorist with twice the life or more of the cross-ply tyre which it has been replacing.

Dunlop, in common with the other tyre makers, has supported the British Rubber Manufacturers' Association in its applications to the Department of Trade and the European Commission to prevent 'dumping' by any foreign manufacturer.

With severe competition, tyre prices have fallen sharply in recent years, so that the real cost to the motorist in pence per mile has fallen, in a decade, by between 30% and 40%. The customer has been exceptionally well-served by the industry in value for money.

The result for the Dunlop European tyre business was a drop from profit into loss at the operating level between 1977 and 1978, reflecting a serious deterioration in the United Kingdom results, only partly offset by slightly better figures in continental Europe. During the year a detailed examination of the situation was carried out. (For report see Appendix 12.)

Other Activities

While grappling with these special problems Dunlop has not stood still in other respects. There was an increase in total operating profit outside the European tyre market, many product divisions and subsidiaries contributing to this improvement.

The broad economic picture in the industrial world in 1978 saw increases in real personal incomes in some countries, notably the United Kingdom. At the same time, there was little sign of a real increase in the pace of industrial output in the major economies. This pattern is closely reflected in Dunlop's own results.

The most dramatic improvement came in consumer goods; in industrial products it was more difficult to make progress, although there were notable achievements. There were also very real signs of advance in many parts of the world with satisfactory profits earned in the Far East, Africa and in the group's plantations.

The Task Ahead

The task facing your board is to ensure that the European tyre business returns to good health speedily. It will be a hard slog, but it will be tackled with realism, vigour and determination. (A review is provided in Appendix 12.)

1979 CHAIRMAN'S REPORT – EXTRACTS

At this time last year, I said that the major task for the company was to restore the European tyre business to good health, and that whilst this would be tackled with vigour and determination, it would be a hard slog. And so it proved in 1979 – a year which began in the United Kingdom with the transport drivers' strike, followed in the autumn by the engineering dispute, by strengthening sterling and by the steady rise in interest rates generally.

The losses due to industrial disputes, taking account of their direct and indirect effects on customers and suppliers, were £10 million for the group worldwide, of which £8 million was in the UK.

Tyres in Europe

I commented last year on the extent of the over-capacity in tyres in Europe and the measures that were in hand to cope with it. In the market place, competition has remained intense, but the closure of several tyre plants in Europe has begun to bring supply and demand a little more into balance. During the year further rationalization and modernization of our tyre facilities in the UK continued, with new product development being given enhanced priority. The UK is the development centre for the group's tyre activities worldwide and we shall continue to strengthen this base. The first results can be seen in the introduction of new ranges of car and commercial vehicle tyres earlier this year, to be followed soon by additional new car tyres. There are, in fact, more new tyres in the development pipeline than ever before.

At the same time, the policy of selective acquisitions to build on our strengths continued. Two companies were bought during 1979 – a specialist manufacturer of printing plates to reinforce our market strength in printers' blankets, and a specialist distributor of health and fitness equipment to enable the Sports Group to build up their stake in this growing part of the market.

Outside Europe, the real growth and profitability of our overseas operations was maintained, notably in the Far East and Africa, where the tyre markets are both expanding and remunerative, and where the group commands substantial market shares. And our plantations companies again achieved record profitability, helped by favourable prices and further increases.

The Way Ahead

There will be no lessening of our efforts to achieve a turnround in the results of our European tyre business – that remains a central task. Good progress has been made, but much remains to be done.

At the same time, we intend selectively to reinforce our other businesses in Europe and to continue to seize every opportunity to capitalize on the real growth that is possible in our overseas businesses.

DUNLOP IN THE EIGHTIES

The eighties began where the seventies left off with rationalization and retrenchment in Europe, particularly with respect to tyres. Much of the rationalization in tyres led to very substantial improvements in productivity. The tyre factory at Inchinnan was closed in 1982, the factory at Cork was closed and the French company was placed into receivership. The union with Pirelli was dissolved with a £21m payment for 'adverse cash flow'. Also the rubber plantations in Malaysia were sold. The National Tyre Service, the group's retail and wholesale distribution chain, increased the number of outlets to over 500 in the UK. The greater geographical spread, increases in volume and operating efficiency significantly improved profitability.

However, continued overcapacity together with increased import penetration persuaded Dunlop to sell its European manufacturing facilities to Sumatomo. Discussions were started in 1983 in which the Japanese company was to pay £82m over a 15-month period and £41m would be paid to Dunlop immediately. Included in the deal was the purchase of Dunlop's tyre inventories which were estimated to be £30m approximately. As the book value of the assets was £94m and there would be additional rationalization costs, there would be a loss on the deal of £25m which would have to be written off as an extraordinary item.

Rationalization and divestment took place in other parts of the group, mostly in those businesses associated with the automotive industry. Whilst top sportsmen were achieving significant results with Dunlop equipment (McEnroe, Bernhard Langer, Geoff Boycott), the Sports Division was operating at very low levels of profitability.

Aviation, oil, and marine hose and belting products were the bright spots in the portfolio, with, in respect of the first two, a world market reputation and leadership and, for all three businesses, products which were technologically advanced for the industry in which they operated.

Chemical products including a range of DIY adhesives produced steady performances, whereas industrial and consumer footwear and the flooring products were subject to much greater volatility in profits.

A new business division was seeking to build up businesses which would be suitable diversification opportunities so that ultimately they could be transferred to a fully commercial operation.

However, by late 1984 the company was in serious financial difficulty. In November Michael Edwardes was appointed to the board to effect a financial reconstruction and turn-round. Before this had really begun, BTR bid for the group and, after increasing the initial offer price, the board eventually recommended acceptance at a price valuing the company at £101m.

THE TYRE MARKET IN THE EIGHTIES

Structure of the Market

In 1982 the world tyre market was worth $27 billion with Goodyear and Michelin being the market leaders as can be seen from table 19.2:

The Japanese companies, although with only a small market share, had grown rapidly and increased share significantly over the previous twenty years as a result of the worldwide success of their motor industry. Furthermore, now that the Japanese car manufacturers were setting up plants in other parts of the world, for example in the USA and the UK, the Japanese tyre firms were following them.

Overcapacity in the European tyre market was still a problem in spite of the closure of 15 plants in Europe over the period 1978–81. In fact, employment in European tyre manufacturing fell from 45,000 (1978) to 25,000 (1983).

TABLE 19.2 The world tyre market in 1972

Company	*Market share*	*Country of origin*
Goodyear	22	USA
Michelin	19	France
Firestone	10	USA
Bridgestone	8	Japan
Dunlop	6	UK
Pirelli	6	Italy
Goodrich	4	USA
General Tire	4	USA
Continental	4	USA
Uniroyal	3	USA
Yokohama	3	Japan
Sumitomo	2	Japan
Others	9	–

Source: *The Economist*

Channels of Distribution

Traditionally tyres were sold through garages but, by 1983, 85% of replacement tyres were sold through specialist distributors offering a 'while you wait' tyre change service. In the UK there were estimated to be approximately 2,500 of the outlets. A large proportion of those outlets were owned by tyre manufacturers as can be seen from table 19.3:

TABLE 19.3 Ownership of tyre distributors in 1983

Name of distributor	*Number of outlets*	*Ownership*
National Tyre	550	Dunlop
Michelin	420	Michelin
Tyre Services GB	280	Goodyear
Motorway Tyres	200	Avon
Kwik-Fit Euro	200	(not owned by tyre manufacturer)

Marketing

Brand loyalty, if it can be called such, results from the car owner replacing the tyres on the car with 'another set of the same'. However, brand awareness is low and it is unlikely that the owner will replace tyres until it becomes legally necessary.

In order to combat this lack of brand awareness tyre manufacturers increased expenditure on direct advertising in the early eighties: Goodyear by £1.9m, Michelin by £1.8m, Dunlop by £1.3m and Kwik-Fit Euro by £2.45m.

Appendix 1

DATA FROM THE COMPANY REPORTS (1968–84) (£m)

Source	*1968*	*1969*	*1970*	*1971*	*1972*	*1973*	*1974*
Sales	450	495	541	585	636	750	888
Operating PBIT	32.6	33.0	34.6	42.6	43.0	47.6	58.2
Total PBIT	35.3	36.1	38.4	50.9	53.4	55.5	70.0
PBT	27.7	27.4	26.9	38.0	39.9	35.7	44.0
Net profit	11.9	11.0	9.1	11.6	13.4	9.8	11.0
Inv. Inc./Assoc. Coy.	1.8	2.1	2.5	6.8	8.8	11.0	10.0
Fixed assets	130.7	144.6		192.8	212.9	237.7	256.9
Investments	10.0	11.6		88.0	54.0	62.0	70.9
Net working capital	132.7	151.1	158.5	174.2	190.1	215.7	252.4
Total	273.4	307.3	326.3	455.0	457.0	515.4	580.2
Shareholders' funds	105.4	122.2	122.6	149.0	123.7	142.5	167.8
Preference shareholders' funds	14.7	14.7	14.7	14.7	14.7	14.7	14.7
Minority shareholders' funds	26.5	27.7	29.2	94.9	105.2	121.3	142.3
Debt & loans	89.1	84.0	101.9	137.1	151.4	163.0	161.1
Overdraft & acceptances	27.2	38.0	35.4	29.2	24.6	38.7	59.0
Other	10.5	20.7	22.5	30.1	37.4	35.2	35.3
No. of Pref. Sh.				14.7	14.7	14.7	14.7
£ of Ord. Sh.				49.1	49.1	49.1	49.1
No. of Ord. Sh. 50p.				98.2	98.2	98.2	98.2
EPS P/Share	11	10	8	11	13	9	12
Exports (£m)				52	49	61	80
Employees (thousands)							
UK					52	52	52
O/seas					54	57	53
R & D (£m)							

1975	*1976*	*1977*	*1978*	*1979*	*1980*	*1981*	*1982*	*1983*	*1984*
1015	1289	1361	1475	1569	1386	1456	1525	1603	1582
66.7	87.0	75	64	64	50	52	41	63	71
80.1	105.9	87	78	76	59	45	49	68	78
52.0	73.3	57	43	29	10	–	(7)	17	27
15.0	19.3	20	11	–	(15)	(41)	(52)	(28)	(15)
13.4	18.9	12	14	12	9	(7)	8	5	7
263.5	302.1	309	340	304	313	332	373	345	237
80.5	101.3	110	115	123	134	46	79	37	25
268.1	347.6	364	386	364	301	332	353	142	136
612.1	751.0	783	841	791	748	710	805	524	398
189.8	229.3	254	251	253	235	253	251	110	48
14.7	14.7	15	15	15	15	15	15	15	15
152.6	180.7	200	200	179	166	73	113	127	57
162.8	228.4	245	294	272	264	288	305	61	66
55.4	75.4	65	78	68	64	135	156	149	163
36.8	22.5	4	3	4	4	(54)	(35)	62	49
14.7	14.7	14.7	14.7	14.7	14.7	14.7	14.7	14.7	14.7
49.1	49.1	65.5	66.2	66.4	68.6	71.9	71.9	71.9	71.9
98.2	98.2	131.0	132.4	132.9	137.2	143.8	143.8	143.8	143.8
16	23	16	8.1	–	(11.3)	(29.4)	(36.7)	(20.4)	(10.8)
98	126	141	152	155	146	129	125	130	139
49	48	48	48	48	36	29	25	22	20
51	54	54	52	54	45	46	34	31	22
			17	20	26	33	36	34	31

Appendix 2

FINANCIAL ANALYSIS

	1968	1969	1970	1971	1972	1973	1974	1975	1976	1977	1978	1979	1980	1981	1982	1983	1984
1. Current ratio	2.4	2.5	2.4	2.6	2.4	2.4	2.4	2.3	1.8	1.8	1.7	1.8	1.6	1.4	1.4	1.0	0.9
2. Acid test	1.2	1.3	1.2	1.2	1.3	1.2	1.1	1.1	0.9	0.9	0.8	0.9	0.8	0.7	0.7	0.5	0.6
3. Gearing	44	43	45	39	42	42	40	38	42	40	44	43	44	55	55	45	66
4. Interest cover	4.5	4.2	3.4	4.0	4.0	2.8	2.7	3.3	3.2	2.9	2.2	1.6	1.2	1.0	0.9	1.3	1.6
5. Stock turnover	4.1	4.1	4.0	3.9	4.1	4.0	3.8	4.1	4.2	4.0	4.0	4.9	4.5	4.1	4.2	4.8	6.1
6. Drs/Sales	82	88	85	80	83	78	77	73	79	75	77	74	72	80	75	10	2.8
7. Sales/Fixed assets	3.44	3.42		3.03	2.99	3.15	3.46	3.85	4.26	4.40	4.34	5.16	4.37	4.39	4.09	4.65	6.45
8. Sales/Total assets	1.71	1.68		1.59	1.58	1.66	1.74	1.91	1.98	2.02	2.03	2.34	2.26	2.19	2.10	3.29	4.24
9. EBIT/Sales	7.24	6.66	6.40	7.28	6.76	6.35	6.57	6..75	5.51	4.34	4.08	3.61	4.26	2.69	2.69	3.93	4.49
10. EBIT/Total assets	12.40	11.19		11.61	10.67	10.51	11.43	12.54	13.38	11.14	8.81	9.58	8.14	7.83	5.65	12.94	19.03
11. PBT/Capital employed	10.13	8.91	8.24	8.35	8.73	6.93	7.58	8.50	9.76	7.28	5.11	3.67	1.33	–	(0.87)	3.24	6.78
12. Dividend	61	78	94	76	39	40	35	40	35	27	26	40	–	–	–	–	–
13. Retained profit	39	22	6	24	61	60	65	73	74	60	–	–	–	–	–	–	–

TOTAL BY PRODUCT (%)

	1971	*1972*	*1973*	*1974*	*1975*	*1976*
Sales						
Tyres	63	63	62	59	61	61
Industrial	12	11	11	13	13	13
Consumer }	17	18	19	19	19	12
Sports }						6
Engineering	7	6	6	6	6	6
Plantations	–	–	–	–	–	3
Other	1	2	2	3	2	–
Profits						
Tyres	70	67	61	50	58	50
Industrial	8	10	15	20	18	23
Consumer }	13	15	16	15	12	6
Sports }						8
Engineering	6	6	4	8	6	8
Plantations	–	–	–	–	–	5
Other	3	2	5	8	5	–

RESULTS BY BUSINESS (£m)

	Sales		*Profits*	
	1984	*1983*	*1984*	*1983*
Turnover				
Dunlop Slazenger	153	128	1	2
Dunlop Consumer	274	274	3	9
Dunlop Engineering	61	63	(1)	(2)
Dunlop Aerospace	53	46	8	7
Dunlop Industrial	135	133	5	4
Dunlop Tire and Rubber	346	273	28	24
Dunlop South Africa	111	118	14	20
Dunlop Overseas	120	113	11	12
Divested discontinued businesses	329	455	2	(13)
Total	1,582	1,603	71	63

DEFINITIONS

Shareholders' funds = Ordinary shareholders' funds + Preference shareholders' funds + Minority shareholders' funds

Total debt = Debt and loans + Overdraft and acceptances

Total assets = Fixed assets + Net working capital

Capital employed = Total assets + Investments

Operating PBIT = Operating profit before interest and tax

Profit before Tax (PBT) = PBIT + Investment income − Tax

Net profit = PBT − Tax

1. Current ratio: $\dfrac{\text{Current assets}}{\text{Current liabilities}}$

2. Acid test: $\dfrac{\text{Current assets} - \text{Stocks}}{\text{Current liabilities}}$

3. Gearing: $\dfrac{\text{Total debt}}{\text{Total debt} + \text{Shareholders' funds}}\ \%$

4. Interest cover: $\dfrac{\text{Earnings before interest and tax}}{\text{Interest payable}}$

5. Stock turnover: $\dfrac{\text{Sales}}{\text{Stocks}}$

6. Average collection period: $\dfrac{\text{Debtors}}{\text{Sales}}$ (days)

7. Fixed asset turnover ratio: $\dfrac{\text{Sales}}{\text{Fixed assets}}$

8. Total asset turnover ratio: $\dfrac{\text{Sales}}{\text{Total assets}}$

9. Operating profit margin: $\dfrac{\text{Operating profit}}{\text{Sales}}\ \%$

10. Return on total assets: $\dfrac{\text{Operating profit}}{\text{Total assets}}\ \%$

11. Return on capital employed: $\dfrac{\text{Total profit before tax}}{\text{Capital employed}}\ \%$

12. Dividend payment: $\dfrac{\text{Dividend}}{\text{Net profit}}$ %

13. Retained profit %: $\dfrac{\text{Retained profit}}{\text{Net profit}}$ %

Appendix 3

RESULTS BY PRODUCT (£m)

	1971	*1972*	*1973*	*1974*	*1975*	*1976*	*1977*	*1978*	*1979*	*1980*	*1981*	*1982*	*1983*
Sales													
Tyres	368	401	463	528	615	776	815	871	897	743	838	872	953
Industrial	68	71	84	114	133	163	182	210	231	244	210	201	198
Consumer } Sports }	101	116	142	170	188								
Consumer						155	167	189	204	170	167	107	218
Sports						77	84	90	96	99	108	119	137
Engineering	40	38	45	52	57	74	77	87	95	73	82	98	97
Plantations	–	–	–	–	–	30	36	40	46	57	51	–	–
Other	8	10	16	24	22	–	–	–	–	–	–	28	–
Total	585	636	750	888	1015	1275	1361	1487	1569	1386	1456	1525	1603
Profit													
Tyres	30.8	30.0	29.9	29.6	38	42	25	18	22	13	24	25	41
Industrial	3.4	4.5	7.3	12.2	12	19	20	10	14	13	9	9	7
Consumer } Sports }	5.7	6.8	7.9	8.7									
Consumer					8	5	8	10	9	7	2	9	11
Sports					–	6	6	4	3	3	2	(1)	1
Engineering	2.8	2.6	1.9	4.7	4	7	8	6	7	5	8	3	3
Plantations	–	–	–	–	–	4	8	8	9	9	7	–	–
Other	1.4	0.7	2.3	4.8	3	–	–	–	–	–	–	(4)	–
Total	44.1	44.6	49.3	60.0	65	83	75	66	64	50	52	41	63

1977	*1978*	*1979*	*1980*	*1981*	*1982*	*1983*
60	59	57	54	60	57	59
13	14	15	18	15	13	12
12	13	13	12	12	14	14
6	6	6	7	8	8	9
6	6	6	5	6	6	6
3	3	3	4	4	–	–
–	–	–	–	–	2	–
33	27	34	26	46	61	65
27	30	22	26	17	22	11
11	15	14	14	4	22	17
8	6	5	6	4	(2)	2
11	9	11	10	15	7	5
11	12	14	18	13	–	–
–	–	–	–	–	(10)	–

OPERATING PROFITS OF UK ACTIVITIES, 1976–80 (£m)

	1976	*1977*	*1978*	*1979*	*1980*
Tyre	10	7	(8)	(13)	(22)
Non-tyre	21	23	26	15	7
Total	31	30	18	2	(15)

Appendix 4

RESULTS BY REGION (£m)

	1971	1972	1973	1974	1975	1976	1977	1978	1979	1980	1981	1982	1983	1984
Sales														
UK	252	259	286	345	393	463	537	591	618	552	498	498	504	506
Rest of EEC	132	149	182	225	255	336	349	384	420	251	243	406	394	277
Rest of Europe	5	5	6	8	10	12	13	14	14	15	12	12	13	15
Asia & Australia	67	77	97	129	133	183	187	204	212	240	283	145	166	181
Africa	49	53	70	78	105	100	104	125	138	169	202	154	165	148
N America	73	85	99	94	119	172	161	160	159	147	203	263	337	428
C & S America	7	8	10	9		9	10	9	8	12	15	19	24	27
Other	–	–	–	–	–	–	–	–	–	–	–	28	–	–
Total	585	636	750	888	1015	1275	1361	1487	1569	1386	1456	1525	1603	1582
Profits														
UK	10.8	12.9	11.7	21.7	21	31	30	18	2	(15)	(13)	(10)	–	8
Rest of EEC	11.6	8.6	7.0	5.3	7	4	2	4	11	9	4	(6)	(4)	3
Rest of Europe	(0.2)	–	–	0.2	–	–	–	–	–	–	1	1	–	(1)
Asia & Australia	7.2	6.6	13.3	15.3	15	21	21	23	27	28	27	17	16	14
Africa	0.7	6.5	9.7	10.5	13	10	9	13	17	23	21	26	26	17
N America	6.0	8.6	8.4	7.3	9	17	12	8	7	4	11	15	22	27
C & S America	8.0	1.4	1.2	(0.3)		–	1	–	–	1	1	2	3	3
Other	–	–	–	–	–	–	–	–	–	–	–	(4)	–	–
Total	44.1	44.6	49.3	60.0	65	83	75	66	64	50	52	41	63	71

TOTAL BY REGION (%)

	1971	1972	1973	1974	1975	1976	1977	1978	1979	1980	1981	1982	1983	1984
Sales														
UK	43	41	38	39	39	36	39	40	39	40	34	33	31	32
Rest of EEC	23	23	24	25	25	26	26	26	27	18	17	27	25	18
Rest of Europe	1	1	1	1	1	1	1	1	1	1	1	1	1	1
Asia & Australia	11	12	13	15	13	14	14	14	14	17	19	10	10	11
Africa	8	8	9	9	10	8	7	8	9	12	14	10	10	9
N America	12	13	13	11	12	13	12	11	10	11	14	17	21	27
C & S America	1	1	1	1		1	1	1	1	1	1	1	1	2
Other	–	–	–	–	–	–	–	–	–	–	–	2	–	–
Profits														
UK	24	29	24	36	32	37	40	27	3	(30)	(25)	(24)	–	11
Rest of EEC	26	19	14	9	11	5	3	6	17	18	8	(15)	(6)	4
Rest of Europe	–	–	–	–	–	–	–	–	–		2	2	–	(1)
Asia & Australia	16	15	27	26	23	25	28	35	42	56	52	41	25	20
Africa	2	15	20	18	20	12	12	20	27	46	40	63	41	24
N America	14	19	17	12	14	20	16	12	11	8	21	37	35	38
C & S America	18	3	2	–		–	1	–	–	2	2	5	5	4
Other	–	–	–	–	–	–	–	–	–	–	–	(10)	–	–

Appendix 5

CAPITAL EXPENDITURE (£m)

	1976	*1977*	*1978*	*1979*	*1980*	*1981*	*1982*	*1983*
By Product								
Tyres	31	35	34	34	37	40	37	39
Industrial	5	9	11	10	9	9	11	12
Engineering	2	2	3	2	2	2	5	8
Consumer	2	3	5	5	3	5	5	3
Sports	2	4	2	2	3	3	3	3
Plantations	1	1	1	1	1	1	–	–
Total	43	54	56	54	55	60	61	66
By Region								
UK	17	23	23	22	25	27	21	22
Rest of EEC	13	14	13	16	10	11	13	10
Asia & Australia	3	6	9	9	8	10	5	8
Africa	8	5	5	5	8	7	9	12
North America	2	6	5	2	4	4	10	13
Central & South America	–	–	1	–	–	1	3	1
Total	43	54	56	54	55	60	61	66

Appendix 6

DIRECTORS, 1972–83

	Age in 1983	*Date joined company*	*84*	*83*	*82*	*81*
Executive						
Lord				CE[a]	CE	CE
Gardener	57	1975		✓	✓	✓
Harvey	51	1959		✓	✓	✓
Hope	51	1976		✓	✓	
Johnson	58	1974		✓	✓	✓
Marsh	56	1951		✓	✓	✓
Wheater				✓	✓	✓
Campbell Fraser		1956			CH[b]	CH
Bexon	60				✓	✓
Dent						
Geddes						
Ward						
Baker						
			84	*83*	*82*	*81*
Non-executive						
Hodgson				CH	✓	✓
Baring				✓	✓	✓
Eng				✓		
Ghafar Baba				✓		
Knight				✓	✓	✓
Menzies Wilson				✓	✓	
Read				✓	✓	✓
Carroll					✓	✓
Lever						
Partridge						
Pirelli						
Shelbourne						
Spinks						
Roberts						
Melville						
Forbes						
Weir						
Flunder						

80	*79*	*78*	*77*	*76*	*75*	*74*	*73*	*72*
CE	CE	✓	✓					
✓	✓	✓	✓	✓	✓			
✓	✓	✓						
✓								
✓	✓	✓	✓	✓	✓			
CH	CH	CE	CE	CE	CE	CE	CE	CE
✓	✓	✓	✓	✓	✓	✓	✓	✓
	✓	✓	✓	✓	✓	✓	✓	✓
		CH	CH	CH	CH	CH	CH	CH
						✓	✓	✓
								✓
80	*79*	*78*	*77*	*76*	*75*	*74*	*73*	*72*
✓	✓	✓	✓	✓	✓	✓	✓	✓
✓	✓	✓	✓	✓	✓	✓	✓	
	✓	✓	✓	✓	✓	✓	✓	
	✓	✓	✓	✓	✓	✓	✓	
	✓	✓	✓	✓	✓	✓	✓	✓
	✓	✓	✓					
✓	✓							
		✓	✓	✓	✓	✓	✓	✓
			✓	✓	✓	✓	✓	✓
					✓	✓	✓	✓
						✓	✓	✓
								✓

[a] *Chief Executive.*
[b] *Chairman*
Source: Company accounts

Appendix 7 Stock market data

FINANCIAL TIMES ACTUARIES' ALL SHARE INDEX

	High	*Wt. ave.*	*Low*
1973	219	184	136
1974	150	106	61
1975	160	133	62
1976	172	153	116
1977	226	191	150
1978	242	216	191
1979	283	245	219
1980	313	271	225
1981	338	308	265
1982	389	342	306
1983	470	435	383
1984	593	517	465

DUNLOP SHARE PRICE

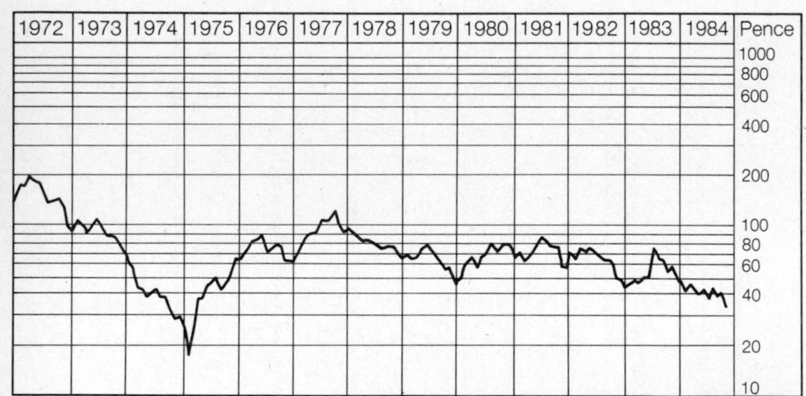

Appendix 8 Tyre market statistics

NO. OF CAR TYRES (MILLIONS)

	Cross ply	*Radial*	*Total*	*Imports*	*Exports*	*Home cons.*	*Inflation index for tyres*
1972	13.0	14.8	27.8	3.5	4.5	26.8	65
1973	9.6	17.1	26.7	3.7	5.2	25.2	67
1974	7.6	16.7	24.3	4.3	5.4	23.2	83
1975	6.2	17.5	23.7	3.9	6.0	21.6	100
1976	5.3	20.2	25.5	4.7	7.6	22.6	113
1977	4.1	19.9	24.0	5.7	6.8	22.9	139
1978	3.6	21.2	24.8	6.5	7.5	23.8	149
1979	3.0	21.2	24.2	7.0	7.6	23.6	167
1980	2.1	22.5	24.6	5.6	10.2	20.0	192
1981	1.6	20.2	21.8	6.7	NA	–	197
1982	1.2	21.4	22.6	6.6	9.1	20.1	211
1983	0.9	22.3	23.2	8.5	9.1	22.6	217
1984	1.0	20.4	21.4	8.5	8.0	21.9	227

ALL TYRES – VALUE (£m)

	Car tyres							
	UK manufacture							
	Cross ply	*Radial*	*Total*	*Imports*	*Exports*	*Home cons.*	*Other UK mftr tyres*	*Total UK mftr tyres*
1972	51.0	72.5	123.5	13.7	20.0	117.2	120.2	243.7
1973	41.1	85.6	126.7	16.2	25.6	117.3	133.4	260.1
1974	41.3	105.1	146.4	24.4	34.1	136.7	164.3	310.9
1975	38.9	138.7	177.6	26.0	47.3	156.3	206.7	384.3
1976	37.1	179.2	216.3	38.9	70.9	184.3	267.0	483.3
1977	35.2	207.8	243.0	54.3	71.2	226.1	291.0	534.0
1978	33.6	235.5	269.1	62.6	80.3	251.4	289.3	558.4
1979	30.7	258.4	289.1	73.5	87.8	274.8	322.7	611.8
1980	23.7	301.2	324.9	66.3	123.4	267.8	326.0	650.9
1981	17.0	254.3	271.3	85.5	NA	–	313.2	584.4
1982	14.9	285.1	300.0	83.7	113.7	270.0	257.6	557.6
1983	11.0	314.8	325.8	117.2	126.4	316.6	282.9	608.7
1984	12.5	307.9	320.4	122.2	124.0	318.6	284.6	609.0

[a] Includes tyres for lorries, buses, tractors, earthmoving equipment, etc.

Source: *Business Monitor* PQ491, PQ4811.

Appendix 9 Car and transport statistics

ESTIMATED ROAD TRAFFIC IN GREAT BRITAIN (THOUSAND MILLION VEHICLE KILOMETRES)

	1974	*1975*	*1976*	*1977*
All motor vehicles	208.09	209.84	220.35	225.18
Cars and taxis[a]	163.90	165.39	173.38	178.23
Two wheeled motor vehicles	3.22	3.84	4.74	4.76
Buses and coaches	2.95	2.90	2.97	2.86
Total goods vehicles	38.03	37.71	39.27	39.33
Light vans[b]	19.01	18.88	19.41	19.77
Other goods vehicles	19.02	18.84	19.85	19.56
Pedal cycles	3.24	3.77	4.21	5.11

[a] This category includes three-wheeled cars: excluding all vans whether licensed for private or for commercial use.

CAR PRODUCTION AND IMPORTS

	Production		*Car imports as % of new UK registrations*
	Cars (millions)	*Comm. veh. (thousands)*	
1969	1.717	466	
1970	1.641	458	
1971	1.742	456	
1972	1.921	408	23
1973	1.747	417	27
1974	1.534	403	28
1975	1.268	381	34
1976	1.333	372	38
1977	1.316	398	45
1978	1.223	384	49
1979	1.070	408	56
1980	0.923	389	56
1981	0.954	229	56
1982	0.888	269	58
1983	1.045	245	
1984	0.909	225	

1978	*1979*	*1980*	*1981*	*1982*	*1983*	*1984*
234.30	223.70	247.58	251.86	259.33	264.20	274.54
185.92	184.93	197.26	201.39	208.77	213.17	221.79
4.74	4.92	5.92	6.69	6.91	6.30	6.24
2.91	2.93	3.06	3.01	3.00	3.11	3.20
40.72	40.92	41.33	40.79	40.66	41.62	43.30
20.34	20.27	21.03	21.26	21.25	21.39	22.40
20.39	20.65	20.30	19.53	19.41	20.23	20.90
4.25	3.80	4.20	4.49	5.27	5.19	5.04

[b] Not exceeding 30 cwt unladen weight.
[c] Provisional.
Source: Department of Transport

Appendix 10 Dunlop review of operations, 1977

EUROPE

Tyres

The keen competition experienced in the markets in 1976 continued throughout the year. Sales of radial car and truck tyres continued to grow; a new radial winter tyre was successfully introduced and fitment of the Denovo safety tyre was increased. Overall results, however, were down on 1976.

In the United Kingdom the strengthened pound brought an increase in tyre imports with consequent pressure on prices in the second half of the year, and the results of both United Kingdom Tyre Division and Pirelli Limited were also affected by industrial relations problems. The tyre distribution companies had a good year.

Dunlop S.A. in France continued to trade throughout the year under the burden of price controls bearing no relationship to cost escalation. Losses were incurred, and the strongest representations were made to the authorities.

In Germany Dunlop A.G. again experienced keen competition in tyre trading, but vigorous management action brought improvements in all parts of the business.

Industrial Products

The Dunlop Industrial Group improved its profitability in 1977, again with an impressive export performance accounting for 34% of total sales.

Hydraulic Hose Division established a new plant for the manufacture of rigid hose assemblies. New product development was a major feature of the group's activities.

With its expanded production facilities in the United Kingdom, Angus Fire Armour Limited achieved record turnover and profits in 1977 and gained its second Queen's Award for the export of irrigation hose; total exports accounted for 69% of the United Kingdom activity.

Engineering Products

Wheel, Suspensions and Redditch Mouldings Divisions all benefited from some improvement in demand from the motor industry whilst Plant and Equipment Division maintained the improvement of the previous year, earning a satisfactory profit and return on funds.

Considerable attention was given during the year to the development of new products and new markets, with both Aviation and Suspensions Divisions undertaking major sales drives in the USA. In addition, a range of new products for industry based on the Dunlop Thermimax Burner was launched.

Consumer Products

The overall profitability of Consumer Group improved in spite of the fact that demand for consumer products remained as depressed as in 1976. Both Dunlop Textiles Limited and Dunlopillo Division showed worthwhile gains and, in particular, Dunlopillo GmbH Germany had a good year.

Sports Products

Owing to the continuing stagnation of consumer spending in many major markets and the over-supply of some major products, 1977 was a difficult year for sporting goods throughout the world. In these circumstances, the sports goods operations did well to increase sales turnover in the United Kingdom and the rest of Europe; but with increased competition, notably from the Far East, operating margins were generally lower.

The main emphasis in capital spending was on improved production methods as part of a continuing cost reduction programme.

During the year, a number of new products including a new range of garden games for the family to be marketed under the generic name Dunlop 'Playsport' was developed for the forthcoming season.

Asia and Australasia

In India a decline in the growth rate for tyres and industrial products coupled with the commissioning of new production capacity resulted in very severe competition and lower margins. In the circumstances Dunlop India Limited did well to achieve a 2% growth in sales volume and to earn a modest profit.

The plantations in Malaysia and New Zealand recorded exceptionally good figures, due mainly to high prices for palm oil and cocoa. Only modest profits were earned from rubber.

In Indonesia construction work was begun during the year on a Dunlopillo factory which should be on stream by the end of 1978 and the new tennis ball manufacturing facility in the Philippines is expected to begin production in April 1978.

The Malaysian golf ball operation continued to improve in efficiency.

Africa

In Nigeria the continued rapid expansion of the economy placed considerable strains on the infrastructure of the country. As a consequence Dunlop Nigerian Industries Limited was short of power supplies throughout the year and this substantially reduced tyre output. Imports of Dunlop tyres were increased, but the results in total were well below those of the previous year.

The South African sports goods business had a particularly successful year with both sales and profits well ahead of 1976.

North America

Intensely competitive conditions in both tyres and sporting goods held back the Dunlop Tire and Rubber Corporation's turnover in each of these product groups to little more than in 1976 in local currency and contributed to some narrowing of margins.

Economy programmes mitigated the effects of this, but profits after taxation were some 20% lower than in the previous year.

During 1977 a new manufacturing plant was established in the USA for the production of both fire and irrigation hose, in line with the policy of expanding Angus Fire Armour's North American activities.

In a generally static market for racquet sports and golf equipment, price competition intensified and results were lower than in 1976.

In Canada, the table market went through a difficult year with falling demand and a serious deterioration of prices. As a result Pirelli Canada Limited sustained a loss.

Dunlop International Projects Ltd

Dunlop International Projects Limited was organized in December 1976 to obtain and manage contracts for the supply of factories and technology to outside customers on a turnkey basis, and the contract signed during 1977 for a factory to produce latex foam articles in the USSR is an example of the type of operation being undertaken.

Appendix 11 Corporate Planning at Dunlop (1977)

Extracts from an article in Long Range Planning *No. 12 (February 1979) pp. 17–21 (Pergamon Press) by A.M. Rossiter, manager of corporate planning. The lecture was originally given on 10 March 1977.*

1 We are much concerned with rebalancing our funds employed, so that new investments are carefully channelled into those areas where profitable growth commensurate with risk can be maximized. equally, we are concerned, without detriment to the quantum of profit upon which we substantially depend, to restrict those parts of our business where the prospects are perceived to be less promising.

2 Operational features of corporate planning (CP) at Dunlop.

(a) CP tends to take the helicopter view which gives a broader view but loses some definition. However, interesting sightings can be examined in closer detail.
(b) CP tries not to get too bogged down in detail, but seeks to spot significant trends and outline their relevance to the firm.
(c) CP seeks to paint a comprehensive picture.
(d) CP is concerned with the right balance between centre-led and bottom-up initiatives.
(e) CP is responsible for the discipline of the planning cycle.
(f) CP develops and disseminates the overall and devolved objectives (usually in terms of profit and profitability) and with allocation of funds to different cost centres.

3 We vet all major capital expenditure plans. We have to try to 'pick the winners'. First we analyse the market in which the business operates and then our own strengths and weaknesses in that market. The results are then plotted on a simple form of 'directional policy matrix'.

Market/Industry Criteria	*Divisional Competitive Criteria*
Market Growth	Profitability
Industry Profitability (particularly margins)	Market Share
Capacity v Demand	Product Quality and Performance
Opportunity for Specialization	Innovative Ability & Resources
Complexity of Products/Services	Marketing Strengths

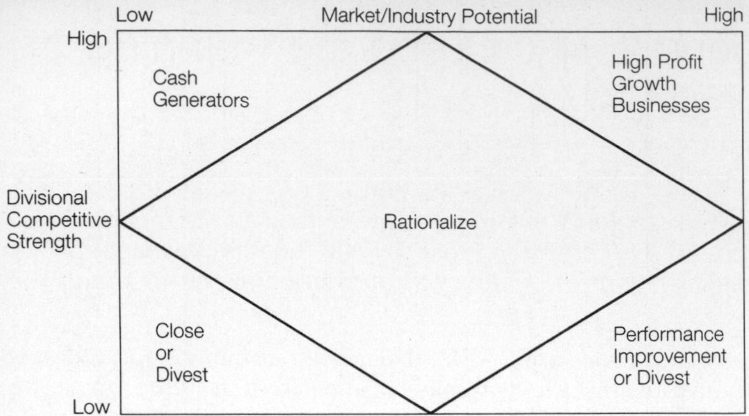

4 Allocation of resources is the actual sum advised to divisions and includes both fixed and working capital requirements for three years.
5 Having categorized each unit according to its prospects for growth and profitability, the object is to expand the funds employed in the growth areas of high profitability, while containing and in real terms contracting those in low-growth and less profitable areas.
6 The CP system will be in a constant state of change as experience is gained and the environment changes. However the change should be evolutionary rather than revolutionary (unless the system is manifestly inadequate) in order not to destroy continuity. Also the system should never be so sophisticated as to deny ready comprehension at all levels.

Appendix 12 Review of European Tyre Operations (1978)

In 1978 Dunlop took steps to strengthen its position as a competitor in the difficult European tyre market. A growing proportion of our output was of the most modern steel radial car and truck tyres, continuing to secure the basis for an improving reputation for our products. There was also progress toward a standardized range of tyres for the European market.

All aspects of the business were scrutinized to find more efficient operating methods, and output per man-hour showed good improvements in France and Germany.

A broader base of business with vehicle manufacturers – the essential original equipment market – was secured and in some markets shares of the replacement tyre business rose. There were two notable improvements in Dunlop technology for tyres and wheels. In November the company announced the 'Denloc' system of keeping the tyre bead in place on the wheel rim in case of puncture or deflation. This major advance in tyre safety commended itself to the National Highway Traffic Safety Administration in the United States of America.

The system has also been incorporated in the improved Denovo run-flat tyre. The Denovo 2 will be available on British, French, Italian and Japanese cars brought out during 1979.

The trading results of the tyre business in Europe were much less satisfactory. Losses were suffered by all the tyre manufacturing businesses, where competition was extremely severe, with markets showing little or no growth as the result of the longer life of tyres. Prices could not be raised to cover cost increases, and in some cases even fell. Some competitors have been forced to withdraw from the business, or scale down operations. Imports into EEC have increased, often at uneconomic prices, which have brought additional pressure on price level.

All the same, the tyre industry in Europe remains the second largest in the world after North America. It has led thc world in tyre technology, and still does so. During the year, Dunlop strategy in this extremely important market was examined in depth, and as a result, the company will attack in Europe the major segments of the market with an appropriate concentration of investment.

The main impact of this policy will be in the UK manufacture of tyres, and in January of this year the ending of tyre making at Speke was announced, and at the same time a plan to invest £75 million in modernization at the three remaining tyre factories at Fort Dunlop, Inchinnan, Renfrewshire, and Washington, Co. Durham. This investment is designed to reinforce Dunlop's position as a leader in the European and worldwide tyre business.

Appendix 13 Review of Operations 1983

Tyres Europe

Competition in tyre markets generally throughout Europe remained intense and, although there was evidence of some recovery in demand as the year progressed, the market for truck tyres remained depressed throughout.

With overcapacity leading to unacceptably low price levels, there was a significant move towards products with demonstrable marketing advantages such as reduced fuel consumption or improved safety features. A number of new vehicles are being equipped with the new TD tyre – most noteworthy is the fitment to Metros.

United Kingdom

Compared with the very low levels of 1982, demand for original equipment car tyres rose by 20%, and for replacement car tyres by 13%. Dunlop sales to vehicle manufacturers rose similarly, but there was little improvement in price levels owing to the continuing unflux of cheap imports.

A minimal loss of market share in the truck tyre market was more than offset by an improving export performance, but during the year production of earthmover tyres ceased as part of the rationalization plan.

France

At the beginning of October, it was decided that the parent company could not continue to support further losses and the judicial receiver was appointed.

Germany

The German company reported a year of considerable progress. The high performance premium range of 'D' tyres gained replacement market share as well as original equipment fitment on prestige vehicles. Dunlop tyres were again successful at the Le Mans 24 Hour race won by a Porsche equipped with special tyres incorporating the Denloc bead-locking system.

The high capacity utilization of car tyre production lines at the two German factories more than offset the difficult market conditions for truck and earthmover tyres.

Ireland

As a result of the unsatisfactory performance of the Cork factory, it was decided to announce closure in the middle of the year.

Rest of Europe

The European selling companies experienced a particularly difficult and unprofitable year with selling prices at very low levels throughout the region.

Diversified Products

Extensive rationalization and reorganization of the diversified products activities in 1982 enabled the group to enter 1983 with a greater degree of flexibility. Consequently, as the year progressed, there was a steady improvement in trading profit which rose by more than 60% compared with that of the previous year.

Engineering

Lower airline traffic worldwide during 1983 affected Aviation Division on two fronts. Demand for replacement equipment for aircraft in service was reduced and the deferment of new aircraft purchases delayed offtake of original equipment. Despite these difficulties, the division was able to exploit its service network to the full and recorded increased profits. The investment programme in new production facilities for the Boeing 757 carbon brake contract continued.

The low level of demand for pipes in the UK municipal and utility sector and the deep recession in the American phosphate mining industry led to disappointing results for Dunlopipe Division factories at Coventry and in Florida.

Automotive Engineering Division returned to operating profit during 1983. The status of sole supplier of steel wheels to BL was maintained, supplemented by significant increases in business with Ford and Vauxhall in the UK as well as BMW in Germany. The latter part of the year saw the commercial introduction of the revolutionary TD wheel which is being fitted to 1984 Metro models and will appear on other new models. Although the commercial vehicle market remained in deep recession, increased sales of the advanced air suspension systems for buses, coaches, and heavy trailers were obtained. A number of development projects, in conjunction with UK, European and American vehicle manufacturers, were initiated during the year. The potential market for both advanced engine and vehicle suspension systems is considerable.

Consumer

Dunlopillo Division consolidated the progress made in moulded car seating during 1982, and with production brought together into one building at Hirwaun, the benefits of rationalization showed through in a return to profit. Retail activities were restructured and a new range of mattress/divan combinations are currently being brought to the market. The continuing research and development effort being devoted to flameproof materials has met with significant success and resulted in a contract from the Department of the Environment for mattresses to be used in prisons and other institutions.

Growth continued at Chemical Products Division with a consequent increase in profits. A new range of structural adhesives and the planned introduction of a range of 'car care' products in 1984 will provide the base for further growth. Contract Services Division maintained profit levels although the level of activity in the construction industry was depressed.

Industrial

Oil and Marine Division continued to dominate the offshore floating hose business with a further increase in market share. The new high-pressure flexible pipe (HPFP) project moved forward late in the year with the installation of initial production equipment and the winning of a substantial order to supply to the new Morecambe Bay offshore gas field. With full production of HPFP scheduled to come on stream in 1984, the division is well placed to maintain its pre-eminence in its field.

Trading conditions for both Hose and Belting Divisions remained difficult throughout the year with the lower demand situation exacerbated by an influx of cheap hose imports. Nevertheless, as a result of rationalization measures taken in late 1982, Belting Division managed to maintain its profit level, and losses were reduced in Hose Division.

In the automotive industry, after a static first quarter, Fluid Seal Division experienced an improving trend for the remainder of the year, increasing their share of business with original equipment manufacturers. For the year as a whole a profit was recorded. Polymer Engineering Division also felt the steady improvement n the UK car market, and made progress in other fields with notable orders being obtained on new rapid transit rail suspension systems in the USA and Canada.

With new orders for the British Aerospace 146 airliner and the SAAB Fairchild SF340 commuter aircraft, and an expansion in the range of products for the medical field, Precision Rubbers Division continued its growth pattern of recent years.

Dunlop Medical Products also increased its product range with the introduction of traction and physiotherapy exercise equipment, and the commencement of clinical trials for carbon implant products.

General Rubber Goods Division significantly improved on the previous year's results with increased sales of Dracones, collapsible containers, and printer's blankets. Benefits also resulted from the computerized mixing facility installed at the Manchester factory.

The Americas

Dunlop Tire & Rubber Corporation again achieved a significant increase in profits. The company is now the undisputed market leader in motorcycle tyres, and taking advantage of the strength of the dollar, made a major penetration into the steel truck tyre market with imported tyres. Productivity improvements were achieved at both factories in Huntsville, Alabama and Buffalo, N.Y., aided by a significant capital expenditure programme and trade union co-operation.

The Caribbean Tyre Company Ltd (formerly Dunlop Trinidad) maintained the profit improvement of 1982, expanding and modernizing to meet growing local demand for tyres.

Dunlop (Canada) Inc achieved a return to profit after the disappointing results of 1982. After a number of start-up problems, the joint venture roofing company now has a good forward order book for both domestic and export markets.

In Brazil, the new printers' blanket company is now fully operational. Dunlop Argentina reported a good year's trading with an expanded product range.

Africa

Dunlop South Africa maintained its level of profitability despite the impact of the recession on supplies to the mining and construction industries. These shortfalls were, however, offset by improved trading results of the tyre and Dunlopillo foam operations.

Foreign exchange shortages for the purchase of certain essential raw materials and replacements parts proved to be a depressing factor for operations in Zimbabwe. Despite productivity gains, government price controls made it impossible to recover all increased costs, so that the company recorded a reduced level of profit.

Far East and Pacific Basin

During the year, a £2 million programme to modernize existing industrial hose production and introduce new product lines was completed by Dunlop India. In contrast, trading conditions in the tyre market, particularly for truck tyres, were extremely competitive, but overall trading profits were ahead of 1982.

The improvement in commodity prices came too late in the year to influence company trading levels in Malaysia where sales and profit levels fell slightly below the previous year. An important diversification was the commissioning of a spring mattress factory to complement the existing Dunlopillo foam plant.

With a government-imposed wage and price freeze, Dunlop New Zealand Ltd maintained profit levels from an increased turnover. During the year the company acquired the tyre manufacturing operations and marketing outlets of the Reid brand from Feltex New Zealand Ltd. Reid was New Zealand's third largest tyre company and its acquisition consolidates Dunlop's market dominance.

Technology

Technology Division placed major emphasis during 1983 on supporting the development programmes in carbon brake technology for Aviation Division and high-pressure flexible pipe technology for Oil and Marine Division. The advances achieved in materials design and application will have potential elsewhere in the group, particularly where the application of high performance composites will give access to high value technology markets such as medical carbon implants.

In the field of dynamic research, new concepts in suspension systems designed to absorb noise, vibration and harshness characteristics in vehicles are also being developed in conjunction with the operating divisions.

PART V

Turnaround

20 International Computers (B)

BACKGROUND

ICL's prospects for 1984 were thrown into confusion by a substantial loss in share value in early December 1983. Considerable efforts by the company to cut overheads, improve profits and reduce borrowings had little impact on the City, which promptly downgraded the ICL share price. In spite of early signs that the new strategy was beginning to show a turnaround, certain observers were less than confident in their expectations.

This was the situation which ICL was taking into 1984 despite a number of strategic successes in 1984 which ought to have made for a more positive outlook. In 1982 ICL had achieved three major objectives which had been set as a conscious part of the recovery programme.

First the company returned increased profits on the previous 12 months and this substantially strengthened the company's financial position. Second, it exceeded sales targets for 2900 series mainframes, bringing in the larger operational profits which only the mainframe machines could provide. Finally, it largely retained the loyalty of its user base. For the year 19892/83 the company again returned increased profits, in spite of increased speculation as to the viability of the new strategy. This speculation was further fuelled by the appointment of Sir Michael Edwardes (former BL Chief) to the ICL board, at the end of 1983.

ICL STRATEGY

Product Strategy

1982 saw the beginnings of the new ICL strategy which was designed to attack the IBM market. Managing Director Rob Wilmot forecast that ICL would be selling mainframe computers – based on Fujitsu technology – by 1984.

Joint ventures with two major UK software house were directed towards developing IBM plug compatibility, and the prospect of two very large hardware orders had prompted ICL to make the next generation of mainframes capable of running ICL or IBM operating systems. British Steel (BSC) and British Aerospace (BAe) had asked ICL for these machines and software to allow them to convert slowly from split ICL/IBM sites to ICL's next generation of powerful hardware.

Wilmot's official strategy was to 'surround' IBM mainframes with smaller ICL systems, with operating systems and software staying independent from each other. The link would be made only to allow data to be exchanged, by emulating a very low level of IBM's Systems Network Architecture (SNA) in ICL's Information Processing Architecture (IPA).

IBM was the international mainframe market leader, but Wilmot claimed that ICL would only seek to sell peripheral systems to an IBM site, or attack the biggest IBM mainframes with the huge Fuhitsu Facom IBM plug compatible mainframes – M382 – which were 15 and 25 million instructions performed a second (mips) machines.

The first major change in direction for the new plan came with the realization that IBM – SNA was 'more important to the future of ICL than ICL's IPA', according to ICL's director of product marketing. This was reinforced by the knowledge that one of the leading IBM systems houses was helping ICL to tackle much more of SNA than it had so far admitted.

ICL's official line was that SNA would not be tackled above the terminal level, and that by emulating IBM's 3274 protocol in IPA, ICL would be able to swap data with any IBM mainframe. The SNA link being developed took ICL much further into the heart of an IBM site and allowed systems up to the ME29 to become nodes in an IBM network.

During early 1983 Rob Wilmot claimed that the only gaps in ICL's product lines were the ones he had chosen to develop. The key elements of the strategy to take ICL through to the 1990s were therefore complete and in the open. The existing 2900 series of mainframes provided much of the cash to keep the expansion plans going and during 1983 the series continued as breadwinner, with improved enhancements and the integration of 'CAFS' (a fast information search device). Collaborative development with Fujitsu for advanced chip technology incorporation into the new generation of mainframes and distributed systems was reported to be on schedule.

ICL's commitment to computer-aided design and manufacturing markets had been enhanced by further joint development of the PERQ scientific and graphics workstation in collaboration with the new management of Perq Systems Corporation (US) (formerly Three Rivers Computer Corporation). The company had also taken a 40% stake in CAD Centre Limited (formerly the government-owned Computer Aided Design Centre, Cambridge).

Other product areas included the DRS office system and the DNX2000 digital exchange system (marketed under an agreement with the Mitel Corporation), although the latter had been troubled with delay due to software problems.

Vertical Marketing

Traderpoint The 'Traderpoint' scheme was initiated by the new management at ICL to improve competitiveness in the area of software support and thereby increase the potential for hardware sales. Third-party ICL software houses willing to develop new supporting software were offered three options.

The first was where the distributor took title to the hardware and received an appropriate cut. The second provided a commission agreement with the software house on packages, while ICL took the hardware contract, and the third provided for collaboration to fill gaps in the computer market.

The second and third options had aroused the most interest in the services industry. The second option generally suited anyone who had already developed ICL applications software or intended to do so, while the third option sought to formalize arrangements where the software house and ICL came together and shared resources and skills.

Towards the end of 1982 there was increasing evidence that ICL was further releasing its hold on software supply and letting in more third-party dealers. Publication of the first edition of the ICL software catalogue showed that over two-thirds of the 600 plus entries for system and applications software came from third-party dealers.

New Management and Strategy There had been problems, however, with implementing Traderpoint. Predictions in the 'pull-through' of hardware sales had not been met, and there were indications that ICL's own sales force had had some problems in adjusting to the new system. At the end of 1982 Ray Piggot who had spent several years with the Data General computer company was appointed head of Traderpoint. He spent several months refining Wilmot's original idea to increase third-party 'added value' sales of ICL hardware, competing first of all with the minicomputer suppliers and then with the micro-computer firms which sold volumes of kit this way. He was given the target of producing 15% of ICL's turnover – a figure of around £150 million – by 1986.

The first major change to Traderpoint came with the launch of a distinct Business 29 annexe, to specifically push sales of the ME29 computer and over a dozen of the most etablished ME29 software houses were offered incentives to prevent sagging sales in the meantime. By mid-1983 ICL was on the verge of becoming the first mainframe vendor to offer its entire range to third parties, and Traderpoint dealers were to have access to everything from the ICL Personal Computer (PC) to the Atlas range of IBM plug-compatible mainframes in the not too distant future.

At this time there were also moves to foster collaboration with consultancies which provided advice to the larger users. Rob Wilmot and Peter Bonfield (marketing director) contacted the big names – Price Waterhouse, Peat Marwick, Mitchell, Deloitte Haskin & Sells, Pactel, Arthur Andersen, etc., in order to try and get ICL closer to them. There was also a plan to work with consultants through Traderpoint, using them as a fourth arm in marketing, and advising both systems and software houses as well as the ICL sales force.

Traderpoint was eventually expanded across the UK, and in ICL's other major markets of Australia, South Africa, Scandinavia and France. It was successful in Italy 'where the style was right', said Piggott. A major marketing effort to win Traderpoint dealers had begun in West Germany, with a second lined up for North America.

Retail Outlets By the end of 1983 ICL had set up nine retail outlets offering the ICL personal computer, DRS, the 8800 record processing system 25, the ME29 and the PERQ computers. These represented the full range of the Networked Product Line (NPL).

The outlets operated within the Traderpoint division under the name of 'Computer point' and the facilities were offered, free of charge, to Traderpoint dealers as well as being used by ICL branch salesmen, for demonstration purposes.

Manufacturing

ICL's new strategy of collaborative agreements with other companies was followed by a considerable reduction in its in-house manufacturing operation. Rob Wilmot had identified ICL's manufacturing group as being seriously overmanned. He said that streamlining would be vital for the company's recovery and that automation of the assembly lines and printed circuit board (pcb) operation must take place to a greater extent than ever before. A month after his appointment he announced 5,200 redundancies with about 1,700 coming from the manufacturing group. This was on top of 2,500 sackings in November 1980 and the closure of the Winsford plant. Collaborative ventures gave rise to only two opportunities for additional manufacturing effort. The Three Rivers 'PERQ' was to be manufactured under licence in the UK and the 'Rair' Black Box (becoming the ICL Personal Computer) also manufactured by ICL under licence. ICL, in common with many other mainframe manufacturers, brought in most if not all its peripherals. Its laser printer was made by Siemens, the disks by Control data, the magnetic tapes by Storage Technology and the front-end processors by Computer Technology.

It had been ICL's aim for some years to approach manufacturing in a modular fashion: where pcbs and other units of assembly were more or less common on the whole ICL range. The idea, as one senior ICL executive explained, was to reduce costs because the same essential process can be applied across the range, and just as importantly ICL could take bulk orders of components at cheaper rates.

To some extent this had been achieved with the 'S' series of machines – built around the 2966. By mid-1982, ICL employed just under 5,000 people in its manufacturing and logistics operation – about a third of the UK workforce. It was the result of the continuous and relentless pressure to reduce the heavy financial burden of designing and making ICL's own computers. Wilmot had trimmed the diversity of the company's in-house products by dropping some machines and software, and increasing the total diversity of the range by buying in from outside.

Finance

The announcement that ICL was to raise £32.2 million through a rights issue came in mid-December 1981. It was a one-for-one, 25p a share offer, though the company's share price at the time stood at the 45p mark. For ICL's shareholders the rights offer was much more important than any short-term gain – it marked yet another step in the new management's bid to turn the company around. In that respect it took on added importance in as much as it contributed to keeping alive UK interest in a key area of economic activity. The company's major shareholders very quickly fell into line behind the new management in backing the offer. It was a further consolation that in opting for a rights issue, ICL was right to the forefront of current fashion in City funding. 1981 saw a record year for the number of companies put forward coming to the Stock Exchange to make a cash call on shareholders through rights issues. The total for the year in fact showed an 86% increase on the previous year, raising almost £2 billion of the £3 billion raised through new issues by the corporate sector.

So, in effect, ICL's move was extremely respectable in so far as it conformed to the example of its more profitable corporate relatives. Against a background of £55 million losses on trading in the year to September 1981 plus a £78.1 million payout to finance the running down of sections of the company's business, the board was forced to act. Those were only the more obvious signs that all was not financially well with the company and that something needed to be done. The company's balance sheet showed some of the classic signs of a company in danger.

Net asset value was down, even in the current cost accounts, as were orders. Short-term loans were up and that was against a decrease in turnover and all-round trading performance. It was against that background and the rundown in shareholders' funds that chairman Christopher Laidlaw put forward his right to shareholders who were given most of January to decide whether or not to accept.

He explained the rights issue as a necessary step towards establishing a stronger capital base and a better balance between shareholders' funds and borrowings. He also explained that the rights issue was likely to be only one of many sacrifices shareholders were going to be asked to make in the interests of their company.

Even before the rights issue, further steps were under consideration to achieve an appropriate level of shareholders' funds. This in fact was the case for, in January 1983, a further rights issue raised £104 million. As a consequence, group worldwide borrowings were reduced to £59 million in March 1983 compared with £180 million as at September 1982. However, some £17 million of the total reduction was attributable to control of working capital.

Gross borrowings continued to fall as profitability improved through 1983. Pre-tax profits shot up 92%, to nearly £46 million as the cost-cutting measures took full effect. The City's response was modest, with the share price continuing to hover between 55p and 65p. Analysts Fielding, Newton and Smith, who accurately predicted a £45 million profit, believed that the new strategy was working, but that the City would await the results of the 1984–5 financial year before 'getting excited'. The company was predicting a steady growth of business in 1984. Chairman Laidlaw announced that development programmes already under way would require additional investment.

Bank Facilities and Government Guarantee[1] By an agreement dated 24 April 1981, between ICL and Midland Bank plc, Barclays Bank plc, Citibank, N.A. and National Westminster Bank plc ('the banks'), facilities totalling £270m were extended by the banks to ICL for the period ended on 31 March 1983.

On 28 September 1981, 50 million Redeemable Preference shares of £1 each were subscribed for by Midland Bank Plc, Barclays Bank Plc and National Westminster Bank Plc and the banking facilities were reduced to £220m. Of this amount the first £70m is secured by floating charges on the assets of ICL, and the balance of £150m is guaranteed by HM Government. In addition, under an agreement between the Secretary of State for Trade and Industry and the relevant banks, HM Government has undertaken to purchase the Redeemable Preference shares from the banks if they are not redeemed on the due dates. 20 million of the Redeemable Preference shares were redeemed at par on 5 April 1983.

By an agreement dated 5 May 1982, the banking facilities were extended for a further year to 31 March 1984. HM Government's guarantee of Redeemable Preference shares and the banking facilities in excess of £70m was limited to £200m until 5 April 1983. The total amount guaranteed was reduced to £150m from 6 April 1983, and will further reduce to 100m from 1 April 1984, to £50m from 1 April 1985 and to nil from 1 April 1986.

[1] Company Report, 1983.

Organization

During 1982 the new management had instituted staff cuts, many of which were at senior level. Wilmot's more open form of management was, in 1983, particularly levelled at reorganizing operations on the basis of new business centres to cover design, marketing and sales of different products in distinctly different areas.

The company was preparing to revamp its sales operations amid speculations that its key Product Marketing Division (PMD) was to be disbanded. At the end of 1983 ICL had set up two specialized Business Centres and a new Office Systems Division drawing staff from PMD and other parts of the company.

The first stage was to comprise a Manufacturing Business Centre at Reading, headed up by manager Gerry Kitzinger and a Small Systems Business Centre at Bracknell, which would be led by Steve Black, the former head of System 25 marketing. A new Office Systems Division would be led by former PMD chief Ninian Eadie and would concentrate on the DRS range, bringing personnel from Bracknell, Kidsgrove, PMD at Slough and Utica in the US.

In December 1983 ICL announced that Sir Michael Edwardes, former chief of British Leyland, had joined the board and that he would succeed the present chairman, Christopher Laidlaw.

Appendix 1 ICL Accounts

CONSOLIDATED PROFIT AND LOSS ACCOUNT FOR THE YEAR ENDED 30 SEPTEMBER 1983 (£m)

		1983		*1982*
Turnover		846.5		720.9
Cost of sales		(533.2)		(422.2)
Gross profit		313.3		298.7
Other operating costs		(252.9)		(251.6)
Operating profit		60.4		47.1
Other income		1.1		3.4
Interest		(15.9)		(26.8)
Profit on ordinary activities before taxation		45.6		23.7
Taxation		(7.0)		(7.8)
Profit on ordinary activities after taxation		38.6		15.9
Minority interests		(0.3)		(0.2)
Profit before extraordinary item		38.3		15.7
Extraordinary item		–		(3.4)
Profit for the financial year		38.3		12.3
Dividends – Preference	(3.7)		(4.8)	
– Ordinary	(3.6)		(0.3)	
		(7.3)		(5.1)
Retained profit for the year		31.0		7.2
Earnings per Ordinary share		8.57p		4.23p
Statement of retained profits				
Balance at 1 October		(13.2)		(23.0)
Retained profit for the year		31.0		7.2
Exchange adjustments		2.5		(17.9)
Acquisition of Computer Leasings Ltd		–		20.5
Balance at 30 September		20.3		(13.2)

BALANCE SHEETS AT 30 SEPTEMBER 1983

	Group		*Company*	
	1983 £m	*1982 £m*	*1983 £m*	*1982 £m*
Fixed assets				
Tangible assets	155.6	161.9	–	–
Investments	6.6	4.5	73.9	73.9
	162.2	166.4	73.9	73.9
Current assets				
Stocks	142.9	129.7	–	–
Debtors	225.9	213.3	187.8	80.3
Investments	3.4	3.6	–	–
Cash at bank and in hand	41.1	32.4	0.1	8.6
	413.3	379.0	187.9	88.9
Creditors: amounts falling due within one year				
Borrowings	(71.4)	(147.4)	(4.0)	–
Other liabilities	(180.2)	(171.6)	(6.9)	(7.6)
Net current assets	161.7	60.0	177.0	81.3
Total assets less current liabilities	323.9	226.4	250.9	155.2
Creditors: amounts falling due after more than one year				
Debenture stocks and loans	(55.9)	(62.8)	(10.5)	(14.5)
Other liabilities	(8.0)	(9.2)	–	–
Provisions for liabilities and charges	(25.9)	(39.4)	–	–
	234.1	115.0	240.4	140.7
Capital and reserves				
Called-up share capital	142.4	116.8	142.4	116.8
Share premium account	69.6	10.1	69.6	10.1
Profit and loss account	20.3	(13.2)	28.4	13.8
Shareholders' funds	232.3	113.7	240.4	140.7
Minority interests	1.8	1.3	–	–
	234.1	115.0	240.4	140.7

GROUP STATISTICS

	1983 £m	*1982 £m*	*1981 £m*	*1980 £m*	*1979 £m*
Turnover and profit/(loss)					
Turnover	846.5	720.9	711.1	715.8	624.1
Operating profit/(loss)	60.4	47.1	(21.1)	46.2	56.8
Profit/(loss) before taxation	45.6	23.7	(49.8)	25.1	46.5
Taxation	(7.0)	(7.8)	(5.4)	(7.4)	(11.2)
Profit/(loss) after taxation	38.6	15.9	(55.2)	17.7	35.3
Dividends					
– Preference	(3.7)	(4.8)	–	–	–
– Ordinary[d]	(3.6)	(0.3)	–	(4.0)	(4.0)
Retained profit/(loss) for the year[a]	31.0	7.2	(133.1)	6.0	31.1
Employment of capital					
Tangible fixed assets	155.6	161.9	126.7	128.8	142.6
Fixed asset investments	6.6	4.5	6.7	5.8	5.2
Net current assets	161.7	60.0	103.9	153.6	140.9
Creditors – due after one year	(63.9)	(72.0)	(78.4)	(113.8)	(117.4)
Provisions for liabilities and charges	(25.9)	(39.4)	(85.8)	(30.9)	(22.3)
Net assets	234.1	115.0	73.1	143.5	149.0
Capital invested					
Called-up share capital	142.4	116.8	83.4	33.4	33.4
Reserves	89.9	(3.1)	(11.8)	108.0	113.4
Shareholders' funds	232.3	113.7	71.6	141.4	146.8
Minority interests	1.8	1.3	1.5	2.1	2.2
	234.1	115.0	73.1	143.5	149.0
Employees					
Number at end of the year	22,573	23,581	25,564	33,087	34,401
Ratios					
Per 25p Ordinary share:					
Earnings/(loss)[b]	8.57p	4.23p	(29.96)p	9.64p	19.14p
Dividends – net[c,d]	0.8p	0.1p	–	2.98p	2.98p
Net assets[c]	£0.52	£0.43	£0.54	£1.06	£1.10
Turnover per employee[e]	£36700	£29300	£24200	£21200	£18300

	1983 *£m*	*1982* *£m*	*1981* *£m*	*1980* *£m*	*1979* *£m*
Percentages:	%	%	%	%	%
Profit/(loss) before taxation to turnover	5.4	3.3	(7.0)	3.5	7.4
Operating profit/(loss) to capital invested and net borrowings	18.9	16.1	(8.9)	15.8	24.5
Profit/(loss) before taxation to shareholders' funds at end of the year	19.6	20.8	(69.5)	17.8	31.7
Net borrowings to shareholders' funds plus net borrowings	27.1	61.0	69.6	51.4	36.2

[a] After extraordinary item of: 1982 – £3.4m; 1981 – £78.1m; 1980 – £7.7m.

[b] All figures adjusted for the December 1982 and December 1981 rights issues and in 1979 for sub-division from £1 to 25p shares.

[c] Figures not adjusted for the December 1982 and December 1981 rights issues but adjusted in 1979 for sub-division from £1 to 25p shares.

[d] The company's securities have maintained their status as wider-range investments for the purposes of the Trustee Investments Act 1961 because the 1980 final dividend was paid in the calendar year 1981.

[e] Based on average of the number of employees at the beginning and end of the year.

Appendix 2

NOTE ON STANDARDS

Chairman's Report[1]

The dominant reason for HM Government support of ICL in the Spring of 1981, by thc loan guarantee package and the appointment of the new management team, was to secure the growth path of the public sector's substantial investment in hardware and software by ensuring the maintenance of a UK computing capability. Our decisions in 1981 to standardise on a single operating system and to access advanced mainframe chip technology from Fujitsu have been fully comprehended and supported by the Government. HM Government now has a major opportunity to support our world-class VME operating system, and Government's demonstrable agreement would be a significant factor in the continuing success of our mainframe strategy.

There is a further vital area where Government has a major role to play. Our overall product strategy rests upon the concept of a Networked Product Line. This concept envisages open systems communicating with each other through networks which confirm with agreed international standards. With the rapid convergence of telecommunications and information processing systems, it is all-important that the open standards recently accepted by the International Standards Organisation are adhered to internationally.

By procuring to agreed international networking standards, Government can ensure that ICL and other British Information Technology companies enjoy their full share of the rapid growth in the industry which will undoubtedly occur. Competition would suffer heavily if instead a de facto monopoly of networking and interface standards were allowed to emerge.

The Information Technology industry operates on a worldwide scale and it is clear that many other countries in this hemisphere are equally concerned that no single country or company dominates or constrains the vital development of this industry. The future will bring considerable changes in the structure of the industry, but these changes must be based upon system communication standards supported by governments and open to all members of the industry.

[1] Extract from Chairman's Statement, *ICL Annual Report*, 1983

Appendix 3

NOTE ON GOVERNMENT – LEGAL ISSUES

Single Tender Policy

In 1982 a Public Accounts Committee (PAC) investigation into ICL's affairs showed that the government was exploiting loop-holes in the new Common Market and General Agreement on Tariffs and Trade (Gatt) rules banning single tender.

Evidence given to the committee confirmed that ICL won the huge £100 million contract to computerize the Inland Revenue's Pay-As-You-Earn income tax system because the Department of Industry was convinced that otherwise the company would collapse.

Complete collapse of the company would have cost the Treasury £300-400 million in conversion and reprogramming costs, according to the PAC.

It was generally held that government computer orders could be exempted from open international tendering, on the grounds of compatibility and security. Since the government already had a large number of ICL machines, the 'compatibility' exemption alone would apply in about half of replaced orders. Additionally it was held that over half the purchases made by the Ministry of Defence would be exempted from open international competition on the grounds of security.

The Department of Industry had decided in 1971 that in the field of computers it was very important, particularly for equipping industry and commerce, to have a domestic capability about to stand up against the multinationals. Support for ICL was provided by procurement preference and some research and development grants.

In June 1982 a move was made to test just how open the UK local and central government tenders were. This case was the first time that the EEC ruling on open tender has been tested and could give it teeth.

IBM sought an injunction to stop the Severn and Trent Water Authority from buying a £15.9 million ICL system. Acting against the advice of its data processing experts, the authority decided to buy an ICL system instead of the recommended IBM. The latter, together with Honeywell, Sperry Univac and ICL bid for the order, and it was IBM's understanding that their proposal was recommended for acceptance by the officers of the authority. However, councillors in the authority's area, who administered its affairs, overruled their experts and picked ICL. IBM's case was based on claims that it was as much a UK supplier as ICL on the basis of jobs, goods made here and investment in the UK industry.

In August 1982, however, IBM withdrew its action for judicial review of the order after ICL's counsel proved that Severn–Trent had approved the decision of its Policy and Resources Committee to overrule a technical panel's choice of IBM and pick ICL.

Appendix 4

MANUFACTURERS LEGIBLE TABLE

UK Market – 1982

Hewlett Packard held the lead at the small end of the systems valued between £15,000 and £29,000; the ICL ME29 model 35 had the biggest installed base among computers between £60,000 and £99,999, and it also had the biggest installed base by value of systems priced between £250,000 and £499,999.

IBM held the top position in all other categories. The biggest value of installed base for any computer in the UK was held by IBM's 3431. A total ot £348 million worth of 4341s was installed at the end of 1982, according to the survey. At the top end of the market, for systems costing £1 million and more, IBM also had the sole position with its 3033 processor. Some £187 million worth of 3033s were installed in the UK at the end of 1982. ICL had been unable to win second place in this sector. Sperry had £106 million worth of 110/80s installed, according to the survey, pushing ICL into third place with £76 million worth of 2972 type computers.

Hewlett Packard's leadership at the bottom end was by only a slim margin. Its HP250 had an installed base value in the survey, at £14 million, followed by IBM's Series 1 at £13 million. Texas Instruments came third with the T1990/12 valued at £10.5 million installed. IBM's System 34 led the field in the £30,000 to £59,999 bracket. Some £200 million worth were installed at the end of the year and shipments during the year were valued at £104 million. As a consolation for ICL, the second machine in this category, the ICL System Ten, had an installed base of £54 million and shipments valued at £980,000.

In the next bracket of value, the ICL ME29 was slightly ahead of the Honeywell Level 6/40 range and both were considerably in front of the CMC Sovereign range at £25 million installed base. ICL's total value of installed base of computers over £15,000 fell back in 1982. It rose to £1.23 billion in 1981 but fell back to £1.19 billion.

The overall position of UK-owned companies did better because of the growth of Ferranti, Systime, and Redifussion. Ferranti's installed base grew to £172 million in the year, achieving 3.3% of the total installed base in the UK, the same proportion as in 1981. GEC just managed to get back to its installed base value of 1980 after losing £2 million in value during 1981.

21 International Computers (C)

In May 1984 ICL celebrated the announcement of improved first-half results with the news that it had got the go-ahead from the French Government to reorganize its French subsidiary. This was part of the company's attempt to make its European operations a major part of its international business and was synonymous with concentrated activity in West Germany, Holland and Scandinavia.

In July 1984, the company faced a takeover bid from STC, the United Kingdom-based electronics group.

ICL'S PROGRESS

The United Kingdom market accounted for just over half of ICL's business by the middle of 1984, the rest being split between continental Europe, Australia, South Africa and the United States.

Australia and South Africa were quite strong subsidiaries and had almost always made a good contribution to ICL's business. However, ICL's position in continental Europe and the USA had, under successive teams of corporate and local management, constantly been in a state of near confusion.

In West Germany ICL had concentrated over the past year on selling the small end of the ICL product range.

The UK management initially sent out to run the West German operation had been replaced with German management, and greater management control had been exerted through the organization put in place. Some 75% of the improvement had been due to better management control and a change from the older style of business.

Better results from Holland and Scandinavia had added to the European performance and, with slimmed-down overheads, profits were beginning to flow.

The biggest international market, the USA, was not ICL's number one priority, as Sir Michael Edwardes, the chairman, had indicated that ICL's objective was to be meaningful in the US rather than to be big. The company's strategy in the US had been to attack one sector at a time and, through one large order, it had taken a lead as top vendor in the DIY sector.

These successes in international marketing contributed to the figures announced in equal measure with domestic UK business. Turnover improved by 8% to stand at £433.4 million for the six months to the end of March 1984 and profit rose by 9.6% to £18.3 million.

The profit figure was somewhat pulled down by the decision of the board to charge a full £4 million of non-recurring losses, caused by the reorganization of the French subsidiary, to the first half of 1984. The balance sheet showed debt down to £74 million from £86 million for the same period in 1983.

PROSPECTS FOR 1984

The City generally expected ICL to generate a profit slightly above £50 million, showing a steady but unspectacular growth from 1983's £46.5 million.

The initial reaction of the City to the results was unclear, because the whole of the electronics sector on the Stock Market was depressed over the discussions between Thorn EMI, Plessey and British Aerospace about possible mergers.

PRODUCT STRATEGY

A general belief on the part of some industry analysts was that large and small computers only would dominate future demand. However, ICL's concentration on the middle sector was re-iterated by Rob Wilmot, ICL's chief executive:

> Nobody, apart from ICL with the DM1, has a middle sector as part of their main thrust. ICL will be able to provide the same architecture, the same operating system and the same levels of security and reliability in both the region and the data processing centre.

Likewise, the chairman, Michael Edwardes, was convinced that such a strategy was viable even in the face of uncertain economic conditions, saying in May 1984:

> If we face higher inflation and interest charges and lower growth in the UK then thank God that my colleagues got it right two to three years ago and that we will have the new product coming through at the beginning of 1985. If we faced those worsening conditions two years ago we would have been in dead trouble.

ICL's directors believed that they were doing all they could in terms of product development, management training and reorganization to revamp the company and give it a future.

THE STC OFFER

On 26 July 1984, Standard Telephones and Cables (STC) acquired over 44 million ordinary ICL shares (which represented approximately 9.8% of the issued share capital of ICL) at a price of 77p per share. Almost immediately, STC announced an offer for ICL equivalent to a value of 77.14p per share. Shareholders were offered 2 new ordinary shares for every 7 ordinary shares held in ICL, or the cash equivalent.

As expected, ICL rejected this offer, basically on the grounds that the offer was considered inadequate, in view of ICL's technological strengths and its significant market position both in the UK and in other countries.

STC'S PRINCIPAL ACTIVITIES AND PERFORMANCE

STC's principal activities were telecommunications, international communications and services, components and distribution, and residential electronics. Most of these activities were supported by substantial research and development in the divisions and laboratories of the group.

Telecommunications

STC's public switching products activity had enjoyed a particularly good period; in 1982 the company had reached agreement with British Telecom to supply the bulk of the latter's TXE telephone exchange requirements. Deliveries against TXE orders from British Telecom continued throughout 1983 at a high rate, and this division was able to achieve sound financial results as a consequence.

The UK market for landline transmission systems was characterized in 1983 by a rapid pace of technological development. In this period of change, the company was able to expand its share of the available market. In addition, the first optical fibre transmission products went into service in 1983, reinforcing the company's position at the forefront of transmission technology.

In 1983, the company's submarine systems division achieved a record level of activity, principally as a result of work on the 7,500 nautical mile ANZCAN system linking Australia and Canada.

In defence systems, 1983 was a satisfactory year for STC. Following reorganization of its defence systems activities in 1980, this business had shown steady growth and improved profitability. Major projects undertaken included work for the Ministry of Defence and increasingly for overseas customers.

In the rapidly expanding area of business communications, STC's results in 1983 were mixed. The STC 3000 'Perfector' teleprinter maintained its position as market leader, despite strong competition, on the basis of superior performance. Satisfactory results were also achieved from a number of other products, particularly the STC radio-pager, which continued to sell well at home and overseas. The results from certain business communications products were less satisfactory, and steps were taken to reduce the associated cost structure as necessary.

International Aeradio, acquired in April 1983, reported operating profit for 1983 some 8% lower than for 1982. This reflected difficult overseas trading conditions, especially in Middle Eastern markets which were affected by instability in the world price of oil. The other companies acquired in 1983 achieved improved trading results.

Components and Distributors

STC's components business saw good growth in both sales and profitability in 1983. Turnover increased over 1982 by some 25% and profit before taxation by more than 70%. These improvements reflected both better underlying trading conditions in the market place and the benefit of new product and process investment in recent years. The components business was substantially strengthened in 1983 by the acquisition of ITT's semiconductor design and manufacturing facility at Foots Cray, Kent. (ITT was STC's former parent company.)

STC Distributors, the company's electrical wholesaling arm, also showed substantial improvement, following rationalization measures taken in 1982, and was able to profit from improved market demand, albeit in very competitive trading conditions.

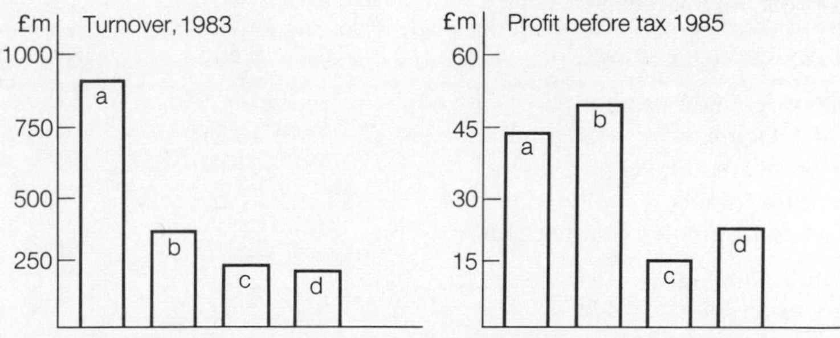

FIGURE 21.1 Main business activities of STC

Appendix 1 International Computers PLC

CONSOLIDATED PROFIT AND LOSS ACCOUNT FOR THE YEAR ENDED 30 SEPTEMBER 1983 (£m)

		1983		*1982*
Turnover		846.5		720.9
Cost of sales		(533.2)		(422.2)
Gross profit		313.3		298.7
Other operating costs		(252.9)		(251.6)
Operating profit		60.4		47.1
Other income		1.1		3.4
Interest		(15.9)		(26.8)
Profit on ordinary activities before taxation		45.6		23.7
Taxation		(7.0)		(7.8)
Profit on ordinary activities after taxation		38.6		15.9
Minority interests		(0.3)		(0.2)
Profit before extraordinary item		38.3		15.7
Extraordinary item		–		(3.4)
Profit for the financial year		38.3		12.3
Dividends – Preference	(3.7)		(4.8)	
– Ordinary	(3.6)		(0.3)	
		(7.3)		(5.1)
Retained profit for the year		31.0		7.2
Earnings per Ordinary share		8.57p		4.23p
Statement of retained profits				
Balance at 1 October		(13.2)		(23.0)
Retained profit for the year		31.0		7.2
Exchange adjustments		2.5		(17.9)
Acquisition of Computer Leasings Ltd		–		20.5
Balance at 30 September		20.3		(13.2)

BALANCE SHEETS AT 30 SEPTEMBER 1983 (£m)

	Group		*Company*	
	1983	*1982*	*1983*	*1982*
Fixed assets				
Tangible assets	155.6	161.9	–	–
Investments	6.6	4.5	73.9	73.9
	162.2	166.4	73.9	73.9
Current assets				
Stocks	142.9	129.7	–	–
Debtors	225.9	213.3	187.8	80.3
Investments	3.4	3.6	–	–
Cash at bank and in hand	41.1	32.4	0.1	8.6
	413.3	379.0	187.9	88.9
Creditors: amounts falling due within one year				
Borrowings	(71.4)	(147.4)	(4.0)	–
Other liabilities	(180.2)	(171.6)	(6.9)	(7.6)
Net current assets	161.7	60.0	177.0	81.3
Total assets less current liabilities	323.9	226.4	250.9	155.2
Creditors: amounts falling due after more than one year				
Debenture stocks and loans	(55.9)	(62.8)	(10.5)	(14.5)
Other liabilities	(8.0)	(9.2)	–	–
Provisions for liabilities and charges	(25.9)	(39.4)	–	–
	234.1	115.0	240.4	140.7
Capital and reserves				
Called-up share capital	142.4	116.8	142.4	116.8
Share premium account	69.6	10.1	69.6	10.1
Profit and loss account	20.3	(13.2)	28.4	13.8
Shareholders' funds	232.3	113.7	240.4	140.7
Minority interests	1.8	1.3	–	–
	234.1	115.0	240.4	140.7

GROUP STATISTICS (£m)

	1983	*1982*	*1981*	*1980*	*1979*
Turnover and profit/(loss)					
Turnover	846.5	720.9	711.1	715.8	624.1
Operating profit/(loss)	60.4	47.1	(21.1)	46.2	56.8
Profit/(loss) before taxation	45.6	23.7	(49.8)	25.1	46.5
Taxation	(7.0)	(7.8)	(5.4)	(7.4)	(11.2)
Profit/(loss) after taxation	38.6	15.9	(55.2)	17.7	35.3
Dividends – Preference	(3.7)	(4.8)	–	–	–
– Ordinary	(3.6)	(0.3)	–	(4.0)	(4.0)
Retained profit/(loss) for the year	31.0	7.2	(133.1)	6.0	31.1
Employment of capital					
Tangible fixed assets	155.6	161.9	126.7	128.8	142.6
Fixed asset investments	6.6	4.5	6.7	5.8	5.2
Net current assets	161.7	60.0	103.9	153.6	140.9
Creditors – due after one year	(63.9)	(72.0)	(78.4)	(113.8)	(117.4)
Provisions for liabilities and charges	(25.9)	(39.4)	(85.8)	(30.9)	(22.3)
Net assets	234.1	115.0	73.1	143.5	149.0
Capital invested					
Called-up share capital	142.4	116.8	83.4	33.4	33.4
Reserves	89.9	(3.1)	(11.8)	108.0	113.4
Shareholders' funds	232.3	113.7	71.6	141.4	146.8
Minority interests	1.8	1.3	1.5	2.1	2.2
	234.1	115.0	73.1	143.5	149.0
Number of employees at end of the year	22,573	23,581	25,564	33,087	34,401
Ratios					
Per 25p Ordinary share					
Earnings/(loss)	8.57p	4.23p	(29.96)p	9.64p	19.14p
Dividends – net	0.8p	0.1p	–	2.98p	2.98p
Net assets	£0.52	£0.43	£0.54	£1.06	£1.10
Turnover per employee	£36,700	£29,300	£24,200	£21,200	£18,300
Percentages	%	%	%	%	%
Profit/(loss) before taxation to turnover	5.4	3.3	(7.0)	3.5	7.4
Operating profit/(loss) to capital invested and net borrowings	18.9	16.1	(8.9)	15.8	24.5
Profit/(loss) before taxation to shareholders' funds at end of the year	19.6	20.8	(69.5)	17.8	31.7
Net borrowings to shareholders' funds plus net borrowings	27.1	61.0	69.6	51.4	36.2

Appendix 2

STC CONSOLIDATED PROFIT AND LOSS ACCOUNT FOR THE YEAR ENDED 31 DECEMBER 1983 (£m)

Turnover	920.6
Cost of sales	668.2
Gross profit	252.4
Marketing, selling and distribution expenses	60.6
Administrative expenses	45.4
Research and development expenses	53.3
Operating profit	93.1
Investment income	4.8
Interest payable	5.7
Profit on ordinary activities before taxation	92.2
Tax on profit on ordinary activities	26.5
Profit on ordinary activities after taxation	65.7
Minority interests	0.2
Profit for the financial year	65.5
Dividends paid and proposed	24.4
Retained profit for the year	41.1
Attributed to:	
The company	25.6
Group companies	14.8
Related companies	0.7
	41.1
Earnings per share	20.6p

STC BALANCE SHEETS AT 31 DECEMBER 1983 (£m)

Fixed assets	
Tangible assets	165.8
Investments	10.3
	176.1
Current assets	
Stocks	193.0
Debtors	242.5
Cash at bank and in hand	24.2
	459.7
Creditors: amounts falling due within one year	
Loans and overdrafts	32.5
Other	280.6
	313.1
Net current assets	146.6
Total assets less current liabilities	322.7
Creditors: amounts falling due after more than one year	
Loans and overdrafts	9.1
Other	29.4
	38.5
Provisions for liabilities and charges	19.8
Net assets	264.4
Capital and reserves	
Called-up share capital	81.3
Other reserve	6.5
Profit and loss account	173.9
Shareholders' funds	261.7
Minority interests	2.7
Total capital employed	264.4

STC FIVE-YEAR RECORD (£m)

	1979	*1980*	*1981*	*1982*	*1983*
Results					
Turnover	436.8	537.7	567.5	628.5	920.6
Operating profit	43.0	55.0	59.0	68.5	93.1
Interest less investment income	9.6	10.9	8.4	4.2	0.9
Profit before taxation	33.4	44.1	50.6	64.3	92.2
Taxation	5.9	15.4	14.1	24.1	26.5
Profit after taxation	27.5	28.7	36.5	40.2	65.7
Minority interests	–	–	–	–	0.2
Profit for the financial year	27.5	28.7	36.5	40.2	65.7
Dividends	8.0	10.0	13.5	18.0	24.4
Retained profit for the year	19.5	18.7	23.0	22.2	41.1
Earnings per share	9.2p[a]	9.5p[a]	12.2p[a]	13.4p	20.6p
Restated for the 2 for 1 issue of 5 November 1982[a]					
Net assets employed					
Fixed assets	70.4	79.0	94.1	111.8	176.1
Other assets (net)	112.3	114.7	119.5	120.9	97.4
	182.7	193.7	213.6	232.7	273.5
Financed by:					
Shareholders' funds	144.0	162.7	185.6	207.8	261.7
Minority interests	–	–	–	–	2.7
Long-term loans	38.7	31.0	28.0	24.9	9.1
	182.7	193.7	213.6	232.7	273.5
Other data					
Plant additions	18.4	21.4	29.6	33.4	58.2
Depreciation	10.9	12.4	14.4	18.5	28.5
Overseas sales	77.3	94.7	125.7	143.3	273.2
Average number of employees ('000)	28.0	27.3	25.0	22.9	28.2
Dividends per share as paid					
Interim dividend	2.0p	4.0p	4.5p	6.0p	2.75p[a]
Final dividend	6.0p	6.0p	9.0p	4.0p[a]	4.75p[a]

[a] After 2 for 1 issue of 5 November 1982

22 Illingworth, Morris

By 1984 Illingworth, Morris (IM) was the largest wool textile company in Europe and second largest in the world. It was a vertically integrated company with interests in wool combing, scouring, commission dyeing, spinning and weaving of woollen, worsted and mixed fabrics and the making up of suitings, though its largest shares of the UK market were in the preliminary processes such as combing and topmaking. (See Appendix 1 for a glossary of textile terms.)

Illingworth, Morris was formed in 1921 when Amalgamated Textiles Ltd changed its name in order to incorporate Daniel Illingworth & Sons Ltd. The main activity at that time was worsted spinning. Many more companies were acquired in the period up to 1975 which considerably increased the size of the group and its involvement in the woollen textile industry. Acquisitions included wool combing, worsted manufacturing, cotton processing, knitwear manufacturing, woollen yarn spinning and clothing manufacturing. The most significant acquisition was that of Woolcombers (Holdings) PLC, the largest wool processing company in the UK, accounting for 30% of UK combing production. From the early seventies, Woolcombers was responsible for importing wool used by the group and converting it into tops. The acquisitions were funded mainly by short-term loans and, to a lesser degree, by the issue of further equity.

As a result of the way that IM grew the company developed several areas of overlap, resulting in excess capacity. Between 1976 and 1981 woollen textiles suffered a considerable decline in demand, exposing faults in IM organization and leaving the company vulnerable to recession. Mr Ivan Hill who was appointed chairman in 1976 had begun a period of rationalization by streamlining the group into four divisions. A large number of mills were closed and the range of yarns and cloths reduced. Nevertheless, the problems continued and after the group reported losses of £2.5 million for year ending March 1980, Mr Donald Hanson took over as chairman in August 1980. He continued the programme of rationalization to eliminate overcapacity in areas where no long-term prospects of a return to previous levels of demand were likely.

The overall programme was carried out in two stages. The first involved the creation of two divisions covering the following activities: (1) Merchanting, topmaking, combing and spinning operations; and (2) Woollen and worsted manufacturing, and cotton and clothing operations. The first stage of the programme was completed in two years, and resulted in the removal of excess capacity in combing, topmaking and spinning, reducing the number of operating units from 16 to 10, and worsted manufacturing being carried out in one semi-bulk unit and three highly specialized units, as opposed to eight units operating before the reorganization.

The second stage of reorganization took place in 1982, when two operating companies were formed, Illingworth, Morris & Company Ltd and Woolcombers (Holdings) plc. The executive directors of these two companies shared responsibility for the day-to-day management of the various units within the group, and were collectively responsible to the directors of the parent company, Illingworth, Morris plc. IM management philosophy was that each unit was developed as a separate profit centre, run by a management team usually consisting of financial, technical, production, marketing and sales specialists. This philosophy was to encourage employees to identify closely with the performance of their unit.

In March each year, each operating unit made a return detailing the forecast results for the financial year ending 31 March, and submitted its forecast and budget for the next financial year for the yearly management review by the group board. Each unit prepared its own management accounts which were submitted monthly to the board of the appropriate management company. Each unit's profit and cash-flow forecast was reviewed quarterly.

This reorganization achieved the following results between March 1979 and September 1982:

1 Stock was reduced from £39m to £17.8m
2 Overdrafts were reduced from £24.8m to £13.2m
3 The number of employees was reduced from 8,542 to 3,805
4 The number of operating units was reduced from 42 to 25.

(Appendix 2 gives financial data on Illingworth, Morris)

Organizationally there were two further changes in 1982. Firstly, in topmaking, IM sold 60% of its interests to the British Wool Marketing Board (BWMB) with the formation between IM and BWMB of Woolcombers (Topmakers) Ltd, in which IM retained 40% interest. Woolcombers (Topmakers) had a 29% share of the UK tops market. Secondly, in combing, later that year IM contracted with Sir James Hill and Sons to buy the latter's combing capacity and undertake Hill's combing on commission. This gave IM a 40% share of UK combing capacity.

A number of IM subsidiaries had famous brand names, for example, 'J & J Crombie Ltd' was the largest manufacturer in the UK of high-quality woollen and cashmere overcoatings with a 10% share of the world market and 1982 sales of £6.4 million. 'Huddersfield Fine Worsteds', incorporating Learoyd Brothers, made very high quality worsted cloth, and IM

TABLE 22.1 IM share of the UK woollen and worsted textile sector by process, 1981–2

	Process	*UK market size (£m)*	*IM sales (£m)*	*% of IM sales which is exported*	*Major competitors*
1	Merchanting	30	8.6	50	
2	Combed specialist fibres (excluding cashmere)	14	4.7	32	
3	Commission wool scouring	8	1.3	–	
4	Wool combing	14	4.6	–	Joseph Dawson Thos Burnley
5	Processing of synthetic fibres	n/a	2.7	–	
6	Topmaking (subsequently through an associated company	65	26.1	27	W J Whitehead Sir James Hill
7	Lanolin	1.5	2.7	59	Croda Chemicals
8	Commission dyeing	3	1.0	–	Bulmer & Lumb
9	Worsted yarns (incl synthetic)	270	15.8	12	Bulmer & Lumb Coats Paton
10	Special fabrics: tennis balls,	2.1	5.8	65	Kenyon
	billiard table cloths, etc.	4.0	2.4	25	A W Hainsworth
11	Woollen fabrics:				
	overcoating,	9	5.8	55	Moorhouse & Brook
	jacketing,	20	0.6	66	Ballantyne
	donkey jacketing	5	1.8	28	Henry Lister
12	Worsted cloth	90	16.9	60	Allied Textile Parkland Textile
13	Mohair cloth	1.5	2.0	85	John Foster
14	Cloth merchandising	6.1	1.9	36	
15	Clothing manufacture	n/a	4.3	63	
16	Knitwear	n/a	1.3	69	
			110.3[a]		

[a] Does not tally with IM sales in 1981 due to inter-company sales.
Source: Monopolies and Mergers Commission

estimated that its shares of the UK output of high- and medium-quality worsted cloths were 60% and 20% respectively.

Table 22.1 shows processes in wool textiles where, in 1981–2, Illingworth, Morris was represented, giving also UK market size, the proportion of IM output exported and IM's main competitors.

UK WOOL TEXTILE INDUSTRY

The UK wool textile industry was concentrated in West Yorkshire which in the early 1980s accounted for about 65% of the net output of the sector. The other major area of the sector was located in Scotland (17% of net output), and the whole of the wool textile sector was one of three within the textile industry generally, the others being cotton and allied fibres/fabrics concentrated in Lancashire and the north-west, and the hosiery and knitwear sector located in the midlands and Scotland.

The textile industry (excluding clothing) as a whole was important in that it represented about 5% of employment in UK manufacturing industry and was responsible for a significant proportion of manufactured exports. Nevertheless, by 1981 employment in textiles generally had fallen to 363,000 from 512,000 in 1977, of which the woollen and worsted sector employed 56,000 in 1981 (from 83,000 in 1977), and of the £35 million of manufactured goods exported in 1980 textiles accounted for 4%.

The 1970s had been a difficult period for all of the textile sectors and the related clothing sector, for there was the extended recession following the 1973–4 oil crisis, the subsequent exploitation of North Sea oil leading to a strengthening in the value of sterling and then the onset of the 1979–83 recession. The cotton sector had undergone rationalization in the 1960s following the Cotton Industry Act of 1959 which encouraged the elimination of excess capacity and installation of new investment. These reorganizations brought about structural changes in that the vertically integrated groups (e.g. Courtaulds) increased their share of capacity, measured in spindles operating, from 60% in 1959 to 68% in 1965 and in looms from 26% to 35%, and the share of employment of the largest five firms rose from 18% in 1961 to 35% in 1964.

Taking textiles and clothing together, yarn and fabric exports over this period had usually outweighed imports of clothing, but in 1973 a substantial balance of trade deficit in textiles/clothing as a whole was built up for the first time. The main argument of the textile industry was that protection was needed against excessive imports to the UK market by low-cost countries, especially cotton yarns, fabrics and clothing. By 1974 some element of protection had been provided with the introduction of G.A.T.T. of the Multi-Fibre Arrangements (MFA) which restricted imports from low-cost countries to an annual growth of 6% p.a., and also by agreement with its European Economic Community partners the burden of imports was agreed to be shared between the European countries.

With such assistance backed by a programme of investment, productivity improvement and new product development, the textile and clothing industries' exports were 30% by volume higher in 1979 than their level in the peak pre-oil crisis year of 1972. The problems associated with the onset of the 1979 recession were attributed to economic rather than commercial reasons, with sterling standing at high rates of exchange with other currencies and interest rates at record level. These encouraged extensive de-stocking by retailers and manufacturers, and increased imports of lower-priced substitutes.

The woollen and worsted sector covered the preparation, spinning, dyeing, weaving and finishing of wool and blended fibres, and was divided into five production sections: tops, worsted spinning, woollen spinning, worsted weaving and woollen weaving. In 1980 there were 732 enterprises operating 865 establishments with a gross output of £1,208 million and employing 60,000 people. (See tables 22.2 and 22.3.)

The process was as shown in figure 22.1.

The decline was highlighted by the fall in production of chiefly wool yarns from 117 million kilograms in 1970 to 50 million kilograms in 1982, and of chiefly wool fabrics from 36 million kilograms to 15 million kilograms over the same period.

Overall output of the woollen and worsted sector fell by 70% between 1973 and 1980, and a further 13% from 1980 to 1983. The decline could be attributed not only to falls in exports but also to increased imports of clothing which had risen from 19% of UK consumption in 1974 to 33% in 1983.

The industry was fragmented, with a large number of companies operating in each of the principal sections. About 40% of enterprises

TABLE 22.2 Wool textiles 1968–1980

Year	*No of establishments*	*No of enterprises*	*No of employees (thousands)*
1968	1,439	965	141.6
1970	1,154	954	134.2
1972	1,015	794	111.1
1973	1,039	831	109.0
1975	1,011	832	92.9
1976	973	802	88.3
1977	949	788	84.9
1978	942	785	81.2
1979	917	764	73.7
1980	865	732	60.1

Source: Census of Production 1980

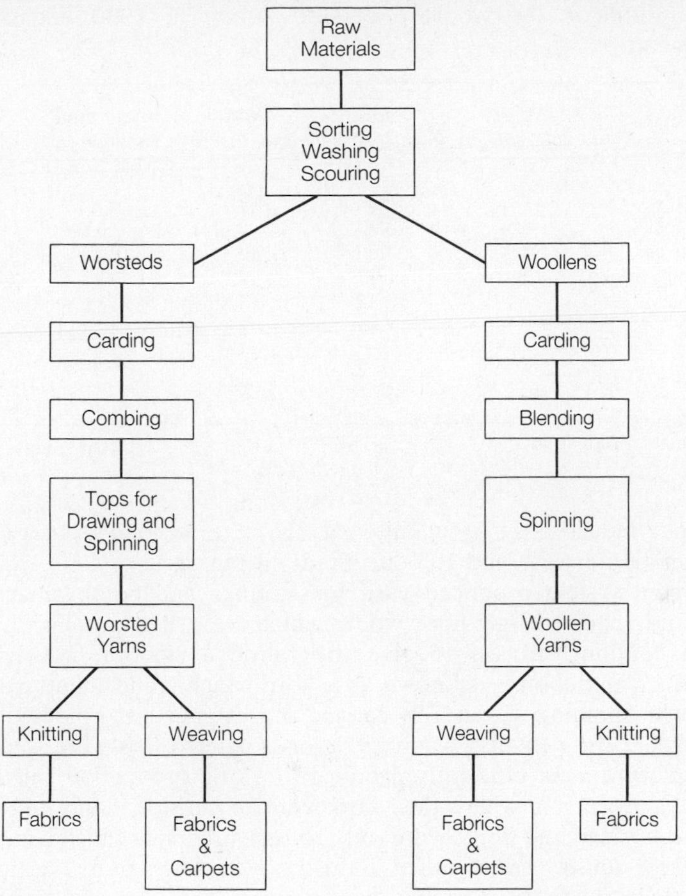

FIGURE 22.1 Production flow in the wool textile industry

were vertically integrated to some extent, involving themselves in more than one process in spinning, weaving, dyeing and finishing, whilst about 20% were specialist weavers and the rest specialized in one of the other processes.

The basic production methods in the industry had remained the same over many years, although the speed of equipment and resulting productivity had risen. There were two series of processes which were different for worsted and woollen which produced two different types of yarn for different end products. Despite the overall decline in the industry, the end product was still highly regarded as a top-quality product in the fabric and clothing trades. Of wool production 43% went

TABLE 22.3 Firms in the woollen worsted sector in 1980 (excluding carpet weaving)

Size of establishment	*No of establishments*	*No of enterprises*	*No of employees*	*% of total employment*	*Sales (£m)*
			(000's)		
1 – 19 employees	495	480	3.6	6.0	322.4
20 – 99 employees	209	200	10.9	18.1	
100 – 199 employees	89	75	12.7	21.1	232.6
200 – 499 employees	51	45	14.8	24.6	300.4
500+ employees	21	15	18.1	30.1	353.1
Total	865	735	60.1	100	1208.5

Source: Census of Production 1980

to the carpet industry, 21% to knitwear, 16% to women's outerwear, 10% to men's outerwear and 10% to handknitting yarns.

The worsted system produced yarn for suitings and botany machine knitwear, and required long-fibre wools which were laid parallel in the gilling and combing process to give the fabric a smooth finish. The resultant sliver or ribbon was known as a 'top' which could then be spun into yarn. The spinning was usually carried out by specialist spinners and sold on to specialist weavers. About 50% of worsted yarns were sold for knitting and were most efficiently produced in long production runs.

In woollen processing where the yarns went to carpets, hand knitting, clothing and hosiery, the fibres were only roughly aligned, which gave the yarn a bulkier finish. The woollen industry was much more vertically integrated than the worsted sector and spinning, weaving and finishing often took place in the same mill.

Spinning reduced the diameter of the sliver by drawing to the appropriate thickness determined by the end product, and the resulting yarn went to knitting or weaving.

Weaving produced the final fabric by placing warp threads on to a beam equivalent in width to the piece of cloth to be woven. Generally the order of the warp threads determined the style of the cloth lengthwise, and the weft thread across the warp face determined the final pattern.

The three main products of the industry, combed tops, yarns and fabrics had fallen steadily over the period to 1982 (shown in figures 22.2, 22.3 and 22.4) due to a number of reasons. Fashion changed from the traditional worsted suit (both men's and women's) to more casual wear with an associated change in retailing. The traditional retailers, e.g. Burton's, with their own tailoring capacities declined and gave way to newer retailers such as Marks & Spencer with about 30% share of the market for all clothing and 15% for men's suits.

UK production of combed tops fell from 140 million kg in 1965 to 120 million kg in 1973 and continued to fall as a result of falls in both home deliveries and exports. (figure 22.2).

The four-year textile cycle would be as observed in figure 22.2, with recovery every four years until 1980, when it failed to materialize.

Similarly there was a continuing fall in UK production of woollen yarns and woven fabrics (figures 22.3 and 22.4). In the case of woollen yarns production fell from 250 million kg in 1965 to 230 mn kg in 1973, and continued whilst fabric production in the UK fell from 270 mn kg in 1965 to 195 mn kg in 1973.

Import penetration was much more severe in the case of woollen fabrics than in that of worsted fabrics, and woollen fabric imports (mainly from the Prato area of Italy) accounted for about half UK consumption, whilst MFA suppliers were of negligible importance. Worsted imports, largely polyester/wool fabrics, were 20% of UK consumption. The more important problem was that of falling exports. Between 1965 and 1982 the proportion of woollen to worsted UK production moved from a ratio of 55:45 to 50:50.

(Appendix 3 gives further statistical information on textile industries including wool textiles.)

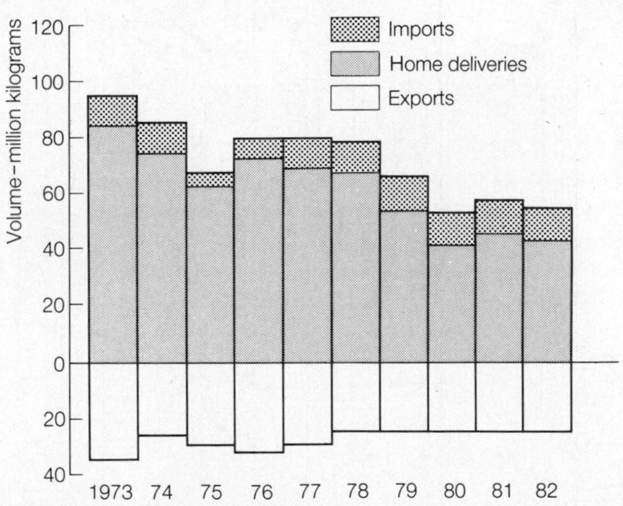

FIGURE 22.2 Cornbed tops. UK wool textile industry: exports, imports and home deliveries of combed tops, 1973–1982 (by weight)

Source: Derived from Wool Industry Bureau of Statistics and Overseas Trade Statistics

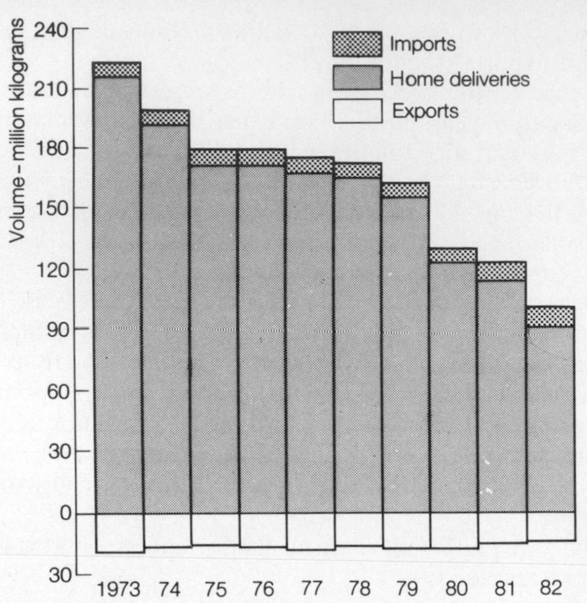

FIGURE 22.3 Yarns. UK wool textile industry: exports, imports and home deliveries of wool yarns, 1973–1982 (by weight)

Source: Derived from Wool Industry Bureau of Statistics and Overseas Trade Statistics

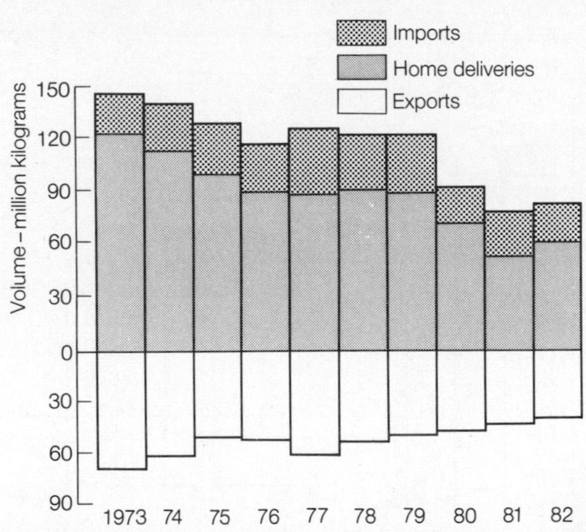

FIGURE 22.4 Woven fabrics. UK wool textile industry, exports, imports and home deliveries of woven wool fabrics, 1973–1982 by volume (excluding blankets)

Source: Derived from Wool Industry Bureau of Statistics and Overseas Trade Statistics

THE WOOL TEXTILE INDUSTRY SCHEME

The government introduced the Wool Textile Industry Scheme in 1973, with a second stage in 1976, with the aim of improving the industry's competitive position by providing assistance to: (a) Modernize production facilities; (b) Improve industrial structure; (c) Eliminate uneconomic excess capacity.

The scheme was reported in 1978[1] to have been well received by the industry, and grants of £16 million were provided towards re-equipment and re-building and towards closure costs of 90 production units. The second stage was more concerned with rationalization within companies rather than the industry structure itself, and grants amounted to £6 million on over 60 projects involving capital expenditure of £31 million mainly in West Yorkshire.

In March 1983 the British Textile Confederation produced a 'Plan for Action', identifying the main need as being to improve competitiveness, especially in relation to other developed countries (particularly in the EEC), and indicated that the main problem was the relatively high sterling exchange rate vis-a-vis other European currencies. For example, the report pointed out that between 1978 when sterling began to appreciate in value and October 1982, costs in the UK had risen by 34% relative to West Germany and by 55% relative to Belgium.

In the 1984 Budget the government announced proposals to aid the UK textiles, clothing and footwear industries with up to £20m government aid. These proposals had to be agreed with Britain's partners in the European Economic Community, and the UK expected to hear the EEC decision on approval early in 1985.

Of obvious importance was the ability of the sector to compete with importers and especially with Italy. The Prato region of Italy had gained almost a complete monopoly of fabrics made from reclaimed woollen materials, and imports from the Prato region were heavily concentrated in fabrics containing less than 50% wool. From 1980 onwards, however, Prato had begun to develop more wool-rich products, e.g. jacket fabrics, and whilst price played an important role, the higher the content of virgin wool then the less the price differential. But price was not the only Italian strategy, for they had proved successful at building a fabric 'story' around a colour and texture theme and presenting target ranges at specific market segments. Although Italy was a developed economy, the Prato woollen industry was a low-cost producer because of the way it was organized.

A concise description of the Prato industry and its approach was contained in a paper given to the Italian Chamber of Commerce in 1978.

[1] 'Wool Textile Industry Scheme – An Assessment', Department of Industry, 1978.

Over the past few years substantial changes have taken place in the pattern of consumption in woollen products. It is no longer a major part of a market which repeats the same pattern year after year, with slight variations to the design or even without changing anything at all. For quite some time now we are seeing an ever increasing demand for products, mainly in the range of clothing, which from season to season, and often during the course of the same season, are subject to quick changes. These kind of changes are not only limited to colours and design, but affect the same basic structure of the products.

The trends in demand have led to a significant shortening of the time lapse between ordering on the part of the retailer, the production and delivery by the weaver. It was not so long ago that each stage felt able to anticipate either the ordering or the manufacturing of a large part of its requirements, without running too much of a risk. Today the increased variety of cloth and styles has, for the most part, made that impossible.

One of the most characteristic aspects of Prato is its articulation on numerous small enterprises which, for the most part lack any manufacturing means of their own, but have an independent commercial structure. The owner of this type of firm is known as an "impannatore", a word that cannot be correctly translated by the English term "converter".

The fabrics that the 'impannatore' sells are usually made by other mills specialising in the work done "on commission", i.e. he does a great deal of market research, ascertains just what the market is looking for, elaborates its suggestions, buys his raw materials, gets the commission firms to make the necessary processing and then delivers the finished product. Therefore, he dedicates most of his time and attention to the market and its trends, which is a job that requires constant attention.

Thanks to his not being tied down to look after his own plant, he is free to choose at any given moment, from the right outside manufacturer, from the many available in the area, to make his product at the best price or in the best quality. This means that, since he can allocate his production over a vast and diversified manufacturing field, the 'impannatore' is always keen to follow the demands of the market, even though this entails frequent changes of quality and style in the production.[3]

The one- and two-man weaving companies which provided the production services on commission to the 'impannatore' were very small,

[3] 'How to Satisfy a Changing Fashion,' Ing Gherardo Cangioli, Managing Director, Lanificio Cangioli of Prato in 'Changing Needs and Relationships in the UK Apparel Fabric Market', NEDO, July 1982.

but there were economies of scale or minimum sizes of operation in the spinning and finishing processes. The advantages were that few vertical relationships existed, and there was complete flexibility to choose a production route through the independent processors to achieve the required product, and consequently there was high motivation.

It was a structure which produced disadvantages such as the social costs of high financial risk, work accidents, low security and low wages for the employees, and an inability on the part of firms to make capital expenditures.

TABLE 22.4 Prato: Number of employees per firm by process (1976)

	No of firms	*No of employees*	*Average employees/firm*
Vertically integrated woollen manufacturing	198	11,051	55
Woollen and worsted spinning	306	5,762	19
Weaving	3,652	6,001	1.6
Finishing	36	1,417	39
Dyeing, washing, milling	44	1,387	32
Warping, packaging	419	808	1.9
Twisting	290	1,594	6.1
Reeling	69	120	1.7

Source: 'The Textile Industry of Prato: A Study of Success in a Mature Sector', an unpublished MBA dissertation by Davide Mariani, Manchester Business School, 1979.

During 1983 the National Economic Development Office organized two successful exhibitions 'Better Made in Britain' by 24 companies of a selection of clothes which were bought abroad, but which they would prefer to buy from British companies in order to meet the shortening lead times required by the clothing fashion markets.

There were differences in the extent to which the woollen and worsted sectors had been penetrated by imports. In woollen fabrics, import penetration was reported to be 55% of home consumption (82% of which came from Italy). The Scottish part of the woollen industry had withdrawn to the higher part of the market, but if the woollen industry at large wished to retain a significant manufacturing base, then it had to meet Italian competition which was based on both lower costs and superior design and performance. By contrast the worsted sector had been penetrated by imports only to 17% of the home market, and these imports from developed countries were largely concentrated in the polyester/wool mixtures rather than the more expensive 100% worsted suitings. However, the industry did suffer from high levels of imported made-up suits from high-cost developed countries which reduced fabric sales to clothing manufacturers.

ILLINGWORTH, MORRIS COMPETITORS

1980 turned out to be the worst year ever for the wool textile companies, and profits fell dramatically and many companies were liquidated, and those which survived cut back on employee numbers. For example, at Parkland Textiles they fell from 4,000 to 1,700 in 1984, and at Illingworth, Morris from 11,000 to 4,000.

Allied Textiles

Allied Textiles was a vertically integrated Huddersfield company mainly involved in worsted spinning and weaving, but it did have some interests outside of the textile industry. When in 1978 it saw the recession approaching, it cut back its textile businesses and closed those which couldn't show profits, and the group which had previously depended for 50% of its sales on fine worsted suitings switched to non-clothing markets such as furnishing fabrics and employees fell from 5,000 in 1978 to 1,400 in 1984. (Table 22.5 gives financial data on Allied Textiles and other principal wool textile companies).

Dawson International

Dawson International was a large Scottish based knitwear manufacturer, but it had interests in the Yorkshire industry through 'Joseph Dawson' which operated at the beginning of the wool process in scouring and combing with a concentration on high-quality cashmere. The Bradford mill was extremely efficient and spent heavily on new productive capacity. Most of its work was on a commission basis, and consequently the higher the volume throughout the better and typically achieved a top to noil ratio of 19:1 compared to the usual 12:1 in the industry. (Joseph Dawson was responsible for about 20% of the sales turnover of Dawson International, and thus the data in table 22.5 do not reflect Joseph Dawson only).

Stroud, Riley Drummond

Stroud, Riley Drummond was a manufacturer of worsted and knitted fabrics with Marks and Spencer accounting for about 20% of sales. After losses in 1980 the company rationalized from three mills to one.

John Foster

John Foster was a spinner and weaver of worsted and mohair and made very high quality products. It was one of the smaller vertically integrated companies which combed and spun its own mohair.

TABLE 22.5 IM competitors in the UK

Company	*Year end*	*Sales (£m)*	*Pre-tax profit (£000)*	*EPS (pence)*	*P/E ratio*[a]	*Capital employed (£m)*
Allied Textiles	Sept 1984	32	4107	13.4	10.6	20.4
Parkland Textile	March 1984	41	1606	27.7	5.1	12.6
John Foster	March 1984	17	602	6.2	8.2	5.2
Bulmer & Lumb	April 1984	35	1643	11.7	8.3	9.8
Dawson Int	March 1984	179	25251	19.8	13.6	92.1
Illingworth, Morris	March 1984	84	2370	4.4	12.7	25.1
Stroud, Riley Drummond	March 1984	15	916	10.4	6.2	5.3

[a] P/E ratio as at 31 December 1984 when the Textiles Sector P/E ratio was 8.7 and the Industrials Sector 13.0.

Parkland Textile

Parkland Textile was a full-line vertically integrated woollen and worsted company which also had interests in garment manufacture and sales to multiple chains.

It was against this background in the industry that IM became involved, between 1981 and 1983 in a takeover struggle which ended when the group was taken over, despite the recommendations of the board to the shareholders not to accept the offer, and a reference to the Monopolies and Mergers Commission by companies owned by Alan Lewis.

It was a very difficult period for the company and the board of directors, as their attention was diverted from commercial considerations to organizational and legal matters at a time when the industry was going through a depressed period. The problems arose when a major shareholder, who had inherited the founder's shares which were vested in a trust, disagreed with the senior management over its strategy and performance. In an attempt to resolve the problems, a group of financial institutions offered, through a merchant bank, to buy the shares of that shareholder and of the trust in September 1981. This offer was not accepted and Mr Alan Lewis negotiated through one of his companies for the purchase of the shares and succeeded in buying 19% in November 1981.

The following two years were taken up by legal proceedings when other inheritors of the shares disagreed with the sale of IM shareholdings on behalf of the trust which held them. During this period a further offer to purchase a part-holding in IM was made by Stroud, Riley Drummond plc, which was not accepted. Eventually in October 1982 the legal proceedings ended, and Mr Lewis was enabled to complete the share purchases such that he bought 46% of the Ordinary Voting Shares, and 41% of the Non-

Voting Shares for £1,486,000, and he then made a cash offer for the outstanding IM shares at 14.75 pence per Ordinary and 10.25 pence per Non-Voting. Eventually he paid a total of £1,719,000 for 48% of the voting shares and 47% of the non-voting shares.

These purchases by Mr Lewis were through one of his subsidiary companies which was controlled by his holding company Alcrafield Ltd, which explained the background to the purchase as in the following statement of the group corporate strategy:

> Alcrafield has changed the direction of its corporate strategy for the 1980s from a property investment emphasis to investment in industry and in financial services, particularly in the textile industry and in consumer finance. This strategy anticipates a decline in the rate of growth of property values, increased opportunities for United Kingdom textile production capacity following a significant contraction in recent years, and an anticipated upturn in demand for British manufactured goods. The anticipated growth in financial services is based on a forecast increase in consumer lending over the next decade. Alcrafield will devote its efforts and resources to developing its interests in these areas, while at the same time continuing a policy of selective property investment and conservative organic growth in its other divisions.[5]

Mr Lewis subsequently became chairman in 1983, and stated

> The ending of the uncertainty concerning the ownership of the group has enabled management to concentrate fully on the conduct of the businesses. In the second half of the trading year a detailed and searching review of all the group's operations has been carried out, and the strategy which will govern the group's future progress has been formulated. The main thrust of the policy will be the continuing control and the considered deployment of our cash resources, with new capital investment being directed at increasing efficiency and profitability in all market areas where long-term growth can be seen.[6]

In a lecture in October 1984 Mr Lewis said

> We cannot afford to put ourselves in the hands of people down the line who may be inefficient. We have got to ensure that the people we are supplying have good communications with the retail firms to ensure that the progression goes through the ranks, so that we have a positive product to sell to our consumer. One of the big problems

[5] Monopolies and Mergers Commission.
[6] Company Annual Report 1984.

was that the cloth manufacturers had let merchants and people of that nature make a niche for themselves in the market. Not that merchants were not needed because they were, but the manufacturers had to ensure that they worked with the merchants and not for them. We cannot allow other people who have got more marketing skills than the actual factory which is producing the quality product to take advantage of us, and I think that is what has happened in Yorkshire.

With respect to imports the real threat was from sophisticated countries and not the Third World, but protection for the industry must be maintained. New retailing trends in Britain could help check the growth of imports. The development of chains of shops like 'Next', 'Principles' and the revamping of 'Richard Shops' would give the advantage to UK production which offered well-styled, good-quality, fashionable and co-ordinated merchandise at moderate prices to high-spending segments of the market. The innovation of these chains was being followed by the multiples with developments on the menswear side. It was important for UK manufacturers to push home their flexibility as the retailers were looking for fashions for four seasons a year. IM was planning to be a vertical textile group, highly specialized, not dependent on suppliers and with closely integrated lines of communication between the raw material processors at one end and the consumer at the other.[7]

Early in 1984 IM sold one of its subsidiary companies (Pepper Lee) which produced mohair cloth with sales of approximately £2 million, which was estimated to be 22% of UK output and 11% of world output. Pepper Lee exported 85% of its output. In a statement IM said that the subsidiary was not large enough to gain economies of scale, and that IM was concentrating on its more important businesses, therefore, it was in the interests of Pepper Lee to join with a large mohair company (John Foster).

[7] Address to the Bradford Textile Society, October 1984, as reported in the *Wool Record*.

Appendix 1

GLOSSARY OF TEXTILE TECHNICAL TERMS

Carding: Opening out, blending and straightening the wool fibres after scouring. The machine used is a carding engine. This process changes the wool into a filament, and eventually into a continuous ribbon or sliver.

Combing: Removal of shorter fibres and remaining vegetable matter in raw wool, and the arranging of the long fibres almost completely parallel by means of the comb which is the machine used in the process. Once the material has been combed the continuous sliver is referred to as a 'top', and the remainder as 'noil'.

Crimp: Waviness of the wool fibre. The regularity of the crimp is one of the criteria in determining wool quality.

Dyeing: Dyeing can take place either in top form, i.e. immediately after the combing process, or in yarn form, i.e. after spinning or in fabric form, i.e. after weaving.

Gilling: Straightening and blending of fibres.

Noil: Short fibres extracted from long fibres by combing.

Sliver: Loose ribbon of fibres without twist.

Spinning: Process of reducing the diameter of the sliver by drafting or drawing out to a thickness determined by the specification of the appropriate yarn according to the type of fabric required.

Top: Sliver with long fibres aligned parallel.

Warp: Threads placed longways and parallel in a loom.

Weft: The cross threads in weaving, i.e. yarn at right angles to the warp.

Weaving: Process of producing fabric or cloth which involves placing of as many as 7,500 warp threads on to a beam equivalent in width to the piece of cloth to be woven. Generally the order of the warp threads determines the style of the cloth lengthwise. The introduction of the weft threads across the warp face determines the final pattern.

Woollens: Fabrics woven from shorter fibres which do not lie parallel in the yarn. Goods manufactured by the woollen process include flannels, blankets and tweeds.

Worsteds: Fabrics made from fine but long wool fibres which lie parallel in the yarn. Worsteds are used for suitings and clear-finish tailored types of material such as serge, gaberdines and steep twills. Worsteds hold their shape better than woollens.

Yarn: Fibres twisted together on the spinning process.

Appendix 2 Financial Information – Illingworth, Morris plc

(i) PROFIT AND LOSS ACCOUNT, YEAR ENDED MARCH (£000)

	1983	*1984*
Turnover	75,475	84,007
Cost of sales	(63,143)	(70,123)
Gross Profit	12,332	13,884
Other operating costs[a]	(10,935)	(11,202)
Operating profit[b]	1,397	2,682
Other income[c]	743	927
Interest payable	(2,119)	(1,239)
Profit before tax	21	2,370
Tax	(71)	(430)
Profit (Loss) after tax	(50)	1,940
Minority interests	(67)	(88)
Profit (Loss) before Extra-ordinary items	(117)	1,852
Extraordinary items[d]	(1,008)	5
Profit (Loss) attributable to shareholders	(1,125)	1,857
Dividends paid[e]	(91)	(91)
Retained profit (Loss)	(1,216)	1,766
Earnings (Loss) per share[f]	(0.5p)	4.4p

Notes

[a] Distribution costs and administrative expenses.

[b] Operating profit is stated after charging (crediting) (£000s)

	1983	*1984*
Depreciation	1,487	2,504
Hire of plant	66	83
Provision for losses	33	148
Auditors	108	108
Surplus on sale of fixed asset	(235)	(83)

[c] From listed investments, bank interest and rents.

[d] Extraordinary items

£000's	*1983*	*1984*
Profit on sale of land	–	3,464
Rationalisation costs	(777)	(2,289)
Legal charges	(231)	(136)
Additional taxation		(1,034)
	(1,008)	5

[e] Dividends on Cumulative Preference Stock.

[f] Calculated on 40,024,733 shares (10 million ordinary voting shares and the balance non-voting shares).

(ii) BALANCE SHEETS, YEAR ENDED MARCH (£000)

	1983	*1984*
Fixed assets	16,116	14,871
Investments	1,475	1,583
	17,591	16,454
Current assets		
Stocks	17,085	19,438
Debtors	10,974	12,559
Cash	119	46
	28,178	32,043
Current liabilities		
Creditors/overdraft	21,946	20,323
Net current assets	6,232	11,720
Total assets less current liabilities	23,823	28,174
Provisions for liabilities and charges	396	3,038
Net assets	23,315	25,069
Financed by:		
Shareholders' funds	21,628	23,403
Minority interests/preference capital	1,687	1,666
	23,315	25,069
Number of employees	3,982	3,849

(iii) GEOGRAPHICAL ANALYSIS OF TURNOVER (£000s)

	1983	*1984*
United Kingdom:		
Home	38,836	44,101
Indirect exports	10,477	11,776
	49,313	55,877
Direct exports:		
Rest of Europe	12,556	14,083
Asia	5,920	5,148
Australasia	402	387
North America	2,354	2,792
South Africa	334	378
Middle East	3,732	4,414
Others	359	505
	74,970	83,584
Overseas subsidiaries:		
Europe	86	41
Australasia	248	382
North America	171	–
	75,475	84,007

(iv) TEN-YEAR RECORD – PROFIT AND LOSS (£000)

	1975	*1976*	*1977*	*1978*	*1979*	*1980*	*1981*	*1982*	*1983*	*1984*
Turnover	80,150	89,621	118,925	119,710	120,797	109,721	97,515	101,423	75,475	84,007
Profit before interest	4,546	3,548	7,694	7,316	6,213	1,441	1,585	4,267	2,140	3,609
Interest	(2,773)	(2,334)	(3,563)	(2,634)	(2,850)	(3,904)	(3,990)	(3,011)	(2,119)	(1,239)
Profit before tax	1,773	1,214	4,131	4,682	3,363	(2,463)	(2,405)	1,256	21	2,370
Profit (loss) before extraordinary items	1,445	484	2,493	3,386	2,958	(1,454)	(1,766)	1,012	117	1,852
Extraordinary items	–	–	–	–	–	(1,992)	(1,526)	(485)	(1,008)	5
Attributable profit (Loss)	1,445	484	2,493	3,386	2,958	(3,446)	(3,292)	527	(1,125)	1,857
Minorities	(136)	(300)	(581)	(134)	(134)	(53)	(119)	(123)	–	–
Dividends	(466)	(500)	(606)	(669)	(753)	(305)	(91)[a]	(383)	(91)[a]	(91)[a]
Retained profit (Loss)	843	316	1,306	2,583	2,071	(3,804)	(3,502)	21	(1,216)	1,766
Employees	9,154	9,997	9,849	9,598	8,943	7,554	5,834	4,743	3,982	3,849

[a] Dividends on preference shares only paid.
Source: Company Annual Reports.

Appendix 3

STATISTICAL INFORMATION ON TEXTILES INDUSTRIES

(i) UK employees (thousands)

	1977	*1978*	*1979*	*1980*	*1981*
Total employment	22,619	22,757	22,920	22,511	21,198
Manufacturing industries	7,292	7,257	7,176	6,807	6,038
Textiles	512	490	478	424	363
of which woollens and worsteds	83	79	75	65	56
Carpets	37	35	34	27	23
Clothing	314	307	311	286	251

Source: CSO Annual Abstract 1983.

(ii) Index of Output (1980 = 100)

			Clothing	
	All textiles	*Woollens & worsteds*	*Men's outerwear*	*Women's outerwear*
1980	100	100	100	100
1981	91.3	90.4	88.8	90.1
1982	87.7	86.0	81.2	83.4
1983	89.4	87.0	81.8	78.5
1984				
1st quarter	89.3	89.7	82.8	78.2
2nd quarter	90.3	89.8	82.3	78.5
3rd quarter	88.4	88.3	94.8	79.3

Source: Monthly Digest.

(iii) Monthly Averages of Output

	Wool tops	*Wool yarn*	*Worsted yarn*	*Wool/mixture fabrics Total*	*Wool*	*Worsted*
	(thousand tonnes)			*(million square metres)*		
1980	3.26	6.8	4.99	9.86	5.39	4.46
1981	3.23	6.0	4.90	8.09	4.03	4.07
1982	2.88	4.4	5.13	8.36	4.05	4.31
1983	2.90	4.7	5.42	7.83	3.86	3.97
1984 (Jan. to Aug.)	3.20	5.0	5.48	7.62	3.44	4.17

Source: Monthly Digest.

(iv) Woollen and worsted fabrics (million square metres)

	1975	*1976*	*1977*	*1978*	*1979*	*1980*	*1981*	*1982*	*1983*
UK consumption									
Woollen fabrics	79.4	72.1	82.8	106.2	110.4	77.1			
Worsted fabrics	49.5	44.8	42.7	41.3	443.8	37.2			
UK production									
Woollen fabrics	76.8	73.6	78.8	78.0	76.1	64.7	47.9	48.6	46.3
Worsted fabrics	74.6	69.4	71.3	66.1	61.7	53.5	48.8	51.7	47.7
Exports									
Woollen fabrics	24.4	27.3	30.2	30.2	30.1	29.9			
Worsted fabrics	26.7	26.2	31.6	28.8	24.3	22.4			
Imports									
Woollen fabrics	27.0	25.8	34.2	58.4	64.4	42.3			
Worsted fabrics	1.5	1.6	3.0	3.9	6.5	6.1			

Source: 'The Changing Needs and Relationships in the UK Apparel Fabric Market', NEDO, July 1982; Wool Industries Bureau of Statistics.

(v) Tops and yarn (million kilograms)

Tops produced	*1976*	*1977*	*1978*	*1979*	*1980*	*1981*	*1982*	*1983*
Woollen yarn output	103.8	97.6	97.6	78.9	65.8	70.1	66.5	70.3
Worsted yarn output	80.8	81.2	77.7	69.0	59.9	51.6	53.7	55.6
Semi-worsted yarn output	–	–	8.7	8.5	7.1	7.2	8.6	9.4

Source: Wool Industries Bureau of Statistics.

(vi) UK woollen & worsted industry (£ billion)

	Sales	*Exports*	*Imports*	*Import penetration (%)*	*Employment (thousands)*
1982	1.0	0.4	0.2	26	50
1983	1.1	0.4	0.3	30	45

Source: Silberston Report (The Multi-Fibre Arrangement and the UK Economy, HMSO, 1984).

(vii) Import Tariffs

Whilst the Multi-Fibre Arrangement with low-cost countries sought to limit the rate of increase of their exports to the developed economies, including EEC countries, exports from the latter generally faced higher tariffs than did imports into the EEC.

Percentage Tariff Rates

Product	*EEC*	*USA*	*Spain*	*Australia*	*S Korea*	*Brazil*
Wool yarns	5	15/20	27	2	30	85
Wool fabrics	13	45	30	50	50	205
Woven outerwear	16	30/40	36/39	70/100	50	205

Source: 'The UK Textile Industry – A Plan for Action', *BTC*, March 1983.

23 S R Gent

In January 1986 the share price of S R Gent plc stood at 64 pence on the London Stock Exchange, having fallen from the 190 pence at which they were sold when the company became a public limited company in June 1983. At that time, enthusiastic employees of the company had bought 900,000 shares when the company offered 25% of its equity to the public which oversubscribed the offer.

S R Gent designed and manufactured ladies' and childrens' clothing, mens' outerwear and household textiles primarily for sale to the large retailing chains, and Marks and Spencer alone took over 90% of company output. Of the 5,000 employees, about 80 were employed in the design department and the company policy was to respond to fashion changes rather than to set fashion trends, and to do this senior managers and designers regularly travelled abroad to keep up-to-date with developments. The objective was to produce balanced product ranges for the winter and summer seasons and this required constant development throughout the year. They produced up to 100 new or amended designs for each principal category of product and these would be presented weekly to the major customers. Following acceptance of the designs, product specifications would be drawn up and quantities and selling prices agreed before volume production started. Over half of the fabrics used were purchased in the United Kingdom, with the balance coming from the rest of Europe, the USA and Japan.

Since the mid-1970s, the management had recognized the need to take advantage of new technology in order to maintain the competitive position of the company, especially with regard to production. The emphasis on technical innovation was inspired by their belief that it was necessary to be able to respond quickly to changes in demand. Even though the company spent over £3 million annually on computer-related equipment which managers agreed was labour-saving and 'de-skilled' staff, the number employed had continued to increase and stood at over 5,000 in 1985. The equipment affected a number of the steps in the process, beginning with designing, which used computer-aided design systems, cutting instructions and computerized sewing machines. In the clothing industry generally, sewing machines were idle about 30% of the time whilst the machinist was preparing material or doing other, related jobs, but Gent's computers enabled this to be cut significantly such that garments took only half the time to sew that they had previously. The biggest impact was, however, in the cutting rooms, which dealt with about 600,000 square metres of cloth every week, whilst each garment would use about ten pieces. The material was cut in layers up to 300 thick, at very high speeds and at a much higher level of accuracy than was possible with traditional methods. In total, the company was producing about 12 million garments a year in over 1,300 different styles.

The company was located in Barnsley, Yorkshire and had sixteen sewing factories within a thirty-mile radius of its headquarters. The finished garments were returned to three central warehouses prior to distribution, which was generally by overnight delivery direct to its customers' retail outlets.

The company had established policies to seek a wider customer base and also to widen its product range. It sought more customers both in the UK and overseas, provided it did not harm its relationship with its major customer Marks and Spencers which had recorded clothing sales in its year ending in 1985 of £1,423 million. Its other customers were five multiples and included Tesco and Richards in the UK and J C Penney in USA. The chairman, Mr Peter Wolff was particularly keen to expand the product range, as he believed that basic products only had a growth rate the same as the economy whereas luxury items or impulse purchases could present high-margin opportunities.

In 1983 the company consolidated the ownership of related companies overseas and it became sole owner of subsidiaries in Australia and Canada, both manufacturers of clothing and the latter a 100% supplier to Marks and Spencer in Canada. There were related companies in South Africa and New Zealand, also in clothing manufacture. Subsequently, the company acquired, in 1984, Sublime Lighting Ltd, a manufacturer of domestic lighting and although they were able to start producing for Marks and Spencer this subsidiary had still not moved into profits in its first two years of S R Gent ownership.

The business had originated in 1945 when Edith Wallace began making ladies' blouses for Marks and Spencer and for many years it operated from two houses in Barnsley under the ownership of Edith Wallace and her subsequent partner, Ruth Wetzel. In 1966, Ruth Wetzel's son and Peter Wolff took over management of the company. Peter Wolff had been a merchandising manager with Marks and Spencer for ten years and he took the opportunity of buying a 50% share of the company, which at that time had sales of £170,000 and profits of £5,000, for an investment of £12,500.

For its financial year ending in June 1985, the company reported sales turnover up to over £82 million, but pre-tax profits were only just over £1 million which was attributed to the problems of the unseasonal weather that the United Kingdom had suffered in both halves of the financial year. (Appendix 1 provides financial information on S R Gent plc.)

THE CLOTHING INDUSTRY

Clothing sales represented a large proportion of UK consumer expenditure, and in 1984 totalled £10.6 billion. In the early 1980s, some radical changes took place in the market place for clothing which had their foundation a decade previously when the cornerstone of the large men's retailers, (e.g. Burton and Hepworths), was undermined by imports of readymade suits. In response, they searched out new markets, including womenswear, and as a result, the whole face of the high street was transformed. Typically, the shopping areas had been dominated by a mix of department stores, multiple stores, variety chains and independents. The multiples – specialist clothing retailers – took a dramatic lead with over 25% of all clothing being bought from stores such as 'Next', 'Principles', 'Top Man', 'Miss Selfridge', etc. Not only did market shares change, but the advent of such stores also increased the proportion of own-label brands at the expense of manufacturers' labels. Figures 23.1 and 23.2 show changes in market shares according to types of outlet in the early 1980s. Figure 23.3 shows changes in brands for the early 1980s.

Such changes presented not only challenges for clothing manufacturers, but also opportunities. One result was for retailers to move away from two seasons, i.e. summer and winter clothing, and towards lifestyle clothing and fashion changes on a much shorter cycle.

Table 14.10 of the Annual Abstract (1985) shows clothing sales for 1983 at £9,804 million in a total expenditure of £182,427 million, i.e. 5.4%.

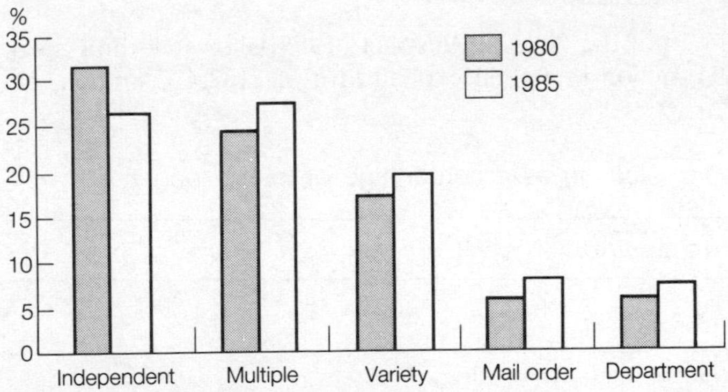

FIGURE 23.1 Men's clothing/retailer market share
Source: Trade estimates

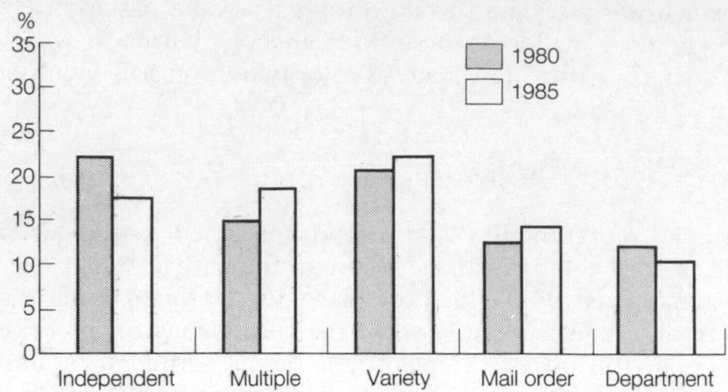

FIGURE 23.2 Women's clothing/retailer market share
Source: Trade estimates

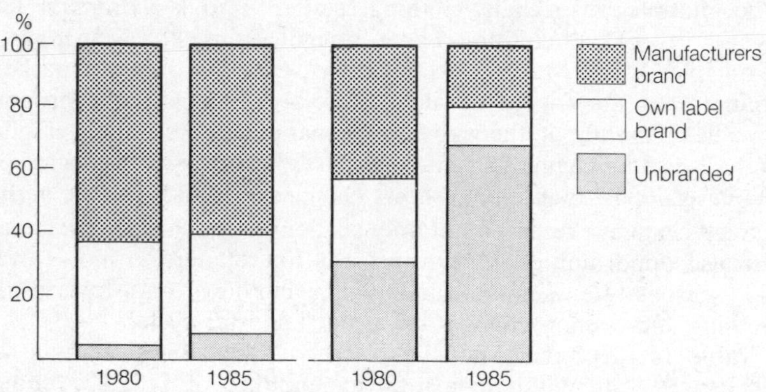

FIGURE 23.3 Brand/women's outerwear
Source: Trade estimates

Table 14.10 of the Annual Abstract (1985) shows clothing sales for 1983 at £9,804 million in a total expenditure of £182,427 million, i.e. 54%.
Similarly:

TABLE 23.1 Clothing as a percentage of total expenditure

1973	*1974*	*1975*	*1976*	*1977*	*1978*	*1979*	*1980*	*1981*	*1982*
7.0	7.1	6.7	6.4	6.4	6.5	6.4	5.9	5.5	5.3

Source: Derived from 'Annual Abstract'.

Nevertheless sales of clothing had grown over the period and the period 1980–3 showed a growth of 9% with a significant increase in men's and boys' clothing.

Of these sales to UK consumers, a significant proportion was imported and the import penetration for various items of clothing varied from 8% for overalls to 86% for woven women's suits.

Table 23.2 shows imports/exports.

TABLE 23.2 Import/Export: Clothing (£ million)

	1980	*1981*	*1982*	*1983*	*1984*
Sales by UK firms	3,241	2,911	2,922	3,253	3,659
Exports	538	558	540	560	644
Imports	871	997	1,051	1,121	1,417
Home market	3,574	3,350	3,433	3,814	4,432
Import penetration %	24.3	29.8	30.6	29.4	31.9

Source: DTI.

RETAILERS

There were approximately 10,000 retailers in the UK specializing in the sales of men's and boys' clothing in addition to the department stores, variety chains and mail-order firms. The specialist stores were estimated to account for 42% of men's/boys' wear sales. The more important retailers were as shown in table 23.3.

TABLE 23.3 Men's/boys' wear retailers (1982)

	% by value
Marks and Spencer	14.0
Burton	4.5
C and A	4.0
BHS[a]	2.9
Littlewoods	2.6
Hepworths[b]	2.3
Fosters[c]	2.0

[a] Now part of Storehouse (owned by Habitat/Mothercare).
[b] Now renamed 'Next'.
[c] No longer independent.
Source: Mintel

There were about 22,000 specialist retailers covering the women's wear market, the most important of which are shown in table 23.4.

TABLE 23.4 **Womenswear retailers (1982)**

	% by value
Marks and Spencer	21.0
C and A	6.0
BHS	4.0
Littlewoods	3.0
Burton	2.8

Source: Mintel.

MANUFACTURERS

There were about 6,000 clothing manufacturers in the UK employing nearly 220,000 people, with exports of approximately £600 million, representing 26% of industry output. Most of these were very small companies, as 74% of all had a workforce of fewer than 20 employees, 53% fewer than 10, and only 5 firms employed more than 1,500 people.

The UK clothing manufacturers varied both in size and in type of clothing made. Some specialized in for example, menswear, which might be branded (e.g. Peter England shirts) or not (e.g. sold through British Home Stores).

Variations in the size of firms is shown in table 23.5.

TABLE 23.5 **Size of UK clothing manufacturers (1978/1983)**

Employees	*No of enterprises*		*Employment (thousands)*		*Gross output (£m)*	
	1978	*1983*	*1978*	*1983*	*1978*	*1983*
1–99	7,399	5,623	118	81	963	1,137
100–199	301	168	42	28	383	403
200–499	184	132	54	47	503	697
500–999	71	40	49	33	454	550
1000 +	55	14	157	25	1,355	383
	8,009	5,761	420	214	3,658	3,170

Source: Census of Production (1983).

Amongst the larger clothing manufacturers were a group of textile companies which were involved in both non-branded and branded clothing. These included William Baird, Coats-Paton, Courtaulds, Dawson International and Vantona-Viyella.[4]

4 Vantona-Viyella and Coats-Paton merged in 1986 and were renamed Coats Viyella.

Also, there was a small group of large firms involved in knitting clothing items, e.g. Corah which supplied 70% of its output to Marks and Spencer. And finally, amongst the large firms in the industry were those involved in clothing manufactured from fabric and who were not part of the textile industry itself. This group included: Aquascutum Group Plc (1,600 employees) which sold its own men's and women's wear through its own retail outlets as well as to other multiples and department stores; S R Gent Plc (5,000 employees) largely involved in women's wear manufacture with 90% going to Marks and Spencer; Lee Cooper Plc (2,400 employees) manufacturing jeans and casual clothing, and I J Dewhirst Plc (3,000 employees) manufacturing men's outerwear and supplying 90% of its output to Marks and Spencer.

(Financial information on I J Dewhirst Plc is provided in Appendix 2 as an example.)

Appendix 1 S R Gent Plc

PROFIT AND LOSS ACCOUNT, YEAR ENDING 30 JUNE (£000)

	1980	*1981*	*1982*	*1983*	*1984*	*1985*
Turnover	46,280	53,566	59,742	70,196	79,591	82,823
Trading profit before depreciation	3,727	5,028	6,771	7,372	8,241	4,581
Depreciation	(1,113)	(1,309)	(1,477)	(1,578)	(2,096)	(2,681)
Trading profit	2,614	3,719	5,294	5,794	6,145	1,900
Interest payable	(2,232)	(2,188)	(1,614)	(1,442)	(741)	(1,305)
Share of profits of associated companies	302	383	581	832	711	432
Profit before tax	684	1,914	4,261	5,184	6,115	1,027
Tax	(114)	(155)	(367)	(359)	(821)	(427)
Profit after tax	570	1,759	3,894	4,825	5,294	600
Extraordinary item	–	–	–	–	–	(263)
Dividends	(64)	(61)	(250)	–	(1,080)	(505)
Profit/(loss) retained	506	1,698	3,644	4,825	4,214	(168)

BALANCE SHEETS, YEAR ENDED 30 JUNE (£000)

	1982	*1983*	*1984*	*1985*
Fixed assets				
Tangible assets	12,749	14,590	16,251	17,707
Investments (note a)	868	1,424	1,613	1,275
	13,617	16,014	17,864	18,982
Current assets				
Stocks	12,981	16,093	20,590	26,130
Debtors	4,510	9,071	4,734	6,296
Issue proceeds	–	4,992	–	–
Cash	88	31	78	82
	17,579	30,187	25,402	32,508
Creditors (due within one year)				
Finance debt (note b)	6,157	10,193	4,022	14,963
Creditors	8,984	10,357	11,932	10,619
	15,141	20,550	15,954	25,582
Net current assets	2,438	9,637	9,448	6,926
Total assets less current liabilities	16,055	25,651	27,312	25,908
Creditors (due after one year)				
Finance debt (note c)	3,430	3,183	811	183
	12,625	22,468	26,501	25,725
Capital and reserves				
Share capital (note d)	214	3,600	3,600	3,607
Share premium account	–	4,692	4,591	4,591
Profit & loss account	12,411	14,176	18,310	17,527
	12,625	22,468	26,501	25,725

Notes

a Investments in subsidiary and related companies including a £46,000 acquisition.

b Short-term bank loans.

c Long-term loans.

d 36 million ordinary shares plus 71,474 allotted on acquisition of a subsidiary (Sublime Lighting Ltd) for a value of £124,364.

SEVEN-YEAR RECORD (£000)

	1979	*1980*	*1981*[a]	*1982*	*1983*	*1984*	*1985*
Turnover	27,601	46,280	53,566	59,742	70,196	79,591	82,823
Operating profit	2,124	2,614	3,719	5,294	5,794	6,145	1,900
Share of profits of related companies	166	302	383	581	832	711	432
Interest payable	(818)	(2,232)	(2,188)	(1,614)	(1,442)	(741)	(1,305)
PBT	1,472	684	1,914	4,261	5,184	6,115	1,027
Tax	(40)	(114)	(155)	(367)	(359)	(821)	(427)
Dividends	–	(64)	(61)	(250)	(83)	(1,080)	(505)
Retained profits/ (loss)	1,432	506	1,698	3,644	4,742	4,214	(168)[b]
Fixed assets and investments	6,944	12,081	12,473	13,617	16,014	17,864	18,982
Net current assets	3,153	134	1,249	2,438	9,637	9,448	6,926
Long-term debt	(3,586)	(4,840)	(4,667)	(3,430)	(3,183)	(811)	(183)
Shareholders' funds[c]	6,511	7,375	9,055	12,625	22,468	26,501	25,725
Average number of employees	3,551	4,582	4,238	4,451	5,444	5,740	5,887

[a] 14-month year.
[b] After charging extraordinary item of £263,000.
[c] Including 33 million shares up to 1982
33.80 million shares up to 1983
36 million shares up to 1984
36.07 million shares up to 1985.

Appendix 2 I J Dewhirst Plc

PROFIT AND LOSS ACCOUNT – YEAR ENDED JANUARY (£000)

	1984	*1985*
Turnover	33,691	43,012
Cost of sales	(29,085)	(37,296)
Gross profit	4,606	5,716
Net operating expenses	(1,634)	(1,977)
Operating profit	2,972	3,739
Net investment income	445	268
Profit on ordinary activities before tax	3,417	4,007
Tax	(915)	(1,363)
Profit after tax	2,502	2,644
Preference dividends	(49)	(49)
Ordinary dividends	(477)	(550)
Retained profit	1,976	2,045
Earnings per share	4.9 pence	5.18 pence
Ordinary dividend cover	5.14 times	4.72 times

BALANCE SHEET (£000)

	1984	1985
Fixed assets	9,252	11,458
Current assets		
Stock	5,763	7,812
Debtors	994	1,511
Investments	3,600	5,029
Cash	7	8
	10,364	14,360
Creditors (due within one year)	(6,525)	(9,279)
Net current assets	3,839	5,081
Total assets less current liabilities	13,091	16,539
Creditors (due after more than one year)	(56)	(763)
Provisions for liabilities	(249)	(799)
	12,786	14,977
Capital and reserves		
Share capital	4,481	5,513
Share premium account	–	108
Revaluation reserve	876	876
Profit and loss account	7,429	8,480
	12,786	14,977

FIVE-YEAR STATEMENT (£000)

	1981	1982	1983	1984	1985
Turnover	20,863	23,186	27,399	33,691	43,012
Operating profit	1,673	2,005	2,441	2,972	3,739
Net investment income	271	512	485	445	268
Profit before tax	1,944	2,517	2,926	3,417	4,007
Tax	403	702	799	915	1,363
Profit after tax	1,541	1,815	2,127	2,502	2,644
Preference dividends	49	49	49	49	49
Ordinary dividends	286	346	404	477	550
Retained profits	1,206	1,420	1,674	1,976	2,045
Ordinary shareholder funds	7,210	8,631	10,306	12,283	14,474
Earnings per ordinary share (pence)	2.98	3.52	4.15	4.90	5.18
Asset value per ordinary share (pence)	14.39	17.23	20.57	24.51	28.89

PART VI

New Business Development

24 York Crest Hotel

In 1984 Pageguild, a substantial York-based property company, acquired a prime site inside the city walls of York, close to Cliffords Tower and the Castle Museum. In October 1984 the company's brokers Cawood, Smithie and Co announced details of a project to build a new hotel on the site, which was to be financed by equity participation and run under a management contract.

YORK AND ITS ENVIRONS

Few cities look as completely medieval as York. With its web of ancient timbered houses and narrow winding streets, the whole city seems to exude an atmosphere of history.

In the fourth century it was a strategic centre for the Romans and even then was a recognized seat of learning. Although the industrial revolution has almost entirely bypassed York, it is today a flourishing city with road and rail links spreading to all parts of Yorkshire.

But the pride of York is the huge and magnificent Minster which towers over the whole city. It contains England's greatest concentration of medieval stained glass – the two most famous windows are the 'Five Sisters' windows in the north transept and the Great East Window which covers 2,000 square feet. It is thought to be the largest area of medieval coloured glass in the world.

The first church to be built on this site was a little wooden building erected in AD 627 for the baptism of King Edwin of Northumbria. The present Minster, the fifth on the site, took masters of every craft 250 years to build and was completed and consecrated in 1472.

For the sightseer, however, there are numerous other sites of architectural and historical interest spanning history back to the Viking days.

With a population of over 100,000, the city also attracts many people who live just beyond the boundary, either to work, shop or for leisure activities. The boundary itself has extended in all directions, but particularly in Acomb, which has developed from a village to a huge residential area. As a result of this, new churches, schools and shops have been built on the outskirts of the city, and old houses cleared from the city itself. There has also been a move to build more residences within the walled city and this is already happening in Aldwark, where old houses have been renovated and new flats and houses built.

Industry and Economic Base

The industries of the nineteenth century had continued and York was still a great railway centre, with its carriage works, huge regional offices and network of lines coming into the city.

In the confectionery trade Terry's, Rowntree's and Craven's had all flourished and moved into new factories. Terry's became part of the Forte group and in 1977 was taken over by Colgate Palmolive; Rowntree's amalgamated with Mackintosh's, but the firms still produced their typical sweets and chocolates. All the firms contributed to the welfare and prosperity of the city; Rowntree's in particular had been pioneers in establishing good conditions for their workers – by having pleasant surroundings, by being the first firm to introduce a five-day week, by having a works council, by having doctors and dentists on the premises, and by having a Day Continuation School for their younger workers – this long before such things were customary. Rowntree's also built New Earswick, a model garden village. A major focus of the economic development strategy was the Clifton Common industrial enterprise (See Appendix 1).

The city's economic base and pattern of employment depended heavily on a small number of employers. The top five employers, for example, (Rowntree-Mackintosh, British Rail, British Rail Engineering, Terry's and Redfearn National Glass) account for 30% of the total number of jobs. In terms of manufacturing jobs the concentration is even more acute, with 40% of the jobs in one company, 58% in the top two, 65% in the top three and 71% in the top four companies. This level of dependence emphasized the need to broaden and diversify the economic and employment base, and so reduce the dependence on the traditional activities – especially British Rail and confectionery.

Furthermore, most of the top employers seemed to have experienced a greater than average reduction in number of employees over the last few years. Taking information from the 1978 Census of Employment and the 1982 County Council Employers Survey, the workforce at York's major companies had dropped by various percentages between 12 and 34%, whereas the average reduction for all York companies over the same four-year period was 8.5%. Although statistically the actual figures needed to be treated with some caution, there did seem to be sufficient evidence to accept the overall pattern. The need to diversify the existing industrial base was recognized within the overall, long-term employment strategy (See Appendix 2).

Tourism

Tourism had developed considerably over the twenty-five years to the mid 1980s. York with its Minster, its walls, its medieval and Georgian buildings, and its quaint streets, had always had a share of visitors, but by 1984 it was one of the foremost centres in the country, with visitors from all over the world. There existed many hotels, some purpose-built, others adapted from Victorian or Georgian houses; new restaurants and coffee bars had opened, and many shops catered particularly for the tourist trade. There was a great deal to attract the visitor – not only the historic buildings themselves, but the Castle Museum, the York Story (St Mary's Heritage Church), the Yorkshire Museum, the National Railway Museum, the Theatre, the Races, and the Festival, when the Medieval Mystery Plays were acted in front of St Mary's Abbey.

Sport

York is one of Britain's most important horse-racing centres. At the city's own famous course there are meetings each month from May to October inclusive.

There are especially good facilities for golf. Some of the best golf clubs in England are situated near the city, and most of these allow temporary membership. There are facilities for fishing in the Ouse and other rivers in easy reach of York.

York is the centre of good hunting country, and visitors are welcome at the meets. There are also three or four riding clubs in and around York with facilities for the visitor.

Popular spectator sports are motor-cycle racing, which takes place at Elvington, hill climbs at Harewood, and harness racing at Green Hammerton. This comparatively new and exciting sport offers a colourful scene with top horses providing the action.

Other Activities

A variety of evening entertainment is available in York and includes theatre, cinemas, six night clubs and discotheques, period banquets, a host of pubs (York has 160) and attractive restaurants as well as many local events, some of which are arranged at short notice.

Round-trip cruises are available from the city centre along various stretches of the River Ouse. Most vessels are equipped with PA systems, and commentaries are given on the thirteenth-century palace home of the Archbishop of York (April–September).

Activities in the arts include experimental theatre, film shows, recitals, children's theatre and folk music, all in a club atmosphere.

THE YORK CREST HOTEL PROJECT

Specification

In October 1984, agreement had been reached between the promoters and Crest Hotels, a subsidiary of Bass plc, to manage the new hotel on a ten-year contract.

The hotel was to be built to four-star specifications with 130 bedrooms, each with a bathroom. The design included a restaurant, banqueting and conference facilities. The site faced Clifford's Tower, a well-known York landmark, which is adjacent to the Castle Museum and the Jorvik Centre and only minutes' walk from the Minster. The exterior design had been carefully planned to blend in with the older buildings nearby.

Operator

Regentcellar Ltd was incorporated to manage the construction and to direct the operating contract once the hotel was completed in spring 1986. Its contract with Crest Hotels was to be renewable at ten-year intervals. (Regentcellar had been incorporated to qualify under the Business Expansion Scheme, which provided for certain investment incentives.)

Crest, one of the largest hotel operators in Western Europe, ran 54 hotels in the United Kingdom. Crest's parent company, Bass plc, had confirmed its belief in the long-term growth potential of its hotel interests, as evidenced by the extent of equity participation (see financial structure below).

Financing

The total cost of construction based on studies prepared by architects and consulting engineers was estimated thus:

		£m
Building work		2.7
Plant, equipment		1.8
Site and management services		1.0
Contingency and interest		0.5
	Total	6.0

The initial proposed financial structure was as follows:

	£m		
Pageguild } Bass plc }	2.00		
Other Ordinary Shareholders	1.35		
Shareholders' Funds	3.35	3.35	
English Tourist Board Grant		0.25	
		3.60	3.60
Bank Finance			2.50
Total			6.10

Cawood, Smithies and Company, the broker, proposed the issue of ordinary shares in the company which were offered at their nominal value of £1 each.

Under the terms of the Business Expansion Scheme these shares would have to be held for five years to qualify for tax relief. However it was hoped that a market could be created for shareholders who needed to dispose of their holdings before this time. At the end of five years, it was the intention of the parties concerned that shareholders who wished to capitalize on their initial investment would have the opportunity to do so, at a price which reflected the value of the business at that time.

Projected Return from Investment

Pageguild had commissioned a feasibility study of the project from Binder Hamlyn Fry, a leading firm of consultants to the hotel industry. Using their figures (updated to take into account the management policies of Crest and the resulting effect upon operating revenues and costs) returns were indicated as in tables 24.1 and 24.2.

TABLE 24.1 Profit and cash-flow projection for Regentcellar Ltd–York Crest Hotel

	Year 1	*Year 2*	*Year 3*	*Year 4*	*Year 5*	*Total*
	(£'000)	*(£'000)*	*(£'000)*	*(£'000)*	*(£'000)*	
Net operating profit	458	519	606	733	770	3,086
Net interest charges	285	260	220	165	100	1,030
Cash flow	173	259	386	568	670	2,056
Depreciation	160	160	160	160	160	800
Pre-tax profit	13	99	226	408	510	1,256

Source: Cawood, Smithie and Co, 1985.

TABLE 24.2 Balance sheet projections for Regentcellar Ltd–York Crest Hotel (Not intended to represent *actual* outcomes)

	Year 1	*Year 2*	*Year 3*	*Year 4*	*Year 5*
	(£'000)	*(£'000)*	*(£'000)*	*(£'000)*	*(£'000)*
Hotel and pre-construction costs	6,100	6,100	6,100	6,100	6,100
Less depreciation	(160)	(320)	(480)	(640)	(800)
	5,940	5,780	5,620	5,460	5,300
Cash at bank	173	432	818	1,386	2,056
Net assets	6,113	6,212	6,438	6,846	7,356
Shareholders' equity	3,350	3,350	3,350	3,350	3,350
Grant	250	250	250	250	250
Medium-term loan	2,500	2,500	2,500	2,500	2,500
Profit retained	13	112	338	746	1,256

Source: Cawood, Smithie and Co, 1985.

Table 24.1 gives a projected pre-tax earnings per £1 share on issued capital of £3.35m of 15.3p in year 5. Subject to commercial considerations, the directors will consider the commencement of dividend payment in year 4. Under current legislation it is anticipated that no tax will be payable in the first five years.

ACCOMMODATION IN YORK

From available records it was estimated that some 113 hotels and guest houses were established in York. Approximately 85% of these establishments charged between £6 and £14 per night and on average, comprised 6 rooms per establishment distributed in the following proportions: single: 14%; double: 57%; family: 29%. The remaining establishments charged £15 per night plus (table 24.3).

CREST HOTELS LIMITED (1984)

Crest Hotels, part of the Leisure Group of Bass plc (see Appendix 4), experienced continued growth in margins and sales during 1984, from a continuation of higher volumes and real improvement in average room rates.

This was a reflection both of more buoyant trading conditions and of extensive capital investment programmes over the years, as the company had applied a consistent policy of improving its product and service to guests.

TABLE 24.3 Hotels in the city (inclusive rate £15+)

Hotel	*No of rooms (with bath/shower)*		*Inclusive rate (at 1984)*
Abbots Mews	26	(26)	£15 – £20.00
Chase	80	(75)	£28.00
Dean Court	35	(35)	£30.00
Disraeli	10	(6)	£15.00
Elm Bank	53	(42)	£16.90
Grasmead	6	(6)	£14.50 – £17.00
Hill Hotel	10	(10)	£17.50
Judges Lodging	14	(14)	£22.00
Kilma	15	(15)	£15.00
Ladbroke Abbey Park	84	(80)	£23.50
Mayfield	7	(7)	£15.00
Mount Royale	19	(19)	£29.50
Post-House	147	(147)	£25.00
Riverside Lodge	24	(11)	£12 – £16.00
Sheppard	20	(20)	£12.50 – £21.00
Viking	187	(187)	£27.75
Voltigner	8	(8)	£18.50

Source: York Tourist Information Office, 1984.

The most exciting development during 1984 in the UK had been the commencement on site of three leisure centre projects at hotels in Maidenhead, Bristol and South Mimms. These were centred around a free-form swimming pool with bar facilities, saunas, solaria and general keep-fit sports areas, including squash courts at Maidenhead.

Spa bathrooms were being provided in eighteen hotels throughout the country, while during 1984 over 1,000 bedrooms in fourteen hotels were completely refurbished in the UK and nearly 800 bedrooms in the continent of Europe.

Crestar II was successfully launched as the company's new international computerized reservations system supported by Crest's first ever European advertising campaign. Results were in line with expectations and further growth was envisaged as the reservations development programme gathered momentum.

A substantial contribution to the year's success had been made through increased penetration of the corporate travel market by the Crest Business Club and of the leisure travel market by the Crest Welcome Breaks, both recognized to be among brand leaders in their sectors.

Improved trading combined with the continued move towards a shorter working week had seen an increase in the actual numbers of staff employed. Training programmes for all staff continued, with increasing emphasis on the provision of friendly and attentive service as well as the basic skills of the profession.

Appendix 1

CLIFTON COMMON INDUSTRIAL DEVELOPMENT[1]

In terms of the economic development of the city and long-term employment trends, Clifton is of fundamental importance – providing, within all land ownerships, some 100 acres of land for development over the next ten years (with the likelihood of a further 70 acres at a later stage).

Within the initial 100 acres, the city owns an area of 55 acres which now has outline planning consent for industrial, warehousing and office use. Twenty-two acres of this can be developed in advance of the Outer Ring Road being available (as soon as services are available). The remaining 33 acres can be started when the Outer Ring Road has been completed – currently programmed for October 1987.

The council's 22 acres, together with the 21-acre North York Trading Estate where development is in progress, will provide the initial thrust of industrial and commercial development at Clifton. In these early stages, therefore, with 50% of the developable land, the council's ability to influence the kind of industrial and commercial growth is of prime importance.

The council's industrial/commercial land must be seen as a resource for creating new economic growth and additional employment. Clearly the development which takes place will need to represent a sound financial investment for the city, but it is important that the question of investment value is related to specific employment and economic objectives rather than forming the sole criterion.

Provisions (in very broad terms) have been made in the capital programme for the 22 acres to be opened up for development. Details of the required works and their programming have now been worked out. . . . Two stages of 11 acres are recommended, (with perhaps a third, earlier stage being introduced) phasing the infrastructure that will be required so that a continuous supply of land is maintained.

[1] Extracted from 'City of York Economic Development Strategy Report', July 1983.

Appendix 2

LONG-TERM EMPLOYMENT STRATEGY – DIVERSIFICATION[1]

While looking for an early contribution towards containing unemployment and providing the opportunities for existing companies to expand or relocate, there is a clear need to take a longer-term view which will influence and shape the economic future of the city.

This must involve a diversification of the industrial base. Although the traditional industries have served the city well in the past and enabled the city to avoid the harsh levels of unemployment that have been experienced elsewhere, the high degree of dependence on a few firms gives rise to a vulnerability that should not be ignored. Failure to take the initiative at this stage – i.e. at the initial marketing of the Clifton land – could have serious implications in the long term.

There is, therefore, a need to attract the growth industries of the future and, in very general items, technology-based activities would meet this requirement. This is not a suggestion that York should join the 'high-tech science park' bandwagon, but to look for a broader range of innovatory activities with a scientific/technological base – e.g. electronics, communications, pharmaceuticals, certain electric/mechanic/chemical engineering industries – or developments within the city's service sector.

Initial job prospects (in terms of employment per square foot) will tend to be lower than in more traditional activities, but this longer-term view (almost a long-term investment) is put forward as an important aspect of a balanced economic development policy. With such a clean and attractive environment to offer, there is every prospect that such activities, which look for high-quality developments, can be attracted to the city.

[1] 'City of York Economic Development Strategy Report', 1983.

Appendix 3

'DOLLAR POWERS HOTELS'[1]

As the politicians bewail the tumbling pound, one section of British industry stands cheering on the sidelines. For hoteliers 1983 was a good year, 1984 was much better, and 1985 is set to be marvellous.

The chart below [table 24.4] shows why. In theory, 1981 should have been a good year for overseas tourists, as the Prince and Princess of Wales obligingly got married and sterling lost a quarter of its value against the dollar by September. In fact, 1981 marked the nadir of the downswing from the 1979 peak. Since then, visitors to the UK have risen steadily. The latest figures show that, by October 1984, 11 per cent more foreigners had landed on these shores than in the same period in 1983.

TABLE 24.4 Overseas visitors and the Exchange Rate

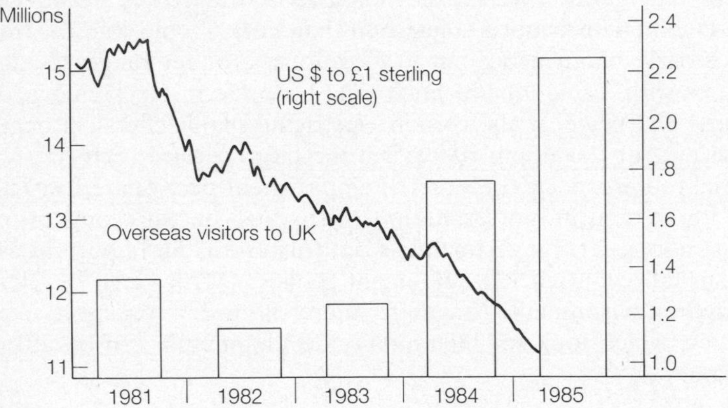

The last two months of the year are relatively unimportant for overseas visitors, but Mr Duncan Black, chairman of the British Tourist Authority and the English Tourist Board, has predicted a 12 per cent rise in overseas visitors to 14m in 1984. The strongest growth has been generated from North America (up to 23 per cent in the first ten months), but Western Europe remains far more important, providing over half the total.

[1] Charlotte Raeburn, *Investors Chronicle*, 1 February 1985 (Reproduced by kind permission of *Investors Chronicle*).

Up-to-date hotel occupancy figures are hard to come by, but reliable estimates are that September 1984 (the peak month of the year) saw London room occupancy top 90 per cent, while for England as a whole it was over 70 per cent. This has meant that, although published tariffs have not risen by much more than inflation for the past two or three years, achieved room rates have improved substantially and discounting, at least in the peak months, has become a thing of the past.

Playing 'pass-the-parcel'

The pressure on room space, particularly in the capital, has pushed hotel prices up sharply. In the almost complete absence of new building, hotel groups have played pass-the-parcel with their properties. Canny operators started in 1982, when Grand Metropolitan sold off the bulk of its UK hotels following the purchase of Intercontinental Hotels from Pan Am, and British Rail put most of its hotels up for auction. Queens Moat Houses picked up 26 provincial hotels, and later its one London property, and Mount Charlotte Investments bought two from Grand Met, one from Ireland's Ryan Hotels and three from Trusthouse Forte.

Further upmarket, big American groups have also moved into London. Marriott paid a reported £14m for Grand Met's Europa Hotel in July 1983, and Regent International bought the Dorchester from an Arab consortium for £45m last year. Now the Dorchester has changed hands yet again, going to the Sultan of Brunei for well over £50m – some sources suggest as much as £65m – though Regent will continue to manage the hotel. The reported price represents pushing £200,000 per room, rising to nearer £300,000 when the planned £20m has been spent on further refurbishment to turn the Dorchester into 'the world's most luxurious hotel'.

Even that is put into the shade by the present value of the Savoy group (taking in the Savoy itself, Claridges, the Connaught and the Berkeley). Its market capitalization is £22.8m, about £350,000 a room, and the properties are not even all freehold. Trusthouse Forte, which bid unsuccessfully in 1981 and holds nearly 70 per cent of the capital, is not interested in bidding again at this price, which chief executive Mr Rocco Forte describes as 'ridiculous'.

Hoteliers have been buying, often at very inflated prices, because the cost of building is seen as prohibitive. Sites with appropriate planning permission are few and far between, particularly in central London, but the American private company, Raleigh Enterprises, thinks it is on to a good thing with its purchase of the former Crown Agents' office on Millbank. Raleigh's London agent, Mr Gary Hersham of Beauchamp Estates, says the price was 'over the asking price of £10m', and a further £20m or so will be spent on constructing 200 suites inside the shell of the building. When completed, the hotel should be in the six-star category, but it must be questioned whether there is a market for such a hotel in

TABLE 24.5 Ratings for some of Britain's busiest hoteliers

Company	*Hotels & holidays as percentage of profits*	*No. of UK hotel rooms*	*Pre-tax profits (£000) latest*	*projected*
Comfort Hotels	89	2,485	2,355	4,000
Ladbroke	28	3,500	41,400	50,000
London Park	100	985	503	–
Mount Charlotte Inv.	98	6,200	4,600	9,000
Norfolk Capital	100	938	504	750
Prince of Wales	100	760	724	750
Queens Moat Houses	100	4,532	4,475	6,300
Savoy	100	649	4,346	7,500
Stakis	56	2,400	9,626	12,000
Trusthouse Forte	79	20,000	96,000	112,000

that location, well away from the heart of Mayfair.

Outside London, building costs fall dramatically. Comfort Hotels, now being taken over by Ladbroke (mainly for the sake of its nine three-star hotels in London) is developing Comfort Lodges in a joint venture with British Land. These two- to three-star properties, sited near major towns and motorways, are being built at the bargain basement costs of £25,000 a room. A more usual and realistic figure is probably the £40–50,000 a room quoted by THF's deputy chief executive, Mr Dennis Hearn, for the chain of Post Houses which THF is currently building in the provinces. These are of four-star standard and cater more for business than tourist trade, and units in Hull, Milton Keynes and Guildford are now planned or under construction.

How to invest in the boom

Hotel shares are expensive. Average PE ratios, even on prospective profits, are well into the 20s, and many shares offer minuscule yields. Three groups primarily involved in hotels are capitalized at over £100m.

Trusthouse Forte is the giant, worth £1.19bn following the latest good results. THF is well represented at the expensive end of the London market, with the Grosvenor House in Park Lane, the Hyde Park Hotel, and Brown's in Dover Street. Its most famous subsidiary is, of course, the Savoy, which is not consolidated in the results, since THF has no management control. Recent speculation that THF might sell its holding is wide of the mark: Mr Rocco Forte also made it clear recently that he still intends to acquire his rival, albeit not at today's prices.

Price (p)	1984–5 high/low (p)	Prospective PE ratio	Yield (%)	Market capitalization (£m)
95	99/33½	29	1.1	73
267	279/182	16	5.0	471
358	358/172	42[a]	2.9	13
80	81/50½	28	1.9	164
23	28/12½	48	1.5	23
100	135/56	25	2.1	12
55½	59/32½	21	3.2	87
395	420/268	23	0.7	228
180	186/86½	17	2.4	132
152	161/93	17	4.4	1,185

[a] Based on latest reported profits.

The Savoy comes next in terms of market value. The management shows no signs of coming to terms with THF, and has concentrated on improving the trading results of its properties following the loss of £1.62m recorded in 1980. Pre-tax profits in 1984 probably reached at least £7.5m, and the hotels are at just the right end of the market to benefit from an influx of wealthy American tourists looking for a well-known name.

The other high player Mount Charlotte Investments, is much less famous, and caters for a different sort of customer. MCI got its foothold of six London hotels in 1982 and 1983, and during 1984 it concentrated on Scotland, with the purchase of Skean Dhu and its five hotels. In November it came storming back into London, buying the Royal Scot Hotel in Kings Cross from Thistle Hotels, part of Scottish & Newcastle Breweries. The cost of £21m represented a fairly modest £29,000 per room, and MCI now has 2,500 rooms in London, making it extremely well placed to accommodate the less well-off tourists from Europe and within the UK. Having issued a mass of paper for its acquisitions, MCI is now capitalized at £164m.

Stakis is not much smaller, at £132m, but has substantial interests in casinos (all but one outside London) as well as its hotels, which are primarily in Scotland. Its London base, the St Ermin's has been so busy since its acquisition from Grand Met in July 1983, that Stakis has not felt able to close it for refurbishment.

Ladbroke, where hotels and holidays contributed only around a quarter of profits in 1983, has jumped into the big league with its takeover of Comfort Hotels. Its terms value Comfort at £73m, a multiple of 29 times probable earnings in 1984. Ladbroke will move into second place behind

THF for UK rooms, and greatly enhance its London presence.

Hotels have historically been a cyclical business. How long will this boom last? Many analysts think it could peak in 1985, when brokers Capel-Cure Myers expect foreign visitors to total 15–15½m. The English Tourist Board is confident in its forecast that the number of foreign tourists in London will go on rising till 1990 at least, but the rest of the country may not share in the bonanza. Barring a return to the $2 pound, though, 1985 has to be a good year, but anyone buying hotel shares at the current high prices should be prepared to unload them when the flood of visitors begins to abate.

Appendix 4 Bass Plc

GROUP PROFIT AND LOSS ACCOUNT (1984) (£m)

	53 weeks 1984	*52 weeks 1983*
Turnover	2,252.3	1,988.4
Costs and overheads, less other income	2,017.0	1,791.2
Trading profit	235.3	197.2
Cost of borrowing	16.9	22.2
Profit on ordinary activities before taxation	218.4	175.0
Tax on profit on ordinary activities	74.7	61.7
Profit on ordinary activities after taxation for the financial year	143.7	113.3
Extraordinary charge for deferred taxation	9.2	–
Attributable to outside shareholders	.9	.6
Preference dividends	.3	.3
Earnings available for ordinary shareholders	133.3	112.4
Ordinary dividends	41.9	36.7
Retained for reinvestment in the business	91.4	75.7
Earnings per ordinary share	44.0p	34.9p

BALANCE SHEETS (1984) (£m)

	Group	
	1984	*1983*
Fixed assets		
Intangible assets	42.6	38.9
Tangible assets	1,280.9	1,209.8
Investments	147.7	119.7
	1,474.8	1,368.4
Current assets		
Stocks	201.9	192.6
Debtors	190.4	198.7
Investments – short-term deposits	62.1	30.2
Cash at bank and in hand	35.1	9.6
	489.5	431.1
Creditors: amounts falling due within one year	422.2	384.6
Net current assets	67.3	46.5
Total assets less current liabilities	1,542.1	1,414.9
Creditors: amounts falling due after more than one year	269.6	238.9
Accruals and deferred income – government grants		
Interests of outside shareholders	15.7	14.9
	1,245.2	1,150.0
Capital and reserves		
Called-up share capital	87.8	87.4
Share premium account	93.8	88.2
Revaluation reserve	235.3	237.5
Other reserves	5.2	5.2
Profit and Loss account	823.1	731.7
	1,245.2	1,150.0

GROUP FINANCIAL REVIEW (£m)

	1984	*1983*	*1982*	*1981*	*1980*
Balance sheet					
Fixed assets					
Intangible assets	46.2	38.9	29.3	22.8	–
Tangible assets	1,208.9	1,209.8	1,156.2	1,122.7	931.4
Investments	147.7	119.7	98.6	81.1	67.6
	1,474.8	1,368.4	1,284.1	1,226.6	999.0
Current assets	489.5	431.1	396.0	392.5	311.8
Creditors: amounts falling due within one year	422.2	384.6	327.0	369.1	243.8
Total assets less current liabilities	1,542.1	1,414.9	1,353.1	1,250.0	1,067
Creditors: amounts falling due after more than one year	269.6	238.9	244.9	199.6	176.6
Accruals and deferred income – government grants	11.6	11.1	10.8	12.0	11.4
Interests of outside shareholders	15.7	14.9	15.3	15.9	15.4
	1,245.2	1,150.0	1,082.1	1,022.5	863.6
Capital and reserves					
Called-up share capital	87.8	87.4	87.0	86.6	76.4
Undistributable reserves	334.3	330.9	332.5	338.3	260.9
Profit and loss account	823.1	731.7	662.6	597.6	526.3
	1,245.2	1,150.0	1,082.1	1,022.5	863.6

	1984 *£m*	*1983* *£m*	*1982* *£m*	*1981* *£m*	*1980* *£m*
Trading results					
Turnover	2,252.3	1,988.4	1,860.8	1,712.6	1,262.8
Surplus on disposal of fixed assets	10.3	14.7	11.5	7.6	7.3
	2,262.6	2,003.1	1,872.3	1,720.2	1,270.1
Bought-in materials and services	(991.8)	(858.4)	(805.7)	(742.8)	(448.9)
Excise duty	(576.2)	(517.5)	(475.5)	(434.5)	(387.5)
	694.6	627.2	591.1	542.9	433.7
Staff costs	(410.7)	(377.8)	(378.5)	(341.0)	(265.3)
Depreciation after crediting grants	(57.6)	(52.2)	(50.6)	(48.5)	(35.9)
Trading profit	235.3	197.2	162.0	153.4	132.5
Cost of borrowing	(16.9)	(22.2)	(25.3)	(20.2)	(19.0)
Profit on ordinary activities before taxation	218.4	175.0	136.7	133.2	113.5
Taxation on ordinary activities	(74.7)	(61.7)	(41.9)	(35.0)	(36.6)

25 The Westbury Homes Group

As Richard Fraser said in his chief executive's statement to the board, 28 February 1985 marked the end of a 12-month period throughout which there had been a great deal of uncertainty about the future ownership of the company. It had in fact been one which began with a feeling of a lot of promise in the air, had pitched into near despair, and yet ended on a high note of optimism with the conclusion of a successful management buy-out and the prospects of strong strategic growth.

At the beginning of the year the directors had announced their decision to apply for a full listing for the Cheltenham-based Westbury Group on the London Stock Exchange. Confidence was high, and a date in July had been set by the issuing house. The rise in interest rates and the sudden decline in the market brought about a temporary halt to the plans. However by the autumn the economy had picked up and the board was ready to revive the flotation. In October the ultimate shareholder changed his mind and announced his intention of disposing of the whole of his shareholding by offering the company for sale by tender on the open market. Faced with this decision the seven senior directors decided to attempt to construct a bid to secure the business. They formed a new company, gained support from two large institutions, and were successful in acquiring the company.

Despite all this corporate activity the Westbury Homes Group yet again achieved record levels of sales units, turnover and pre-tax profits, and, as to the future, the annual report commented that although the ownership of the company had changed, the management had not, that the market remained good, and that the group had the skills and resources to continue its historic profits growth.

The year was one in which a lot of lessons had been and could be learned, and yet one which may have paved the way for a significant level of strategic initiative.

THE DEVELOPMENT OF A BUSINESS

Westbury Homes evolved out of the initiative and imagination of the two brothers, Bob and John Joiner. In 1966 they sold their existing business to ITT after a period of credit squeeze and a consequent loss of profit. They were not inclined to work for another company as employees, and forbidden by the terms of the sale to re-enter the television business in opposition; they felt that their only real alternative was to set up another business. Their capital gave them the time to think carefully upon the options and to start on a well-planned basis.

They pored over government statistics to find suitable opportunities for their limited resources and decided upon the main criteria to govern their choice. First, the market had to be large enough to accommodate their entry. It had to be able to allow a business to start up and develop without attracting too much competitive attention and aggression. It had to have low entry barriers, given the scale of their capital, and to allow for growth opportunities. Secondly, they wanted to deal with large-value items that might produce rapid cash flow – a unit selling price that was high enough to avoid the need for large selling teams. Thirdly, the product should involve a high labour content which might be sub-divided and sub-contracted out in order to reduce managerial time, attention and risk.

Only house-building and tour-operating fitted the bill and, as the housing business was then in a healthy state of growth, the brothers bought some land at the beginning of 1967. A small estate was contract designed and the construction was subcontracted. Start-up was slow but steady, and the first year saw the completion of just five houses. In 1970 they took on a larger site of 23 units, and profitability was rapidly improved due to the concentration of work in the one site area, thus setting a pattern for future contracts. This was an operation that was largely run by the seat of the pants, with the family making all operational and strategic decisions.

Between 1970 and 1973 Westbury Homes really took off, and company targets were doubled each year. Rapid growth brought with it problems of liquidity and, with a gearing ratio of 9-1 the company was not only under-capitalized, but vulnerable to adverse economic changes.

True to form, in May 1973 interest rates climbed and prices nose-dived. Like Alice in Wonderland who grew too large to get through the door, so too was Westbury Homes faced with a slump of 30% in the market and a mounting backlog of unsold houses. Wisely the brothers swallowed their medicine and took drastic action by slimming down staffing levels and virtually halting new work in order to complete and sell outstanding and uncompleted units.

1974 saw many large housebuilders go to the wall but Westbury just survived and this experience was largely responsible for the introduction and development of an effective financial and management control system which was to serve the company well in the future. Towards the end of 1974 the market improved and the company expanded its geographic coverage. By 1979 the Centre for Inter-firm Comparison had placed Westbury Homes as heading the top ten for return on capital employed of 71%, and second in the league for the fastest growing housebuilder.

THE JOINER BROTHERS

Bob Joiner was the extrovert and visionary of the two brothers, customer-oriented, dynamic and with an ability to motivate his staff; John Joiner could be described as an introvert, planning-oriented, rather uncommunicative, but with attributes which complemented those of his brother. Both brothers typically set themselves objectives which were consistently too high, and consequently operational and financial aspects of the business tended to suffer from a lack of realism.

The two brothers, although professionally unqualified, successfully managed the company from 1964 until the property slump of 1974, when facing imminent financial collapse they handed over management to Geoff Hester as managing director in 1976 and retired into chairmanship positions. It is doubtful that Westbury would have survived the crisis and grown to its present size had they not stepped aside as they found themselves unable to manage a business facing severe problems. This interference in the operational management of the company and the removal of capital sums for private and venture needs, hampered the efficient development of Westbury and left behind little capital for re-investment and re-capitalization.

The brothers certainly could be described as entrepreneurs. Stepping out of operations management, they spread their wings and were responsible for setting up overseas housebuilding operations, one in Canada in 1975 and two in the USA in 1979 and 1983. This 'have a go' attitude of the Joiners enabled them to exploit opportunities as they arrived and was the basis of their business success.

A CHANGE IN MANAGEMENT STYLE

In 1970 Geoff Hester joined Westbury Estates and by 1973 became a director of the company. As managing director in 1976 there can be no doubt that he was largely responsible for taking the company from its relatively small beginnings through to a major housebuilder by the time of his departure in June 1981. Geoff Hester's style of management was a hands-on approach in which typically most operational and strategic decisions were made by him. Known as Mr Westbury, his 'hire and fire' approach to management provided a high staff turnover and earned the company a poor outside image. He was, however, uncomfortable with the large divisionalized company that he had created and, finding himself unable to delegate responsibility adequately, he departed. John Joiner assumed day-to-day control of the company.

For a short period John Joiner's style proved to be a complete contrast; he sought a decentralized form of growth with only a limited amount of control coming from the centre, indeed so much so that it became almost impossible to prepare plans and budgets. This was an exciting period of development – from autocracy to democracy within eight months. The period produced much frustration, especially at top level. John Joiner clashed with the board and its traditional view of growth. In 1981/2 profits dropped for the first time as John Joiner was prepared to lose half a million pounds to get his ideas through. However the tensions were too great and in a boardroom clash John Joiner left and moved off to the United States, leaving his brother Bob as the sole owner of Westbury UK.

Bob Joiner had moved to live in the West Indies in 1977 where the group was now legally registered. His control was thus distant but he still remained financially insistent and demanding.

Richard Fraser was appointed to the position of managing director to bring some sense of control over the erratic pattern of activity. An accountant by profession and with the company since 1973, he had to determine upon a style of management that might rebuild a sense of corporate mission. The new MD encouraged the development of a top-down planning, bottom-up communications style of management. The culture is presently that of a family atmosphere in which employees are encouraged to take pride in their work and in Westburys, in return for higher than average salaries and a management responsive to the needs and development of its staff.

'The company's main resource is its people' says Richard Fraser, 'and I am very much concerned with the welfare and development of my staff, but I have no time for those who cannot shape up to my company expectations. We have to be a slim-line, thinking-based organization in a competitive business and we cannot afford to carry passengers.' The reputation and image of Westburys in the industry and in the public eye is seen as a major concern, and public relations is increasingly occupying both his and the personnel manager's working time. Considerable effort has been necessary to achieve a balanced style after the earlier contrasts, and an incremental and more open method of decision-taking has contributed much to a higher standard of decision-taking. Westburys' image, both internally and externally, was in the process of being changed to fit in with the management's vision of its future role. By March 1984 things had settled down once again and growth was evident in all indices. Bob Joiner and the board wished to go to the market to increase the finance available for fast expansion.

THE PRESENT BUSINESS

Subcontracting is anything and everything in this organization to enable top management to spend its time on doing what it knows best – making money. This principle is still valid today. Subcontractors are part of the family and many of them have been with the firm longer than most of the staff. There are in fact some 300 management and associated staff within Westburys; there are some 2,000 people externally employed.

Table 25.1 illustrates growth in the group's unit sales over the 10-year period to 1984, compared with total private-sector dwelling completions in Great Britain, making it today the twelfth largest housebuilder.

The group develops housing estates of from 15 to 400 houses for sale to private buyers. Estates typically include a range of detached, semi-detached and terraced houses and in some cases flats. In addition, the group undertakes a limited amount of contract housebuilding for housing associations and local authorities. In the year ended February 1984 such contract housebuilding amounted to less than 3% of group turnover.

The group's head office is located at Westbury House, Cheltenham. This accommodates the group's centralized design, marketing, land acquisition, planning and finance functions. The operating subsidiaries, which are also based at Cheltenham, are responsible for production and sales in the four operating regions. Figure 25.1 outlines the organisation structure.

AREA AND SCOPE OF OPERATIONS

The group's four operating regions are South-West, Severnside, Midlands and Wales (see Figure 25.2). Currently the group has 40 estates under development in 12 counties of England and Wales. It is likely that future operations will extend to cover mid and southern England. Within its area of operations, the directors estimate that the group has a market share of approximately 12% locally and about 1% in the national market.

LAND ACQUISITION AND LAND BANK

The success of the group has been founded partly upon an in-depth knowledge of land and planning matters within its expanding area of operations, and to this end a small specialist team exists to deal exclusively with this important aspect of the business.

The group has consistently been able to acquire land with outline planning consent in good locations. Land is not usually acquired without such consent, but the group has developed the use of options on those sites where it is felt that the group's expertise can be used to accelerate the planning consent procedure.

At 31 May 1984 land controlled by the group represented a stock equivalent of two years' usage based on anticipated sales for the year ending February 1983. In addition, at 31 May 1984, the group had options on sites equivalent to a further 2,500 plots. None of these sites presently has planning consent.

ESTATE DESIGN

Reflecting the importance that the group attaches to this key element of the business, a staff of 34 is engaged in the design of housing estates and in carrying out the legal and planning work necessary before site development can commence. These staff have the skills necessary to maximize the estates' appeal to prospective housebuyers and to ensure speedy resolution of planning matters.

HOUSE DESIGN AND PRODUCT RANGE

The group currently has a range of 19 designs for houses, varying in size from one to five bedrooms. In order to maximize customer appeal, each of these designs can be built in a range of external styles. There are currently three distinct styles: Rural, Georgian and Tudor, each of which can be built in a variety of elevations and treatments. Current prices of one-bedroom houses range from £17,750 to £25,000 and of four-bedroom houses from £35,000 to £70,000. In the year ended February 1984 some 43% of turnover was made up of sales of one- or two-bedroom homes and the average sale price of all units sold in that year was £27,800.

PRODUCTION AND CONTROL

All construction is carried out by sub-contractors, many of whom have developed with the group and therefore understand the group's strict requirements for construction to be completed on time and to high standards of finish. Most sub-contractors work almost exclusively for the group. This close relationship with sub-contractors has helped the group achieve a production-line approach to building. House construction is divided into eight stages (appropriate to particular sub-contract trades) and is closely supervised on each estate by a manager employed by the group and based on that estate. All homes are constructed to National House Building Council Standards and are sold with a 10-year NHBC structural warranty.

Control over house production is achieved by means of a detailed

TABLE 25.1 Recent performance of top ten U.K. housebuilders

Parent	*Company*	*Year end*	*No. of homes sold*	*Pre-tax profit (% to T/Over)*	*Return on investment*	*Approx. land bank (No. of years)*
	1. Barratt	June 82	14000	11.1	18%	3
	2. Wimpey	Dec. 81	7400	6.4	6%	
	3. Tarmac	Dec. 81	3980	9.0		
Guardian Royal Exchange	4. Broseley	Dec. 81	3027	3.3	7%	
P & O	5. Bovis	Dec. 81	2029	11.0	51%	5
	6. Leech	Aug. 81	1880	4.2	6%	4½
	7. Bryant	May 81	1700	13.2	32%	4¾
	8. Westbury	Feb. 82	1420	6.9	43%	1¾
Carlton Industries	9. Comben	Dec. 81	1402	6.1	16%	5
Trafalgar House	10. Ideal	Sept. 81	1300	3.5	20%	
			38138			

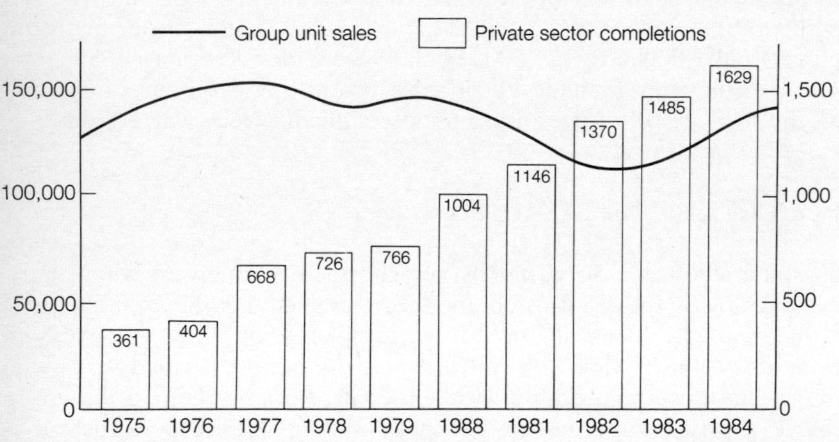

Note: Industry figures (Source: Department of Environment) are for the calendar year and are compared with Group unit sales for the year to end February in the following year.

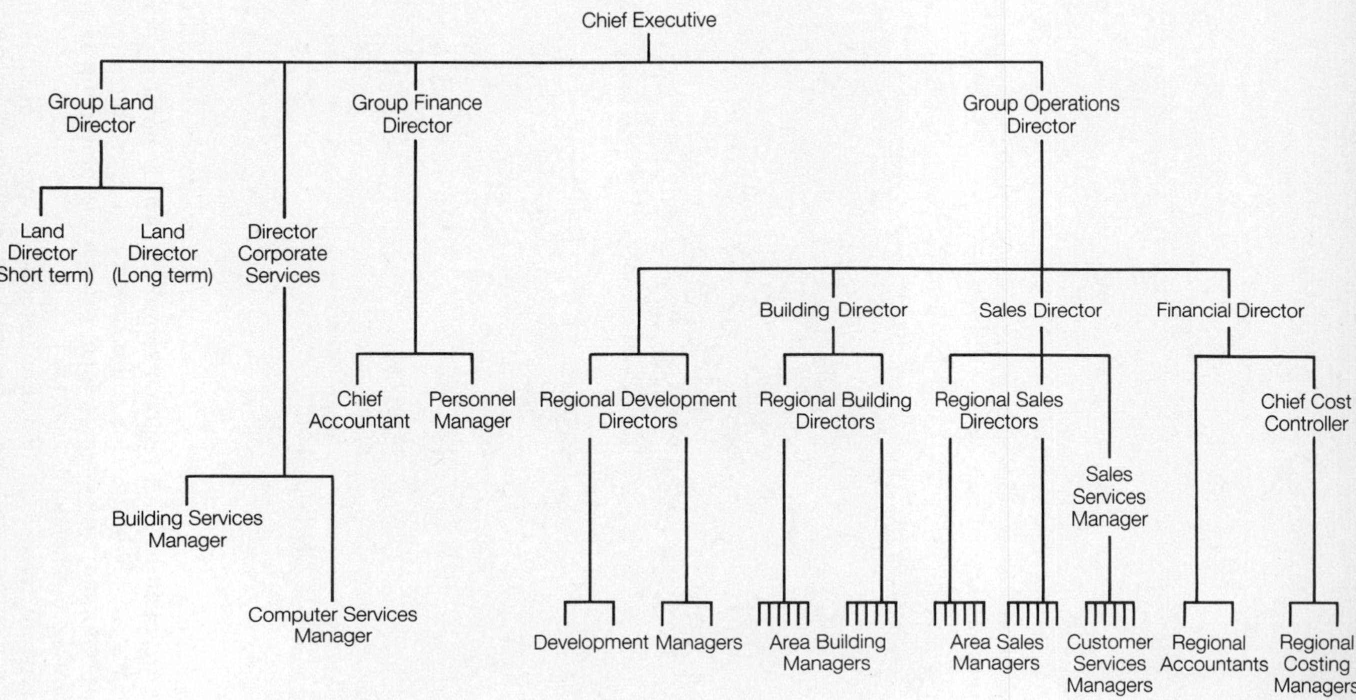

FIGURE 25.1 Company organisation chart

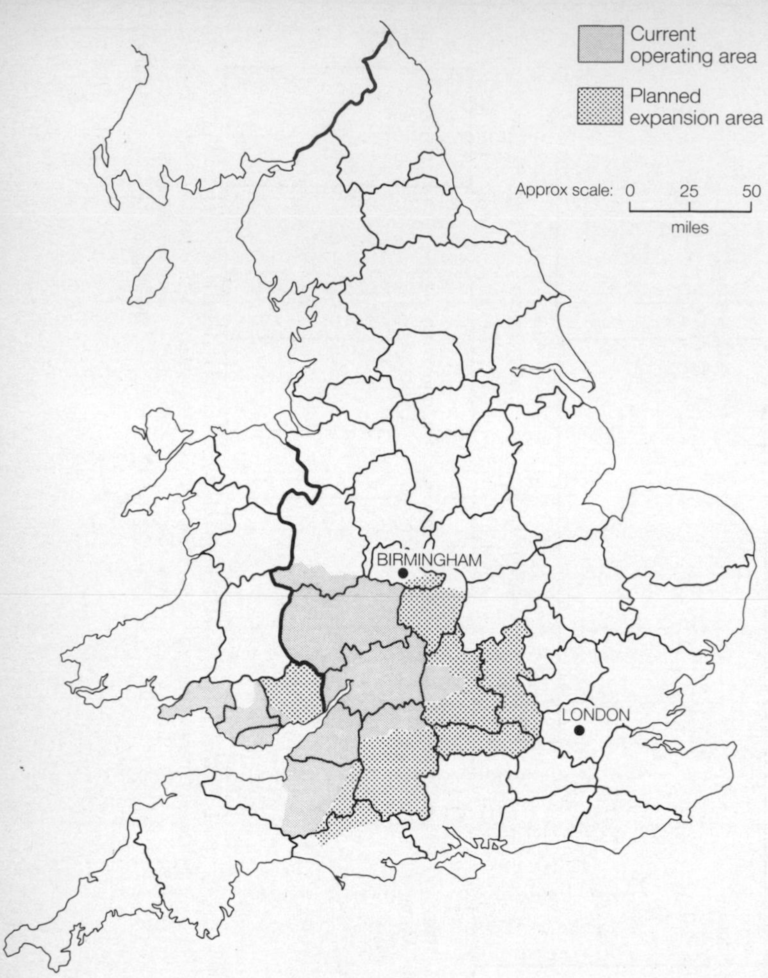

FIGURE 25.2 Areas of UK operation

programme, operated by each regional subsidiary, which monitors house production on a weekly basis. This is linked to the group's computerized management information system which provides comprehensive and regular operating and financial reports.

The policy is 'to get it right first time, produce a quality product that the market can afford, and never to miss a completion date for our customers'.

SALES AND MARKETING

The group places great importance on effective on-site presentation and on ensuring that both the house and the estate are presented to customers as attractively as possible. On each estate there is one or more fully furnished show home open seven days a week and staffed by a full-time member of the sales team. Advertising in the local press is controlled by area sales management, who are best placed to assess local conditions and requirements. This is supported, as required, by special promotions and corporate advertising on television and in the national newspapers. On the majority of sites, at least one estate agent is appointed on a 'no sale no fee' basis.

The group considers it important to provide a comprehensive sales service to customers, and to this end employs eight full-time customer service managers who are responsible for accepting houses from production and liaising with customers both before and after sale. The directors believe that this service leads to increased trade-up sales to satisfied customers as well as to new introductions provided by such customers. The group has extensive mortgage allocations with several major building societies and is able to offer the benefit of mortgage assistance to many customers. The group also runs a home exchange plan which operates within strict limits on the number of second-hand houses that can be held by the group at any one time. Each house has a fitted kitchen; however, the group does not normally equip houses with 'white' goods, carpets or curtains as this conflicts with the group's policy of providing maximum value in the building itself.

Effective control, monitoring and target setting are considered vital ingredients of the group's sales success. The sales teams are given targets against which performance is measured. Reservations, contracts and legal completions are all monitored weekly and this information is linked to the group's computerized management reporting system.

OPERATIONAL AND MANAGEMENT CONTROLS

A key feature of the Westbury approach to house building is the emphasis that is placed on effective monitoring and control over all aspects of the business. To this end the group prepares:

weekly reports of sales, reservations and production by region;
profit and loss reports after six, eight, ten, 11 and 12 weeks of each quarter for each operating company and for the group as a whole;
monthly information packs containing a detailed statistical digest plus a cash-flow projection for the next six weeks, and cash-flow comparison with the previous month; and

quarterly management accounts containing detailed profit and loss accounts and balance sheets compared with budget, backed up by statistical and financial detail; a rolling 12 months' budget which amends the current year's budget; and a detailed management information book which contains a wealth of financial and statistical historical data on the group. This information is produced for each operating company and for the group as a whole.

FINANCIAL STATUS

General

In the year ended February 1984 the group sold 1,629 units, achieving turnover of £45.3 million and pre-tax profits of £3.6 million. Apart from a dip in profits in 1982, the group's unit sales, turnover and pre-tax profits have increased in each of the last ten years.

In the year ending 28 February 1985 the latest management accounts, covering the first 26 weeks of the year, show a net profit before taxation of £1.86 million. The directors expect unit sales of 1,711 and a turnover of £53.3 million for the full year. In the absence of unforeseen circumstances, the directors also expect that the group profit before taxation for the year ending 28 February 1985 will be in the region of £4 million. The directors estimate that net tangible assets of the group as at 28 February 1985 will be approximately £9.5 million.

The group had intended to seek a quotation on the Stock Exchange in July 1984. These plans were postponed in the light of the market conditions at that time.

Trading record and 1984–5 budget

Set out below is a summary of the trading record of the group for the five years ended February 1984, together with the budget for the year ending February 1985. Further financial information is set out in the Accountants' Report.

ENVIRONMENTAL ISSUES

Of major importance to the growth of the company is the government's ability to control interest rates.

The growth of pressures upon planning authorities to restrict house building means that political power is increasingly occupying the group's time. Contacts with planning authorities, land agencies, solicitors, estate agents etc. are vital relationships which, if managed well, can facilitate the lead time to construction start-up.

Demographic changes and population movement to the south of England tend to work in Westbury's favour. Previously, 70% of families lived in rented accommodation, whereas now 60% own their own homes, and present government policy is to increase that percentage.

The first-time-buyer market, however, peaked in 1967 and potentially the largest market segment is in upmarket houses and residential buildings for the elderly. This is presently contrary to Westbury's market focus, which is on the lower end of the housing price scale.

There is now greater emphasis on inner-city sites for urban renewal and public support for the refurbishment of old buildings, often with the co-operation and support of local authorities.

The requirements of housebuyers are changing, with more demand for houses with purchase appeal and superior living environments.

The technology of this industry is low and traditional building materials and construction methods are favoured. Fortunately, the industry is not highly unionized, and Westbury's policy of making the employees feel part of the company has promoted a highly motivated and loyal workforce.

THE BOMBSHELL

In April 1984 confidence in the company's prospects and the market for housebuilding was high. Expansion prospects existed, but capital for land acquisition was scarce. Bob Joiner was disinclined to invest any further; indeed he wished to liquidate some of his investment tied up in the business.

The proposal to float the company, to draw in outside funding, was a positive and logical move. It did, however, demand a greater knowledge of the market and a greater self-awareness than hitherto. It precipitated a search for greater understanding about both policy and strategy, which was to be a great plus when the board came round to negotiating the management buy-out. In the March – June period of 1984 the preparatory work was done, but in June interest rates rose by 2% and a lot of other flotations were on the stocks of the City institutions, and the decision was taken to hold the offer. Everything was flattened out; there was a loss of impetus and emphasis; but by the autumn, with BT out of the way, the merchant bankers recommended a flotation for June 1985. Thus a re-writing of the prospectus was put in hand at some quarter of a million pounds' cost. The board meeting was scheduled for Friday 12 October with the prospectus as the single item on the agenda. Bob Joiner attended that meeting, abrupted the agenda, and announced that he was going to sell.

Bob Joiner had been in ill-health for some time, approaching retirement age and with no immediate family to succeed him. The coming was sudden. He had been advised by his doctor that week to stop work.

BALANCE SHEETS AT 29 FEBRUARY 1984 (£000)

	The Group
Fixed assets	
Property, plant and equipment	1,116
Investment in subsidiary	–
	1,116
Current assets	
Stocks	22,916
Debtors	1,555
Bank balances, deposits and cash	169
	24,640
Creditors falling due within one year	
Loans (secured)	3,165
Bank overdrafts (secured)	6,548
Creditors	6,554
Dividends	338
Taxation	1,230
	17,835
Net current assets	6,805
Total assets less creditors falling due within one year	7,921
Creditors falling due after more than one year	272
Deferred taxation	160
Net tangible assets	7,489
Shareholders' funds	
Share capital	465
Reserves	7,024
	7,489

PROFIT AND LOSS ACCOUNTS YEAR ENDED 28 OR 29 FEBRUARY (£000)

	1980	*1981*	*1982*	*1983*	*1984*
Turnover	18,697	25,572	31,525	38,354	45,284
Cost of sales	(13,755)	(18,429)	(22,894)	(27,689)	(33,389)
Gross profit	4,942	7,143	8,631	10,665	11,895
Selling costs	(741)	(1,869)	(3,189)	(3,977)	(4,379)
Administration costs	(912)	(1,266)	(1,774)	(2,001)	(2,182)
Operating profit	3,289	4,008	3,668	4,687	5,334
Investment income	13	55	35	92	19
Interest payable	(782)	(1,292)	(1,486)	(1,660)	(1,707)
Profit before taxation	2,520	2,771	2,217	3,119	3,646
Taxation	(19)	(229)	(619)	(738)	(1,537)
Profit after taxation	2,501	2,542	1,598	2,381	2,109
Extraordinary items and non-recurring proprietorial expenses	(428)	(469)	(867)	(577)	(1,070)
	2,073	2,073	731	1,804	1,039
Dividends	(361)	(369)	(212)	(1,113)	(917)
Retained profit	1,712	1,704	519	691	122
Earnings per share	13.4p	13.7p	8.6p	12.8p	11.3p

STATEMENTS OF SOURCES AND APPLICATIONS OF FUNDS YEAR ENDED 28 OR 29 FEBRUARY (£000)

	1980	*1981*	*1982*	*1983*	*1984*
Sources of funds					
Funds generated from operations					
Profit before taxation	2,520	2,771	2,217	3,119	3,646
Depreciation	71	80	122	124	119
Losses/(profits) on sales of fixed assets	–	6	28	(14)	(14)
	2,591	2,857	2,367	3,229	3,751

	1980	1981	1982	1983	1984
Funds from other sources					
Proceeds from sales or fixed assets	13	91	70	173	459
Loan received	–	398	–	–	–
Total sources of funds	2,604	3,346	2,437	3,402	4,210
Applications of funds					
Purchases of fixed assets	261	859	236	124	220
Long-term loan repayments	20	–	58	137	106
Tax paid	82	293	421	301	616
Dividends paid	136	694	147	1,150	625
Extraordinary items and non-recurring proprietorial expenses	428	469	867	577	1,070
Total applications of funds	927	2,315	1,729	2,289	2,637
Net sources of funds	1,677	1,031	708	1,113	1,573
Increases (decreases) in working capital					
Increases in stocks	2,743	4,075	2,886	1,857	5,462
Increases (decreases) in debtors	543	163	166	254	(330)
(Increases) in creditors	(1,874)	(3,344)	(2,223)	(819)	(3,546)
	1,412	894	829	1,232	(1,586)
Movements in net liquid funds	265	137	(121)	(119)	(13)
Increases in working capital	1,677	1,031	708	1,113	1,573

He determined to cut all UK connections, to sell the company, and concentrate his activities in Florida and the Bahamas where he had lived since 1977.

The sudden nature of the statement was serious enough, but equally significant to an astonished board of directors was the immediacy of the decision. It left so little margin of discretion to them. The announcement to sell was made on Friday 12 October; the timetable for the sale was for close of bid offers by 23 November, and completion of the sale by 20 December. The time period was indeed very short, and therefore it seemed only major companies with large resources could be invited to bid.

All promises were broken and seemingly no options existed. The initial reaction of the board was one of despondency. It could be expected that any new owners would replace or phase out much of the senior management and bring in their own people.

THE MANAGEMENT FIGHT-BACK

Barrie Hall was the architect of the buy-out. Over the weekend he read up an article on MBOs and decided to raise the issue on 14 October at a further board meeting.

As group financial director and Richard Fraser's right-hand man, Barrie Hall had played a major role in shaping the outcome of most major decisions, particularly on financial and control aspects. 'When the Westbury sale was announced, I was motivated more by self-preservation than entrepreneurship. I was determined not just to lie there and do nothing so I started phoning around for details on MBOs and soon the idea became a possibility'. The problem was, of course, whether they could produce the sort of money that would make a credible bid. They needed financial advice and they needed it fast. They needed venture capital and they needed a lot of it. They had to build a credible position out of nothing.

The owner and non-executive directors were against the feasibility of a buy-out from personal views and on the advice of Samuel Montagu, the merchant bankers handling the sale.

Unconvinced by any opposition to his idea, Barrie Hall, and on persuasion, Fraser, decided that further action was necessary and during the first week made active enquiries in London for backers and secured the interest from three venture capital companies, Investors in Industry, Candover and Charterhouse.

The other five senior executives were now approached and they rapidly decided to support the buy-out deal, either because of the opportunity to own their own business and reap the financial rewards, or because failure to secure a deal meant redundancy.

One of the problems was that this was an inexperienced board. Arguments in favour of making a bid were that:

the company was well-known in building industry circles;
it had a small landbank which was rapidly turned;
the only real asset was people;
thus the buying prospects for an outsider were somewhat limited;
the board knew their people and their potential;
the prospectus had already been designed and thus the board knew far more about the potential than could any outside bidder;
all the data were at hand.

Against this there was, of course, the time factor and the fact that in the ultimate the main concern of the vendor was to have a signed and sealed contract for cash with immediate delivery.

The first problem was to find a broker to put together the venture capital. Investors in Industry hit it off with Westburys from the first, both in style and penetration. They had ample experience in MBOs. Their past records showed that their success rate on MBOs was high. The company promoted an active policy of liaison negotiation and post-MBO monitoring. The company could secure finance in the time available. They were to take a stake in the equity and therefore were not only committed but personally interested in the success of the deal. Relationships were good right from the initial stages. They put together a deal with, amongst others, the Prudential, sorted out other partners and formulated a proposal. By 10 November a shell company had been set up to acquire the business should the bid succeed.

The buy-out team together with advice from Investors in Industry were able to put together a feasibility plan and, armed with an accountant's audit of Westbury, secure the initial financial backing. Investors in Industry acted as sole agent for a consortium of financial investors representing their interest in the buy-out deal. As the legal and taxation issues in MBOs are complex, a firm of solicitors was engaged to act on Westburys' behalf, but all parties were still under the direction of Investors in Industry.

MBO TACTICS

Richard Fraser was in a difficult position and facing conflicting interests. He was now in the market as a potential bidder. He was also still running the company for the owner and expected to show the company to any alternative bidder in honest and open fashion. He decided that as far as other competitors were concerned his responsibilities entailed that he should willingly answer any questions concerning the company and the sale, but that he was not obliged to volunteer information.

His role as far as the bidding period was concerned was thus a passive one and, in order to allay suspicions, all bidders were fairly informed of his involvement in a buy-out package.

The advantages that the MBO team had over other businesses were that, firstly, they knew the business inside out and were therefore more likely to appreciate its true worth and potential and, secondly and more importantly, they knew exactly what the owner wanted. Surprisingly none of the other competitors actually took the trouble to fly out to the Bahamas where the owner was residing as a tax exile to discover more about him and his needs. Alternative bidders thus had little apparent notion of the personalities involved in the battle and particularly that what Bob Joiner was really after was to be paid in cash on 20 December.

The buy-out team were able to successfully exploit these conditions in their preparation of the bid:

1 The MBO bid/offer was on one page, simple and unaccompanied by masses of legal jargon (made subject to contract) – and was tailored to the owner's needs.

2 The offer was for cash. Other bidders made offers including delayed payments, share offers, and indeed some required extension to the bid deadline.

3 The MBO team had found it possible to raise money and complete the deal within the time stipulated by the owner. Indeed they knew that time was a key factor in the successful outcome of the buy-out team.

4 The working relationship with Investors in Industry was excellent, and this facilitated the process of raising the finance and shortening the negotiating period.

5 Some bidders were put off once they realized that the entire management team was involved in the buy-out. Should the buy-out fail, the new owner was likely to purchase a company divorced from its senior executives and divorced from their goodwill.

Fraser and Hall pitched the offer price just above the expected market level, but they acknowledged that they had very little margin to play with even if it had not been the best offer. In fact the bid was lower than that suggested by Investors in Industry after much deliberation by the three-man board. Fraser felt the need to notify the next level down in the management team as early as possible. Westburys had always been a very open firm and he felt the need to share the problems and the proposals with 25 of the senior managers to enable them to foresee the options open. The main board of seven, of course, owned the problem.

Rumours had got around, indeed many were based upon fact. One sub-contractor heard the full story from his bank! The search was now for a secure business. The search told the board a lot about how to run an exposed business, dependent wholly upon market forces. In particular it taught it how to raise its sights to the future. The prospectus had to rise beyond immediate opportunities or threats within the construction industry, and in particular beyond the options limited in the south-west.

Bob Joiner did not really believe that the board could find the money and asked Richard Fraser to sell at the best possible price. When it became evident that an MBO was not only possible but financially acceptable he came round enthusiastically to the idea. It was obvious that with an MBO team involved the competition was increased and indeed the buy-out team might well offer the best price. If he sold to the management the company that he had built up and had had some considerable pride in would maintain its identity and name and would not be lost in a corporate swallow-up. The top management, with whom the owner had worked, would not lose their jobs and additionally the employees would benefit from their years of service.

The management were under no illusions as to the owner's concern with obtaining the highest price and realized that therefore all other influences were of a very secondary nature. However they made every effort to tailor their bid to his needs and sale requirements, and this was seen to be an influencing factor in the success of the offer.

The week-end following Friday 23 November was spent waiting. Would the tender be accepted? On Monday the bid was successfully received. Richard Fraser notified the press and the staff had the immediate notice of success.

VALUATION OF THE COMPANY

The assets of the company totalled some £9.5 million but it was obvious that book value did not represent the going market value of Westburys.

Investors in Industry and Prudential (the key financial backers) were prepared to go up to £14 million and, having spent so much time and effort on the deal, were particularly anxious to achieve a successful bid.

Based on their knowledge of the company and the housebuilding industry and supplemented by snippets of information gathered from private sources and competitor reactions, the buy-out team soon realized that they could substantially drop the price below the ceiling imposed by their backers.

A price incentive deal was therefore negotiated with Investors in Industry, in which the management's share of the company would be 12% for a purchase price of £14 million, but for each £0.5 million below the top price the buy-out team gained an extra 0.5%.

A complicated organic method of valuation was not employed to arrive at the bid offer, but rather a subjective method was used, based on these questions:

What is the highest bid our competitors are likely to make, based on formal and informal sources of information available to the buy-out team?

What is the minimum price the owner will accept for his company?

Against advice from their backers, the MBO team trusted their instincts, and their offer of £12 million was successful (only just).

The management stake in Westburys consequently went up to 14%. The £2.5 million over book price represented valuation of goodwill, intangibles, quality of the company's management control systems, and Westburys market position and growth potential.

THE MBO DEAL

In order to represent the interests of the financial investors, three non-executive directors joined the board, although maintaining a sensible policy of non-interference in the management of Westburys'.

TABLE 25.2 Capital structure of the Westbury Homes buy-out

Investors	*Share price*	*Type*	*Amount*	*Ownership*
			£m	%
Bank	–	Secured	2.0	–
Investors in Industry and Prudential	£7.67	Preference	9.8	38
Others	£8.45	Preference		48
Buy-out	£1.00	Ordinary	0.2	14
			12.0	100

The MBO period is expected to last some three to five years before taking the company into public ownership. The issues at stake here are to continue company growth and profitability, and simultaneously to convince the financial community that Westburys is a well-managed company with a highly attractive appeal to potential investors.

The Westbury Homes buy-out consisted of a straight purchase of assets; however, legal and taxation problems posed some major headaches during the contract period. The sale transaction did not initially achieve tax clearance from the Department of Inland Revenue.

The importance of tax warranties and indemnities cannot be over-stressed in any deal of this kind, and both sides took time to arrive at mutually agreeable positions. Discrepancies in the accounts and back tax were typically met by the seller.

In the Westbury Homes deal, £10 million was paid on the due date and the balance with interest, but minus tax debts, paid one year later.

The capital structure was as set out in Table 25.2.

Investors in Industry, Prudential and the buy-out team together held 52% of the new company's stock, giving them a majority stake.

WHAT HAS CHANGED?

The MBO has been successfully negotiated and the board has settled down to a programme of strategic development designed to build a prospectus for a market launch in two to three years' time. Barrie Hall sees the company continuing to expand on a steady basis. 'Sticking to what it's good at' is his view of the company.

There has been no change at the lower levels of the enterprise and none in basic operational practices. The firm has always had to operate on tight site controls and that is ever more necessry now. At the top, the group has lost its two founders who built the company. Now the board is able to use its own projected earnings to plan future developments and growth. The venture capital was fixed for two years; if any major shareholder wants to get out then he is required to sell to one of the others. This is a young and hungry company, says Richard Fraser with great and natural pride.

There has been a change of emphasis since the buy-out. The company has become more professional and this has been accompanied by a quicker flow of decisions, says Roger Hughes, the group operations director. 'But our immediate problem concerns lack of finance for growth due to the buy-out debt burden. We can however take an enterprising stance on the future of Westburys and would in due course like to see both internal growth and diversification into related fields.' He argues that the buy-out has enabled the company to get its house in order, particularly on consistent decision-making, more effective planning, the use of profits within the business and the encouragement of professional people managing the company without over-interference.

Now the issues are strategic. Richard Fraser is familiar with the operational needs and difficulties but now he says, due to increasing size and complexity, he confines himself to the strategic issues. He now has to adopt an arbitrating role. Although power is vested in his position, his approach to management is to keep in touch with the other key senior executives, looking at the angles, soliciting advice as necessary, listening to the views of interested parties but taking the ultimate responsibility. Strategy is largely developed on an incremental basis still, and although present policy is largely reactive to market needs and geared to short-term horizons, the company is now forced to view long-term planning with equally increasing importance. The structure of the new prospectus will be such as to demand a formal statement of growth strategy. 'Our immediate plan is to go public at the right time and with the right price in order to repay debt and raise finance for corporate growth, and therefore I intend to make Westbury Homes an attractive buy to outside investors.'

26 An Alternative Corporate Plan

INTRODUCTION

Against a background of nationalization, the possibility of defence spending cutbacks and the threats of redundancy in the mid 1970s, Lucas Aerospace Combine Shop-Stewards Committee (LACSSC) embarked upon proposals designed to safeguard its members' jobs, whilst ensuring the continuing application of human skills and technical capability. Implications of social responsibility and the threat of nationalization were to shape the proposals through their various phases up to the introduction of the interim report[1] finalized in February 1979.

BACKGROUND

Between 1960 and 1975 the total number of workers in the UK aerospace industry had been reduced from 283,000 to less than 200,000. Some concern had been expressed with the growing tendency to implement rationalization in the industry through co-production within the European Community (e.g. the 'Jaguar' project shared by Britain and France), thus leading to a possible further spread of production sharing among the aerospace component industry, of which Lucas Aerospace was a part.

The vulnerability of component suppliers in the aerospace industry is reflected in their role as sub-contractors to the major suppliers of engines, aircraft and other large systems. The recipient prime contractor may often possess the capability of manufacturing components, and in a time of reduced activity it may elect to 'pull back' work from its sub-contractors. The exclusion of Lucas Aerospace from the nationalization programme was seen as a further increase in this vulnerability:

[1] 'Turning Industrial Decline into Expansion', Lucas Aerospace Confederation Trade Union Committee (CAITS North-East London Polytechnic, February 1979). Subsequent quotations for which no source is given are also from this report.

> As trade unionists we do not wish to see a relationship between the aerospace component firms and the nationalized sector of the industry which would be similar to the relationship of the equipment manufacturers to the National Coal Board. Such a relationship would provide the opportunity for those forces in society hostile to nationalization to point out that nationalized industries were economically unsuccessful. (LACSSC)

LUCAS INDUSTRIES

Lucas Aerospace Ltd is a wholly owned subsidiary of Lucas Industries, a complex organization whose activities extend from design through sales in the aerospace, defence and automotive industries. The company was founded in 1877 and since the early 1960s has been transformed into a large multinational organization with interests in Europe, the Far East, South Africa and South America (Appendix 1). UK subsidiaries include Lucas Defence Systems, Lucas Batteries and Lucas Electrical, in addition to Lucas Aerospace, with sites spread across the West Midlands, South-West, South-East and North-East England.

In 1978 the company employed approximately 70,000 people in the UK although this figure was nearer to 80,000 in 1970. During this period, overseas production had risen from 22.4% to 33% of total company production (Appendix 2).

LUCAS AEROSPACE PRODUCTS AND CAPABILITY

Lucas Aerospace represents the largest supplier of aerospace components in Europe, of its kind. Research facilities include: engine high altitude testing; combustion chamber testing; radio interference, laboratories and environmental test facilities, in addition to a substantial manufacturing capability. Products manufactured by the company include gas turbines; aircraft engine fuel systems; flight control systems; medical equipment; power generation sets and nuclear equipment.

Lucas Aerospace components are used for a variety of complex operations in modern aircraft and other transports, e.g. the Concorde supersonic airliner, hovercraft, the Polaris submarine and the Tornado multi-role combat aircraft (MRCA).

LUCAS AEROSPACE PROPOSALS FOR CHANGE

Company proposals in March 1978 announced various measures for rationalization.

1 In the Engine Management Division, gradual transfer of manufacturing from the Victor Works at Liverpool to the Birmingham-based factories. Reduction of labour force at Liverpool from 1,450 to 500. Plans for a new plant at Huyton, Liverpool, would mean employment of 500 people. Reasons given for proposals included: lack of workload, uncompetitiveness, batch size problems and technological change from purely hydromechanical fuel systems to electrically controlled systems.

2 Changes in the Electrical Division included:
 (a) the closing of existing sites at Bradford and Shipley, transfer of generating systems and gas turbines to Hemel Hempstead
 (b) transfer of control gear manufacture from Bradford to Hemel Hempstead
 (c) closure of No 2 Building at Hemel Hempstead
 (d) closure of Coventry foundry
 (e) closure of Bashley Road Site (Willesden)
 (f) discontinuation of manufacture of industrial ballscrews
 (g) building of new actuator factory at Bradford employing 400 people.

Job losses totalled 537: 68 at Hemel Hempstead, 358 at Bradford, 46 at Coventry, 43 at Willesden and 22 at other sites.

Reasons given include: lack of profitability; inadequate reinvestment; uncompetitiveness; marketing and engineering effort thinly spread; low market shares, organizational complexity; excessive capital employed, therefore low return on investment.

In response to these management claims and proposed actions, the Committee carried out extensive examinations into the various operations and in particular, those relating to the Coventry site.

PRELIMINARY UNION PROPOSALS

During 1975 detailed plans covering alternative products, markets and use of existing resources were compiled by the Lucas Aerospace Shop Stewards' Committees across the several divisions of Lucas Aerospace. The need to guard against possible defence and aerospace cuts was not a sole reason for proposing a policy of diversification as there existed among most Trade Unions general support for a policy of reduced defence spending. The LACSSC proposals suggested a positive swing in direction towards the application of resources to 'more socially useful production'.

> There is something seriously wrong about a society which can produce a level of technology to design and build Concorde but

cannot provide enough simple urban heating systems to protect the old age pensioners who are dying each winter of hypothermia. (LACSSC)

THE UNION PLAN

The Lucas Aerospace Corporate Plan (LACP) compiled by the LACSSC looked at the major areas of diversification, restructuring and the plan implementation. The committee put forward the following preliminary plans for consideration by the company.

Alternative products

Of the 150 products drawn up in the plan, some related to *alternative energy technology*. The company's expertise in heat-pump technology and aerodynamics was considered well suited to the development of large-scale windmills for both direct and (friction) heating devices and electricity generation on a 'community scale'. Control and switching circuits for solar heating systems were proposed as viable opportunities for utilization of the company's experiences in the area of control systems and fluid dynamics.

In the field of *medical technology*, the plan underlined the emphasis given to 'social' products. Proposals for artificial-limb control systems development, research into aids for the blind and transportable life support systems were considered complementary to the company's general aerospace and control systems know-how.

Transportation composed a major consideration of the proposals for alternative products: a hybrid road/rail vehicle capable of driving in cities and rail-track (a prototype of which has been developed and tested in conjunction with the North-East London Polytechnic); the development of a hybrid powerplant making use of the I.C. engine and the electric motor; a new type of airship utilizing the vectored thrust principle developed for the Harrier VTOL aircraft; electro-magnetic braking systems with in-built fail-safe devices.

Other products included: auxiliary power units for use in third-world countries, oceanic exploration support equipment and off-shore maintenance and fire-fighting systems.

Restructuring proposals

The impact of diversification called for a reversal in the trend towards fragmentation, de-skilling and ever-increasing work pace that the existing business operations imposed. The plan proposed a major reappraisal of the employee development programme, pointing to the need for autonomous work groups and project teams, and emphasized the need for the close integration of shopfloor 'commonsense' with the technical staffs' 'scientific knowledge'. Existing company plans for employee development came under criticism.

> Very little is being done to extend and develop the very considerable skills and ability still to be found within the workforce . . . there is little indication that the company is embarking on any real programme of apprenticeships and the intake of young people. . . . The company is making no attempt to employ women in technical jobs, and apart from recruiting these from outside, there are many women doing routine jobs well below their existing capabilities. (LACSSC)

Markets

Public sector organizations were seen as a major potential for the proposed alternative products. The authors of the plan, however, realized that a fuller assessment of market potential for the alternative products would be needed. Although many of the products would be competitive on the open market, a more 'direct' means of meeting community needs was required to be developed, for example, through contacts with the local community, trade associations and environmental groups.

Implementation of the plan

Whilst recognizing the impracticalities of sweeping changes and 'opt out' from the aerospace industry, the committee hoped to negotiate implementation in advance of any redundancies.

The proposal was to introduce alternative products in a phased manner such that industry contraction would to some extent be halted and then gradually reversed through the programme of diversification.

The committee had envisaged a number of problem areas in spite of this cautious approach.

> There is obviously the danger that the discussions with the management about the implementation of the Plan (if it were agreed that such discussions should take place), could gradually degenerate into formal collaboration. There is also the danger that even if collaboration were carefully avoided the company might simply take parts of the corporate Plan and have all this technology on the free. ¨he Plan has taken a very considerable length of time to prepare and involved many evenings and weekends of work. It has also meant that outside experts have been prepared to give generously of their detailed knowledge in order to help the development of the Corporate Plan. In these circumstances the greatest care will have to

> be taken to ensure that the company does not succeed in drawing off the 'money spinners' from the Plan, and perhaps even having these produced abroad, whilst declining those products which would be socially useful. It is even conceivable that whilst the company would take sections of the Plan, our members may still be confronted with the perennial problems of redundancy. Because of these dangers it is suggested that the correct tactic would be to present only part of the Plan to the company, and then to test out in practice the manner in which the company will attempt to deal with it. (LACSSC)

As a result of the above reservations, the committee submitted only 12 of the originally planned 150 products.

The company subsequently resisted moves to use the plan as the basis for a voluntary planning agreement between the Government, Unions and the company, and in February 1976 they rejected the plan in favour of a continuation of existing business. However, some interest was expressed by the local management at the Burnley site, and plans were negotiated for the development of small heat pumps powered by natural gas and which could be used for domestic heating systems.

FURTHER ALTERNATIVE PRODUCT PROPOSALS

As a result of more detailed research up to the end of 1978, the committee put forward further support for a number of alternative developments. These are listed below, along with the rationale for consideration.

Gas turbines

Growth in the use of gas turbines for generation is expected to rise by about 3% per annum over the next 10 years (Sources: Rolls Royce and *Turbomachinery International*, Nov/Dec 1978).

Small gas-turbines could be used as power source for generator set up to and beyond 0.5 MW. The company have considerable experience in the design development and manufacture of small gas-turbines. The Lucas GG220 is considered to be a world leader in terms of lower levels of pollution and high combustion efficiency.

Gas powered heat-pump systems

The domestic sector presents the largest coherent market for heat pumps.

The potential market for heat-pump systems is regarded as substantial, owing to increasing fuel costs. Reports indicate that the market in 1985 will reach values of £897m (commercial) and £225m with the EEC (1975 prices, Frost and Sullivan survey).

Although a British invention, the country has no pump available 'which might satisfy the biggest potential UK market . . . insufficient design and manufacturing effort has been expended to yield reliable technology at a sufficiently attractive price' (*The Energy Daily*, 12 December 1977).

Haemodialysis machines (kidney machines)

The company already manufacture kidney machines, but has lost the lead to Dylade of Runcorn and to other foreign manufacturers.

The company manufactured 135 units in 1977 and 116 units in 1978, with 100 projected for 1979. Of these, 27 were exported in 1977 and 33 exported in 1978. 'The only thing which stops us selling those kidney machines is Her Majesty's Government, who won't give us an order for any more kidney machines.' (Mr James Blyth, Lucas Aerospace, Independent TV interview, 20 September 1978)

Oceanics

Exploitation of the ocean bed is likely to take at least three forms:

(a) exploitation and extraction of oil and natural gas;
(b) collection of mineral bearing nodules;
(c) submarine agriculture.

The percentage of the world's oil which is extracted from coastal waters is increasing. The real growth area is seen to be in a whole range of automatic and remotely controlled electronic equipment. Subsea activity is likely to require a range of submersible vehicles, plus generating and handling equipment. Westinghouse and Lockheed are both actively engaged in oceanics. British Aerospace has also undertaken significant work in this field.

Hybrid power-pack technology

With the problems of energy and pollution the development of alternative forms of power plants or improvement of present form is regarded as imperative.

Battery-powered vehicles have the advantage of being virtually silent and non-polluting. With the huge amount of resources spent on research into solar, wind and wave energy to produce electricity, the electrically powered vehicle has a very bright future.

Company product philosophy on the question of alternative power-plant technology seemed to point towards the hybrid system.

> It is clearly the case that the potential rewards from the introduction of a commercially successful battery electric vehicle are large . . . but it has become increasingly clear that the development of a

> commercially successfully electric vehicle requires a total system approach.
>
> However, until entirely satisfactory electric private cars can be produced, there is little or no chance that the introduction of the new generation of electric vehicles will make any significant impact on the rate at which oil resources are being used. At the present stage of development it is not possible to see the solutions to the problems of producing viable electric private cars for the private market.[2]

Volkswagen, General Motors, Bosch, Toyota and Minicars Incorporated of California are each concerned in hybrid power-plant development. (The latter development being concerned with vehicle emission studies.)

With the exception of the internal combustion engine itself, all of the expertise and technology for the development of hybrid drives are contained within the Lucas company. In addition, Lucas manufactured components seem complementary to such developments, e.g. batteries, generators, switchgear, control units, pumps and solar panels.

CONCLUSION OF THE INTERIM REPORT

The proposals to reduce the Aerospace workforces from its present 11,500 to 10,000 were seen to come within the wider strategic framework of Lucas Industries' policy of transforming itself into a trans-national company. They were viewed as part of a logical extension of a rationalization originating from the late 1960s, resulting in a reduction of the UK workforce from 18,000 to 11,500 in 1978.

The company's redundancy proposal was considered to have been a centralized bureaucratic decision. Nor was there considered to be any clear indication at technical or divisional management level of how it could be put into effect. In making its proposals public the company was considered by the committee to have:

1 concealed important information, e.g. the major structural defects in the existing Victor Works factor, which would involve provisional cost of £450,000 for rectification, with construction work in the affected area lasting approximately 10 months.

2 deliberately misled Members of Parliament and others as to the employment and other significance of the growth of electronic control systems as distinct from fuel systems as a whole. (LACTUC)

The proposal to move the Shipley team to Hemel Hempstead would, the committee concluded, result in the break-up of a highly talented gas

[2] M.G.G. Harding, *Conference on Report on Electrical Vehicle Development*, 1982.

turbine research and development team whose efforts resulted in the Queen's Award to Industry in 1970. Moving the Bradford generating design team to Hemel Hempstead would also result in the breaking-up of a team whose skills have previously won two additional Queen's Awards for technological achievement and who are acknowledged by the company to be the world's leading design team in this field.

The proposals would finally impose extensive hardship, suffering and disruption on some 1,400 workers and their families.

UNION AND MANAGEMENT DEBATE

In the early part of 1981 the committee claimed that foreign competition beat their parent company to the punch in the development of new projects.

An aspect which was annoying the Unions most was their feeling that the UK company could now be trailing well behind foreign manufacturers in relation to projects such as the road-rail vehicle and the hybrid power engine, which local shop stewards had 'on the stock' under their corporate plan some years ago.

Phil Asquith, union representative and chairman of the Joint Shop Stewards' Committee, commented:

> If you look back at the projects which were proposed under our Corporate Plan, which were relative to Lucas, you will find that just about all of them are now being made outside the Lucas set-up . . . and outside the United Kingdom.[3]

Mr Asquith had uncovered information showing German interest in, and development of, the rail/bus system and American research into the hybrid electric car, and how the trend, all over the world, was to develop energy conserving transport.

He considered that Lucas's recently forged link-up with UK battery manufacturer Chloride constituted the biggest boost yet for their development of a British electric vehicle. Lucas also had carried out extensive research into electric vehicles and, working in conjunction with Bedford, had produced a large number of proto-types. The company was also working on a hybrid engine for passenger cars.

Current developments at home seemed to back up Asquith's claims. A House of Lords select committee concluded that both hybrid and electric vehicles were a serious strategic option, with environmental and energy advantages over conventional powered vehicles, and urged government backing for such projects. Arguing for the management's case a spokesman for Lucas at Birmingham stated:

[3] *Burnley Express*, 16 April 1981.

Ever since the Corporate Plan was first mooted, in 1976, the Lucas Group has increased its spending on research and development. In the current year it is running at £55m, and last year it was £45m. That is a thumping good figure – made more so in these extremely difficult times.

The Corporate Plan was examined carefully by the management – and in great detail. Items and suggestions were rejected for a variety of reasons. There were also items which were not rejected, but which have been explored.

Take electric vehicles. We have been developing these for some time. We are, we think, world leaders today in this field.

Another point in the Corporate Plan related to kidney dialysis machines. At the moment we have a surplus stock of these machines in that part of the Lucas group which makes them.

We were making them before the recommendations in the plan. Many of the problems which arose involved social aspects.

We have our own electric vehicle project which is associated with our battery company – which is the logical place for it to be. It is better development which will make or break electric vehicles.

We think it will make them. We think our efforts in this direction are being made in the right place, industrially, within our group.

There is no need for it to be associated with Aerospace. If you are a Lucas person, you belong to a group of companies and must resist the temptation to be parochial and must think on a group scale.[4]

[4] *Burnley Express*, 16 April 1981.

Appendix 1

LUCAS INDUSTRIES: SOURCES AND USES OF FUNDS – MAJOR ITEMS OF INVESTMENT, 1960–77

Year	*Ordinary shares (£m)*	*Overdraft/ short-term loans (£m)*	*Bonds and long-term loans (£m)*	*Net change (£m)*	*Usage*
1960	14.32				
1961	14.32	1.35	–	+ 1.35	Acquisition
1962	14.32	5.17	–	+ 3.82	Site expansion; acquisition at Coblessy; extension of distribution in France; Argentina, Germany and Switzerland
1963	14.32	0.70	–	– 4.47	
1964	35.4	0.37	4.1	+24.85	Swiss bonds bought to reduce overdraft. 1:4 issue raised £3.58m 1:1 ord. raised £16.09m 1:1 pref. raised £1.5m
1965	35.4	1.20	4.1	+ 0.83	Acquisition – established Condiesel SA
1966	35.4	1.5	4.1	0.17	Established Sao Paolo plant and CAV Mexico
1967	35.4	1.5	4.1	+ 0.13	Established Friens Girling; acquisition of 26% of Martin Amato
1968	38.1	1.97	11.1	+10.17	Acquisition; established Girlock Subtration; expansion Roto Diesel; extension in Mexico
1969	38.3	4.9	13.9	+ 5.93	Acquisition; Horstmann; Dawe Instruments; Special Prods Divs of GEC; Rists site in Calais
1970	39.3	20.2	20.9	+23.3	Acquisition; new factory in South Africa
1971	39.3	4.4	38.8	+ 2.11	Revaluation of property; establishment of Lucas Aerospace
1972	47.1	2.1	43.1	+ 9.8	Conversion of loan stock; acquisitions overseas

Year	Ordinary shares (£m)	Overdraft/ short-term loans (£m)	Bonds and long-term loans (£m)	Net change (£m)	Usage
1973	69.1	4.7	44.8	+26.3	1:2 Scrip issue; acquisitions, extensions establishments, Eire; Thailand; Spain
1974	69.1	26.3	44.5	+21.3	Acquisitions and extensions in Brazil, Mexico, Germany and Spain. Agreements in Rumania and Yugoslavia
1975	69.1	47.6	46.6	+23.4	Interests acquired; mergers, establishments in Spain and Germany
1976	92.5	36.4	50.0	+15.6	Rights issue 1:3 ord; and 1:2 pref. Acquisitions: UK and France; expansion Brazil and Mexico
1977	92.55	45.5	50.6	+ 9.75	Expansion: CAV USA (£2m), South Korea (£3,5m), Brazil (£5m), Michigan site

Source: Lucas, a British Company? B. Bolton, Ruskin College, Oxford, 1978.

Appendix 2

GROWTH OF LUCAS OVERSEAS PRODUCTION (£m)

	1978	1977	1976	1975	1974	1973	1972
(1) Sales – United Kingdom[a]	562.2	508.1	420.3	344.7	286.7	269.4	239.7
(2) – Overseas	409.0	378.0	299.5	225.5	166.1	129.8	100.1
(3) Total sales	971.2	886.1	719.3	570.2	452.8	399.2	339.8
(4) Exports from United Kingdom (included above)[b]	154.6	139.9	111.7	93.8	71.5	60.7	49.1
(5) Production by home subsidiaries[c]	666.0	611.0	498.0	409.0	337.0	315.0	277.0
(6) Production by overseas subsidiaries	306.0	275.0	222.0	162.0	116.0	84.0	62.0
(7) Overseas production sold in United Kingdom[d]	50.0	37.0	35.0	31.0	22.0	15.0	11.0

[a] Sales of goods originally within the group (home or overseas) (1) in UK, (2) overseas.
[b] Included in (2) above.
[c] Sales of goods at home and abroad originating in (5) home and (6) overseas subsidiaries.
[d] (6) + (4) − (2) above, i.e. overseas production plus united Kingdom exports minus overseas sales.
Source: Compiled from: 'Turning Industrial Decline into Expansion' (LACTUC-NELP) February 1979

Appendix 3

CONSOLIDATED PROFIT AND LOSS ACCOUNT (£m)
LUCAS INDUSTRIES PLC

	1983	*1982*
Turnover	1,216·8	1,220·3
Costs less other income	1,171·3	1,160·7
Trading profit	45·5	59·6
Share of profits/(losses) of related companies	(·8)	3·2
	44·7	62·8
Interest payable less received	24·6	27·5
Operating profit	20·1	35·3
Redundancy and closure costs	18·0	15·1
Profit on ordinary activities before tax	2·1	20·2
Taxation	12·3	14·2
Profit/(loss) on ordinary activities after tax	(10·2)	6·0
Minority interests	2·6	2·1
Earnings/(loss) attributable to shareholders	(12·8)	3·9
Extraordinary items	–	(·9)
Profit/(loss) for the financial year	(12·8)	3·0
Dividends	8·2	8·2
Amount withdrawn from reserves	(21·0)	(5·2)
Earnings/(loss) per share	(13·5p)	4.1p

CONSOLIDATED BALANCE SHEET (£m)

	1983	*1982*
Fixed assets:		
Tangible assets	359·0	353·0
Investments	28·3	31·1
	387·3	384·1
Current assets:		
Stocks	291·1	308·3
Debtors	260·7	250·8
Cash	23·9	14·8
	575·7	573·9
Creditors: Amounts falling due within one year	(328·4)	(343·0)
Net current assets	247·3	230·9
Total assets less current liabilities	634·6	615·0
Creditors: Amounts falling due after more than one year	(132·1)	(121·5)
Provisions for liabilities and charges	(40·4)	(39·2)
	462·1	454·3
Capital and reserves:		
Called-up share capital	93·9	93·9
Share premium account	24·4	24·4
Revaluation reserves	62·6	54·5
Other reserves	10·8	13·4
Profit and loss account	222·8	242·5
Related companies' reserves	6·1	8·6
Total shareholders' funds	420·6	437·3
Minority interests	41·5	17·0
	462·1	454·3

SUMMARIZED RESULTS (£m)

	1983	1982	1981	1980	1979
Sales					
United Kingdom	585·7	607·9	606·3	654·0	606·4
Overseas	631·1	612·4	579·9	541·9	465·3
Total sales	1,216·8	1,220·3	1,186·2	1,195·9	1,071·7
Exports from United Kingdom (included above)	238·2	250·9	234·6	223·9	191·4
Operating profit	20·1	35·3	5·0	53·2	70·7
Redundancy and closure costs	18·0	15·1	26·4	12·2	
Profit/(loss) before tax	2·1	20·2	(21·4)	41·0	70·7
Profit/(loss) after tax	(10·2)	6·0	(34·5)	30·9	52·9
Earnings/(loss) attributable to shareholders	(12·8)	3·0	(34·7)	27·8	51·0
Shareholders' funds	420·6	437·3	459·0	486·4	450·2
Minority interests	41·5	17·0	16·3	13·8	10·4
Total capital employed	462·1	454·3	475·3	500·2	460·6
Profit before tax as percentage of total capital employed	0·5%	4·4%	(4·5%)	8·2%	15·3%
Ordinary and redeemable preference shares Called-up capital	93·6	93·6	93·6	93·6	92·5
Assets per ordinary share	460p	479p	502p	532p	498p
Earnings/(loss) per ordinary share	(13·5p)	4·1p	(38·6p)	29·2p	54·3p
Dividends per ordinary share	8·6p	8·6p	11·0p	11·0p	11·0p

ANALYSIS OF SALES

RESULTS OF THE PRINCIPAL CLASSES OF BUSINESS

The sales to third parties, including the Lucas share of related companies' sales, and the profit/(loss) attributable to the principal classes of business were as follows:

	1983 Sales £ million	*1983* Profit/(Loss) before tax £ million	*1982* Sales £ million	*1982* Profit/(Loss) before tax £million
Automotive	997·8	(17·2)	976·0	3·7
Aerospace	255·0	15·4	270·6	13·9
Industrial	111·2	3·9	113·2	2·6
	1,364·0	2.1	1,359·8	20.2
United Kingdom companies	769·8	(17·6)	790·4	(3·4)
Overseas subsidiary companies	447·0	20·5	429·9	20·4
Share of related companies	147·2	(·8)	139·5	3.2
	1,364·0	2·1	1,359·8	20.2

GEOGRAPHICAL ANALYSIS OF SALES

Sales by Lucas and its subsidiary companies to third parties in the following areas were:

	1983 *£ million*	*1982* *£million*
United Kingdom	585·7	607·9
Rest of EEC	266·2	250·4
Europe outside EEC	89·5	86·6
North America	82·9	81·6
Central and South America	31·8	31·5
Australasia	50·0	58·0
Asia	78·2	69·4
Africa	32·5	34·9
	1,216·8	1,220·3

The Lucas share of related companies' sales was as follows:

EEC	104·1	96·3
Europe outside EEC	·6	·8
North America	·7	·6
Central and South America	3·7	6·7
Australasia	19·9	17·2
Asia	10·5	10·0
Africa	7·7	7·9
	147·2	139·5
Total group sales	1,364·0	1,359·8

Appendix 4

BUSINESS REVIEW (1983)[1]

The group's trading results for the year are shown in the consolidated profit and loss account.

Sales by the UK companies for the year were £20m lower than last year at £770m. A loss of £17.6m was incurred after a £16.3m charge for redundancies and closures compared with a £3.4m loss after charging £14.7m for redundancy and closure costs in 1981/82. Sales by the overseas subsidiary companies amounted to £447m, an increase of £17m over last year, but profits before tax, at £20.5m, were unchanged. The Lucas share of related companies sales was slightly higher at £147m but there was an overall loss before tax of £800,000 compared with a profit of £3.2m the previous year.

Direct exports from the UK suffered from the difficult world trading conditions, but at £238m, were only £13m lower than the previous year. In the vehicle equipment companies, Lucas Electrical and Lucas CAV suffered from reductions in demand from overseas customers, but these were partly offset by higher exports from Lucas Girling and Rists. Lucas Aerospace exports were marginally lower but represented over 40% of its total sales.

The group's liquid resources have been kept under close control throughout the year and at the year-end the net borrowings amounted to £177.5m compared with £206m at the start of the year.

The number of people employed by the group in the UK has been reduced by 2,329 in the year after transferring 1,636 from Smiths Industries on the formation of Lucas Electrical Electronics & Systems, and overseas the number employed was reduced by 1,049. At 31 July the total number employed was 64,600.

Automotive Products

World wide vehicle equipment sales, including our share of related companies' sales and the additional sales arising from the merger of the Smiths Industries vehicle equipment business into the newly established Lucas Electrical Electronics & Systems company, were 2% higher than last year at £998m. This sector of the business incurred an overall loss of £17.2m after charging £14.2m redundancy and closure costs, compared with a small profit in the previous year.

In the UK demand for original equipment did not pick up until the

[1] *Source*: Company Report, 1983.

second half of the year and there has been little indication of a recovery in the aftermarket. As a result, it has been necessary to make further cuts in our UK manufacturing facilities during the year and the loss in the UK, after redundancy and closure costs of £12.5m, amounted to £33.1m.

In Europe our subsidiary companies had a better year overall. Lucas CAV diesel fuel injection equipment businesses in France and Spain successfully gained new business and both companies increased their profits substantially. The Lucas Girling brakes company in Germany performed well with higher sales and profits, but the French business, while remaining profitable, suffered from the recession. Our French partnership company, Ducellier, manufacturers of automotive electrical equipment, had another extremely difficult year, and were particularly badly hit by severe reductions in aftermarket sales. The Italian related company, Carello, made good progress with substantially higher sales and profits.

Outside Europe, although there were very good performances in some areas, the vehicle equipment subsidiaries had a disappointing year overall with profits down 25% at £9.7m. In the USA the results were particularly poor and reflected the collapse in the demand for diesel cars which caused our microjector production at Greenville, South Carolina, to be stopped for several months in the first half of the year. Lucas Girling's plant for manufacturing commercial vehicle drum brakes at Cincinnati is now operational and their results reflect the start-up costs. In Australia our businesses suffered from the effects of the recession and after some years of deteriorating results the loss-making rotating machinery business was sold. In New Zealand, also, our businesses were affected by the continuing economic recession and profits were substantially lower than the previous year. Our Brazilian companies performed well and increased profits overall in spite of a deteriorating economic situation. In Argentina, despite significantly lower vehicle production, profits were increased. Our service company in Mexico had a good year whilst our related company manufacturing diesel equipment there made lower profits but did well against the adverse background. In India our partnership companies earned profits only slightly below the record established last year notwithstanding more difficult trading conditions. In South Africa the small loss-making battery business was sold; the remaining businesses achieved significant improvements although the economic climate was poor.

Aerospace

Sales of aerospace equipment at £255m were £16m lower than the record level achieved in the previous year but, by improved operating efficiency and lower redundancy costs, the profit before tax was increased at £15.4m. The UK results for the year reflected the lower demand for equipment for both civil and military aircraft particularly the run-down of the RB211 powered TriStar programme and the stretching out of the Tornado programme. The subsidiaries in the USA, Canada and Australia all performed well. Our French partnership company, Thomson-Lucas, suffered from lower demand which resulted in slightly lower profits but the results of the German partnership, Pierburg, were greatly improved.

Industrial

The industrial businesses which supply a range of electronic and hydraulic equipment made further progress during the year. Although sales were slightly lower at £111m, profits were £1.3m higher at £3.9m. Our businesses in the UK had a very satisfactory year and benefited from special receipts from Syalon technology. The businesses in North America, after a poor start, saw some recovery in the second half of the year and Ledex, which was acquired last year, performed well finishing the year buoyantly.

Research and development

The group continued to maintain a high level of expenditure on research and development. Expenditure amounting to £78m was incurred during the year both on basic research and on developing products and manufacturing processes to ensure that the company is able to meet customers' requirements at competitive prices. Royalty income arising from the use by others of group technology continued to be an important source of income and for the year amounted to £6.6m.

Outlook

Towards the end of the financial year, though output of commercial vehicles, agricultural tractors and automotive diesel engines remained depressed, there were signs of recovery in UK car production. Likewise, in Continental Europe and in North America, demand for our vehicle and diesel engine equipment has been uneven. In the 1983/84 financial year we see demand for automotive equipment in the UK and Continental Europe stabilizing at about the current levels. Recovery in North America should be maintained at a more lively rate and vehicle output in 1983/84 could be 6% up on the previous year. In South America and Mexico vehicle production may rise more sharply.

Although the aerospace business has its production base mainly in the UK, it has growing overseas interests and 75% of total sales are supplied, directly or indirectly, to overseas customers. Sales of aerospace equipment were lower in 1982/83 than in the previous year and no significant upturn in world demand for civil or military aircraft is anticipated during the next eighteen months. However, spending on guided weapon systems is increasing and this sector offers continuing prospects for Lucas Aerospace.

Demand for industrial systems and products is likely to show further improvement in 1983/84, particularly in the fields of telecommunications and defence.

With these prospects, and building on the measures taken to restructure our resources, we look to 1983/84 as being a period of consolidation with a modest improvement in performance in the first half of the year and a stronger recovery in the second. We shall maintain and intensify our programmes of cost cutting and productivity improvement to enhance further our profitability – our aim being to achieve worldwide competitiveness in all operations. With the help of all Lucas people we are determined to achieve these objectives and we plan continued progress so that our financial performance reaches acceptable levels.

27 Trusthouse Forte (B)

BACKGROUND

Trusthouse Forte Limited is the largest hotel and catering group in the UK. It was formed in 1970 by the merger of the Trust Houses Group Limited and Forte Holdings Limited.

Trust Houses were formed in 1903 with the main objective of restoring the standards of the old coaching inns, many of which had fallen into decline with the development of the railways. Over the years the company grew into a nationwide group of hotels, with overseas hotel interests as well.

The major expansion of the company began in the post-war period and soon activities spanned the whole range of catering: popular and exclusive restaurants, banqueting, airports and in-flight catering, duty-free shops, motorway service areas, and from 1958, hotels in Britain and overseas. By 1970 the company had 41 hotels, a number operating in partnership with BEA and BOAC (now British Airways).

THF is primarily an hotel company with almost three-quarters of its profits currently coming from the United States and Japan. In 1980 THF had a total of 810 hotels throughout the world. These hotels ranged from exclusive hotels such as the Hotel George V in Paris to the Post Houses and Inns found in the UK.

The second most important profit centre to the THF organization is catering, which includes several high-class restaurants and goes down the scale to in-store catering. The Little Chef restaurants run by the group are particularly popular with tourists and travellers. The activities of Gardner Merchant can be included in this section. This company carries out industrial catering contracts using the facilities provided by the client firm.

In 1984 the company had revenues exceeding £1.1 billion with profits of around £105 million, and by this time, Lord Forte had handed over executive control to his son Rocco, but remained active as chairman.

DEVELOPMENT IN THE 1980s

Many of THF's development policies and actions had already been predestined, i.e. much of 1980's and 1981's acquisitions were just the start of a much larger future development. During the course of the 1980 financial year, more than £95 million was spent worldwide to build new hotels, to acquire others, to refurbish and redecorate properties, to buy new equipment and to develop new markets. THF had stated that its priority regions for expansion were Britain, the USA, Europe and the Middle East.

Further expansion of the Little Chef catering establishments was implemented in 1981, with the company developing a further 30 new restaurants. A catering innovation in 1980 was the Julie's Pantry fast-service hamburger restaurants. The first 'in-town' operation of Julie's Pantry was in London's Knightsbridge, and there were two others at Scratchwood (M1) and Corley (M6) motorway service stations. Five others were planned to open during 1980.

The Kardomah chain of restaurants which is aimed at shoppers was restyled during 1981, and there were plans to open or acquire further restaurants during the year. There were also plans for the catering partnership, which specializes in catering in departmental stores, to increase the number of its outlets by 50%.

In October 1980 THF took over the management of the Hotel des Bergues in Geneva, a 143-bedroomed hotel which was ranked highly among the world's exclusive hotels. THF spent in excess of £1m on refurbishing and redecorating this hotel.

During 1981 THF added luxury hotels in Tulsa, Little Rock and Miami in the USA, and Toronto in Canada, to complement its existing properties in New York, Dallas and Philadelphia.

In early 1983 Donald Durbin, a director of THF reiterated the company's strengths in hotels and catering and its concentration in doing what it was good at. He was, in fact, referring to the sale of the company's leisure division to Lord Delfont – one of Britain's leading impressarios – for around £37 million.

The following year saw the disposal of the Colony Foods restaurants, and Eastern Foods Inc (industrial catering), two of the company's US operations.

Little Chef catering lodges

In October 1985 THF opened the first of its 'Little Chef Lodges' at Barton-under-Needwood on the A38 near Burton-on-Trent, and sited adjacent to the existing Little Chef restaurant.

The 'lodge' concept was based on low-cost accommodation with simplicity as the key theme. For example, there are no conference facilities, no reception area and hardly any staff. The lodge is managed by the same person currently managing the restaurant, the latter having undergone extra training.

Specification Every lodge is designed to look the same from inside, although the construction can be extended in any direction and go up to three storeys high. Being of modular design, each room is 'factory made' and therefore can be delivered complete with fittings, to the appropriate site.

Each lodge was planned to have a mixture of between 20 and 30 double and single bedrooms incorporating very basic fittings. A standard double room offers a king-sized bed and a sofa bed which converts into a full-sized single bed, and includes a pull-out 5 ft × 2 ft 6 in. child's occasional bed in its base. Rooms are provided with tea- and coffee-making facilities and combined television and radio alarm. In 1985 tariffs were £19.50 for single occupancy and £24.50 for a double/family room (including VAT).

Bookings Guests – who may or may not have booked in advance – check in at the restaurant reception area and pay on arrival. After 10 pm a night supervisor merely hands over the room key.

Building costs The lodge at Barton-under-Needwood was built in just 16 weeks (after ten weeks of site preparation). Although exact costs had not been disclosed, THF's catering managing director, Alan Hearn, had intimated that the company were building the lodges at less than half the cost of a Post House. (Post Houses were estimated to cost £41,000 per room (1985).)

Future developments In January 1986 a further lodge (30 bedrooms) was opened in Bebington, Cheshire, closely followed by a third development in East Horndon, Essex.

Two more firm sites were under review and more than 20 other planning permissions had been obtained around the country.

Although across the UK there were 130 suitable sites, the company had indicated it had no plans to use all of them.

Appendix 1

A 'LITTLE CHEF' OPENING EVERY NINE DAYS[1]

The Little Chef name first came to public attention in 1959 when a snackbar with 11 stools opened in Reading, Berkshire.

Last week, the company had 235 Little Chefs in operation but more are opening at the rate of 25 – 30 a year; 'one every nine days' as Mr Hearn pointed out. The 250th opens just after Christmas. This financial year should see the arrival of 28 – 13 more are under construction.

Originally conceived as a roadside catering operation for the traveller, Little Chef is now developing local business.

The basic formula, though, has not changed – waitress service; limited, graphic, grill-based menu; 60 seats on average; open 364 days a year from 7 am to 10 pm.

A three-year redevelopment programme now 18 months away from completion will give all the units a new, softer look; change of emphasis from bright, bold primary colours to pastel shades, from fluorescent to softer lighting. Tables are larger, as are reception areas. Toilet facilities are being improved too. Three-year-old Barton-under-Needwood's ladies' room features fresh flowers for Mr Hearn believes: 'You can judge a business by the quality of the toilets – you can't walk around the kitchens but you can walk around the loos.'

The change of direction is not intended to encourage longer stays but is an acknowledgement of the increasing variety of reasons for visiting.

'These are evolutionary moves, not revolutionary moves,' Mr Hearn said. 'We're still averaging 60 seats although some units can go to 80. We have to be consistent and work within our existing management skills. Remember, nothing is pre-cooked at a Little Chef and if the number of seats were trebled, we'd have trouble running it.'

Staffing is around 12 – 15, starting with a manager; a deputy (or two); two or three supervisors to cover the seven-day-a-week, 7 am – 10 pm operation; and restaurant catering assistants who cover all duties, with some majoring on griddle work.

The management structure allows upward movement – Little Chef lodges will add a greater career dimension by extending job opportunities. Every manager within Little Chef must have managed a unit at one point in his or her career even if only for a fortnight.

Director-in-charge Peter Smith is not exempt. 'Little Chef,' Alan Hearn said, 'is a super breeding ground for young managers. It's probably the quickest route there is within THF.'

[1] Extracted from Kate McDermid 'Lodges Chain Offers Family Rooms at £24,' *Caterer and Hotel Keeper*, 3 October 1985.

'If managers want more variety, we've got the whole of THF to offer them.'

Little Chef limits its operation to 'A' roads, equivalent trunk roads or motorways – 11 are operated under franchise by THF's motorway service area division, one at Luton Airport by the airport catering division.

Only one site, in Lewdown, Cornwall, is fanchised – to a former Little Chef manager, a relic of a short-lived franchise policy, ditched when it was realized that standards could be better maintained through direct managership.

Little Chef's meteoric development is slowed down by only one thing – the country's road improvement programme, which can knock sites out for a year, or in some cases for ever if, for example, a new by-pass is built.

But Mr Hearn reports 100 per cent co-operation from local authorities.

Half the stock is THF-owned, half on lease. 'Our problem is finding, acquiring and building sites. On a 30-mile stretch, for example, there may be only one feasible site.'

The key to Little Chef, offering not a gourmet experience but a consistent, no-risk food formula, is a reluctance to introduce new ideas until management knows they can succeed at 250 units.

'Our managers spend 70 per cent of their time communicating policy and standards to their staff. You'll get the same answers from everyone in the company. Consistency of thinking is the key to consistency for the customers.'

The tables will always be laid in the same way, the food should be of the same standard whether in Glasgow or Gaewan.

The Little Chef consistency has even been noted by *The Tatler*, (whose readers one may not expect to see in a Little Chef), which, much to Mr Hearn's delight, recently praised the company for producing food exactly like the picture on the menu.

Appendix 2

WEIGHING UP HOTEL SHARES[1]

If hotels spell glamour, luxury and deep-pile sophistication to you then you're right in step with the stockmarket. There are less than a dozen publicly quoted hoteliers and they have attracted quite an exclusive image. Not to mention pretty fancy share ratings. Though, in fact, few of them operate at the top-notch five-star end of the market.

PE ratios in the late teens to mid twenties are par for the course. That's quite a premium to the rest of the stockmarket, where the average share changes hands on a PE of, say, 12.

But before you settle down for a vicariously cossetting read, be warned that this special status for hotels is a recent phenomenon.

A run of good years is not exactly exceptional in the hotel business, which is characterized by boom or bust cyclicality. When times are good they are very, very good. But in the past the stockmarket has never lost sight of the other side of that refrain – when times are bad they are horrid.

The industry has done its best to make itself less vulnerable to these cyclical jolts. But currency swings and the business cycle remain two big bogies in the hotel business.

Soggy sterling mops up tourists

Foreign tourists are the bread and butter business for many hotels, especially those in London and Scotland. American tourists are often more interested in rediscovering their roots north of the border than in paying homage to Shakespeare! (Most of the quoted hotel companies have little interest in the resort hotels concentrating on tour customers, which tend either to be family owned or part of the large package holiday specialists like Saga and Horizon.) (Scottish tiddler Norscot is an exception in selling to coach operators.)

The tourist trade is international, which means that British hotels are competing for customers with hotels in many other countries. And though Britain has enviable historical attractions, what matters as much to the tourist is how far his buck goes.

Following the three-year surge in the dollar North America is now the largest source of foreign visitors to the UK; almost one in every four. Previously our continental neighbours held number one slot.

So the reversal in the dollar's fortunes since spring does not augur well for the London-based hoteliers. The Savoy group, for instance, which

[1] Reproduced from *Investors Chronicle*, 1 November 1985.

takes in the Connaught, Berkeley and Claridges as well as its namesake flagship, gets about two-thirds of its London trade from Americans.

However, too strong a dollar can hurt provincial hotels. Their tourists often spend one night in London, the rest round the country. If they can't get that London bed – because the capital is overcrowded – they may avoid Britain altogether.

Many hotel companies tend to make the greater proportion of their profits during the tourist season. So always check a company's financial year end when weighing up any set of figures. At the tiny Prince of Wales Hotels, for instance, the latest six months trading (to early July) produced a pre-tax loss.

Business customers are less fickle

The pound's gyrations on the foreign exchanges can, however, be overemphasized when looking at many hotel shares. Hoteliers are only too aware of the need to secure a balanced mix of business.

For many provincial hotel chains, such as Queens Moat Houses, bedrock is the business traveller, who more often than not is a local Brit, and hence not directly affected by exchange rates. Moreover, this sort of business is less seasonally skewed to the benign spring and summer months.

It is, however, closely tied to corporate prosperity. Just as Uncle Sam may forego his tour of Europe for Disney World if the dollar falls through the floor, when there's a squeeze in the UK, the business traveller tends to trade down to a no-frills 2-star rather than the usual THF 3-star.

Hotels linked to the conference trade, such as the Birmingham Metropole – near the National Exhibition Centre – are often hardest hit when recession bites, because conferences tend to be treated as disposable luxuries. But on the whole the cyclicality of hotels serving the business traveller is not as savage as for the tourist hotels.

How operating costs work

But why should hotels be any more sensitive to currency or business swings than any other trade serving the same markets? The reason lies in the enormous fixed overhead costs of a hotel compared with the small variable cost related to the actual sale of a room.

An awful lot of rooms – at least 50 per cent of the total – must be filled before most hotels can merely break even. That's not really very surprising. Just think of the bills for rent, rates, heating, lighting and wages for the armies of visible and behind-the-scenes staff in any goodish-sized hotel.

Once that magic break-even point has been turned, however, the costs to service each extra body thereafter (just laundry and room cleaning) are small. So most of the extra revenue passes straight down to the bottom line. (The jargon for this sort of cost structure is 'high operational gearing'.)

Airlines – that classic volume game – face the identical cost structure. In the flying business it's known as getting bums on seats; in the hotel trade it's bodies into beds. And don't let the plush image of many hotels persuade you otherwise. That's why even the plushier hotel groups jumped aboard the 'bargain break' bandwagon some years back. Even cut-price bodies in beds were better than no bodies.

The nice side of heavy operational gearing is that small increases in demand can mean proportionately much bigger surges in profits on the up-swing. The nasty side is that a small shortfall in turnover can play havoc with the profit forecasts.

London hotels are by far the most volume-sensitive. Expensive London rates and salaries mean that the occupancy levels necessary to reach breakeven are higher. But most London hotels also rely much more on room revenues than provincial hotels, which can often attract local custom to their restaurant and bar in town. In London most visitors only take breakfast in the hotel. Few groups attract much local bar and restaurant trade.

It's worth knowing, therefore, how London figures in the portfolios of the quoted hotel chains. Only for the Savoy and the tiny London Park is it the dominant feature. More typical is Mount Charlotte, for whom the capital accounts for half of all revenues, or Trust House Forte, where it brings in a third of the total. For Stakis and Queens Moat Houses, the figure is under a tenth.

Growing by acquisition

We've mentioned already that building costs, especially in London, are astronomic. Well over £100,000 per room the pundits reckon. That's if you can find a decent-sized plot in Central London in the first place; not to mention arm-twisting your local authority to grant planning permission.

This latter point can often be the biggest headache. A typical case is the Hyde Park Corner hospital, St George's, which has now reverted back to the Grosvenor estate. But has the Duke of Westminster been able to wangle planning permission? No way.

There is an alternative to building for hoteliers anxious to share in the boom in visitors to the capital – acquisitions. On a per-room basis buying an existing hotel can often work out at a fraction of the cost of building from scratch. And if you bought at the bottom of the cycle, as Mount Charlotte did with its clutch of acquisitions in 1982, then subsequent profits growth can be dramatic.

Acquisitions don't just make sense on per-room cost basis. With a chain of hotels there is often scope to cut out central administrative functions such as booking, marketing and accounting personnel.

Hotels are one of the many businesses where the specialist quoted companies own only a smallish slice of the cake. Some of the largest hotel chains belong to diversified holding companies like Grand Met or Lonrho, in which they are overshadowed by other activities. The biggest quoted chain, THF, gets about two-thirds of its profits from its UK hotels. And Ladbroke, now the second largest hotelier in the country after its takeover of the quoted Comfort Hotels, gets less than a third of total profits from hotels. So when you try to decide what Ladbroke shares are worth, you have to value the betting and property interests as well as the hotels.

Buying individual hotels can sometimes be a better bet than buying whole companies. In the early eighties there was a steady stream of cast-offs from the large chains (notably Grand Met and British Rail, but also THF) which were snapped up by the smaller quoted specialists. But that supply now seems to be drying up. Either because the big groups have now got their empires in order, or because no one wants to sell when their rooms are choc-o-bloc.

So from now on acquisition-fuelled growth by leaps and bounds may be more difficult to come by.

Trading up

Another attraction of acquisitions – though the same treatment can be applied to a hotel group's existing stock of properties – is that they often offer the scope to 'trade up'. In plain language this means tarting up a hotel in order to charge higher room rates.

In the eighties trading up has been all the rage. In some cases it led to that off-loading of peripheral properties by the big chains. More often it meant closing down a hotel over the slack winter months and doing a complete overhaul of the property's facilities. The payback was often as dramatic as it was immediate.

Before you get too carried away, though, remember that most properties cannot be upgraded beyond a certain level – it all depends on what the area will bear. So if a hotel group has already spent substantially on refurbishments the scope to continue trading up may be virtually nil.

So it's worth checking where – if anywhere – a particular company's growth can be expected to come from in future. Some hotel chains, such as Mount Charlotte, still have plenty of potential on the prettification, if not on the acquisition, front. But most don't.

Appendix 3 Trusthouse Forte PLC and Subsidiaries

CONSOLIDATED PROFIT AND LOSS ACCOUNT FOR THE YEAR ENDED 31ST OCTOBER 1985 (£m)

	1985	*1984*
Sales	1,244.5	1,131.4
Operating Costs	(1,060.2)	(979.3)
Gross trading profit	184.3	152.1
Depreciation	(42.0)	(37.2)
Trading profit before interest	142.3	114.9
Interest	(27.2)	(19.5)
Trading profit after interest	115.1	95.4
Surplus on disposals of property and trade investments	8.0	9.2
Share of profits of subsidiary company not consolidated	6.5	4.3
Profit on ordinary activities before taxation	129.6	108.9
Tax on profit on ordinary activities	(41.0)	(29.5)
Profit on ordinary activities after taxation	88.6	79.4
Minority Interest	(1.9)	(2.6)
Profit before extraordinary items attributable to Shareholders	86.7	76.8
Extraordinary items	(3.7)	(6.6)
Deferred taxation provision	–	(8.3)
Ordinary and Trust dividends	(42.5)	(37.0)
Profit retained for the year	40.5	24.9
Earnings per share (net)	11.11p	9.84p
Dividends per share	5.45p	4.74p
Dividend cover	2.0 times	2.1 times

BALANCE SHEETS AT 31st OCTOBER 1985 (£m)

	Group	
	1985	*1984*
Fixed assets		
Tangible assets	1,099.3	1,019.2
Investments	137.6	143.7
Current assets		
Stocks	33.6	30.2
Debtors	200.6	189.9
Short-term deposits and cash	42.4	50.4
Total current assets	286.6	270.5
Creditors – amounts falling due within one year		
Bank and other borrowings	73.2	77.7
Creditors	257.6	229.4
Total current liabilities	330.8	307.1
Net current assets (liabilities)	(44.2)	(36.6)
Total assets less current liabilites	1,192.7	1,126.3
Creditors – amounts falling due after more than one year		
Bank and other borrowings	244.5	242.7
Creditors	17.7	20.0
Total net assets	930.5	863.6
Capital and reserves		
Called up share capital	195.1	195.1
Share premium account	68.8	68.8
Revaluation reserve	384.3	325.5
Profit and loss account	267.7	239.4
Shareholders' investment	915.9	828.8
Minority interest	14.6	34.8
Total equity investment	930.5	863.6

FIVE-YEAR RECORD, 1981–85

	1985	*1984*	*1983*	*1982*	*1981*
Sales (£m)	1,245	1,131	963	907	833
Gross trading profit (£m)	184.3	151.1	121.7	107.8	97.7
Trading profit before interest (£m)	142.3	114.9	89.6	77.3	71.9
Profit on ordinary activities before taxation (£m)	129.6	108.9	84.0	57.4	52.3
Profit attributable to shareholders (£m)	86.7	76.8	63.8	47.6	44.2
Earnings per share (net) (p)	11.11	9.84	8.18	6.10	6.94
Dividends (£m)	42.5	37.0	32.2	27.5	22.2
Dividends per share (p)	5.45	4.74	4.125	3.5	3.0
Dividends cover (times)	2.0	2.1	2.0	1.7	2.0
Total assets less current liabilities (£m)	1,193	1,126	871	805	763
Shareholders' investment					
Total (£m)	916	829	642	583	553
Per share (£)	1.17	1.06	0.82	0.75	0.71
Net borrowings (£m)	265	270	215	238	168
Current costs					
Earnings per share (net) (p)	9.65	8.33	6.52	4.60	5.12
Divided cover (times)	1.8	1.8	1.6	1.3	1.5
Shareholders' investment per share (£)	1.42	1.24	0.97	0.88	0.83
Assets employed (£m)	1,391	1,281	1,002	949	837